"Everything about this book is wonderful: the contributors, the essays they've written, the topics they address, and their main subject, Robert P. George. *Social Conservatism for the Common Good* is a must-read for any believing Christian interested in bringing faith and reason together to advance human dignity, human flourishing, and human rights."

Ryan T. Anderson, President, Ethics and Public Policy Center

"Robert P. George is not only, as he is often called, one of today's leading public intellectuals; he is also a devout Catholic who has much to teach the whole body of Christ, including evangelical Protestants, as these splendid essays attest. In the best tradition of Chuck Colson and Richard John Neuhaus, Robby George helps us, Catholics and evangelicals alike, live faithfully on our difficult journey toward a common mission."

Timothy George, Distinguished Professor of Divinity, Beeson Divinity School, Samford University

"The pro-life movement in America today has rarely had an advocate as articulate and intellectually commanding as Robert P. George. A professor of law at Princeton and a constitutional scholar, George has collaborated closely with a number of evangelical thinkers, including my late friend Chuck Colson. Even more, he's a true role model of how we can treat those who oppose us in the culture with civility while defending our most cherished and sacred beliefs."

Jim Daly, President and CEO, Focus on the Family

"This volume is not just a celebration of and deep engagement with Robert P. George's work; it is also worthy of that work. Which is to say that it is rigorous, illuminating, and concerned, above all, with discerning the truth. It is an important contribution to the essential project of sustaining a Christian morality in the public square."

Rich Lowry, Editor in Chief, *National Review*

"Few thinkers of any age have been as influential in as many ways as Robert P. George. On paper, George is something of an enigma: an Ivy League professor who has not only remained a faithful Catholic but has become one of America's foremost intellectual leaders on the sanctity of life, marriage, and religious freedom. Remaining a member in good standing in the academy and the church is unusual today, but George has managed to do that, which likely explains his ability to appeal across many would-be divides. The Protestant contributors to this volume effectively engage with George's moral, political, and legal philosophy and make a case for why it must be taken seriously in the public square. George's work, undaunted courage, charitable heart, and energetic willingness to do the right things, even if hard, offer the next generation hope and a model to influence the culture for good while faithfully bearing witness to Christ."

Kristen Waggoner, CEO, President, and General Counsel, Alliance Defending Freedom

"It's no easy task to assemble a collection of essays on important topics that are serious, informed, and fair, but Andrew Walker has accomplished this in *Social Conservatism for the Common Good*. While my own conclusions about natural law and political theory have sometimes differed from Robert P. George's, reading his work has always stretched me intellectually and inspired me to think better about whatever subject was at stake. Evangelicals wishing to think sharply and be good citizens do well to grapple with George's work, and those looking for an appreciative analysis of it have picked up the right book."

David VanDrunen, Robert B. Strimple Professor of Systematic Theology and Christian Ethics, Westminster Seminary California

"In *Social Conservatism for the Common Good*, readers will find not only a well-deserved homage to Robert P. George, one of the greatest political theorists of our time, but also a compendium on how to understand liberalism and social conservatism in an age diametrically opposed to all we hold dear."

Alexandra DeSanctis, fellow, Ethics and Public Policy Center; coauthor, *Tearing Us Apart: How Abortion Harms Everything and Solves Nothing*

"What an incredible resource! Not only does this book provide the best summary of Robert P. George's significant contributions to Christian conservative thought (as if that would not be enough), it also offers an incredible collection of scholars engaging, rejoining, critiquing, and clarifying his ideas. Andrew Walker has given us all quite a gift."

John Stonestreet, President, Colson Center; Host, *Breakpoint* podcast

"Andrew Walker has assembled a brilliant collection of essays that engage fruitfully with the pioneering and courageous work of Robert P. George. This is the rare multicontributor book in which every chapter shimmers with insight and wisdom."

Trevin Wax, Vice President of Research and Resource Development, North American Mission Board; author, *The Thrill of Orthodoxy* and *This Is Our Time*

Social Conservatism for the Common Good

Social Conservatism for the Common Good

A Protestant Engagement with Robert P. George

Edited by Andrew T. Walker

Foreword by Ben Sasse

CROSSWAY®

WHEATON, ILLINOIS

To my friend, mentor, fellow protégé of Robert P. George,
and colaborer in defense of "the permanent things,"
Ryan T. Anderson

Contents

Foreword

ROBERT P. GEORGE—or Robby, as he is known—is the most influential banjo player in the conservative movement. Throughout his life, this great West Virginian has dedicated himself to what James Madison called "the sacred rights of conscience."[1] He is a patriot and a great thinker, and for that reason, he deserves a place in the conservative canon.

For Christians, the two greatest commandments are to love our God with all our being and to love our neighbors as ourselves. Robby's work in defense of liberalism—both in interpersonal relations on campus and in our constitutional settlement—is persuasive precisely because it makes this command of love a political principle. Robby George's liberalism is the kind of political witness Christians need to bring to the forefront of our civic discourse.

In his Farewell Address, George Washington told the American people that the Constitution is the "palladium" of our liberty and that "religion and morality are indispensable supports" of the Constitution.[2] In other words, the Constitution supposes that limited government can protect the people when their leaders lack what *Federalist Papers* no. 51 refers to as "better motives," but free government cannot long endure if a people lacks those better motives altogether.[3]

For Robby, as for the founders, the word *freedom* does not merely signify a release from tyrannical restraint. In the highest sense, rather,

1   James Madison, "July 23, 1813: Proclamation on Day of Public Humiliation and Prayer," University of Virginia, Miller Center, accessed May 15, 2022, https://millercenter.org/.
2   George Washington, "September 19, 1796: Farewell Address," University of Virginia, Miller Center, accessed May 15, 2022, https://millercenter.org/.
3   *The Accessible Federalist: A Modern English Translation of 16 Key Federalist Papers*, adapted by S. Adam Seagrave (Indianapolis: Hackett, 2017), 40.

freedom is the free pursuit of the good. The good is the source of our "better motives."

Throughout his work, Robby has frequently cited an aphorism of James Madison: "A well-instructed people alone can be permanently a free people."[4] We need to know what good we should pursue, and for that we rely on wise instructors—teachers like Robby—to show us the way we should go.

In a meaningful way, Robby's work has served as more than a defense of "the sacred rights of conscience"—he has acted as a voice of conscience itself. On issues from abortion to religious liberty, Robby has been a fearless truth teller even in a culture that would rather be told lies.

Robby's ideas aren't the only way he teaches us to live up to the promise of the American founding though. His way of life is a model of the kind of virtue he believes our republic needs. His students, both at Princeton and among his wider readership, are inspired to live better lives thanks to his example.

Take his friendship with former fellow Princeton professor Cornel West. Despite the vast divide separating their political views, Drs. George and West share an unshakable friendship. Theirs is a beautiful example of the way we can all live together as Americans and how the kind of confident pluralism Robby teaches can help us love one another.

America is an experiment, and as the founders knew, an experiment can fail. Most, if not all, of the republics that came before the United States collapsed into anarchy or were conquered by stronger tyrants. If our experiment is to succeed, it needs strong defenders like Robby George to guide and enlighten it.

As a confessional Protestant, I—and many other contributors to this volume—disagree with Robby George about a whole host of important theological questions. Robby and I can have spirited conversations about soteriology, but that's precisely why we agree about civics. Without minimizing our disagreements, we can remember that we share so many important political principles. One of the great idolatries of the twenty-first century has been the deification of politics. Robby, taking to heart the psalmist's admonition, has never been one to put his trust in princes or parties.

---

4 James Madison, "December 5, 1810: Second Annual Message," University of Virginia, Miller Center, accessed May 15, 2022, https://millercenter.org/.

We can—we must—work together for the defense of the human person, the preservation of a free and open society, and the promise of religious liberty. In this cause, Robby George's work can serve as a beacon. All Americans—theist and atheist, Jew and Gentile, Protestant and Roman Catholic alike—can be grateful for this great scholar's contributions to our shared intellectual life.

Senator Ben Sasse

Acknowledgments

THE IDEA FOR THIS VOLUME came to me in December 2019 while I was sitting at my desk on the campus of the Southern Baptist Theological Seminary. As a newly minted ethics professor, I was struck, looking at the number of volumes by Robert P. George that I had on my bookshelves, at just how much I had been influenced by his thought. It also convinced me that more evangelicals needed to be aware of George's work. That same day, I emailed Dr. George, suggesting a project of this nature to gauge his own interest. More than three years later, that idea is now in your hands.

Many individuals should be thanked for their assistance in the project. First, Robert P. George should be acknowledged for his willingness to give this project a green light. My friend and agent, Andrew Wolgemuth, is always a trustworthy guide for writing projects. Justin Taylor at Crossway is owed appreciation for letting a unique book project like this see the light of day. Project assistance also came from my former or current students Alex Ward, Flynn Evans, Alex Richey, Caleb Newsom, and Christopher Parr. Their work on miscellaneous and tedious tasks is deeply appreciated. Lastly, I want to thank each of the contributors for their willingness to sacrifice time and energy for the sake of a volume that introduces, honors, and interacts with a thinker we all so dearly and deeply admire.

As always, the source of my greatest joy in this earthly life is my family: Christian, Caroline, Catherine, and Charlotte. Their love and support awaken me each day to the goods and promises of this life lived under God's providential hand.

Andrew T. Walker

Introduction

Tenacious Civility

The Spirit of Robert P. George for Contemporary Times

Andrew T. Walker

"I'M GOING TO MAKE THEM regret this every day of their lives."

These were the words that went through the head of the conservative Catholic philosopher Robert P. George after receiving the news that he had been granted tenure at Princeton University, one of the most prestigious universities in the world, notorious for its secular atmosphere. He knew he would be a gadfly at Princeton with his unabashed yet genteel and genial social conservatism, but George could not have foreseen at the time just how much he would also thrive and become one of the university's most famous professors and an intellectual icon within American conservatism.

With a career spanning over thirty years to date and now holding the title of McCormick Professor of Jurisprudence, Robert P. George is one of the world's most prominent and respected public intellectuals. Even if others disagree with him, there is no doubt that he is one of the most important living social-conservative thinkers and someone critics must contend with if they wish to live with intellectual honesty. He is taken seriously by friend and foe alike. His stature is that of a grand admiral of social conservatism. If you ever step into his office at the Witherspoon Institute, you'll see a wall bedecked with awards and accolades. He has been consulted by US presidents, has served on numerous governmental commissions, and has received the Presidential Citizens Medal from President George W. Bush.

Alongside a bevy of other public profiles, George's 2009 profile in *The New York Times Magazine* called him, to use the article title, "The Conservative-Christian Big Thinker."[1] It is hard to classify George as only one type of scholar. With degrees from Swarthmore College, Harvard Law School, Harvard Divinity School, and Oxford University, he's known primarily as an analytic legal philosopher. The themes of his work in legal philosophy, however, have necessarily entailed serious incursions into and contributions within the fields of political philosophy, moral philosophy, constitutional law, and even theology. He has made his mark on the academy primarily by advancing a particular form of natural law theory that understands morality as rationally derived from certain "basic goods" that are constitutive of human flourishing (I delve into this subject in depth in chap. 4). From his belief that society can order itself and its laws to obtain these goods, George criticizes secular views of society that would deny the existence or distort the meaning of concrete moral norms and moral goods. Fundamentally, George is animated by an aim to obtain the ideals of the just society—one whose common good is defined by respect for the human person in all its dimensions.

I first became familiar with the thought of Robert P. George sometime in 2007. I somehow came upon *The Clash of Orthodoxies* and recall thinking to myself how I had never read arguments that were so powerful and clear—and not explicitly religious—while also aligning with biblical ethics. Though I was still very young and largely ignorant of the tradition I was embarking on, I was grasping that the moral convictions of the Bible were based not only on divine rules but on reason as well. In other words, Christians did not believe their morality was intelligible by pure religious fiat *alone*. Rather, God inscribed reasons that can be grasped as true for the morality he commands. What were those reasons? Ultimately, to glorify himself but also, as a secondary matter, to order a creation within which humans would be able to prosper. These truths are ones I'm still wrestling with more than a decade and a half later, ones I have quite literally given my career to exploring, defending, and expounding. I believe that Christianity

---

1 David D. Kirkpatrick, "The Conservative-Christian Big Thinker," *New York Times Magazine*, December 16, 2009, https://www.nytimes.com. For an additional intellectual profile of George, see "Robert P. George" at the Contemporary Thinkers website: https://contemporarythinkers .org/robert-george/.

is the answer for everything—from how we need salvation to escape God's wrath to how to live a well-ordered life. Robert P. George's body of thought helped ignite that spark.

I wish I could remember the details of how I happened upon a book that would become life altering. That is lost to the annals of time, I guess. But books come upon us in ways that change us and help us see the world in fresh, enlivening ways. Though several living individuals have shaped my thinking in immense ways, I must admit that George's thought is first among equals. I am persuaded by his articulations of natural law and his defenses of the coherence of morality, the dignity of the human person, marriage, and religious liberty, and frankly, I am teaching my students these ideas with evangelical expression and writing and speaking about them in public forums. This, in summary, is the joy of the intellectual tradition: to recognize an indebtedness to systems of thought that have been advanced by prior generations and to carry those patterns forward for the sake of the common good—ultimately all for God's glory.

I have gotten to know Robert P. George through various connections. From interactions with him when I served at the Ethics and Religious Liberty Commission to visits to Princeton for workshops at the Witherspoon Institute, I have had the pleasure to get to know George not only as an intellectual but personally. I'm also part of a younger network of scholars, including Ryan T. Anderson and Sherif Girgis, that has arisen out of George's tutelage. I've come to know Dr. George as someone who possesses the virtues of statesmanship, scholarship, and intellectual charity.

I still remember the first time I met him. It was in 2012 when I was working at the Heritage Foundation alongside Ryan T. Anderson. At that time, we were entering the later stages of the Obama administration's attempts to redefine marriage. The Heritage Foundation was routinely hosting events and seminars to help Capitol Hill staffers learn the truth about what marriage is and why it is worth protecting. George was a mentor to Anderson, and Anderson had brought George to the Heritage Foundation for an event on the necessity of protecting marriage. Given that the event was happening later in the afternoon, George spent the day in a spare office at the Heritage Foundation. I knew he was going to be there, and so I sheepishly approached him and asked him to sign one of the books he had written. He was, of course, unflappably kind. He signed my book, and off I went (I thought to myself, "Don't be that guy who lingers around bothering him with twenty questions").

But what strikes one about Robby (as he insists on being called) is how preternaturally down-to-earth he is and how willing he is to invest in a rising generation of intellectuals. You will learn more about his humble origins later in the volume. But from his banjo picking to his collegiality with those across the ideological aisle, George does not carry himself with an air of pride or self-righteousness. He's laser sharp, and one better be prepared to defend every utterance one makes, as though standing before an interrogator or tribunal. But George makes no cruel put-downs and exudes no hubris, despite his stature. I know this from experience. One personal story serves to illustrate the kind of intellectual Dr. George is—zealous for valuing ideas and truth as virtues in themselves yet also attentive to young voices.

Though I consider myself an advocate for natural law, a few years ago I wrote an article criticizing a particular formulation of natural law around issues of contraception. I still stand by most of my original claims but acknowledge that I could have communicated my argument with greater precision.

Within a day or two, I awoke—bleary-eyed—to see an email from Robert P. George. I opened it with great curiosity to discover an eight-hundred-word rebuttal of my comments. My heart pulsing, then sinking into my stomach, I read as George rebutted my argument line by line. He did so, of course, with characteristic grace. But a few things struck me after reading his comments: (1) he took the time to read the thoughts of a young, ambitious evangelical, which itself is an honor; and (2) he took time to correct. But he did so in a way that invited me to journey with him in the quest toward greater understanding. He was not dismissive. He was not harsh. He didn't frame his rebuttal with towering Princetonian condescension that one could expect from a respected, accomplished intellectual. He was admonishing and encouraging, as though he was still a student on the journey as well. I came away with this: *I had never felt so affirmed in being told I was wrong.*

One of the reasons this book is a valuable enterprise is because it focuses not only on the intellectual fruits of George's work but also just as much on the implications of character and institution building. We need arguments, but we also need right character and the formation of institutions that work to produce both. George embodies this. He has done the work, and as you will read further in this volume, he has also cultivated a character and posture toward academia and truth seeking that is an antidote to the stifling, cruel illiberalism incubating in our day. Moreover, he has invested in younger scholars (he regularly brags about them on Facebook) and has worked tirelessly in the background to form allegiances in defense of "the permanent things" that, were it not for his relational networks, would never have come to fruition. In George we see an institution builder, a networker, and an intellectual. There's a formula therein for how ideas take effect and metastasize. Ideas are not simply platonic forms; they influence only to the degree that networks and institutions are there to cultivate and expound them. Ideas, if they are to influence, are inseparable from individuals and institutions.

It's easy, as a conservative Christian, to want to be the gadfly who stands athwart liberalism yelling, "Stop!" But what Dr. George's witness communicates is that what matters is being the *right type* of gadfly—the kind of person who is winsome and gracious but astute in an argument, one who must be taken seriously by ideological counterparts.

His is a combination of scholarly output, acumen in building diverse coalitions, fierce yet honest examination of differing viewpoints, and care for and attentiveness to the next generation. Each facet is a model for us to follow as we enter the next generation of debate about issues integral to Christian faithfulness but also vital to a healthy, functioning social order.

Anyone who knows Professor George knows of his admiration for his students who venture out in defense of "the permanent things"—among them life, marriage, and religious liberty. Indeed, this is a moment when we confess that we, as young scholars and activists in defense of "the permanent things," stand on someone else's shoulders. Dr. George has spoken of how the days for "comfortable Christianity" are now over. But he should know that the legacy he's passing on is being picked up by a generation that is willing to take up its cross to follow Christ.

The book you are holding in your hands offers evangelical explorations into the thought of Robert P. George. I've tried to assemble a network of scholars who know the various contours of George's work well. But you may wonder: Why is there a book such as this written by evangelical Christians about a conservative Catholic? The answer is that George's thought is profoundly influential among evangelical intellectuals, and now, more than ever, the continuation of his thought for future generations is all the more urgent as the secular winter grows even colder. We need his thought to help us endure coming storms.

There's a particular reason why this is necessary for evangelical audiences. In my experience, evangelicals have the wonderful instinct to believe the Bible at face value, which means they do not need to be convinced of its accuracy. I love this about evangelicals. We humbly and eagerly submit ourselves to the word of God as his authoritative, inerrant, and all-sufficient revelation. I also notice, however, that despite our confidence in the Bible's teaching on such subjects as the family or sexuality, evangelicals often lack either the confidence or ability to explain the reason, purpose, or intelligibility of biblical ethics rationally. For example, most evangelicals I know believe unswervingly in the enduring reality of the male-female binary, but if you asked them how to define what a man or woman is, they would cite a Bible verse yet be unable to speak intricately about the way the human body and its embodied forms are designed for specific ends that both complete it and, in turn, dictate how the body is understood and respected. If our answer cannot make sense apart from the Bible, what we have told our audience is that our ethics make sense only as a sectarian matter, rather than as a public matter with public implications for public policy and public morality. A failure to understand how the Bible speaks about creation order leaves Christians with a deficient understanding of the Bible's relationship to public ethics.

The Bible's presentation of morality, however, is universal in scope, objective in its truthfulness, and intelligible in its reasons for commanding our obligation to obey it. Biblical morality is, therefore, a matter of law. It summons our obedience because biblical morality constitutes a truthful standard of measurement, action, and restraint. It exists for our good. This is where George's thought proves immensely valuable to evangelicals. George's work helps give colorful and rational expression to the ethics that evangelicals hold dear.

Social Conservatism for the Common Good seeks to explain the broad contours of George's work and demonstrate its ongoing relevance to the moral concerns in the public square facing evangelical Christians. To that end, this volume is a project of social and public ethics, but more than that, I hope it serves students in the broader project of developing a public theology that is faithful to Scripture and beneficial to neighbor and world.

Where necessary, of course, authors here explain the divergences of his thought from how evangelicals develop certain arguments within the public square. We are evangelicals, after all, and there are areas where George's thought differs from our own. In this book we are by no means wishing to downplay the very important differences between Rome and Geneva. Thus, this book is both explanatory and, by nature, critical at points, but it is still complementary to an evangelical worldview.

One of the most important reasons for this book is that it aims to inspire courage. I know of few others like Robert P. George who have been willing to withstand ridicule and contempt for their faithfulness to Christ. Our natural inclination is cowardice, and when Scripture speaks of the transaction of one being blessed in proportion to encountering persecution, it strikes us as bizarre. How can suffering be a blessing? One way is that it draws those who are suffering to an even greater dependence on Christ. But it also fortifies the relationships one can look to when experiencing suffering or persecution. The cross is indeed a place of suffering and liberation—where the Christian learns to live unencumbered by the shallow dross of the world and where intimacy with Christ is most visceral. But the cross is not the last word either. We stand as people who are promised resurrection, which means our persecution, cultural rejection, and scorn are not in vain.

George has powerfully articulated the need for courage as the virtue du jour. At the National Catholic Prayer Breakfast in 2014, George spoke the following words on how the days of "comfortable Christianity" are over:

To be a witness to the gospel today is to make oneself a marked man or woman. It is to expose oneself to scorn and reproach. To unashamedly proclaim the gospel in its fullness is to place in jeopardy one's security, one's personal aspirations and ambitions, the peace and tranquility one enjoys, one's standing in polite society. One may in consequence of one's public witness be discriminated against and denied educational opportunities and the prestigious credentials they may offer; one may lose valuable opportunities for employment and professional advancement; one may be excluded from worldly recognition and honors of various sorts; one's witness may even cost one treasured friendships. It may produce familial discord and even alienation from family members. Yes, there are costs of discipleship—heavy costs. So for us there is no avoiding the question:

Am I unwilling to stand with Christ by proclaiming his truths? The days of comfortable Christianity are past.[2]

George demonstrates an indefatigable and, frankly, cancel-proof courage. Years ago, he wrote the following on Facebook. It is something I come back to regularly:

Surely no one is surprised that many Christians are swept along by cultural trends, no matter how antithetical they are to Biblical principles and the firm and constant teaching of the faith. 'Twas ever thus. (Indeed, 'twas thus for the ancient Hebrews, too, as scripture makes more than abundantly clear.) And Christians who fall in line with a trend always find ways to say that the trend, whatever it is, is compatible with Christian faith—even dictated by it! It's hard for human beings to actually be countercultural, and Christians are human beings just like everybody else. So, when Marxism is trendy, there will be self-proclaimed Christian Marxists. When Fascism is fashionable, there will be self-identified Christian fascists. When racial subordination and segregation is the cultural norm, we'll baptize it. When eugenics is in vogue, there will be Christians claiming that eugenic practices and policies constitute Christian love in practice. If polyamory becomes the next cause embraced by the beautiful people and the cultural elite, we will start hearing about the Christian case for group marriage—"love cannot be arbitrarily confined to pairs." And on and on. Being human, we crave approval, and we like to fit in. Moreover, we human beings are naturally influenced by the ways of thinking favored by those who are regarded in a culture as the sophisticated and important people. When push comes to shove, it's really hard to be true to Christian faith; the social and personal costs are too high. We Christians praise the martyrs and honor their memories, but we are loath to lose so much as an opportunity for career advancement, or the good opinion of a friend, much less our lives. So, we tend to fall in line, or at least fall silent. We deceive ourselves with rationalizations for what amounts to either conformism or cowardice. We place the emphasis on whatever happens in

2   Robert P. George, "Ashamed of the Gospel? The End of Comfortable Christianity," *Touchstone*, May/June 2015, 3–4.

the cultural circumstances to be the acceptable parts of Christian teaching and soft-pedal or even abandon the parts that the enforcers of cultural norms deem to be unacceptable. We make a million excuses for going along with what's wrong, and pretty soon we find ourselves going along with calling it right. Jesus says, "if you want to be my disciple, you must take up your cross and follow me." We say, "um, well, we'll get around to that at some point." May God have mercy on us.[3]

In an age like our own, when culture seems to religious conservatives to be growing increasingly secular and hostile to Christian ethics, the fact that someone of George's convictions can prosper at a place like Princeton is evidence that though the times are challenging and increasingly so, they are not as bad as they could be. But that will continue only if there are individuals and institutions that exist to carry the torch forward with the dispositions of courage, joy, rigor, and tenacity.

George's adversaries may regret that he was ever given tenure to promote the views he does, but no one—even at Princeton—should say that his tenure was wasted.

---

3   Robert P. George, "A thought and a prayer for my fellow Christians (and for myself)," Facebook, June 13, 2012, https://www.facebook.com/robert.p.george.39/posts/3914005561246.

1

A Socrates for Our Athenian Age

A Short Life of Robert P. George

John D. Wilsey

THE SWARTHMORE COLLEGE academic year of 1973–1974 was the freshman year for a young country boy from Morgantown, West Virginia. Robert P. George—he welcomes people to call him Robby—grew up as the oldest of five boys, the sons of Joseph and Catherine George. As with most boys in his station, his childhood was marked mostly by days spent hunting and fishing, walking and running through the woods and over the hills in country claimed over time by the Cherokee, Iroquois, Shawnee, English, and French, and later by Virginia and, as a result of national fratricide in the nineteenth century, West Virginia. George was a precocious boy, talented especially at playing what he calls "Appalachian classical music" (that is, bluegrass) on the banjo,[1] and he was the first of his family ever to attend college. His high school education was adequate for a boy headed for the coal mines but not suited to preparing an academic. Finding himself poorly equipped for the intellectual rigor and challenges of Swarthmore, he wondered during his first semester whether he would make it to the end of the academic year.[2]

---

1   Robert P. George, "Humble Beginnings: A Conversation with Robert P. George," interview by Nino Scalia, *Madison's Notes*, May 27, 2020, https://jmp.princeton.edu/podcast.
2   Guy Denton, "The Making of Robert P. George," *The Dispatch*, October 16, 2021, https://the dispatch.com/.

At this critical time, a professor who believed in George stepped in on his behalf. James Kurth, who taught political science, recognized George's strengths as a critical thinker with a strong desire to succeed. Feeling that a poorly written paper George had submitted did not reflect the young West Virginian's true ability, Kurth called him into his office and tutored him on how to approach academic writing. He gave George a second chance at the paper, and his pupil did much better—earning a B+. And as a result of Kurth's instruction and encouragement, George's performance dramatically improved in his other courses as well.

In George's sophomore year, Professor Kenneth Sharpe, who taught an introductory course in political theory, assigned George's class Plato's dialogue *Gorgias*.[3] Reading *Gorgias* was a life-changing event for the young man. Up to that point, George had always believed that the value of education and, indeed, knowledge itself was instrumental, a means to the end of getting a good job and making a decent income. But *Gorgias* was as a bolt out of the blue sky. Plato portrays Socrates—in his engagement with the Sophist characters Gorgias, Polus, and Callicles—demonstrating that knowledge of truth is actually an end in itself, a thing fundamentally valuable for its own sake. "As soon as Plato led me through the exercise of leading to the conclusion that knowledge is an intrinsic aspect of our well-being and fulfillment as human beings," George notes, "I could see it! I had to . . . rethink everything."[4] Plato's *Gorgias* impelled George toward a lifetime of truth seeking through teaching, writing, debating, and engaging in the public square that has inspired thousands of people over nearly four decades.

Today, George has accumulated a list of impressive credentials. He serves as the McCormick Professor of Jurisprudence in the Politics Department at Princeton University, a chair held previously by distinguished figures such as Woodrow Wilson and Edward Corwin. He was appointed to the US Commission on Civil Rights by President George H. W. Bush, served on the President's Council on Bioethics, was chairman of the US Commission on International Religious Freedom, represented the United States in UNESCO's World Commission on the Ethics of Scientific Knowledge and Technology, and was a judicial fellow of the Supreme Court of

---

3   Denton, "Making of Robert P. George."
4   George, "Humble Beginnings," interview by Scalia.

the United States. He is the founder and director of the James Madison Program in American Ideals and Institutions, a program at Princeton devoted to building the undergraduate curriculum in constitutional studies; advocating for American ideals and institutions; hosting visiting scholars in history, philosophy, law, and political theory for half-year and yearlong appointments; and promoting scholarly cooperation between Princeton students and postdoctoral and visiting fellows in the Program.[5] He is a 1977 graduate of Swarthmore College, and he received a JD (juris doctor) degree from Harvard Law School and an MTS (master of theological studies) from Harvard Divinity School. George also holds degrees of DPhil (doctor of philosophy), BCL (bachelor of civil law), DCL (doctor of civil law), and Dlitt (doctor of letters) from Oxford University.

One of George's proudest moments was when he was awarded the United States Presidential Citizens Medal from George W. Bush in a ceremony in the Oval Office of the White House on December 10, 2008. George's friend Charles Colson, a recipient of the same honor, urged him to wear the lapel pin signifying the medal as a matter of civic duty, and George wears it everywhere he goes. He has given lectures all over the world, holds twenty-two honorary degrees, was awarded the Bradley Prize for Intellectual and Civic Achievement, the President's Award for Distinguished Teaching at Princeton University, and several other prestigious recognitions. His name appears as author or editor on thirteen volumes, and his scholarly articles and reviews can be found in the *Harvard Law Review*, the *Yale Law Journal*, the *Columbia Law Review,* and other renowned publications. His public writings appear in such auspicious outlets as the *New York Times*, the *Wall Street Journal*, and *First Things*.[6] And yet, when one spends a few hours with George, one finds a man devoted to his family, to his students, to his friends, and to ideas. He is known for being the same man when he relates to presidents, popes, Supreme Court justices, and scholars as he is to undergraduates, parishioners, restaurant servers, and janitors.

George's ready smile, customary three-piece suit, familiar shock of neatly parted salt-and-pepper hair, and dignified yet unassuming manner naturally

---

5   Mike Sabo, "The Importance of Civic Education in a Creedal Nation," *RealClearWire*, January 8, 2021, https://www.realclearwire.com/.

6   "Robert P. George," Princeton University, Program in Law and Public Affairs, accessed September 11, 2021, https://lapa.princeton.edu/.

draw people to him. His friends are deeply devoted to him, and his philo-sophical opponents are some of his oldest and most committed companions. George is acknowledged by many to be among the most sincere and consis-tent truth seekers alive today. In 2009, David D. Kirkpatrick of the *New York Times Magazine* called George "this country's most influential conservative Christian thinker,"[7] but George charmingly laughs off this salient description by jesting, "I don't believe a word the *New York Times* says, and I don't believe anyone should believe that claim!"[8] It is an easy claim to believe nonetheless.

Plato's *Gorgias* serves as something of an analogy to George's life and career, as he has pursued truth courageously since his youth and shown others by his example how to be truth seekers themselves. He is a Socrates in our Athenian culture, a culture corrupted by an unquenchable thirst for power; fueled and justified by baseless, sentimental rhetoric; and devoted to the pursuit of the pleasures of unbridled passions. George has devoted his life to the countercultural mission of practicing humility, extending charity, and demonstrating what Socrates taught about the good life, that "this is the best way of life—to live and die in the pursuit of righteousness and all other virtues. Let us follow this, I say, inviting others to join us."[9] George is a partner to anyone who would seek after the good, the true, and the beauti-ful. Though he is a committed Catholic, he counts Jews, Muslims, mainline Protestants, and evangelicals among his friends and collaborators. Prominent evangelicals such as Chuck Colson, Timothy George, Albert Mohler, Peter Lillback, and Richard Land have each found common cause with George over the decades, working alongside him to advocate for the sanctity of life, the sanctity of marriage, and religious freedom. George has proved himself to be a close Catholic ally to evangelicals for his whole career, a fact that this book attests to.

Early Years

George was born on July 10, 1955, as a third-generation American. His grandparents were immigrants—his paternal grandfather came to America

7   David D. Kirkpatrick, "The Conservative-Christian Big Thinker," *New York Times Magazine*, December 16, 2009, https://www.nytimes.com.

8   George, "Humble Beginnings," interview by Scalia.

9   Plato, *Gorgias*, trans. W. D. Woodhead, in *The Collected Dialogues of Plato, Including the Let-ters*, ed. Edith Hamilton and Huntington Cairns, Bollingen Series 71 (New York: Pantheon, 1961), 527e.

from Syria and was of the Antiochene Orthodox tradition, which George proudly observes was the first tradition in the world in which the followers of Christ were called "Christians."[10] His maternal grandfather, a Catholic, arrived from southern Italy. Both of George's grandfathers worked in the coal mines, although his maternal grandfather was able to save enough money to eventually become a grocer. Joseph, George's father (whom he refers to as "the Chief"), was drafted at the age of eighteen in 1944 and served with the Sixty-Sixth Infantry Division (the Black Panthers) in Normandy and Brittany. He was aboard the troop transport SS *Leopoldville* when it was torpedoed by a German U-boat on December 24, 1944, as it carried the division from England to France during the Battle of the Bulge. Hundreds died, but Joseph was among the soldiers who were rescued. A few years after returning home from the war, Joseph met and fell in love with Catherine Sellaro. They were married in 1953 and had five sons: Robert, Leonard, Kent, Keith, and Edward.[11]

The family was tight knit, and the boys were particularly close. George remarks, "At times I couldn't remember which one I was."[12] They stuck together. George recalls, "Rarely did any of us get picked on by other kids, but if we did, it was a case of 'woe unto him by whom transgressions come.'"[13] And while George was the first of his family to go to college, all five boys ultimately earned undergraduate and graduate degrees. Three of George's brothers—Kent, Keith, and Edward—followed him to Oxford. The other, Leonard, holds graduate degrees from Harvard and Yale.

As a boy, George discovered his love of music, especially mountain music played on the banjo. He began playing at age twelve and got so good at the banjo and the guitar that he played for square dances, for rod and gun clubs, and at the West Virginia University folk music scene. He played often on Friday nights at a coffee house run by the Catholic chaplaincy on campus that was known as the Potter's Cellar. On Saturday nights, he would play for the campus Protestants at their chaplaincy, which they called the Last Resort. When he played for the miners, he could make up to twenty

---

10 Robert P. George, interview by the author over videoconference call, September 29, 2021.
11 Anne Morse, "Conservative Heavyweight: The Remarkable Mind of Professor Robert P. George," *Crisis Magazine*, September 1, 2003, https://www.crisismagazine.com/.
12 George, interview by the author.
13 Morse, "Conservative Heavyweight."

dollars a night, which George described as a "fortune" for a country boy in Morgantown in the sixties.[14] George has always loved banjo picking. His banjo playing could be heard from his rooms while he studied at Oxford, and he continues to be an avid bluegrass and folk musician. During the months of the pandemic lockdown in 2020, George would record himself playing and singing songs like "Keep on the Sunny Side," then would post his songs on his social media accounts. Each year at the James Madison Program's annual Robert J. Giuffra Conference, George can be counted on to play and sing informally for a relaxed and joyful crowd after the concluding dinner.

George's parents were the most important shapers of his character. "My life was built on their success," George says, and he learned from them how to cultivate a generous spirit.[15] He remembers his Catholic family being closely integrated with the religious life of Morgantown, which was defined mainly by Scotch-Irish Protestantism dating back to the eighteenth century. While George does not recall the term *evangelical* being used as a descriptor of Protestants when he was growing up, he did consider evangelicalism to be a powerful religious and cultural influence in his community. There were Southern Baptists, independent Baptists, Pentecostals, and mainline Protestants in the Morgantown of the 1950s and 1960s, and the Catholic Georges fit in well, since theirs was a working family like everyone else's. Joseph was a salesman and then a wine and spirits broker in Morgantown, and he encouraged his boys to get to know the religious traditions of their friends by going to church with them, provided they also attended Mass on Sunday.[16]

Encountering Evangelicalism

George's first exposure to evangelicalism was through his boyhood best friend and, particularly, the influence of his friend's mother. They were Southern Baptists, and while his friend's father had died before George knew the family, these Baptists had become a second family to him. They spoke to George of having a personal relationship with Jesus and of the importance of making a decision to follow Christ. While the spirit of this

14   George, "Humble Beginnings," interview by Scalia.
15   George, "Humble Beginnings," interview by Scalia.
16   George, interview by the author.

language was not foreign to George—as Catholics, they would have affirmed those things—George says, "It was just not an idiom in which we spoke."[17] Still, conversations they had together spurred George on to learn more about his own Catholic faith and Christianity more broadly.

It was through George's friendship with this Southern Baptist family that he was introduced to the ministry of Billy Graham. Films of Graham's crusades would periodically be shown in the movie theater in town, and they would attend those films together. George remembered how the crusades would close with Graham's altar call, accompanied by George Beverly Shea's singing of the hymn "Just as I Am." Since Graham's sermon was being displayed on the movie screen, the people in the theater were invited to come behind the curtain backstage to receive counseling and literature. Responding publicly to the altar call was something, as George recalls, "I always felt that, as a Catholic, I shouldn't do, so I didn't do it. But I rejoiced that so many in the audience did." Since those early days, George says, "I developed an enormous admiration for Billy Graham, and a certain kind of envy that the Protestants and evangelicals *had him*!"[18]

By the time George went off to Swarthmore, he was struck by how many academics disparaged evangelicals. "They didn't know [evangelicals]," George says. "I did. I knew that their depiction of them was a caricature, and I was offended that Protestant evangelicals would be thought of in this way by people who purported to be learned, to be intellectuals."[19] Even as a college student, George aligned himself with his evangelical peers, defending them and identifying with them, refusing to distance himself from them or make sure that others knew he was Catholic, attending their Bible studies and prayer meetings, and merely sticking up for his evangelical friends. "I didn't want to leave [their detractors] with the impression that I was embarrassed by evangelical Protestants," George recalls, "so I didn't mind if they thought that's what I was."[20] George's earliest friendships with evangelicals, his admiration for Billy Graham, and his identification with evangelicals who were mocked by secular professors in college formed the basis for what later became strong relationships and partnerships with evangelical leaders.

17 George, interview by the author.
18 George, interview by the author.
19 George, interview by the author.
20 George, interview by the author.

Educational Journey

As a student at Swarthmore, and after having read *Gorgias* under Sharpe's guidance, George became fascinated with law, ethics, and jurisprudence under the tutelage of Swarthmore professor Linwood Urban, an Episcopalian clergyman and specialist in medieval philosophy. He later became acquainted with the work of new natural law scholar John Finnis. It was through Finnis's work on Aristotle and natural law that George broke through David Hume's embrace of subjectivity in ethics to, as George describes it, "a positive account of the objectivity of practical reason and morality that does not fall to the Humean critique."[21] George came to believe that knowledge of the good is real, that humans can possess that knowledge directly, and that we can accept the knowledge of the good as an end in itself. "My grandmother," George says, "who had less than a fifth grade education, understood perfectly well that friendship, for example, was good not merely for instrumental purposes, but was intrinsically valuable."[22] After his graduation from Swarthmore, George studied at Harvard Law School and Harvard Divinity School, where his fascination with the connections between law and morality deepened further. In 1981, upon finishing his studies at Harvard, George received the Frank Knox Memorial Scholarship from Harvard and was accepted to study at Oxford University for the DPhil degree under the supervision of John Finnis and Joseph Raz. Finnis and Raz, protégés of H. L. A. Hart, were taking on a student who would prove to be as significant to the field of legal philosophy in the twenty-first century as their teacher was in the twentieth.

During this time, George was dating Cindy Schrom, an English literature student and classical guitarist whom he had met as a sophomore at Swarthmore. Together, they finished Swarthmore, went to Harvard, and were engaged by the time George went to England to study at Oxford. While bluegrass music wafted from George's rooms ("A bit of Appalachia had taken over the city of dreaming spires," George jests) and natural law philosophy flowed from his pen, his thoughts were ever on Cindy back home in the States. The couple was married at Andover Chapel on Harvard's campus in December 1982. Today they have two adult children,

---

21 Denton, "Making of Robert P. George."
22 Denton, "Making of Robert P. George."

David and Rachel, and George's family is his life's first priority, followed by his students.[23]

In 1986, George submitted his doctoral dissertation, titled "Law, Liberty, and Morality in Some Recent Natural Law Theories." Charles Beitz, who had taught George political science at Swarthmore, contacted him while he was working on his dissertation to let him know that Princeton was looking to fill a position in their Politics Department. Beitz suggested George write to the department, which George did. He was invited to interview and was offered the position. In 1985, George settled into his teaching post at Princeton. Aside from visiting professorships, including one at Harvard Law School, George remarked, "My one and only [full-time] job has been at Princeton."[24]

Evangelical Relationships

After George was granted tenure at Princeton in 1993, George's relationships and partnerships with evangelicals deepened. He joined with Richard John Neuhaus in bringing Catholics, Protestants, Jews, and Eastern Orthodox Christians together through the Institute on Religion and Public Life and *First Things*. The Ethics and Public Policy Center, under the leadership of its then–vice president Michael Cromartie, convened a conference on Protestants and the natural law tradition. At that conference, George found himself in a spirited debate with Carl F. H. Henry on natural law, which attracted the attention of Chuck Colson. As a result of George's exchange with Henry, Colson invited George to speak to the board of Prison Fellowship on natural law, an invitation George accepted. A lifelong friendship ensued.[25]

In Princeton's broad community of students and residents, George has become a well-known friend to evangelicals. Since George founded the James Madison Program in 2000, it has welcomed Protestant and evangelical scholars each year as postdoctoral and visiting fellows, such as Allen C. Guelzo, J. Daryl Charles, Matthew Wright, Adam MacLeod, Adeline Allen, Carl Trueman, Daniel K. Williams, Jonathan Den Hartog, Roberta Bayer, and many others. George has also maintained close ties with evangelical students through involvement with Princeton Christian Fellowship (known

23 Morse, "Conservative Heavyweight."
24 George, "Humble Beginnings," interview by Scalia.
25 George, interview by the author.

as Princeton Evangelical Fellowship prior to 2017), Manna Christian Fellowship, and Athletes in Action. And George has worked closely with Stone Hill Church, an evangelical congregation in Princeton. Matt Ristuccia, Stone Hill's longtime pastor (retired in 2018), is one of George's dear friends, having partnered together with him for many years. Each year, Stone Hill has opened its doors to evangelical visiting scholars at the James Madison Program as they looked for a church home during their yearlong appointments. George has on many occasions given talks at the church.

As a Catholic, George has found common cause with Protestants and evangelicals for over three decades, particularly with regard to issues such as civility, the sanctity of life and marriage, and religious freedom. Still, for George, those issues, as important as they are, must be based in the most important common cause of all, "the spreading of the gospel," specifically, "what [C. S.] Lewis called 'mere Christianity,' the ancient creeds of the Christian church . . . with the essential doctrines of the Trinity and the incarnation."[26] Nicene doctrines and evangelism must form the basis for fellowship between Catholics and evangelicals "because it is a profound sharing."[27] If Catholics and evangelicals can base their fellowship on the essentials of the Christian faith, it follows that their partnership in civic engagement will be marked by the love of Christ. Rather than a sentimental abstraction, the love of Christ serves as the impetus behind an active defense of human dignity, of bearing witness to the truth "when it's easy and when it's hard, and these days it's hard," George says.[28] George insists that Christianity, with love as its essential and animating attribute, "is the ground of possibility of mustering the courage to have somewhat uncomfortable conversations about deep issues that people do not always want to talk about."[29] Protestants and Catholics have pronounced theological differences that keep them from uniting with one another under the same ecclesiastical authority. Those differences aside, what characterizes George is his warmth toward evangelicals and his willingness to partner with them in the defense of "the permanent things."

---

26 George, interview by the author.
27 George, interview by the author.
28 George, interview by the author.
29 Ashley McKinless, "Cornel West and Robert P. George on Christian Love in the Public Square," *America*, March 8, 2019, https://www.americamagazine.org/.

Tough Topics

George has spent his career directly addressing uncomfortable topics because those topics are at the heart of what it means to be human. Conversations about abortion, sexuality, and rights of conscience may not necessarily ease digestion for family members around the table after a Thanksgiving meal, but those issues transcend political, social, and religious tribal concerns and pertain to the most significant elements of how we know the good, the true, and the beautiful. Central to George's philosophy is the idea that human law is necessary and good but only to the extent that it is consistent with divine and natural law, which is superior to human law.[30]

Take abortion as an example. As a member of the President's Council on Bioethics, George heard testimony from Anne Lyerly, MD, who was then serving as chair of the Committee on Ethics of the American College of Obstetrics and Gynecology (ACOG). Lyerly's testimony concerned a report produced by ACOG titled "The Limits of Conscientious Refusal in Reproductive Medicine," in which physicians laid down their opinions of what should count as the concerns of conscience, thereby stepping far outside the scope of their expertise. Specifically, in the members of ACOG's judgment, pregnancy should be considered a matter of health care rather than a decision between a man and a woman about having a child. This judgment was philosophical and political, not scientific. Thus, as George said to the Society of Catholic Social Scientists in 2012, the report's "analysis and recommendations for action do not proceed from a basis of moral neutrality."[31]

One of the recommendations for action in the report was notably troubling. Because ACOG judged that pro-life physicians in recommending their patients elect against abortion would be inappropriately foisting their religious beliefs on them, it advocated barring those physicians from doing so. In an effort to prevent force, the report recommended force! In George's analysis,

> Those responsible for the report and its recommendations evidently *would use coercion* to force physicians and pharmacists who have the temerity to

---

30 McKinless, "Christian Love in the Public Square."

31 Robert P. George, "Conscience and Its Enemies," *Catholic Social Science Review* 18 (2013): 284.

dissent from the philosophical and ethical views of those who happen to have acquired power in the American College of Obstetrics and Gynecology, either to get in line or to go out of business.[32]

The inherent contradiction in ACOG's report was fueled by political commitments that informed their approach to medicine. This was a naked power play in the guise of neutrality and was supposedly, to put it in colloquial terms, "merely following the science." George argued, "In itself, a direct (or elective) abortion—deliberately bringing about the death of a child in utero—does nothing to advance maternal health. . . . That's why it is wrong to depict elective abortion as health care."[33]

George takes a historical and philosophical perspective in his critiques of abortion, same-sex marriage, and transgenderism. Considering today's ethical permissiveness and comparing our contemporary philosophical environment with that of the first- and second-century West, George asserts that the ancient heresy of Gnosticism is making a comeback. The ancient Gnostics divided reality into two distinct spheres, the spiritual and the physical. The spiritual was over and above the physical, superior to it in every way. The physical, marked by change and decay, was evil. Gnostic "Christians" taught that salvation from the world lay in a secret, esoteric *gnosis*, or knowledge of the divine. Today's gnostics echo the ancients in stressing the immaterial over the material. "Applied to the human person," George writes, "this means that the material or bodily is inferior. . . . The self is a spiritual or mental substance; the body, its merely material vehicle."[34]

The obvious consequences of contemporary gnosticism play out in ethical policy matters, namely, matters pertaining to abortion, euthanasia, and sexuality. If personhood is found only in the mental, and not the physical, then a fetus, which is apparently merely physical, possesses no personhood. Conversely, if personhood is found only in the mental, then being same-sex attracted or feeling as if one is a woman trapped in a man's body is the real, and biological corporeality is of no account. Therefore, marriage and sexuality are defined solely in terms of individual sentimentality and sexual passion. Finally, if personhood is found only in the mental, what of

32 George, "Conscience and Its Enemies," 285.
33 George, "Conscience and Its Enemies," 286.
34 Robert P. George, "Gnostic Liberalism," *First Things*, December 2016, 34.

those who have lost or have never had mental competence? They cannot be persons. George writes that, for adherents of the new gnosticism,

> those in the embryonic, fetal, and early infant stages are *not yet* persons. Those who have lost the immediate exercise of certain mental powers— victims of advanced dementias, the long-term comatose and minimally conscious—are *no longer* persons. And those with severe congenital cognitive disabilities aren't now, never were, and never will be persons.[35]

Citing Steven Smith's book *Pagans and Christians in the City*,[36] George accounts for this rise of contemporary gnosticism in the value placed by figures such as John Rawls and Ronald Dworkin on neutrality in law and government.[37] Neutrality, as George has frequently argued, is a disguise for secular ideology pertaining to human nature and the human good. Furthermore, neutrality is meant to be taken as a guard of freedom against religious dogmatism and persecution, but in reality, it is a threat to freedom in two ways, according to George: "freedom as self-mastery (so called 'positive liberty') and freedom as immunity from unwarranted and unjust imposition or coercion ('negative liberty')."[38] Neutrality, detached as it is from objective reality and hanging in the air of epistemic and ethical subjectivity, turns against traditional American understandings of freedom. It constitutes a fundamental redefinition of liberty as something other than the ability to experience human excellence.

On marriage, an institution with human good as an essential attribute, the federal government officially jettisoned biblical and natural law understandings of its nature, once it handed down the 2015 Supreme Court decision *Obergefell v. Hodges*, which requires states to issue licenses for same-sex marriages. For George, neutrality has proved to be a "pretense" that the left has "abandoned,"[39] now that entertainment, Hollywood,

---

35 George, "Gnostic Liberalism," 34.

36 Steven D. Smith, *Pagans and Christians in the City: Culture Wars from the Tiber to the Potomac* (Grand Rapids, MI: Eerdmans, 2021).

37 Robert P. George, "The Pagan Public Square: Our Christian Duty to Fight Has Not Been Cancelled," *Touchstone* 33, no. 3 (May/June 2020): 24–27.

38 Robert P. George, "On Peter Simpson on 'Illiberal Liberalism,'" *American Journal of Jurisprudence* 62, no. 1 (2017): 104.

39 George, "Pagan Public Square," 25.

government, and corporations have adopted a secularist ideology animated by passion, advocated through empty rhetoric based on sentimentality, with its object being increased political power. While George classifies secular ideology in gnostic terms, Smith calls it paganism. But both descriptions seem accurate. As with both ancient Gnosticism and paganism, George argues that while "contemporary secular progressivism" may not contain "*all* the ideas and beliefs of ancient Romans," it is still true that "*some* of the central ideas and beliefs that distinguish secular progressives from orthodox Christians and Jews today are ideas and beliefs they have in common with the people whose ideas and beliefs Judaism and Christianity challenged in the ancient world."[40]

Thus, the culture we live in today bears striking similarities to that of the ancient Greco-Roman world in the first centuries of church history. Whereas the ancient Greco-Roman world was pre-Christian, contemporary Western culture is rejecting Christian norms as informed by divine and natural law. In an essay for *National Review*, George reflects on the thought of the nineteenth-century German poet Heinrich Heine, who wrote in 1814 that Western culture was on the verge of discarding Christian norms and returning to the paganism of the ancients. Heine prophesied,

> This talisman [the cross, Christianity] is fragile. And the day will come when it will collapse miserably. Then the ancient stony gods will rise from the forgotten debris and rub the dust of a thousand years from their eyes. And then Thor, with his giant hammer, will jump up and smash the Gothic cathedrals.[41]

What struck George about Heine's lines was his recognition that what happens in the mind ultimately finds expression in reality. The rejection of premodern, ordered thought, beginning with metaphysics, followed by epistemology and ethics, became disordered in the Continental Enlightenment of the seventeenth and eighteenth centuries. First epistemology, then ethics became the starting point for philosophy and theology, representing a rejection of Christian orthodoxy in favor of autonomous reason first and

---

40 George, "Pagan Public Square," 25.

41 Robert P. George, "Realms Visible and Invisible," *National Review* 72, no. 23 (December 17, 2020): 34.

of experience and feelings later. Reflecting on Heine's prognostication, George writes,

> There is an ideology, a set of beliefs, a worldview . . . that has long been in place in the minds and hearts of opinion-shaping elites and influencers that now plays out in the realm of the visible. The time to have fought was long ago in the realm of the intellect, the invisible domain of the spirit.[42]

But there is no reason to give up hope. Whereas bad ideas yield bad results, good ideas yield good results: "Good thinking, good education, good formation can produce good results every bit as much as bad thinking, bad ideas, and bad formation will produce evil results."[43] So courage, not defeatism, is required. The need for courage is, in fact, a ubiquitous theme in George's public voice.

Courage finds its voice in the expression of the conscience. For George, knowledge is an intrinsic human good, and the pursuit of knowledge is a unique feature of human personhood. Truth seeking, knowledge acquisition, and the asking and answering of ultimate questions—George has spent his career arguing that these elements of conscience formation are essential to being human. Comparing John Stuart Mill with John Henry Newman on freedom and conscience, George has written that Newman's concept of conscience is not based on subjective individuality: "It is not a writer of permission slips."[44] Conscience is understood as an exchange of duties and privileges, rights and obligations, as seen through the lens of natural law. Rights of conscience—the basis of religious freedom—are based on a search for truth and demand action based on what the truth reveals. Sometimes the truth reveals reality that goes against what a fallen human nature desires. But conscience is not autonomous, individual, and thus divorced from reality. As George explains it, "Conscience as 'self-will' is a matter of feeling or emotion, not reason. . . . Conscience as self-will identifies permissions, not obligations."[45] In contrast to conscience as self-will,

---

42 George, "Realms Visible and Invisible," 36.
43 George, "Realms Visible and Invisible," 36.
44 Robert P. George, "John Stuart Mill and John Henry Newman on Liberty and Conscience," *Saint Anselm Journal* 10, no. 2 (Spring 2015): 43.
45 George, "Liberty and Conscience," 44.

the right of conscience does press obligation on us. Thus, even when the right of conscience results in duties that a person does not want to fulfill, it is still essential to human flourishing since it is the conscience that acts as a conduit to human understanding.

As Americans, our rights of conscience are expressed in the religion clause of the First Amendment. Freedom of religion is first among four other freedoms: freedom of speech, freedom of the press, freedom of assembly, and freedom of petition. George notes that freedom of religion is first because religion is "architectonic in the way we lead our lives."[46] People engage with the most significant questions of the universe through religion. Does God exist? What are his attributes? Has God spoken? How do we know what he has revealed to us? Who am I as God created me? What does God require of me? What must I do to be saved? Religious questioning of this sort, George writes, "helps us to view our lives as a whole and to direct our choices and activities in ways that have *integrity*—both in the moral sense of that term and in the broader sense of having a life that hangs together, that makes sense."[47] Americans must exhibit courage to ask ultimate questions, to allow their consciences to be formed by religion, because religion is an intrinsic good.

But religious freedom and rights of conscience do not pertain to Americans alone. Americans must guard the freedoms identified in the First Amendment, but they must also remember that religious freedom is under threat elsewhere in the world. In 2013, George received the John Leland Award for Religious Liberty from the Ethics and Religious Liberty Commission of the Southern Baptist Convention. In his acceptance address, titled, "Those of Us Who Care about Religious Freedom Have a Job to Do," George reminded his hearers that "religious freedom entails the right to be who we truly are as human beings."[48] Religious freedom means being free to believe and to act on that belief concerning ultimate questions and how those questions bear on immanent reality. Governments that trample on their citizens' rights of conscience violate the humanity of their citizens and harm their societies politically, economically, morally, and socially.[49] In the

---

46 George, "Liberty and Conscience," 45.
47 George, "Liberty and Conscience," 45.
48 Robert P. George, "Those of Us Who Care about Religious Freedom Have a Job to Do," *Vital Speeches of the Day* 80, no. 2 (February 2014): 35.
49 George, "Job to Do," 36.

year that George received the Leland Award, more than five billion people were living in repressive regimes—countries such as Burma, China, Egypt, Iran, Nigeria, Pakistan, Russia, Saudi Arabia, even Germany and Sweden. Western nations that restrict religious freedom, George said, aim to ensure the absolute power of secularist ideology over competing ideas, a secularist ideology that stems from "an extremist view of state-church separation which seeks to relegate religion to the purely private domain."[50] Such a view of church-state separation fosters the doctrine of neutrality, which, as we have seen above, leads to paganism. But American citizens do not have to wait for their own government to act. Through active support and advocacy, ordinary citizens can and ought to defend religious freedom and pressure the government to take steps to protect religious freedom at home and abroad.[51]

To properly stand for truth in a culture that so often opposes it, civility and academic freedom are necessary. George has exemplified civility and commitment to academic freedom consistently from Princeton and is known by his friends and opponents as a true Christian gentleman. Both honest dialogue between parties with sincere convictions and sharing a deep desire for knowledge for its own sake are prerequisites for civility, according to George. In institutions of higher learning, civility can flourish only where there is academic freedom. George has defined academic freedom as "freedom *for* something, something profoundly important—namely, the intellectual excellence that makes self-mastery possible."[52] Political correctness, the cousin of neutrality, shuts down conversation in the name of tolerance. But the true casualty of political correctness is knowledge. Since knowledge is an intrinsic good and is necessary to human flourishing, the liberal arts curriculum ought to be unshackled from the constraints of false tolerance in order for true dialogue to occur and thus truth to be discovered. Even in confessional institutions, truth provides the boundaries for academic freedom, so that ideas can be explored and debated without fear. "Freedom," George argued, "is as necessary to the intellectual life of man as oxygen is to his bodily life."[53]

---

50 George, "Job to Do," 39.

51 George, "Job to Do," 40–41.

52 Robert P. George, "Why Academic Freedom Matters (Now More Than Ever)," *Intercollegiate Studies Institute* (blog), June 18, 2018, https://isi.org/.

53 George, "Why Academic Freedom Matters."

Academic freedom is necessary also for Catholics and Protestants to understand one another and join in common cause together. True civility fostered in an environment of academic freedom allows for intellectual humility, which is necessary in the pursuit of truth. Both Catholics and Protestants must acknowledge that they have much to learn from one another. George observes that Catholics have developed an intellectual and theological tradition drawing on thought dating back to Plato and Aristotle; Protestants, in their commitment to Scripture, have taught by their example the profound value of the devotional study and applica-tion of the Bible.[54] Since the 1960s, Catholics and Protestants have forged partnerships in contending for human dignity together. George notes that this partnership "began in the trenches of the pro-life movement where Catholics and Protestants found themselves together because of shared devotion to the sanctity of human life."[55] Ultimately for George, Catholics and Protestants today recognize that, with regard to ethical issues per-tinent to the public square, much more unites them than divides them. To be sure, George acknowledges, there are real differences between the two, and those differences must be addressed: "I've never been the sort of ecumenist that says, ah, the differences aren't important." He insists that the work of restoring Christian unity is the work of the Holy Spirit, and people get in the way of his work with their pride and tribalism: "When we lose humility, we impede the work of the Holy Spirit. Conversations in which we are dealing with differences must be in the spirit of humil-ity, and we must be praying together to have a spirit of Christian unity."[56] George's wisdom and example have served the cause of both Catholics and Protestants well, resulting in the advance and defense of truth and human flourishing.

Socrates Redux

Plato's *Gorgias* was instrumental to George's becoming a legal philosopher, natural law theorist, professor, and public intellectual. In the dialogue, Socrates engages Gorgias with the question of "what it is you claim to be

---

54 George, interview by the author.

55 Robert P. George, "What Protestants Can Learn from Catholics, and Vice-Versa," *Catholic Herald*, January 23, 2021, https://catholicherald.co.uk/.

56 George, interview by the author.

the greatest blessing to man."[57] Gorgias attempts to argue that the greatest blessing is the power to persuade others through rhetoric—"I mean the power to convince by your words the judges in court, the senators in Council, the people in the Assembly, or in any other gathering of a citizen body."[58] Socrates pursues this argument with Gorgias, patiently walking him down the corridors of the logical consequences of such an argument. Socrates ultimately silences Gorgias, convincing him that rhetoric's value is only chimerical, "a creator of a conviction that is persuasive but not instructive of right and wrong."[59] Rhetoric, in the final analysis, leads to false conclusions, fails to serve the purposes of truth, and is, according to Socrates, "a form of flattery, and I claim that this kind of thing is bad . . . because it aims at what is pleasant, ignoring the good."[60] Socrates's instruction to Gorgias is reminiscent of our own culture's preoccupation with rhetoric turned against logic, against reason, against the good—a rhetoric used in arguments that undermine the institution of the family, militate against human dignity through the destruction of the unborn, and violate human dignity by attacking freedom in the name of tolerance. Today, George serves as a Socrates to those who would view rhetoric, the power to persuade the culture, as the greatest of all blessings.

Plato continues the dialogue, with Gorgias leaving the scene and Polus, a young man, taking it on himself to engage Socrates with the argument that the power to tyrannize others is the greatest blessing: "to be at liberty to do what I please in the state—to kill, to exile, and to follow my own pleasure in every act."[61] But Socrates confronts the young man with his ill-conceived argument, saying that rather than envying those who do evil, we should pity them, because of all men, the wicked are the most miserable. For Socrates, "to do wrong is the greatest of evils," and if given a choice between doing and suffering wrong, Socrates said, "I would choose rather to suffer than to do it."[62] Furthermore, the wicked man is marked by misery, but the wicked man who is never punished is even more miserable than the one who is held to account. The wicked man who is punished has at

---

57 Plato, *Gorgias*, 452d.
58 Plato, *Gorgias*, 452e.
59 Plato, *Gorgias*, 455a.
60 Plato, *Gorgias*, 465a.
61 Plato, *Gorgias*, 469c.
62 Plato, *Gorgias*, 469b.

least received instruction in wisdom, but he who has not been punished is bereft of wisdom.[63] By the force of reason and common sense through dialogue, Socrates convinces Polus that he is wrong and "that a man must take every precaution not to do wrong." And if he were to do wrong, he should immediately seek punishment "to prevent the distemper of evil from becoming ingrained and producing a festering and incurable ulcer in his soul." Polus sheepishly replies to Socrates's question "What more can we say?" with the answer "What else indeed can we say, Socrates?"[64]

As with Gorgias, we see in Polus a striking picture of so much of what our own culture values—a quest for power to dominate others and to do what pleases the self in the name of freedom. The cause that unites faithful Catholics, Protestants, Jews, Muslims, and all people of good will is to confront forces that insist that liberty is license, that power over others satisfies, and that one's enemies must be completely destroyed. George has been a model of courage in standing up against such an ethos and what devastation that ethos has wrought on the unborn, on the family, and on the vulnerable.

Finally, Plato introduces the reader to Callicles. Callicles hears Socrates dispatch Polus's argument and asks his friend Chaerephon, with a mocking tone, "Is Socrates in earnest or joking?" Callicles thinks self-mastery to be absurd, an excuse that the weak employ to hide their cowardice and incompetence. Whereas Socrates defines self-mastery as "the popular notion of being temperate and in control of oneself, and mastering one's own pleasures and appetites," Callicles responds by calling Socrates naive and those who are temperate "simpletons." Instead, Callicles argues that the chief blessing of life is found in unleashing the passions and appetites, in having the courage to pursue one's desires wherever they lead: "Anyone who is to live aright should suffer his appetites to grow to the greatest extent and not check them . . . and to satisfy every appetite with what it craves."[65] Furthermore, true happiness and blessedness are found in unbounded desire, and to deny this is to be a fool. Callicles says to Socrates, "Luxury and intemperance and license, when they have sufficient backing, are virtue and happiness, and all the rest is tinsel, the unnatural catchwords of mankind,

63 Plato, *Gorgias*, 472e.
64 Plato, *Gorgias*, 480b.
65 Plato, *Gorgias*, 491e–492a.

mere nonsense and of no account."[66] Could a more accurate description of American culture in the twenty-first century be offered?

What is needed in our own culture is the same thing that was necessary to check such unbalanced and disordered notions of the good, the true, and the beautiful in the fourth century BC. Socrates answers Callicles, who by the end of the dialogue sits in sullen silence, while Socrates offers his unassailable argument. Contrary to Callicles, Socrates says that the temperate soul is good and the intemperate soul evil. He who is possessed of self-mastery knows his duty, and the doing of just duty is always, in itself, just. The temperate man knows his nature, knows that at times it is against his nature to do his duty, but still he must remain steadfast to what he knows is true: "There is every necessity, Callicles, that the sound-minded and temperate man . . . must be completely good, and the good man must do well and finely whatever he does, and he who does well must be happy and blessed, while the evil man who does ill must be wretched."[67] For Socrates, the most blessed state in life is to be temperate above all, in control of one's own passions, aware of one's own nature, and committed to the right even when one's passions militate against the right. Sometimes, the good man will suffer hardship, physical pain, even death, but to suffer wrong is far better than doing wrong: "Of these two then, inflicting and suffering wrong, we say it is a greater evil to inflict it, a lesser to suffer it."[68]

Socrates gives his final appeal in the dialogue, making the case that a man should do more than merely seem good but truly be good, both in public and in private. Rhetoric, that power of persuasion, should be used in the pursuit of justice.[69] And in answering the question he posed to Gorgias at the beginning of the dialogue, Socrates makes the statement I referenced above and will repeat here: "This is the best way of life—to live and die in the pursuit of righteousness and all other virtues. Let us follow this, I say, inviting others to join us."[70]

George is a Socrates in our Athenian culture, many of whose members seem driven by an empty and sentimental rhetoric in pursuit of the power

66 Plato, *Gorgias*, 492c.
67 Plato, *Gorgias*, 507c.
68 Plato, *Gorgias*, 508d–509d.
69 Plato, *Gorgias*, 527b.
70 Plato, *Gorgias*, 527e.

to undermine freedom and tyrannize others in the name of license and passion. As George has argued, our world has much in common with the world of the ancients. Socrates was the man to point people to truth in his day. Robert P. George is a man pointing us to truth in ours. Thank God for giving us such a man.

2

From Separatism to Cobelligerency

Evangelicals, Other Christian Traditions,
and the Common Good

David S. Dockery

MORE THAN TWENTY YEARS AGO, I was introduced to Professor Robert P. George by our mutual friend Chuck Colson.[1] After reading George's book *The Clash of Orthodoxies*, I invited him to speak at Union University. A few years later, he graciously wrote the foreword for my book *Renewing Minds: Serving Church and Society through Christian Higher Education*. We served together on the Manhattan Declaration board and were both involved in the work of *Touchstone* magazine. This chapter is about the changes in North American evangelicalism and in the world of Roman Catholicism that have made possible joint efforts between someone like George and myself. My focus in this chapter entails tracing the developments

---

1   Parts of this chapter have been adapted from David S. Dockery, ed., *Southern Baptists and American Evangelicals: The Conversation Continues* (Nashville: Broadman and Holman, 1993), 1–25; Dockery, "Evangelicalism: Past, Present, and Future," *Trinity Journal* 36, no. 1 (Spring 2015): 3–21; Dockery, "Southern Baptists, Evangelicalism, and the Christian Tradition," in *Baptists and the Christian Tradition: Towards an Evangelical Baptist Catholicity*, ed. Matthew Y. Emerson, Christopher W. Morgan, and R. Lucas Stamps (Nashville: B&H Academic, 2020), 267–92; Dockery and John Stonestreet, eds., *Life, Marriage, and Religious Liberty: What Belongs to God, What Belongs to Caesar; Essays for the Tenth Anniversary of "The Manhattan Declaration"* (Nashville: Fidelis, 2019), ix–xii; Dockery, "Baptist Higher Education, Evangelicalism, and the Global Church," *Baptist Educator* 83, no. 2 (2019): 7–16, https://baptistschools.org/. Used by permission.

in evangelical life over the past century that have led to opportunities for evangelical-Catholic cobelligerency. The chapter also attempts to identify the evangelicals who are engaging Professor George.

Here I seek to understand how the fundamentalist movement, which in the initial decades of the twentieth century was so deeply committed to separatism, has moved toward evangelical-Catholic cooperation, collaboration, and eventually cobelligerency. As the story unfolds, it becomes clear that the move toward evangelical-Catholic cobelligerency did not take place in a vacuum but developed in response to key events during the second half of this past century.[2] The chapter concludes with a brief word regarding shared service for the common good.

Evangelicals: Identity and Current Challenges

The titles of key publications in the early decades of the twenty-first century point us to current concerns related to the evangelical movement. Luder Whitlock has authored *Divided We Fall*, Mark Labberton has put together a multiauthored conversation titled *Still Evangelical?*, Iain Murray has written *Evangelicalism Divided*, and Kenneth Stewart has penned *In Search of Ancient Roots: The Christian Past and the Evangelical Identity Crisis*. In some ways this question is not new. More than half a century ago, in 1967, Carl F. H. Henry published *Evangelicals at the Brink of Crisis*.[3]

Still, the question has intensified. Some, such as Harvard sociologist Robert Putnam and Notre Dame political science professor David Campbell in their volume *American Grace*, point to the enhanced connection between the evangelical movement and political ideologies, noting the priority that these political leanings now take for many people.[4] Dallas

---

2   See Millard J. Erickson, *The New Evangelical Theology* (Westwood, NJ: Revell, 1968).

3   Luder G. Whitlock Jr., *Divided We Fall: Overcoming a History of Christian Disunity* (Phillipsburg, NJ: P&R, 2017); Mark Labberton, ed., *Still Evangelical?: Insiders Reconsider Political, Social, and Theological Meaning* (Downers Grove, IL: InterVarsity Press, 2018); Iain H. Murray, *Evangelicalism Divided: A Record of Crucial Change in the Years 1950 to 2000* (Carlisle, PA: Banner of Truth, 2000); Kenneth J. Stewart, *In Search of Ancient Roots: The Christian Past and the Evangelical Identity Crisis* (Downers Grove, IL: IVP Academic, 2017); Carl F. H. Henry, *Evangelicals at the Brink of Crisis: Significance of the World Congress on Evangelism* (Waco, TX: Word, 1967).

4   Robert D. Putnam and David E. Campbell, *American Grace: How Religion Divides and Unites Us* (New York: Simon and Schuster, 2010).

Theological Seminary professor Ramesh Richard has gone so far as to propose replacing the term *evangelical*, even while noting that the term remains a positive and inviting one across the Global South.[5]

The word *evangelical* is transliterated from the Greek term *euangelion*, which primarily means good or glad news. It also describes the theological identity of a particular group of Christ followers and their calling to proclaim to a lost and dying world the loving and gracious message of eternal salvation provided by the atoning death and resurrection of Jesus Christ. Unfortunately, the term has been tainted by sociological and media descriptions of evangelicals as merely a political category, categorizing people who are seemingly opposed to much of what twenty-first-century cultural shapers seemingly affirm. In the next section of this chapter, I explore the words *evangelical* and *evangelicalism* as understood in North America from a theological, historical, and cultural perspective. Let us begin by attempting to understand who evangelicals are, whence they have come, what they believe, what they do well, and where they have challenges.

Evangelicals are men and women who love Jesus Christ, love the Bible, and love the gospel message. They are gospel people. Evangelicalism, a cross-denominational movement that emphasizes classical Protestant theology, is often best understood as a culturally engaged, historically shaped response to mainline liberalism, on the one hand, and reactionary fundamentalism, on the other.[6]

The evangelical movement finds its roots in the teaching of the apostles, in the early church consensus as it developed through the great church councils, and in the Reformation of the sixteenth century. The movement developed through the influence of Puritanism and Pietism in the seventeenth century and is perhaps best traced to and through the revivals of the eighteenth and nineteenth centuries. Evangelicals are heirs particularly of the postfundamentalists coming out of the twentieth century's

---

5 Ramesh Richard, "Should We Still Be Called 'Evangelicals'?" *Christianity Today*, February 22, 2021, https://www.christianitytoday.com/.

6 See David F. Wells and John D. Woodbridge, eds., *The Evangelicals: What They Believe, Who They Are, Where They Are Changing* (Nashville: Abingdon, 1975); Brian Stanley, *The Global Diffusion of Evangelicalism: The Age of Billy Graham and John Stott*, History of Evangelicalism 5 (Downers Grove, IL: InterVarsity Press, 2013); Gabriel Fackre, *Ecumenical Faith in Evangelical Perspective* (Grand Rapids, MI: Eerdmans, 1993); Thomas Oden, *Rebirth of Orthodoxy: Signs of New Life in Christianity* (San Francisco: HarperSanFrancisco, 2003).

modernist-fundamentalist controversies.[7] Though much has been made today of many evangelicals' involvement in the political arena, including the extremely insightful work by Kenneth Collins, *Power, Politics, and the Fragmentation of Evangelicalism*,[8] evangelicalism is best understood as a confessional identity focused on (1) the gospel message announcing the redemptive work of Jesus Christ, (2) personal conversion or the response to the gospel message, (3) the Bible as the source of that gospel message, and (4) service or activism that lives out that message (adapted from David Bebbington's evangelical quadrilateral). Alister McGrath, in his fine book *Evangelicalism and the Future of Christianity*, suggests similar markers.[9]

Shaping Influences: A Brief Historical Overview

The two Reformation doctrines of *sola Scriptura* (the Bible is the church's ultimate authority) and *sola fide* (salvation is by faith alone) still inform and shape twenty-first-century evangelicalism in a way not unlike the emphases proposed by Kenneth Kantzer half a century ago. These two defining emphases are often called the "formal principle" (the Scriptures) and the "material principle" (the gospel).[10] The seventeenth century added to these doctrinal essentials the need for personal, heartfelt, life-transforming, experiential faith. The influential movements known as Puritanism and Pietism stressed conversion and grace and downplayed liturgy and sacraments, maintaining that a conversion to Jesus Christ made a difference for all aspects of life.[11]

Both the Puritan and Pietist movements were used of God to awaken a cold orthodoxy and to revive scholastic Protestantism. While seeking

---

7   Donald W. Dayton and Robert K. Johnston, eds., *The Variety of American Evangelicalism* (Downers Grove, IL: InterVarsity Press, 1991); Martin E. Marty, *A Nation of Behavers* (Chicago: University of Chicago Press, 1976).

8   Kenneth J. Collins, *Power, Politics, and the Fragmentation of Evangelicalism* (Downers Grove, IL: IVP Academic, 2012).

9   David W. Bebbington, *Evangelicalism in Modern Britain: A History from the 1730s to the 1980s* (London: Unwin Hyman, 1989); Alister E. McGrath, *Evangelicalism and the Future of Christianity* (Downers Grove, IL: InterVarsity Press, 1995), 53–87. Also see Douglas A. Sweeney, *The American Evangelical Story: A History of the Movement* (Grand Rapids, MI: Baker Academic, 2005); Mark Ellingsen, *The Evangelical Movement: Growth, Impact, Controversy, Dialog* (Minneapolis: Augsburg, 1988), 136–73.

10 Kenneth S. Kantzer, "Unity and Diversity in Evangelical Faith," in Wells and Woodbridge, *The Evangelicals*, 38–67.

11 See F. Ernest Stoeffler, *The Rise of Evangelical Pietism* (Leiden: Brill, 1965).

to address the spiritual decline in the Lutheran, Reformed, and Anglican churches, these movements stressed experiential faith, emphasizing prayer, warm-hearted fellowship, and evangelistic zeal. The Pietists influenced both the Moravians and the eighteenth-century revivalists, seen in the conversion account of John Wesley.[12] By the end of the eighteenth century, the most evangelistic of the churches in both North America and Great Britain were the Baptists and Methodists, clearly the fastest-growing groups, which, as Joel Carpenter has noted, even affected the slave communities in which Jesus was found to be a "rock in a weary land."[13] During the last decade of the eighteenth century, William Carey set out for India, launching a worldwide missionary movement that would shape what would become a global evangelical movement by the twenty-first century.[14]

The evangelical movements at the beginning of the nineteenth century looked somewhat different from the Reformation and post-Reformation movements three centuries earlier.[15] While the Reformed theology at Princeton, led by Charles Hodge, A. A. Hodge, and B. B. Warfield, shaped the thought leaders of the day, evangelicalism as a whole placed a greater emphasis on personal, warm-hearted, experiential faith and on cooperation across denominational lines, aggressive evangelistic efforts, conversionist views of salvation, pious living, and revivalist expectations.[16] D. L. Moody became the most influential figure in this regard on both sides of the Atlantic in the nineteenth century, not only for his evangelistic preaching but also for his efforts in social and urban renewal and his collaborative, transdenominational emphasis.[17]

---

12 See F. Ernest Stoeffler, ed., *Continental Pietism and Early American Christianity* (Grand Rapids, MI: Eerdmans, 1976).

13 See Joel A. Carpenter, "The Fellowship of Kindred Minds: Evangelical Identity and the Quest for Christian Unity," in *Pilgrims on the Sawdust Trail: Evangelical Ecumenism and the Quest for Christian Identity*, ed. Timothy George (Grand Rapids, MI: Baker Academic, 2004).

14 See Timothy George, *Faithful Witness: The Life and Mission of William Carey* (Birmingham, AL: New Hope, 1991).

15 See Timothy George, *Theology of the Reformers*, rev. ed. (Nashville: B&H Academic, 2013); also, Bernard L. Ramm, *The Evangelical Heritage* (Waco, TX: Word, 1973), 23–40.

16 See W. Andrew Hoffecker, *Piety and the Princeton Theologians: Archibald Alexander, Charles Hodge, and Benjamin Warfield* (Phillipsburg, NJ: Presbyterian and Reformed, 1981).

17 Michael S. Hamilton, "The Interdenominational Evangelicalism of D. L. Moody and the Problem of Fundamentalism," in *American Evangelicalism: George Marsden and the State of American Religious History*, ed. Darren Dochuk, Thomas S. Kidd, and Kurt W. Peterson (South Bend, IN: University of Notre Dame, 2014), 230–80.

After the Civil War, evangelicals wrestled with the changes taking place all around them, including the rise of Darwinism, naturalism, biblical criticism, a postslavery society, pragmatism, and expanding urbanization and industrialization. As the twentieth century began, new movements were launched to revive, renew, correct, and even to separate from the established Protestant denominations—which evangelicals viewed as growing more liberal and more worldly.[18] And so came the rise of the modernist-fundamentalist controversy. In 1910, the "five fundamentals" were clarified by the Northern Presbyterians, reflecting on earlier versions spelled out in the final decade of the nineteenth century by the Niagara Bible Conference movement. These doctrinal tenets—the full and complete inspiration and authority of Scripture, the virgin birth of Jesus Christ, the deity of Christ, the substitutionary and atoning death and resurrection of Christ, and the historical reality of biblical miracles—sought to address the primary challenges of liberalism.

The publication of *The Fundamentals*, a multivolume work that included ninety articles to address challenges to historic Christianity, edited by R. A. Torrey and funded by Lyman and Milton Stewart, were well-reasoned, serious, calm, thoughtful, not shrill, and generally quite persuasive.[19] More than thirty of these articles dealt with the inspiration, truthfulness, and authority of Scripture. Authors included representatives from diverse denominations and various theological traditions including Calvinistic, Wesleyan, dispensational, covenant, and Keswick movements, together with what some considered to be more moderate voices like the Southern Baptist leader E. Y. Mullins and British theologian James Orr. These volumes represented a different tone and approach than what would characterize the forthcoming fundamentalist movement.

18 See Joel Carpenter, *Revive Us Again: The Reawakening of American Fundamentalism* (New York: Oxford University Press, 1997); Stewart G. Cole, *The History of Fundamentalism* (Hamden, CT: Archon Books, 1963); Norman F. Furniss, *The Fundamentalist Controversy, 1918–1931* (New Haven, CT: Yale University Press, 1954); Andrew Himes, *The Sword of the Lord: The Roots of Fundamentalism in an American Family* (Seattle: Chiara, 2011); George M. Marsden, *Understanding Fundamentalism and Evangelicalism* (Grand Rapids, MI: Eerdmans, 1991), 7–61; Bill J. Leonard, "The Origin and Character of Fundamentalism," *Review and Expositor* 79, no. 1 (1982): 5–17; Louis Gasper, *The Fundamentalist Movement, 1930–1956* (Grand Rapids, MI: Baker, 1963).

19 R. A. Torrey, ed., *The Fundamentals*, 12 vols. (Los Angeles: Bible Institute of Los Angeles, 1917).

A key moment took place in 1919, when fundamentalist leader William Bell Riley said the five fundamentals were not enough. He wanted to also stress separation, dispensationalism, and lifestyle taboos, equating these issues with primary doctrines.[20] A distinguishing mark of the fundamentalist movement over the next three decades was the prioritizing of this expanding list of primary issues.

In 1922, Harry Emerson Fosdick preached his famous sermon at the First Presbyterian Church of New York City "Shall the Fundamentalists Win? No!"[21] In 1923, representing the more conservative perspective, Princeton scholar J. Gresham Machen published *Christianity and Liberalism*; the word *and* in the title was key because Machen maintained that liberalism was a different religion from orthodox Christianity altogether.[22] The publication of this work led to Machen's withdrawal from the faculty of Princeton Theological Seminary to start Westminster Theological Seminary. In 1925 in Dayton, Tennessee, the Scopes trial gained the attention of the nation. The fundamentalists won the battle but seemingly lost the war.[23]

Prior to the modernist-fundamentalist controversy, Protestant denominational distinctives were much more clearly recognized and understood:

- Lutherans: word and faith
- Reformed and Presbyterians: Scripture and the sovereignty of God
- Anglicans: prayerbook and worship
- Baptists: Bible, conversion, and baptism
- Quakers: inner light
- Methodists: heartfelt religion
- Holiness: piety and separation
- Restorationists: New Testament church

20 Timothy P. Weber, "William Bell Riley," in *Baptist Theologians*, ed. Timothy George and David S. Dockery (Nashville: Broadman, 1990), 351–65; William Vance Trollinger, *God's Empire: William Bell Riley and Midwestern Fundamentalism*, History of American Thought and Culture (Madison, WI: University of Wisconsin Press, 1990).

21 Gary Dorrien, *The Making of American Liberal Theology: Idealism, Realism, and Modernity, 1900–1950* (Louisville: Westminster John Knox, 2003), 203–8.

22 J. Gresham Machen, *Christianity and Liberalism* (1923; repr., Grand Rapids, MI: Eerdmans, 1987).

23 Edward J. Larson, *Summer for the Gods: The Scopes Trial and America's Continuing Debate over Science and Religion* (New York: Basic Books, 1997).

- Pentecostals (though newcomers in the early twentieth century): the power of the Spirit[24]

Such clarity began to dissipate as these groups rapidly fragmented in the wake of the modernist-fundamentalist controversies and as fundamentalism became a movement characterized by separatism.

Fundamentalism and the Call to Separation

In the 1920s, groups such as the Fundamentalist Fellowship and the Baptist Bible Union developed, seeking to encourage pastors and churches to separate from their parent denominations, starting the independent church movement in addition to creating new denominations.[25] There was less tension in the South than in the North since the Southern churches were more conservative, though there was discordance among Southern Baptists led by J. Frank Norris.[26]

Separation became a dominant theme among American fundamentalists, calling for the faithful to withdraw from the places where apostasy, modernism, and liberalism were on the upswing in churches, colleges and universities, seminaries, and publishing houses, as well as among denominational leaders.[27] Apostasy was understood as the conscious denial of the expanded list of essential beliefs and practices. Biblical passages such as Romans 16:17–18; 2 Corinthians 6:14–18; and 1 Timothy 6:3–5 were employed as a part of this clarion call to separate from false doctrine and moral impurity. This practice became known as first-degree separation.

Second-degree separation went further, calling for faithful believers to separate from those who refused to separate from liberals, even if their own lives and doctrinal beliefs were in order. Aimed at those who compromised by refusing to separate, second-degree separation led toward a type of isolationism. The call to "come out and be separate" became the watchword of

---

24 David S. Dockery, "Denominationalism: Historical Developments, Contemporary Challenges, and Global Opportunities," in *Why We Belong: Evangelical Unity and Denominational Diversity*, ed. Anthony L. Chute, Christopher W. Morgan, and Robert A. Peterson (Wheaton, IL: Crossway, 2013), 209–31.

25 David S. Dockery, "Separation," *Theological Educator* 41 (1990): 135–39.

26 See O. S. Hawkins, *In the Name of God: The Colliding Lives, Legends, and Legacies of J. Frank Norris and George W. Truett* (Nashville: B&H, 2021).

27 Erickson, *New Evangelical Theology*, 22–30.

extreme fundamentalists like those at Bob Jones University as well as those associated with John R. Rice, the founding editor of *The Sword of the Lord*. Some have even suggested a third-degree form of separation,[28] which called for true fundamentalists to separate from other fundamentalists who failed to practice second-degree separation. During the 1930s, fundamentalists were quite active in publishing newspapers, magazines, tracts, books, and other forms of literature. New colleges, especially Bible colleges, and seminaries were started to prepare a new generation of faithful fundamentalists.[29] The 1940s saw the development of the American Council of Churches, led by Carl McIntire, who, in his book *Outside the Gate*, stressed the importance of separation as a marker of authentic faith.[30]

The Beginnings of Evangelical Renewal

In 1942, new winds began to blow, pushing back against the excesses of fundamentalism, with the formation of the National Association of Evangelicals, which initiated a type of evangelical ecumenism in which commonalities were seen to be more important than denominational distinctives. In 1947, a new theological seminary was founded by evangelist Charles Fuller, designed to create a new and scholarly evangelicalism. Fuller Theological Seminary's young faculty included E. J. Carnell, Carl F. H. Henry, Wilbur Smith, and Harold Lindsell. Carnell held a terminal degree from Harvard, and Henry had completed doctoral work at Boston University. The Evangelical Theological Society, with a shared commitment to biblical inerrancy, was birthed in 1949. That same year, Billy Graham's evangelistic crusade in Los Angeles put Graham on the map, thanks to the unbelievable attention provided by the Los Angeles media. Now Graham had become the movement's architect and spokesman; Henry, the movement's theologian; and Harold Ockenga, pastor of the historic Park Street Church in Boston, the movement's organizer. Prior to his tragic death, Carnell had become the leading apologist while serving as president of Fuller Seminary. Others such as Kenneth Kantzer, Ted Engstrom, and Bernard Ramm, to name a few, also carved out significant roles.[31]

---

28 See Himes, *Sword of the Lord*, 274–85.

29 See Gasper, *Fundamentalist Movement*, 93–120.

30 See Carl McIntire, *Outside the Gate* (Collingswood, NJ: Christian Beacon, 1967).

31 See Erickson, *New Evangelical Theology*, 13–45; Matthew J. Hall and Owen Strachan, eds., *Essential Evangelicalism: The Enduring Influence of Carl F. H. Henry* (Wheaton, IL: Crossway, 2015).

The 1957 New York crusade was pivotal for defining the nonseparatist approach of Billy Graham and the new evangelicals. The fundamentalist leaders labeled Graham apostate because he violated the separatist tendencies of the fundamentalist movement when he invited Roman Catholic and mainline Protestant leaders to sit on the platform at the New York crusade. This story is told with great insight by historian Grant Wacker in his work on Graham titled *America's Pastor*.[32]

In 1959, E. J. Carnell, the brilliant theologian at Fuller Seminary, authored *The Case for Orthodox Theology*, which really should have modified the title of Machen's 1923 work by calling it *Christianity and Fundamentalism*. Carnell declared fundamentalism to be suspicious, separatistic, and divisive. He pointed out that those involved in the movement failed to agree on core beliefs, thus declaring that fundamentalism was "orthodoxy gone cultic."[33]

By contrast, the new leaders of the evangelical movement—Billy Graham, Harold Ockenga, and Carl F. H. Henry, who authored the important volume *The Uneasy Conscience of Modern Fundamentalism*[34]—focused on central core beliefs stressing the importance of convictional cooperation, serious scholarship, and cultural engagement. The new impulse in evangelical renewal had moved from isolation and separation to cooperation and engagement. By the 1960s, the mainline denominations had seemingly lost their way. Living in a time of racial unrest, protests, rock-and-roll celebrations, love-ins, and sit-ins, all amid the sexual revolution, the mainline denominations shifted their focus away from the gospel to social issues like the Vietnam War, civil rights, and gender and sexuality.[35] The emphasis on issues other than the gospel, in the words of former *Los Angeles Times* writer Russell Chandler, moved the "mainline" to the "sideline."[36]

---

32 Grant Wacker, *America's Pastor: Billy Graham and the Shaping of a Nation* (Cambridge, MA: Belknap Press of Harvard University Press, 2014), 12–15.

33 E. J. Carnell, *The Case for Orthodox Theology* (Philadelphia: Westminster, 1959).

34 Carl F. H. Henry, *The Uneasy Conscience of Modern Fundamentalism* (1947; repr., Wheaton, IL: Crossway, 2022).

35 Helen Lee Turner, "Fundamentalism in the Southern Baptist Convention: The Crystallization of a Millennialist Vision" (PhD diss., University of Virginia, 1990).

36 Russell Chandler, *Racing toward 2001: The Forces Shaping America's Religious Future* (San Francisco: HarperSanFrancisco, 1992).

Evangelical Essentials: Bible, Gospel, Missions, and Engagement

Evangelical leaders in the middle of the twentieth century rejected fundamentalism and fundamentalist separatism, while holding on to the fundamental beliefs represented in the best of the Christian tradition that runs through the Reformation, Puritanism, Pietism, and the Great Awakenings. Twentieth-century evangelicals could be characterized as historically orthodox, gospel centered, culturally engaged, and transdenominational. Graham, Henry, and others stressed the importance of biblical inerrancy but viewed it primarily as a matter of evangelical consistency more so than one of evangelical identity.[37]

It has been said that the evangelical movement is a protest against a Christianity that is "not Christian enough." Critiques of the traditional church and calls for renewal have been central features of evangelical-type movements for almost five hundred years.[38] By the middle of the twentieth century, fundamentalism had grown hard-line, harsh, and isolationist;[39] the renewed evangelical movement attempted, instead, to stress Christian unity, cooperation, and collaboration, seeking to distinguish primary matters from secondary and tertiary ones while encouraging a form of convictional evangelical ecumenism.[40] It is best to understand evangelicalism as a large umbrella group that includes many submovements and thousands of parachurch organizations. Robert Wuthnow, the Princeton sociologist, brilliantly argues that these changes were key to the major restructuring of American religion that had taken place by the end of the twentieth century, resulting in the decline of denominationalism.[41]

---

37 Carl F. H. Henry, ed., *Revelation and the Bible* (Grand Rapids, MI: Baker, 1958). Contributors to this volume included, among others, G. C. Berkouwer, F. F. Bruce, and Paul K. Jewett, who did not affirm biblical inerrancy.

38 Sweeney, *American Evangelical Story*, 17–26.

39 Fundamentalism, best understood as a reaction to theological liberalism, modernism, Darwinism, and the expression of these movements in culture, developed through six phases in the twentieth century, moving (1) from a defense of historical orthodoxy, (2) to the fundamentals, (3) to fundamentalism, (4) to harsh legalism and separatism, (5) to withdrawal from denominations, (6) to becoming hard-line and isolationist, splintering into several groups. See C. Allyn Russell, *Voices of American Fundamentalism: Seven Biographical Studies* (Philadelphia: Westminster, 1976); Barry Hankins, ed., *Evangelicalism and Fundamentalism: A Documentary Reader* (New York: New York University Press, 2008).

40 Carpenter, *Revive Us Again*, 141–60; Donald G. Bloesch, *The Evangelical Renaissance* (Grand Rapids, MI: Eerdmans, 1973); Carl F. H. Henry, *Evangelicals in Search of Identity* (Waco, TX: Word, 1976).

41 Robert Wuthnow, *The Restructuring of American Religion: Society and Faith Since World War II* (Princeton, NJ: Princeton University Press, 1988).

For evangelicals, as with historic orthodoxy throughout the centuries, the church's basic beliefs are centered on and grounded in Jesus Christ. We can understand evangelicalism through the window of both historical meaning and ministry connectedness, but it also includes important truth claims, giving the movement a theologically shaped meaning.[42] As Kenneth Kantzer has reminded us, we cannot and must not miss the fact that evangelicals have prioritized the authoritative Scripture and the gospel message focused on the person and work of Jesus Christ.[43]

Evangelicals believe that salvation is by God's grace alone through faith alone in Jesus Christ alone. By grace believers are saved, kept, and empowered to live a life of service. Evangelicalism is more than an intellectual assent to creedal formulas, as important as these confessional statements are. It is more than a reaction to error and certainly more than a call to return to the past. It is the affirmation of and genuine commitment to the central beliefs of orthodox Christianity, as these beliefs have been carefully and clearly articulated. These core strengths, representing commitments to the Bible, the gospel, missions, and engagement, reflect the best of the evangelical movement.[44]

Toward a Transdenominational Evangelical Ecumenism

Most of the larger denominations in North America have been divided over whether evangelicalism as a movement has been a help or a hindrance to them. More than forty years ago, Foy Valentine, who at the time served as the leader of the Southern Baptist Christian Life Commission, the forerunner to the Ethics and Religious Liberty Commission, claimed, "Southern Baptists are not evangelicals; that is a Yankee word."[45] Part of that claim had to do with the left-of-center leanings of most Southern Baptist leaders at the time; part of it was a failure to understand the differences between the newer evangelicalism and the older fundamentalism. But the confusion represented in Valentine's response points to the confusion present among a variety of leaders across all denominational lines.

42 John Stott, *Evangelical Truth* (Downers Grove, IL: InterVarsity Press, 1999), 13–34.

43 Kenneth S. Kantzer, "Systematic Theology as a Practical Discipline," in *Doing Theology for the People of God: Studies in Honor of J. I. Packer*, ed. Donald Lewis and Alister McGrath (Downers Grove, IL: InterVarsity Press, 1996), 21–42.

44 McGrath, *Evangelicalism and the Future of Christianity*, 53–60.

45 Quoted in Kenneth L. Woodward, "The Evangelicals," *Newsweek*, October 1976, 76.

The emphasis on cooperation reflected the best of the historical evangelical movement from the time of the awakenings and revivals in the eighteenth century with George Whitefield, from the nineteenth century with D. L. Moody, and from the expanded efforts during the twentieth century with Billy Graham. Evangelicalism, which during this time primarily functioned without a developed ecclesiology or a shared funding approach, created networks that worked through parachurch groups and around denominational structures, resulting in a distinctive type of evangelical ecumenism.[46]

Evangelicals are best understood as people committed not only to essential orthodox Christian beliefs but also to transdenominational movements, working together in special-purpose groups and across shared networks. These interlocking networks, more so than denominations, form the center of evangelicalism. D. L. Moody popularized these special-purpose-group movements. Billy Graham blessed and expanded these organizations, which emphasized lay leadership and entrepreneurial development. Evangelicals rarely started new denominations, but they poured their energy into an untold number of organizations.

Changes in our twenty-first-century context can be seen in technology, in the economy, in globalization, in government, in the social realm, in population patterns, and elsewhere. Evangelicalism is clearly not exempt from the impact of these issues. It is important to be aware that the movement's unity, or perceived unity, is threatened by politics, key doctrinal differences, a variety of approaches to church and worship patterns, methods of ministry, and diverse opinions on ethical and social issues, including social justice, in order for efforts toward missional and ministry collaboration, including evangelical-Catholic cobelligerency, to proceed.[47]

46 See Christian Smith, *American Evangelicalism: Embattled and Thriving* (Chicago: University of Chicago Press, 1998), 9–19; John C. Stackhouse Jr., *Evangelical Landscapes: Facing Critical Issues of the Day* (Grand Rapids, MI: Baker Academic, 2002), 13–120.

47 The restructuring of American religion includes a more horizontal than vertical understanding of affinities within the Christian movement, particularly for evangelicals, as described by Wuthnow in *The Restructuring of American Religion*. It is certainly an interesting day when evangelical Baptists and evangelical Presbyterians find that they have more in common with traditional Roman Catholics and Eastern Orthodox than with progressives in their own denominational tradition. Such common ground has opened the door for cobelligerency opportunities discussed in this chapter. See Charles Colson and Richard John Neuhaus, eds., *Evangelicals and Catholics Together: Toward a Common Mission* (Nashville: Thomas Nelson, 1995).

A century ago, liberalism began to flourish by adapting the Christian faith to the changing culture, even identifying with it. Shaped by the influence of Friedrich Schleiermacher and Horace Bushnell, as well as their popularizers, such as Harry Emerson Fosdick, Henry Ward Beecher, and Philips Brooks, liberalism and its wide-ranging influence seemingly had great momentum. By the time of World War I, at least half of all denominational leaders in America were self-identified liberals, as well as about one-third of all pastors, and more than half of all publishing house leaders and college and seminary faculty. During this time, the unique historic and orthodox claims of the Christian faith were being rejected or at least redefined.[48]

In our world today, we see the rise of secularization and pluralization, a growing interest in a vast and amorphous spirituality, a new atheism, the rise of the "nones" (those with no religious affiliation), all shaped by and within a rapidly changing postmodern culture.[49] While there are things for evangelicals to learn from the trends of the early and mid-twentieth century and from our own period as well, before some go rushing toward the trending post-evangelical trajectories of our day, it would be good to be reminded of the overall assessment of the progressive movement from H. Richard Niebuhr, one of the twentieth century's most profound thinkers: "Liberalism has created a God without wrath who brought men without sin into a kingdom without judgment through the ministry of Christ without an atoning cross."[50]

Yet just as evangelicals need not fall into the waiting arms of a revisionist progressivism, so they would be equally wise to avoid a reductionistic, raucous, and separatistic fundamentalism. Neither a new form of liberalism nor a reactionary fundamentalism, however, are wise options. What is needed at this time are thoughtful efforts to strengthen cooperative and collaborative work, including a type of evangelical cobelligerency for the sake of the common good.[51]

---

48 See Luigi Giussani, *American Protestant Theology: A Historical Sketch* (Montreal: McGill-Queens University Press, 2013), 53–99.

49 James Emery White, *The Rise of the Nones: Understanding and Reaching the Religiously Unaffiliated* (Grand Rapids, MI: Baker, 2014).

50 H. Richard Niebuhr, *The Kingdom of God in America* (New York: Harper, 1959), 193; also see Sydney Ahlstrom, *Theology in America: The Major Protestant Voices from Puritanism to Neo-Orthodoxy* (Indianapolis: Bobbs-Merrill, 1967), 587–618.

51 See J. I. Packer and Thomas C. Oden, *One Faith: The Evangelical Consensus* (Downers Grove, IL: InterVarsity Press, 2004); Stott, *Evangelical Truth*, 13–34; H. E. W. Turner, *The Pattern of*

Cooperation, Collaboration, and Cobelligerency

Commitments to cooperation and collaboration, as well as efforts toward evangelical cobelligerency, have developed for evangelicals from a theological understanding of the kingdom of God. In a distinguishing manner, Carl F. H. Henry articulated a concern for personal and social ethics, which was informed by an understanding that Christ followers live in a sinful world until God unveils his glory in an eschatological revelation of power and judgment, vindicating righteousness and justice.[52] During Henry's tenure as editor of *Christianity Today*, many of his editorials focused on these themes.

Henry's understanding of the kingdom provided a framework for cultural engagement that would pave the way for opportunities of evangelical cobelligerency.[53] Henry reflectively offered strategies for how evangelicals could serve together in the work of cultural engagement and social action. Recognizing that evangelism, winning individuals to Christ, has been a priority for evangelicals, Henry stressed the importance of evangelism while calling for believers to be benevolent, compassionate, and engaged citizens, suggesting that the work of social justice be seen as a parallel calling. Recognizing that all governments and individuals are imperfect, he stressed that salvation remained America's only ultimate hope. Social action grows out of evangelism; at times Henry seemed to imply that evangelism and social action are equal partners, that individual conversion through preaching and political restructuring for greater social justice through social action are joint priorities.[54] He did not, however, advocate for the strategy put forth by Jim Wallis through *Sojourners* and Ron Sider through Evangelicals for Social Action (now Christians for Social Action). These groups, influenced by the Anabaptist tradition and suspicious of all political power and governmental institutions, have been committed to rigorous discipleship, corporate lifestyle, and social critique, associating the church with the powerless and dispossessed.[55]

Christian Truth: A Study in the Relations between Orthodoxy and Heresy in the Early Church (London: Mowbray, 1954).

52 See Carl F. H. Henry, *Aspects of Christian Social Ethics* (Grand Rapids, MI: Eerdmans, 1964); also, Henry, *Christian Personal Ethics* (Grand Rapids, MI: Eerdmans, 1957).

53 See Carl F. H. Henry, *God, Revelation, and Authority*, 6 vols. (Waco, TX: Word, 1979), 4:522–91.

54 See Carl F. H. Henry, *A Plea for Evangelical Demonstration* (Grand Rapids, MI: Baker, 1971).

55 See Robert K. Johnston, *Evangelicals at an Impasse: Biblical Authority in Practice* (Atlanta: John Knox, 1979), 77–112.

From the time he penned *The Uneasy Conscience of American Fundamentalism*, Henry pushed for a combination of evangelism and social action. He believed that God is intimately involved in the effort to rescue society from its woes and that Christians have the obligation to serve as redeeming agents of Christ.[56]

Even while articulating these ideals and creating transdenominational networks to attempt to implement them in the middle of the twentieth century, evangelicals were still quite uncomfortable working with Roman Catholics.[57] It should be noted that the reverse was also the case, certainly prior to Vatican II (1962–1965).[58] In the broader context of forming ecumenical alliances in the twentieth century, starting with John R. Mott and the 1910 Edinburgh Conference, which eventually led to the founding of the National Council of Churches and the World Council of Churches, both evangelicals and Roman Catholics largely remained on the sideline.[59]

When President Harry Truman appointed an envoy to the Vatican in the early 1950s, both Francis Schaeffer and Carl F. H. Henry voiced their opposition to such a move.[60] In *The Fundamentals*, key articles addressed not only liberalism but also Romanism.[61] The anti–Roman Catholic mindset was on full display when John F. Kennedy ran for president of the United States.[62] After the Supreme Court decision in 1973 in *Roe v. Wade*, however, things began

---

56 Henry, *God, Revelation, and Authority*, 2:1–24; also see his personal reflections in Carl F. H. Henry, *Confessions of a Theologian: An Autobiography* (Dallas: Word, 1986).

57 See Loraine Boettner, *Roman Catholicism* (Phillipsburg, NJ: Presbyterian and Reformed, 1962).

58 At Vatican II, some Orthodox and Protestants, who have received a Trinitarian baptism, were categorized as "separated brethren." Several Roman Catholic theologians, over the past fifty years, have been exploring further soteriological understandings. See Timothy George and Thomas G. Guarino, eds., *Evangelicals and Catholics Together at Twenty: Vital Statements on Contested Topics* (Grand Rapids, MI: Brazos, 2015). Also see Gregg R. Allison, *Roman Catholic Theology and Practice: An Evangelical Assessment* (Wheaton, IL: Crossway, 2014); Gregg R. Allison, *40 Questions about Roman Catholicism* (Grand Rapids, MI: Kregel Academic, 2021).

59 See Ruth Rouse and Stephen Neill, eds., *A History of the Ecumenical Movement*, vol. 1, *1517–1948* (Philadelphia: Westminster, 1954), 405–15.

60 See Timothy Padgett, ed., *Dual Citizens: Politics and American Evangelicalism* (Bellingham, WA: Lexham, 2020).

61 See T. W. Medhurst, "Is Romanism Christianity," in Torrey, *The Fundamentals*, 3:288–300.

62 More than 150 Protestant leaders joined together to voice their opposition to a Roman Catholic president in the presidential election of 1960. Supporters of the protest included Billy Graham and Norman Vincent Peale. Peale was quoted as saying, "Faced with the election of a Catholic, our culture is at stake." "The Religious Issue: Hot and Getting Hotter," *Newsweek*, September 19, 1960, cited in Thomas C. Reeves, *A Question of Character: A Life of John F. Kennedy* (New York: Forum Books, 1991), 191.

to change. Francis Schaeffer called for evangelicals and Roman Catholics to work together as cobelligerents against abortion.[63] Roman Catholic thinkers and leaders had been more consistent advocates for a pro-life ethic than many evangelicals prior to this key court decision. The issue of abortion became the rallying cry for various Christian traditions to work together, seeking to penetrate the culture and to engage the political arena and the justice system, as well as the rest of society.

These cobelligerency efforts led to collaborative responses not only to issues like the sacredness of life but to matters related to human sexuality and marriage, the importance of racial reconciliation, the meaning of religious liberty, and calls for collaboration in the public square. While it is challenging, to say the least, to address all these matters, the failure to do so has led to the loss of a theological compass in some sectors of the evangelical world, resulting in a growing lack of consensus regarding both ethical issues and cultural challenges.[64]

Chuck Colson, founder of Prison Fellowship, and Richard John Neuhaus,[65] founding editor of *First Things*, built on the call of Francis Schaeffer and the kingdom vision of Carl F. H. Henry to encourage what Colson often called an ecumenism of the trenches.[66] In fall 2009, guided by the leadership of Chuck Colson, more than 150 religious leaders came together to address three of the key cultural issues of the twenty-first century: life, marriage, and religious liberty. At Colson's request, Timothy George, founding dean of the Beeson Divinity School, and Robert P. George, McCormick Professor of Jurisprudence at Princeton University, served as primary authors

---

63 See Francis A. Schaeffer, *A Christian Manifesto* (Westchester, IL: Crossway, 1981); Schaeffer, *How Should We Then Live?* (Old Tappan, NJ: Revell, 1976). Also see Barry Hankins, *Francis Schaeffer and the Shaping of Evangelical America* (Grand Rapids, MI: Eerdmans, 2008). Furthermore, in *Strength for the Journey: An Autobiography* (New York: Simon and Schuster, 1987), Jerry Falwell credits Schaeffer for helping him see how to build coalitions across theological boundaries.

64 See John S. Dickerson, *The Great Evangelical Recession: Six Factors That Will Crash the American Church . . . and How to Prepare* (Grand Rapids, MI: Baker, 2013), 11–122.

65 Richard John Neuhaus, *The Naked Public Square: Religion and Democracy in America*, 2nd ed. (Grand Rapids, MI: Eerdmans, 1988).

66 Colson and Neuhaus refer to "an ecumenism of the trenches born out of a common moral struggle to proclaim and embody the gospel of the Lord Jesus Christ." Quoted in Timothy George, "Unity," in *Evangelicals and Catholics Together at Twenty*, ed. Timothy George and Thomas G. Guarino (Grand Rapids, MI: Brazos, 2015), 2–3. It should be noted that fundamentalist and conservative evangelical leaders such as John MacArthur and R. C. Sproul did not support the efforts of the Manhattan Declaration.

of a significant statement known as the Manhattan Declaration. Colson and Timothy George were Southern Baptist evangelicals, Robby George, a faithful Roman Catholic.

Included among the 150 religious leaders were Roman Catholics, Orthodox, and evangelical Protestants from various denominations and nondenominational backgrounds. Deep theological differences would have made it nearly impossible for this group to reach consensus about things such as the work of evangelism or church life, and especially to share Communion together, but they were able to find broad agreement in their concerns for these pressing cultural issues. To be clear, the Manhattan Declaration, which was a portrait of cobelligerency, was no attempt at a mushy ecumenism. Rather, the statement was an affirmation built around genuine, shared conviction. The participants also recognized their joint commitments to the Nicene Creed (and even then, they acknowledged historical differences in the understanding of the creed) and their collective concern regarding the issues of life, marriage, and religious liberty, among other important cultural and societal challenges. Within months of the statement's release, more than 550,000 people added their names in support of the Manhattan Declaration.

A decade later, at a somewhat different cultural moment, some came together once again to express their ongoing commitments on these three key issues.[67] During that decade, the board of the Manhattan Declaration passed on the responsibility for the oversight of the declaration to the Colson Center for Christian Worldview, under the direction of John Stonestreet. The ten-year anniversary of the statement provided an opportunity not only to renew and reaffirm the commitments articulated so clearly in 2009 but also to once again bring the work back to public attention. Building on their work as primary authors of the original statement, Timothy George and Robby George wrote the bookend chapters for the volume. The Beeson dean offered a ten-year reflection, while the McCormick professor penned a concluding and defining word regarding the conflict of worldviews in our cultural context.[68] Between these two brilliant chapters were thoughtful contributions related to the themes of life, marriage, and religious liberty,

---

67 See Dockery and Stonestreet, *Life, Marriage, and Religious Liberty.*
68 Robert P. George, "Postscript: A Contest of Worldviews," in *Life, Marriage, and Religious Liberty,* 172–83.

including a word from Chuck Colson, a piece that was written in 2010, just one year after the release of the declaration.

Among the Roman Catholic contributors were Ryan T. Anderson, Timothy Cardinal Dolan, Mary Eberstadt, Robert P. George, Jennifer Roback Morse, and R. R. Reno. The Orthodox contributors included Chad Hatfield and Frederica Mathewes-Green. The other contributors—Randy Alcorn, Bruce Ashford, Joni Eareckson Tada, Michael Farris, Timothy George, Russell Moore, Kristen Waggoner, Andrew Walker, Rick Warren, Trevin Wax—represented various traditions within the evangelical movement. One could not have imagined such a volume during the first half of the twentieth century.

The group of influential thinkers contributing to the book, speaking from their respective and distinctive theological, vocational, and ecclesiastical backgrounds, provided a symphonic, up-to-date commentary on the three primary principles affirmed in the Manhattan Declaration. The substantive, convictional, and readable chapters attempted to be charitable to those with whom they differed, modeling kindness, humility, and civility—again, something quite different from the raucous voices of fundamentalism a century earlier. Genuine civility and kindness are much needed in our polarized and fragmented culture. Civility, rightly understood, is not merely a diplomatic posture nor a code of conduct but a virtue. The volume produced a chorus that attempted to "hold fast what is good" (1 Thess. 5:21), while faithfully "holding fast to the word of life" (Phil. 2:16). Speaking and living with convictional civility and convictional kindness reflect lessons that all the contributors learned from Chuck Colson and that are exemplified in the work of Robby George.[69]

While the authors attempted to reflect and model faithful cultural engagement, real differences of theological conviction remained among the contributors. They shared substantial agreement on the issues of life, marriage, and religious liberty, but authors spoke from, and not always for, their particular traditions and denominational perspectives. The work exhibits real tensions, which reflect the challenges involved in the work of cobelligerency. Not every participant in the volume agreed with the conclusions or implications

---

69 See L. Ben Mitchell, Carla D. Sanderson, and Gregory A. Thornbury, eds., *Convictional Civility: Engaging the Culture in the 21st Century; Essays in Honor of David S. Dockery* (Nashville: B&H Academic, 2015).

of other contributors. The work of cobelligerency must not attempt to ignore the real theological differences that exist between the traditions.[70] Yet where there is common ground to speak to shared affirmations for the sake of the common good regarding crucial matters such as the sanctity of life, the sacredness of human sexuality and marriage, and the of religious liberty, it seems wise and prudent to do so, providing a witness both to Christians and to the watching world of how devoted men and women can wrestle seriously with these matters of central importance while taking up the call to engage the culture in a way faithful to the best of the Christian tradition, doing so for the sake of the common good.[71]

Evangelical-Catholic Cobelligerency and the Common Good

We now find ourselves in the global context of the third decade of the twenty-first century. This moment presents us with what many believe to be one filled with great challenge and change but also one characterized by renewed hopefulness. If we look around us and see only trends and signs such as secularism, the expanding pluralization of the culture, the new atheism, the new liberalism, and various fundamentalist reactions, we will likely become discouraged. We can become discouraged when we hear talk of the decline of Christianity in North America and an embattled Christian movement whose young people are characterized by what Christian Smith has called "moralistic therapeutic deism."[72]

We can learn from those on whose shoulders we stand, finding hope to work together for the sake of the common good. As evangelicals, we are called first and foremost to a commitment to gospel commonalities that are more important than and precede callings to collaboration or cobelligerency—such as a commitment to the divine nature and authority of God's written word; the deity and humanity of Jesus Christ; a heartfelt

---

70 See George Weigel, *Evangelical Catholicism: Deep Reform in the 21st-Century Church* (New York: Basic Books, 2013), 218–32, which illustrates the serious reflection on matters related to cultural engagement and public policy among Roman Catholic thinkers.

71 See Jake Meador, *In Search of the Common Good: Christian Fidelity in a Fractured World* (Downers Grove, IL: IVP Books, 2019); Robert P. George, "Engagement, Constitutional Structures, and Civic Virtues," in *Worship, Tradition, and Engagement: Essays in Honor of Timothy George*, ed. David S. Dockery, James Earl Massey, and Robert Smith Jr. (Eugene, OR: Pickwick, 2018), 318–32.

72 Christian Smith and Melinda Lundquist Denton, *Soul Searching: The Religious and Spiritual Lives of American Teenagers* (Oxford: Oxford University Press, 2005).

confession of the Holy Trinity; the uniqueness of the gospel message; the enabling work of God's Spirit; salvation by grace through faith alone; the importance of the church and the people of God, who are both gathered and scattered; the expectant hope of Christ's return; and the sacredness of life, marriage, and family.[73] May God grant us wisdom and courage for this important calling in the days and years to come.

---

73 See Packer and Oden, *One Faith*; David S. Dockery, *Southern Baptist Consensus and Renewal: A Biblical, Historical, and Theological Proposal* (Nashville: B&H Academic, 2008), 16–98.

3

Son of Thomas, Heir of Theoden

Faith and Reason in the Work of Robert P. George

Carl R. Trueman

AS THE UNITED STATES enters a period of history when religious arguments are regarded not simply as implausible in the public square but even
as positively harmful and immoral, Christians are faced with a number of
questions regarding the connection of faith and reason. First, how are faith
and reason to be understood in the dogmatic task of theological formulation? Second, what role should reason play in the pastoral and apologetic
tasks of strengthening the convictions of those who are already Christian
and persuading those who are not to take the faith seriously? And third,
to what extent should Christians relate to their faith commitments when
engaging in the public square? It is this last question that is most pressing
when examining the relationship between faith and reason in the work of
a public intellectual such as Robert P. George.

In tackling this topic, it is important to address three specific aspects of
George's life and work. First, there is the matter of his own personal Christian life and its relevance to his public work. Second, it is useful to look
at a couple of specific examples of public policy issues on which George
has opined to see how his Christianity shapes his wider engagement. And
third, given the fractious nature of our times, it is important to reflect on
how George's example of a publicly engaged Christian may, or may not, be
useful in the future.

Robert George's Religious Background[1]

George was raised in a devout Catholic home. He describes his father, Syrian Orthodox in background, as a man of simple, childlike, yet very deep faith. His prayers witnessed to a direct relationship with God and clearly impressed George. His mother, an Italian and a Latin-rite Catholic, taught him the standard form of Catholic prayer—the Hail Mary and the Our Father. His young life was also shaped by Sunday Mass and the rhythm of the church's liturgical year, and he continues to follow his childhood pattern of devotion as an adult. In particular, he notes Jesus's comment in Mark 10:13–16 about the exemplary nature of childlike prayer. This childlike faith was something that he witnessed in his father and that has profoundly shaped his own piety. Though as a Roman Catholic he may not immediately appreciate the comparison, this is very similar to the approach of Martin Luther, for whom children were the paradigm of true faith and childlikeness a state of mind much to be pursued.

To those who know George, it is not surprising that he says that he has never really experienced the dark night of the soul that so many Christians have faced over the years. Personality and disposition surely play a part in this, and George is irrepressibly cheerful. But he does use the Psalter as a deep source for devotion, appreciating especially the movement from darkness to hope that many of the psalms of lament represent.

This personal piety is clearly the foundation of George's approach to the whole of life. But it is significant not simply for how it has shaped his religious imagination over the years. It has also connected him to two important streams that have shaped him intellectually. It is interesting that his preferred posture for prayer is that of kneeling, and that is indicative in a profound way of a heart that wishes to submit to and obey God. For a Catholic, this must be understood in an ecclesiological sense, whereby the voice of the church is decisive for the thinking of the individual. Thus, this act of practical piety finds its intellectual counterpoint in his commitment to being guided by the tradition of Catholic social teaching, specifically papal encyclicals, on matters of faith and reason in general and on specific issues

1   This section relies on information from George's interview with *America* magazine, which provides a more thorough account of George's childhood. The complete text is available at Robert P. George and Kevin Spinale, "Attend to Your Spiritual Life," *First Things*, July 12, 2016, https://www.firstthings.com/.

such as abortion. The attitude of childlike faith is, therefore, the foundation for a sophisticated Catholic approach to the most complex and pressing moral issues of our day.

George is happy to acknowledge that this commitment to Catholic teaching does not mean that there is always a "one size fits all" answer to applying the principles of this teaching to every situation. But it does mean that there are certain ideas that he believes Catholics need to be unconditionally committed to. The list takes us to the heart of George's own priorities:

> What Catholics are bound to believe . . . are the propositions about the requirements of justice and political morality which the magisterium of the Church, and notably the Pope himself, has so powerfully asserted in the language of human rights. For example, no Catholic may deny the Pope's teaching regarding the right of Sudanese Christians—and other human beings—not to be enslaved or tortured; or, the right of Chinese Christians, Tibetan Buddhists, and all believers freely to practice their faith; or, the right of the unborn child, the frail elderly person, the handicapped individual, and every innocent human being not to be directly killed.[2]

Abortion, euthanasia, religious freedom—these are all issues on which the church's position is unequivocal and thus binding on all Catholics. They are all also, as we shall see below, matters that do not stand in isolation from each other but that each rest on a common Christian understanding of human personhood.

In seeking to deploy both faith and reason in his teaching and public witness, George has drawn deeply on the intellectual tradition of Catholicism, particularly in the area of natural law, for his own work. A student of Catholic philosopher John Finnis, at Oxford, George stands as representative of a way of thinking that has sought to bind together faith and reason. But it is important to note that this is not "reason" in the Kantian or utilitarian sense; it is reason perhaps in the more Thomistic or even Anselmic sense, which sees the foundation of knowledge as lying in revelation, even as reason is the human means by which the nature and implications of

---

2 Robert P. George, *The Clash of Orthodoxies: Law, Religion, and Morality in Crisis* (Wilmington, DE: ISI Books, 2001), 240.

such revelation can be explored and explicated. As he says of Christianity in his interview with *America* magazine, which was posted in unabridged form at *First Things*,

> It is a rational hope. It is a trusting of God, not irrationally, not as a purely blind faith, but because we know something about God. God has already manifested himself. Jesus gave us "signs," so that when the trial came, when the cross came, when the darkness rolled in, there were still grounds for hope that death would be defeated, that even if people destroyed that temple as Jesus said they would, God would rebuild that temple in three days. So I see the Christian faith as a faith that integrally involves a hope that is not an irrational hope or a blind faith, but a rational hope.[3]

This principle, applied here specifically to a rational defense of the cross and resurrection, can be applied to other areas; for George, moral thinking is rational when it takes God's revealed reality seriously and seeks to be consistent with that reality.

George elaborates this principle in more detail in an essay on Pope John Paul II's encyclical letter *Fides et Ratio* (*Faith and Reason*).[4] In this document, the pope used an image that recurs several times in George's work, whereby faith and reason are characterized as two wings on which the human spirit ascends to the contemplation of truth. Both are thus necessary for the task of thinking about truth. They are not to be set in opposition to each other or seen as modes of thinking that can be considered alternatives. Both are vital.

Underlying the encyclical's argument is a commitment to the idea of reality, of there actually being a real world that is not simply constituted of matter but that also has a specific moral shape. The world is not a subjective psychological construction. It possesses an objective reality and integrity, and the role of thinking is to explore and elucidate this reality. Reality is God-given and extends beyond the matter of which the world is made to its deeper moral structure and telos.

This realism means that there is thus no possibility of some double-truth theory, whereby something might be legitimately asserted as true by reason

---

3 George and Spinale, "Attend to Your Spiritual Life."

4 The text of *Fides et Ratio* is available at John Paul II, *Fides et Ratio* (encyclical letter), Vatican, September 14, 1998, https://www.vatican.va/.

but be legitimately declared false by revelation. This is because both reason and revelation connect to the same consistent, objective reality and thus cannot stand in contradiction to each other.

Fides et Ratio also assumes (as does George) the point made at the very start of the *Summa Theologiae* by Thomas Aquinas, that there are truths of revelation that transcend (but never contradict) reason, such as the Trinity and the incarnation.[5] Even here, *Fides et Ratio* and, following the encyclical, George himself assert the usefulness of reason for exploring the doctrines that are available only via revelation. The Anselmic notion of faith seeking understanding gives space for reason in the dogmatic task.[6] What is important to understand here, however, is that this distinction between, on the one hand, truths available via reason and revelation and, on the other, those available only via revelation rests on a distinction between ends. Human beings have both natural and supernatural ends, the former referring to how the good life is to be lived on this earth, the latter referring to the supernatural destiny of Christians in the heavenly city. The former has relevance to all human beings, the latter to Christians. And it is these shared natural ends, ends that can be discerned by the use of reason, that are the focus of George's work. If something falls into this category, then it is something that Christians should be interested in and should confidently use in rational (i.e., natural law) arguments.

We should note that this high view of reason, based on a metaphysical realism whereby reality has a given moral structure and telos, does not, of course, mean that any particular claim of reason (or any personal interpretation of a biblical passage) is necessarily correct. Human reason has been damaged by sin and thus cannot in and of itself always be a perfectly reliable guide to reality. In practice, this means that revelation (faith) is necessary as the ultimate criterion for judging the truth claims of reason. But it does not mean that revelation is necessary for a claim of reason to be intrinsically true. Reason can speak truth, even though (to paraphrase Thomas in *Summa Theologiae* 1a.1.1) those relying solely on reason can never know in an absolute sense that their arguments and claims are valid. But this overlap of faith and reason is the space in which thinkers such

---

5   See Thomas Aquinas, *Summa Theologiae* 1a.1.1.
6   See John Paul II, *Fides et Ratio*, 66; George, "On *Fides et Ratio*," in *Clash of Orthodoxies*, 312.

as George can make their arguments in the public square, which must be consistent with Catholic dogmatic teaching but can be articulated using a commonly accepted rational foundation.

In summary, George's own personal commitment to the church and Catholic teaching motivates and shapes his thinking on matters in the public square. More than that, it makes public engagement an imperative, for God is interested in the city of man, even as his ultimate goal for the human being is that of heaven. The Christian, therefore, has obligations to this world on this side of heaven. As George stated in an interview for *Plough* in March 2020,

> Christians understand the difference between the city of God and the city of man, but we also understand that it's part of our vocation to do what we can for the sake of the common good. That means taking part in public life in some way, to the extent that we can do so in good conscience.[7]

The Christian's task is to engage this city of man in a manner that is faithful to Christian witness but that also draws on the common tools that God, in his goodness, has given to all who are made in his image: the tools of reason.

Two Examples of Faith and Reason in Robert George's Work

To elucidate the way that George engages the city of man by exploiting the overlap of faith and reason and pursues his task as both a public advocate and a Christian for specific ethical positions, I want to consider two obvious examples: abortion and gay marriage. Both are highly contentious and high-profile public issues, both collide with traditional Christian moral teaching, and both, in their different ways, raise the issue of what exactly it means to be human. Both are also areas to which George has made passionate and influential contributions.

Abortion

The issue of abortion has been a matter of considerable interest and concern to George throughout his career. Indeed, it was the Democratic

---

7   Cornel West and Robert P. George, "The Politics of the Gospel: An Interview," *Plough*, March 25, 2020, https://www.plough.com/.

Party's increasingly strident stand on this issue that pushed George away from his youthful identification as a Democrat to the more conservative side of politics.[8] He has also authored numerous articles and coauthored a monograph on the issue.[9]

The abortion debate offers a valuable opportunity to explore how George practically connects faith and reason because, as is well-known, a significant number of politicians who ostensibly share George's Catholic faith adopt a very different, indeed, militantly pro-choice, stand on the issue as it relates to public policy.

Of these figures, George has identified Mario Cuomo, the late governor of New York, as perhaps the most significant example, not so much because of the office he held as the fact that he was a learned Catholic who was prepared to deploy his church's own teaching as a means of defending his "privately opposed but publicly supportive" position. Cuomo's primary articulation of this position was a 1984 speech he delivered at the University of Notre Dame.[10]

In this speech, Cuomo pointed to the fact that a free, pluralist society must accept that many practices condemned by some religious and moral traditions are not appropriate candidates for legal prohibition. It is easy to think of examples: the Catholic objection to contraception, for example, or the Southern Baptist opposition to the consumption of alcohol are not typically regarded as legitimate bases for politicians belonging to those traditions to strive to make it a criminal offense to own a condom or consume a gin and tonic. To quote the key paragraphs of Cuomo's speech,

> Certainly, we should not be forced to mold Catholic morality to conform to disagreement by non-Catholics however sincere or severe their

8   See David D. Kirkpatrick, "The Conservative-Christian Big Thinker," *New York Times Magazine*, December 16, 2009, https://www.nytimes.com.

9   E.g., Patrick Lee, Christopher O. Tollefsen, and Robert P. George, "Marco Rubio Is Right: The Life of a New Human Being Begins at Conception," *Public Discourse*, August 18, 2015, https://www.thepublicdiscourse.com/; Robert P. George, "'A Republic . . . If You Can Keep It': Why Lincoln Defied *Dred Scott* and We Must Defy *Roe*," *First Things*, January 22, 2016, https://www.firstthings.com/; Robert P. George and Christopher Tollefsen, *Embryo: A Defense of Human Life* (New York: Doubleday, 2008).

10 The text of the speech is available at Mario Cuomo, "Religious Belief and Public Morality: A Catholic Governor's Perspective" (lecture, University of Notre Dame, Notre Dame, IN, September 13, 1984), http://archives.nd.edu/.

disagreement. Our bishops should be teachers not pollsters. They should not change what we Catholics believe in order to ease our consciences or please our friends or protect the church from criticism.

But if the breadth, intensity and sincerity of opposition to church teaching shouldn't be allowed to shape our Catholic morality, it can't help but determine our ability—our realistic, political ability—to translate our Catholic morality into civil law, a law not for the believers who don't need it but for the disbelievers who reject it.

And it is here, in our attempt to find a political answer to abortion—an answer beyond our private observance of Catholic morality—that we encounter controversy within and without the church over how and in what degree to press the case that our morality should be everybody else's, and to what effect.

I repeat, there is no church teaching that mandates the best political course for making our belief everyone's rule, for spreading this part of our Catholicism. There is neither an encyclical nor a catechism that spells out a political strategy for achieving legislative goals.

In short, while it is important for Catholics to follow the church's teaching in their own private lives (as Cuomo stated he and his wife did), they need to accept that theirs is a minority religious position that cannot simply be imposed on others who do not hold to the Catholic faith.

For George, Cuomo represents a catastrophic failure to think in a clearly Catholic way—a failure made even less forgivable by the governor's evident intellectual ability and theologically informed intellect.[11] He also offers a case study in how a failure to understand the relation between faith and reason can prove catastrophic.

For George, Cuomo's fundamental error is to see abortion as a religious matter that can thus be carefully detached from other concerns. To recast this in the terms used above, Cuomo makes the ethical principles that guide the pro-life cause into matters of personal faith that cannot be defended in the public square. In short, the pro-life cause lies outside the common ground between faith and reason and the overlap of com-

---

11   See Robert P. George, "The Mario That Might Have Been," *Public Discourse*, January 6, 2015, https://www.thepublicdiscourse.com/.

mon concerns between the city of God and the city of man. It can no more be mandated by a government, therefore, than daily confession or weekly Mass.

George describes the problem as follows:

> This way of presenting the issue . . . fails to come to grips with the core of the very teaching that Cuomo claims to accept as a matter of his own religious conviction, namely, that abortion constitutes the unjust taking of an innocent human life. As such, abortion simply cannot be considered "private" in the sense that Cuomo attempts to depict it. It always involves the violation of the rights of another human being, namely, the unborn baby whose death is precisely what is sought in an act of direct abortion.[12]

The abortion debate is therefore not the equivalent of the debates surrounding contraception (at least not contraception of a nonabortifacient variety) or the consumption of alcohol. In using a contraceptive or consuming a gin and tonic, no human life is terminated, and no innocent person necessarily suffers.

Peter Steinfels, a Catholic journalist of a more liberal stripe than George, also finds Cuomo's stand on abortion problematic. Though expressed in different terminology from that used by George, the similarities between the two are clarifying. Here is Steinfels comparing Cuomo on the death penalty to Cuomo on abortion:

> Although Cuomo sometimes justified his opposition to the death penalty with utilitarian arguments about reducing crime overall, he believed deep down that executing people was wrong in itself, not because of what some moral authority stated or what public consensus would or would not tolerate. When it came to abortion, however, did he believe that the church rejected abortion because it was wrong or that it was wrong—for him, that is—because the church rejected it? More and more, it seemed the latter, an old-fashioned Catholic view of morality as "following the rules" because the church taught them.[13]

12 George, *Clash of Orthodoxies*, 246.

13 Peter Steinfels, "Mario the Pre-Conciliar Catholic," *Commonweal*, January 4, 2015, https://www .commonwealmagazine.org/.

Seen in this light, Cuomo's "privately opposed but publicly supportive" argument makes specious sense. He considers the prohibition on abortion not to connect to the rational, moral structure of the world (the natural end of human existence) but instead to declare a revealed positive law on the part of the church that has significance only to the faithful and then only as they seek to find their way to the heavenly city (the supernatural end of Christian existence). As Steinfels hints, this stands in significant tension with Cuomo's approach to the death penalty. It is a matter of faith, disconnected from reason, of no relevance to the natural ends of being a human.

George's direct response to Cuomo's argument is that the issue of abortion (the taking of an innocent life) is such that to will that an individual have the freedom of choice in the matter is to "will" (i.e., to accept as legitimate) acts of abortion.[14] Underlying this, of course, is an anthropology, two points of which are of particular interest.

First, George is clear that life begins at conception. The fertilized egg is alive. This is a point that could easily be established on biblical premises. The conception of Jesus is the obvious example, even if exceptional: from the moment Jesus is conceived in Mary's womb, the Word has "taken flesh" (cf. John 1:14). But this is also a point that science can establish without referring to revelation, as George does, for example, in his essay "When Life Begins."[15] In this essay he is clear that it is a fundamental error to place the question of when life begins purely in the category of faith. It is one of those matters in which the content of faith and the content of reason overlap.[16]

Second, George is clear that personhood does not depend on a certain level of self-consciousness, of the kind that his Princeton colleague Peter Singer sees as the key to life issues.[17] There is an organic (George uses the term "intentional") process whereby we develop from embryos to babies to children to adults.[18] There is continuity here, and one could argue for it on a faith premise, such as being known from conception by God, but one could

---

14   George, *Clash of Orthodoxies*, 245–47.

15   The essay "When Life Begins" is reprinted in Robert P. George, *Conscience and Its Enemies: Confronting the Dogmas of Liberal Secularism* (Wilmington, DE: ISI Books, 2013), 165–67.

16   George, "When Life Begins," 167.

17   For Singer's views, see his *Writings on an Ethical Life* (New York: Ecco, 2000), 130, 137–38. Singer agrees with George that life begins at conception, but he considers life as an isolated category to be irrelevant to questions about the morality of abortion.

18   George, "When Life Begins," 166.

also base it on a rational premise, such as the embodied continuity from conception onward. In short, George's objections to his fellow Catholics' "personally opposed but publicly supportive" arguments for abortion do not rest solely on the church's teaching; rather, he makes the case against abortion on rational grounds. Abortion does not simply speak to people as Catholics; it speaks to them as human beings.

Gay Marriage

George is probably the most high-profile intellectual critic of gay marriage. His book *What is Marriage?*, coauthored with Ryan Anderson and Sherif Girgis, was arguably the most articulate defense of traditional marriage in the buildup to *Obergefell v. Hodges* in 2015.[19] As with the abortion issue, the Catholic Church has clear teaching on the matter of marriage. Indeed, given the fact that the Catholic Church regards marriage as a sacrament, the issue of gay marriage is arguably even more theologically intense for Catholics than for Protestants. Yet George's work offers an interesting defense of traditional marriage that is rooted in reason, again predicated on the overlap that he sees existing between reason and revelation on the matter of natural human ends. Yes, marriage for the Christian has a Christological basis as an analogy for the relationship between Christ and the church and thus a supernatural basis, as Paul argues in Ephesians, but it is also connected to natural ends and is therefore defensible on rational grounds.

George does this most notably in his essay "Same-Sex Marriage and Moral Neutrality."[20] Here he addresses the idea that the state should adopt a neutral stance on the issue of marriage and thus not enshrine the notion of it as a heterosexual union. In a manner analogous to the issue of abortion, he frames the argument as a response to the claim that one can be personally committed to the traditional definition of marriage and yet argue that the state should take no position on the matter.

After briefly addressing the logical problems entailed in the idea of state neutrality on marriage, the burden of George's case rests on the significance of the act of sexual union as central to the definition of marriage. Indeed, he defines marriage as follows:

---

19 Sherif Girgis, Ryan T. Anderson, and Robert P. George, *What Is Marriage? Man and Woman: A Defense*, 2nd ed. (2012; repr., New York: Encounter Books, 2020).

20 In George, *Clash of Orthodoxies*, 75–89.

Marriage is a two-in-one-flesh communion of two persons that is con-summated and actualized by acts that are reproductive in type, whether or not they are reproductive in effect (or are motivated, even in part, by a desire to reproduce). . . . Marriage, precisely as such a relationship, is naturally ordered to the good of procreation (and to the nurturing and education of children) as well as to the good of spousal unity, and these goods are tightly bound together.[21]

Indeed, George proceeds to point out that the reproductive act of human beings is by definition a two-flesh union. One male or one female, in isola-tion, cannot reproduce the species.[22]

One obvious objection to this, and one that George anticipates, is that this definition's emphasis on the significance of reproductive sex for a real marriage excludes heterosexual couples who, for some reason or other, cannot reproduce. What of the marriages, therefore, of postmenopausal women or men who cannot produce fertile sperm? In response, George asserts the uniqueness of heterosexual acts, even when they do not end in reproduction. Male and female sex organs are designed to fit together, and even when conception is not the end result, heterosexual sexual union is reproductive in type, that is, the act involves the sex organs being used in the appropriate manner, in a way that other sexual acts do not do so.[23]

What is striking about this defense of traditional marriage is the weight that George places on biology but within a framework assuming that biology itself reflects a moral structure. The human body—the sexed body—is more than just its biological matter; it has a telos, an end, which should shape how that body is used. His assumption, in other words, is of a moral realism reflected in physical reality. And thus, the plausibility of his argument depends on whether the audience to whom he is speaking accepts the plausibility of that assumption. That plausibility is a function of what Charles Taylor calls the social imaginary—that set of intuitions that shapes how we understand the world to be. And that raises the ques-

---

21 George, *Clash of Orthodoxies*, 77. George does not explicitly cite Catholic teaching in this essay, but his thinking is clearly consistent with Catholic teaching on the issue, of which the work of Dietrich von Hildebrand is a good example. See the latter's *In Defense of Purity: An Analysis of the Catholic Ideals of Purity and Virginity* (Steubenville, OH: Hildebrand, 2017).

22 George, *Clash of Orthodoxies*, 83.

23 George, *Clash of Orthodoxies*, 85.

tion whether George's strategy of public engagement can remain plausible as this social imaginary shifts. It is to that question that I wish to turn in the final section.

Faith and Reason in the Future Public Square

It is clear that George has been exemplary in his engagement in the public square, defending natural goods with rational arguments. The pressing question of the moment, however, is whether this strategy can continue to prove helpful in the future.

Such a question is, of course, speculative, and I offer my thoughts here in the knowledge that I could be proved wrong and, indeed, rather hoping that that might well be the case regarding my pessimistic outlook. As it stands, however, I suspect that the framework of public discourse in which George has operated is rapidly coming to an end, if it has not already ended.

If we take abortion and gay marriage as examples, it is clear that George's rational case for each depends on a number of suppositions. The most obvious is perhaps that of a tacit assumption that human nature is something that all, believers and unbelievers, can agree on. That then allows for rational discussion about human flourishing and human ends. The problem is that this assumption has come under severe attack in the academy in recent decades, and all the signs are that this animosity to such thinking is now percolating down through our culture.

Two obvious strands to this shift are the utilitarian pragmatism of, for example, a Peter Singer and the various critical theories that have come to dominate the humanities in the United States. For Singer, moral arguments based on human exceptionalism present themselves as rational but are in fact built on the theological premise that human beings are made in the image of God. Regarding abortion, Singer expresses this thinking as follows: "The belief that mere membership in our species, irrespective of other characteristics, makes a great difference to the wrongness of killing a being is a legacy of religious doctrine that even those opposed to abortion hesitate to bring into the debate."[24] In saying this, Singer is claiming that there is no real overlap between reason and revelation; indeed, reason (at least as deployed by thinkers such as George) is really revelation in disguise.

---

24 Singer, *Writings on an Ethical Life*, 156.

Singer is no critical theorist, but critical theory tends to the same conclusion. For critical theorists, human nature and human rationality are constructs of the dominant group that holds power. Arguments based on human nature are thus disingenuous attempts to normalize concepts that support the same. "Human nature" and "reason" thus become code for "white, male heteronormativity." And while few read the turgid prose of the Judith Butlers and Kimberlé Crenshaws of this world, the clichés of critical theory ("white privilege," "white gaze," "heterosexism," "cisgenderism") have made their way into popular culture, reinforced by the increasing social orthodoxy that victimhood in and of itself is virtuous.

To this we might add the manner in which technology and media such as Twitter are reshaping public engagement. On the technological front, for example, there is the massive expansion of reproductive technology in particular and indeed how technology tilts the social imaginary toward myths of total control of reality. These make intuitively plausible the notion that the world and all it contains (including us) is just so much stuff with no given moral structure or telos. In such an imagined world, arguments based on the moral significance of biological reality (as in George's case for heterosexual marriage) will carry little or no immediate plausibility in the wider world.

As to Twitter (with a few honorable exceptions, one of which is George himself), the model of engagement and argument that it promotes could not be further from that espoused by George. It prioritizes emotion and sound bites over nuance and truth and typically depends for its rhetorical power on the demonizing, rather than the careful refutation, of the perceived opponent. It is a medium more for "Gotchas!" than for the establishment of the truth. In such a world, the careful, nuanced, and gracious work of George seems implausible to many, precisely because of those things that many of us regard as its strengths.

These factors have indeed changed everything, not least the ability to engage in civil discourse in the public square. The advance of critical theory among cultural elites is why the First Amendment is under severe pressure. Freedom of speech, like rational argument, is simply a ruse, a way of maintaining the status quo while giving people the illusion of freedom. And the increasing plausibility of a universe that lacks any meaning beyond the atoms by which it is constituted makes natural law arguments look more and more like faith-based claims. And that means that reasonable interlocutors like George will not find that their reasonableness wins them a hearing. A recent essay at *Public Discourse* by George's friend Hope Leman makes precisely this point.[25]

This then raises the question whether George's strategy of public engagement, based on the continuity between faith and reason, remains a viable option for the future. Notwithstanding the concerns I've laid out above, I am inclined to say yes, for two reasons.

First, the call of the Christian is to bear witness to the truth. On this level, the question whether the public argument is won or lost is irrelevant. Truth matters. The vulnerable and innocent need people to speak on their behalf. How else is a Christian to do this other than by asserting the realities that others choose to deny?

Second, by engaging in the manner in which he does, George does a twofold service to the rising generation of Christians. He offers an example of what gracious refutation of falsehood looks like. The Bible has much to say about kind words turning away wrath, about not growing weary in doing good, and about reflecting the character of God in our interactions with others. In a day of Twitter outrage, George models something important: grace under fire. And he also offers arguments that reinforce Christian beliefs. It may be that his writings on marriage persuaded no proponents of gay marriage, for example, to change their minds, but they have certainly proved helpful in showing younger Christians that the Bible's teaching on marriage not only is true but (if this does not sound odd) actually makes sense as well.

A Personal Postscript

To end on a personal note, I have benefited tremendously from reading Robby's work and watching him as he operates in both public and private settings. It is an honor to have been asked to reflect on his significance in this volume. I remain more pessimistic than he is about the immediate prospects for conservatism, political and religious, in the United States, but (to risk ending with a clichéd quotation from J. R. R. Tolkien), when it comes to the big issues of our day, he has encouraged me to think like Theoden:

---

25 Hope Leman, "My Problem with Truth-Seeking, Open-Mindedness and . . . Robert P. George," *Public Discourse*, July 27, 2021, https://www.thepublicdiscourse.com/.

GAMLING: "We cannot defeat the armies of Mordor."
THEODEN: "No, but we will meet them in battle nonetheless."[26]

Yes, Robby has taught me that, regardless of the outcome, Christians must meet the enemy on the field of battle—graciously, yes, but in a manner that cedes no ground without a fight. For his example in this, many of us owe him a debt of real gratitude.

---

26 *The Lord of the Rings: The Return of the King*, directed by Peter Jackson (Los Angeles: New Line Home Entertainment, 2004), DVD.

4

Robert P. George and (New) Natural Law Ethics

Philosophical and Biblical Considerations

Andrew T. Walker

NATURAL LAW HAS A LONG TRADITION in Christian ethics. Throughout church history, theologians considered it the grounds to find a common moral grammar with an unbelieving world and a mechanism to advance the universal truth claims of Christian morality. Sadly, due in large part to Karl Barth's influence on Protestant ethics in the mid-twentieth century, the natural law tradition fell out of favor, leading to its current dormancy. There are signs, however, of a Protestant natural law renaissance.

Whenever the topic of natural law comes up, especially in evangelical Protestant circles, the first response is usually some form of apathy, suspicion, or doubt. "Everyone who believes in natural law is already committed to its existence; it does not persuade non-Christians," one person objects. Or, in a similar refrain, "Because of sin, the moral law is not self-evident, so morality is completely reliant upon divine revelation." Other voices accuse natural law of relying too strongly on the powers of so-called autonomous reason. Of course, one should note, these types of statements issuing from Protestants are in historical discontinuity with their own tradition.[1]

---

1   For resources looking at the Reformation's embrace of natural law, see John T. McNeill, "Natural Law in the Teaching of the Reformers," *Journal of Religion* 26, no. 3 (1946): 168–82; Stephen J.

The purpose in raising these objections is not to refute them, at least not in full. It is instead to demonstrate from the outset that much Protestant malaise and antipathy toward natural law is a result of wrongly defining it, which leads inexorably to misconstruing it. These misconstruals then lead critics of natural law to overlook the multitude of ways natural law principles indisputably undergird our everyday existence.

To understand Robert P. George's theory of natural law is not to defer immediately to questions of natural law's divine origins but to seek basic explanations for why individuals act the way they do in their individual and social capacities. In other words, what *reasons* do people have for acting how they do, and toward what *end*? As this chapter argues, Robert P. George's explanation of natural law offers a powerful account of moral theory that *parallels*, *explains*, and *confirms* the Bible's account of morality.

Rather than diving immediately into George's *theory* of natural law, which can be admittedly complex, an illustration of what his natural law theory seeks to articulate would be apropos and clarifying as we begin our journey into this topic.

Everyday Action

On any given summer day, schedule permitting, I enjoy going to a nearby swimming pool with my family. One day I watched as a young mother helped her toddler learn to jump off the diving board. She had to lovingly coax him into jumping, assuring him as he stood on the end of the diving board that she would be right there to catch him and bring him to safety. As I observed this scene, something struck me about the child and his mother: the child did not have to be convinced to pursue his safety (it was, rather, self-evident), and the mother did not have to deliberate or be convinced to act in such a way as to secure her son's life. All this may seem so patently self-evident that pointing it out borders on the absurd. "Of course the mom wants to save her child's life," you might be thinking.

Nevertheless, how did this mom know to protect her child? I do not know whether the young mom was a Christian. That, however, raises an important question: Supposing she was not a Christian, what theory of

---

Grabill, *Rediscovering the Natural Law in Reformed Theological Ethics* (Grand Rapids, MI: Eerdmans, 2006).

moral action guided her actions? How did she have justified knowledge that she should act to care for her child? She seemed to operate according to a morality of some sort. What was it, and where, ultimately, does it originate?

While at the pool, I will also pursue a range of activities I consider worthwhile. Perhaps I will exercise by swimming laps in the pool since swimming is a uniquely helpful way to stay fit. Or maybe my wife and I will play a game with our daughters. Then, after a little while, I might take a nap, read a book, enjoy a poolside snack, or even pray quietly to myself—all these activities occurring while I behold the beauty of my surroundings by using my cognitive faculties. That I innately desire to pursue these activities raises a question: Why do I choose to engage in them? On what basis are they compelling so as to order my behavior?

So why point out the mundane, the routine, and the obvious? Why did the child want his mother to care for him? Why did the mother not have to deliberate whether saving her son's life was a good thing to do? Why do I pursue a range of activities while at the pool? *Because every action described above assumes that there is a worthwhile pursuit of a known, discerned objective.* The reason I act and the reason the mother acts is to pursue *ends* or *goods* that we both grasp as beneficial to either my own or someone else's flourishing. This process occurs in every human being: every action we pursue assumes an intelligible end worth pursuing for its own sake. That may sound circular, yet it helps explain the theory of natural law advanced by Robert P. George and his philosophical compatriots, known as *new natural law* (hereafter, NNL).[2]

Why then do I act the way I do? I do so because I understand and grasp it as intrinsically valuable and worth doing or as bringing about something intrinsically valuable and worth having. In the same way, something that is intrinsically valuable informs why I would *not* act, so as to avoid potential risk to experiencing that intrinsically valuable thing. Natural law is simply the body of reasons for acting in the pursuit of a good or abstaining from acting in the avoidance of a good's negation.

2   George is unhappy with the designation of his natural law approach as "new." He calls such a label a "misnomer" because all approaches trace their origins to Thomas Aquinas. For more, see Andrew T. Walker and Robert P. George, "An Interview with Robert P. George and Andrew T. Walker on the Natural Law," *Eikon: A Journal for Biblical Anthropology* 2, no. 2 (Fall 2020): 15.

Defining Robert P. George's Natural Law Theory

The opening illustration above allows us now to establish the more formal definition of natural law. George posits the following definition of
natural law:

> Theories of natural law are reflective critical accounts of the constitutive
> aspects of the well-being and fulfillment of human persons and the com-
> munities they form. The propositions that pick out fundamental aspects
> of human flourishing are directive (that is, prescriptive) in our thinking
> about what to do and refrain from doing (our practical reason)—they
> are, or provide, more than merely instrumental reasons for action and
> self-restraint. When these foundational principles of practical reflection
> are taken together (that is, integrally), they entail norms that may exclude
> certain options and require other options in situations of morally signifi-
> cant choosing. Natural law theories, then, propose to identify principles
> of right action moral principles—specifying the first and most general
> principle of morality, namely, that one should choose and act in ways that
> are compatible with a will towards integral human fulfillment. Among
> these principles is a respect for rights people possess simply by virtue of
> their humanity—rights which, as a matter of justice, others are bound to
> respect and governments are bound not only to respect but, to the extent
> possible, also to protect.[3]

The essential component of George's definition centers on his understanding of natural law as fundamentally "reflective" and practical rather
than purely theoretical or speculative. George's definition is theoretical
insofar as it advances a theory of moral action, but George is concerned
primarily with demonstrating how, practically, an agent grasps the principles
of natural law. For George, the power of reason helps discern what activities further human flourishing. Actions that facilitate the goal of human
flourishing obtain the force of law.

George's view stands out because it does not *immediately* invoke a concept
of God or abstract theories about human nature for its justification. For

---

3   Robert P. George, "Natural Law," *Harvard Journal of Law and Public Policy* 31, no. 1 (Winter
2008): 172.

George, to insist on the existence of human nature requires learning what activities fulfill human nature. We can know human nature indirectly by establishing what basic goods tend to perfect rational beings. We establish what human nature is and the actions and norms necessary to nature's fulfillment by identifying those goods (I explain more about these "goods" below).

Upon reflecting on the sources of everyday experience that inform us of whether something is worth doing, we derive norms directing our action to intelligible ends and norms directing us away from privations of these goods. Reflection is the innate, often instantaneous capacity to consider what is good and evil. Hence, NNL understands this formula to parallel Thomas Aquinas's "first principle of practical reason," which famously states that "good is to be pursued and evil avoided." The principle is unprovable because it is self-evident and underived; hence it is "indemonstrable."[4] Thus, all rational, moral action assumes the intelligibility of willing good and shunning evil. According to Germain Grisez, whom George builds on in his own work, "In voluntarily acting for human goods and avoiding what is opposed to them, one ought to choose and otherwise will those and only those possibilities whose willing is compatible with a will toward integral human fulfillment."[5] Any moral theory that intentionally wills harm or intentionally thwarts well-being is not only invalid but irrational. This is what George and his school of thought refer to as "the first principle of morality."

To put it in the plainest of terms, the capacity to reason enables individuals to understand and act to promote and protect their own and others' well-being. Well-being, however, is not defined by "emotion, feeling, desire or other subrational motivating factors."[6] In other words, the "good" is not synonymous with intuition or whatever is supposedly "natural." Natural instincts well up inside of us that we should all agree are dangerous to act on. The existence of a desire does not mean it is good. The desire to steal does not mean one *ought* to steal. We can only derive a norm against stealing when the power of reason realizes that stealing violates a good. As George writes, "Knowledge of the natural law . . . is the fruit of insights

---

4   Thomas Aquinas, *Summa Theologiae* 1a2ae.94.2.

5   John M. Finnis, Germain Grisez, and Joseph Boyle, "Practical Principles, Moral Truth, and Ultimate Ends," *American Journal of Jurisprudence* 32, no. 1 (1987): 128.

6   George, "Natural Law," 178.

which, like all insights, are insights into data: data which are supplied by experience."[7]

Thus, well-being is discussed in terms of obtaining basic goods understood by reflecting on the data of everyday experience (discussed further below). Proper moral action is willed action to achieve human flourishing. Human flourishing thus directs us in that it guides action and explains action. When humans act in ways that benefit themselves and their political community, moral norms of justice are established. George and the NNL tradition refer to proper action as "modes of responsibility," which include the Golden Rule (Matt. 7:12) and the Pauline principle (Rom. 3:8).[8] Another mode of responsibility, "human integral fulfillment," means acting to pursue goods. All rightly ordered action is intelligible and justified by how it guides and directs us toward individual goods and common goods. A law that prevents murder, for example, is protecting the good of life while also creating a norm that all society must abide by if the political community is to flourish.

While NNL is not opposed to theoretical or speculative reasoning about moral knowledge and human nature, what distinguishes George's thought is a primary concern for practical reason as the means for obtaining moral knowledge concerning goods and moral norms.[9] According to George, "Practical knowledge (i.e., knowledge of human goods and moral norms and the reasons they provide) is a *source* of our knowledge of human nature."[10]

---

7   Robert P. George, "Natural Law, God and Human Dignity," in *The Cambridge Companion to Natural Law Jurisprudence*, ed. George Duke and Robert P. George (Cambridge: Cambridge University Press, 2017), 58.

8   For more on the modes of responsibility, see Germain Grisez, "A Contemporary Natural-Law Ethics," in *Moral Philosophy: Historical and Contemporary Essays*, ed. William C. Starr and Richard C. Taylor (Milwaukee, WI: Marquette University Press, 1989), 131–36.

9   In a footnote in *Making Men Moral*, George urges caution in forming a major divide between practical and theoretical reason: "Our knowledge of basic reasons has its truth, rather, in the adequation of those reasons to possible human fulfillment that can be realized in and through human action. Of course, our knowledge of the possibilities of such fulfillment will depend, in any particular circumstances, on various types of theoretical knowledge, including a knowledge of empirical possibilities and environmental constraints. To hold that the basic reasons for action, as self-evident first principles of practical reasoning, are not inferred from prior theoretical principles is by no means to imply, then, that there is a 'wall of separation' between practical and theoretical reasoning." Robert P. George, *Making Men Moral: Civil Liberties and Public Morality* (Oxford: Oxford University Press, 1993), 13n15.

10 Robert P. George, "Natural Law Ethics," in *A Companion to Philosophy of Religion*, ed. Philip L. Quinn and Charles Taliaferro (Malden, MA: Wiley-Blackwell, 1999), 462.

NNL does not deny the ontological existence of "nature" but instead argues that *knowledge* of nature is derived practically. There is no antecedent concept of human nature apart from determining what goods—and the norms to achieve those goods—fitly serve the constitutive whole of human nature. Goods achieved by positive action and, correspondingly, thwarted by illicit action formulate rules for moral action. According to George,

> An entity's nature is understood by understanding its potentialities or capacities; these are in turn understood by understanding its activities and performances; and these finally are understood by understanding the *objects* of its acts or performances. Human nature, then, is known by understanding the objects of human acts; and these are the basic human goods which, by providing non-instrumental reasons, give human acts their intelligible point.[11]

In light of this explanation, let us revisit our pool example. Why did the young mother intuitively act to safeguard her son's life? She did so because the action to protect and care for her son accords with, first, the basic good of her motherliness (family life) and, second, the basic good of preserving her son's being (life). Her actions testify to the desirability of willing whatever activity furthers the good of family life and life itself.

Basic Goods

Thus far, I have spoken broadly of such concepts as basic goods, well-being, and human flourishing. To speak of a "good" means acting to attain the right end or goal. The good of a baseball team, for example, is to play the game cooperatively such that they win the game. The goal or good of winning directs what activity is necessary to accomplish that end. Thus, a moral norm is established: to win a baseball game (the good), all players should use their talents to score runs (the norm). NNL is fundamentally a teleological ethical approach in that it establishes norming rules in order to achieve proper ends.

This focus on "goods" differentiates George and the NNL tradition from other ethical theories, namely, deontology or utilitarianism. In deontological

11 George, "Natural Law Ethics," 463.

ethics, moral action is governed by positing abstract rules and duties. George, on the contrary, does not believe that norms can be established apart from the goods those norms are said to direct people toward. In utilitarianism, whatever action accrues the greatest aggregate benefit to the largest number of persons is moral. While George appreciates utilitarianism's concern for human well-being, he rejects the hierarchy of goods behind the utilitarian framework (e.g., lying is okay if it serves a good end). In the NNL tradition, all goods are "incommensurable," meaning there is no hierarchy of goods that allows the pursuit of one good at the negation or thwarting of another good.

It is not as though deontology and utilitarianism can be discarded entirely. For George, the pursuit of intelligible goods better explains why humans act and counteracts the utilitarian temptation to pursue whatever action benefits the most people, which is inherently unstable and subject to human passions. According to George, "The content of the human good shapes the moral norms applied in moral judgments about right (and wrong) choices and actions. Moral norms themselves are entailments of the primary practical principles that direct us to basic aspects of human well-being or fulfillment."[12] Thus, a focus on basic goods shapes the practical principles and norms of morality.

It is necessary to specify what these "basic good" concepts concretely are. The goods listed below are "domains" that organize all rationally motivated activity. In other words, when people are acting in their right mind, they are pursuing aspects of the goods below. NNL theorists debate the full range of goods, but among them are the following:[13]

- Life: One acts to preserve one's life—something as mundane as brushing one's teeth serves the end of oral health, which inexorably contributes to the totality of health.
- Marriage and family life: Fostering family life is founded and centered on the conjugal union of husband and wife.
- Friendship (sociability): Human beings enjoy companionship with like-minded persons.

12 George, "Natural Law," 185.
13 For more on basic goods, see John Finnis, *Natural Law and Natural Rights*, 2nd ed. (Oxford: Oxford University Press, 2011), 85–95.

- Knowledge: Learning is inherently beneficial.
- Aesthetic appreciation (beauty): Beauty motivates persons to pursue it in various expressions.
- Practical reasonableness: People in their right mind using their faculties appropriately makes possible all other basic goods.
- Religion: Knowing God and aligning oneself with God's plan is always good.
- Play: Rest, leisure, and skillful activity are intrinsically beneficial for their own sake.

These goods, then, are said to be "noninstrumental" in that they are pursued for their own sake. That means that they provide reasons for action whose intelligibility as reasons depends on no further or deeper ends than that they are mere means. We benefit from each good in and of itself. The attainment of the good is the purpose of pursuing the good. This is a crucial aspect of George's natural law theory and the key to unlocking its essence.

Let us take the good of aesthetic appreciation. When I attend a concert and find myself enraptured by the beauty of skillful artistry on stage, experiencing the good of beauty is the goal of my activity and the purpose for why I ordered my actions to buy concert tickets. Take another example: family life. To protect my marriage, I should allow no corrupting influence to undermine the sanctity and unity of my marriage. For if I allow something to pollute my marriage, it can have a detrimental impact on my marriage and my children's well-being. Pornography is a destructive industry that objectifies women and corrodes men's minds. It would violate the integrity of my marriage vows to my wife, were I to indulge it. It is habit-forming and vile. Because experiencing the felicity of family life is intrinsically valuable for its own sake (the good), I must order my actions according to a norm that protects the flourishing of my family life—thus, I should not watch pornography (the norm). Pleasure is an instrumental good to be experienced toward the furtherance of a noninstrumental good, such as marriage. To that end, it cooperates toward a basic good if experienced properly. If I isolate an instrumental good (such as pleasure) to the level of a noninstrumental good, I am apt to pursue that good in whatever context enables its achievement. Pleasure, torn from marriage, licenses several individual and social pathologies. Instrumental goods must always serve noninstrumental goods. Money, for example, is an instrumental good in that it allows us to purchase objects that serve noninstrumental goods, such as shelter and food, that work to protect the basic good of family life.

These goods posit a "basic reason for action," which is a "reason whose intelligibility as a reason does not depend on further or deeper reasons for action."[14] A noninstrumental good needs no other reason for action than its own attainment. "Only those ends or purposes that are intrinsically worthwhile," writes George, "provide basic reasons for action."[15] Why does one act to preserve one's life? Because the sanctity of life is intrinsically valuable.

In personal correspondence, George disclosed to me that he does not subscribe to either a limited or unlimited set of "basic goods":

> Whatever provides an intelligible reason for action that does not depend for its intelligibility on any further or deeper reason, or subrational motivating factor, to which it is a means, is a basic human good—no matter the label or how one categorizes it as part of a schema, or what have you.[16]

God and Natural Law in Robert P. George's Work

The biggest question and the source for most Protestant criticism of the sort of natural law theory Robert P. George promotes is the place and role of God in it. Is NNL a godless moral theory? Is it futilely attempting to create morality absent God? George freely admits that "most, but not all" proponents of natural law are theists.[17] New natural law proponents are not hesitant to confess that God's existence is what stands behind their theory. Patrick Lee, one of George's coauthors, writes that "since God is the author of both our nature and our intelligence, these moral principles are indeed directives from God, a part of God's wise plan for his creation."[18] What distinguishes the NNL tradition from others is the belief that moral principles are in fact *known* through practical reason and that these principles can be considered binding regardless of whether one believes in God's existence. Lee writes,

---

14   George, *Making Men Moral*, 11.
15   George, *Making Men Moral*, 11.
16   Robert P. George, email message to author, June 23, 2021.
17   George, "Natural Law," 108.
18   Patrick Lee, "God and New Natural Law Theory," *National Catholic Bioethics Quarterly* 19, no. 2 (Summer 2019): 280.

One need only distinguish between knowing certain moral truths and knowing their source, that is, between knowing moral precepts that in fact are part of the natural law and knowing that they are part of a law— which of course by definition includes the notion of a legislator. NNLT holds that the former occurs—people who do not know that God exists still know some moral truths. But it also holds that, of course, to know that these moral truths are part of the natural law requires knowing or believing in God the legislator.[19]

Thus, brought to its absolute foundation, natural law is admittedly a function of the eternal law, which posits that God upholds the whole of the cosmos. When it comes to God and NNL, it is not that God's existence is a nonfactor. If morality truly is natural in that it "obtains as a body of reasons" that requires no more extraordinary proof for its existence apart from its own self-evidence, it follows that some basic principles of morality exist that all persons could, in principle, grasp and effectuate.[20] In short, if natural law is true, it ought to be true naturally. George believes that a divinely ordered universe allows for theists and nontheists alike to develop principles of human dignity and human rights since both are alike in their ability to reason. The ability for self-professed nontheists to possess moral comprehension reflects the human's creaturely participation in the eternal law. According to Thomas Aquinas, "The human being has a share of the Eternal Reason, whereby it has a natural inclination to its proper act and end: and this participation of the eternal law in the rational creature is called the natural law."[21]

While I wish that the NNL tradition were more apt to mention God than it generally is, its claim about the inevitability of morality is, prima facie, true. If morality truly exists, then we should expect those who do not believe in God to know some facet of natural law at its most rudimentary level. For morality to be truly binding, it should be binding on its own accord and rational desirability, regardless of whether one has intricate details of the source of that morality. It is not that God is altogether unessential to morality. He is essential. The question is whether morality can be coherent if

19   Lee, "God and New Natural Law Theory," 287.
20   Walker and George, "Interview," 13.
21   Thomas Aquinas, *Summa Theologiae* 1a2ae.91.2.

the interlocutor in question rejects God. On George's approach, the answer is yes—which I would accept, at least superficially. Any sustained moral discourse, ultimately, is going to require transcendent authority for its intelligibility. If morality exists, God must exist. Still, one could hypothetically affirm morality's existence without having confidence in God's existence. Though one's confidence in a moral order would stand on irrational, shaky, tentative, and potentially culturally destabilizing grounds, one could hypothetically affirm the existence of morality without the full confidence of where that inclination to moral certitude originates.

The natural law tradition does not teach that all persons know all contours and depths of natural law equally, only that there are basic, underived principles that persons cannot vitiate without moral action becoming an entirely futile enterprise. Rejecting even the most basic moral principle would constitute a fundamental denial of reason and nature (e.g., the first principle of practical reason and the first principle of morality). Thus, for George, agreement on the reasons for action factors more significantly than agreement on God's exact nature. He explains,

> In my view, anybody who acknowledges the human capacities for reason and freedom has good grounds for affirming human dignity and basic human rights. These grounds remain in place whether or not one adverts to the question whether there is a divine source of the moral order whose tenets we discern in inquiry regarding natural law and natural rights. I happen to think that the answer to this question is yes, and that we should be open to the possibility that God has revealed himself in ways that reinforce and supplement what can be known by unaided reason. But we do not need agreement on the answer, so long as we agree about the truths that give rise to the question—namely, that human beings, possessing the God-like (literally awesome) powers of reason and freedom, are bearers of a profound dignity that is protected by certain basic rights.[22]

As this quotation suggests, for George, the true test of natural law is its persuasiveness, *regardless* of whether one is a theist or nontheist. As he writes, "Natural law ideas, like theocratic ideas or secularist liberal ones,

---

22 George, "Natural Law," 182.

must stand or fall on their own merits."[23] In other words, the success of natural law does not depend on whether everyone believes in God but whether persons of variegated convictions can agree on basic, immutable moral first principles with reason as their foundation.

Of course, George would prefer that everyone subscribe to his theological worldview, but he is concerned with proposing a theory in which those who reject the theological aspects could still subscribe to the practical aspects. George is concerned with demonstrating the intelligibility of goods and norms laid down by his theory of natural law, not ultimately finding agreement on their source. A theory of natural law, by definition, would imply that there are unchanging first principles that individuals can grasp regardless of their theological commitments. And indeed, the young mom who acted to protect her son at the pool witnesses that this is indeed true.

Classical Natural Law versus New Natural Law

Thus far, the use of *new* to describe Robert P. George's approach to natural law might leave one wondering what its newness is measured against. Is there an "old" natural law? Disagreements between classical natural law theorists and new natural law theorists stem from differing interpretations of Thomas Aquinas's work in the *Summa Theologiae*. Germain Grisez's 1965 article on Thomas's view of natural law upended traditional interpretations of Thomas by insisting that for Thomas, practical reasoning rather than speculative reasoning is how we obtain moral knowledge.[24] Is a moral norm deduced or inferred? As one new natural law proponent helpfully states the debate: "It is not because we have an inclination to X that we may infer that X is good for us. It is our prior grasp of X as good that justifies the claim that our inclination to X is a natural inclination."[25] For example, the desire for sex does not mean that acting on every sexual desire is moral just because it is *natural*. The new natural law tradition argues that it is the mind's grasp of the good of family life using reason that forms the moral norm governing what constitutes licit and illicit sexual activity.

---

23 George, "Natural Law," 184.

24 Germain G. Grisez, "The First Principle of Practical Reason: A Commentary on the *Summa Theologiae*, 1–2, Question 94, Article 2," *Natural Law Forum* 10 (1965): 168–201.

25 Alfonso Gómez-Lobo, *Morality and the Human Goods: An Introduction to Natural Law Ethics* (Washington, DC: Georgetown University Press, 2002), 127.

This debate is important because the new natural law tradition believes that the classical natural law tradition is guilty of committing the naturalistic fallacy: deriving an *ought* from an *is*. The new natural law tradition argues that practical reason is the only way to yield an *ought* and that blunt assertions about human nature cannot, on their own, yield confident insights about moral norms.

Space prevents me from attempting to resolve this debate, but I tip my hat in the direction of the NNL tradition by granting to them that regardless of who promulgates these laws and norms of morality, we know them by practical reasoning. Even Steven A. Long, a critic of George and NNL, concedes that the experiential grasp of natural law precedes immediate awareness of God when he writes, "In the order of our discovery of the natural law, and in precision from grace, our awareness of God comes later rather than earlier."[26] At the same time, this is one area where a weakness of George's perspective comes into view. According to J. Budziszewski, where natural law is God ordered, the naturalistic-fallacy accusation (the idea that one cannot derive an *ought* from an *is*) loses its punch:

> An "is" which merely "happens to be" has no moral significance because it is arbitrary; that is why it cannot imply an "ought." But an "is" which expresses the purpose of the Creator is fraught with an "ought" already. Such are the inbuilt features of our design, including the design of deep conscience.[27]

Regardless of whether one accepts the metaphysical presuppositions surrounding classical natural law theory, new natural law seeks to establish a grounding for natural law around reason and reason alone under the pretense that individuals, whether religious or not, are all invariably, and thus inevitably, aiming at grasping and fulfilling specific goods that are intuitively worth choosing. Consequently, critics of new natural law believe George and his school of thought are gutting the natural law tradition of its metaphysical richness and thus its authority. George would reply that

---

26 Steven A. Long, "God, Teleology, and the Natural Law," in *Natural Law: The Present State of the Perennial Philosophy*, ed. Christopher Wolfe and Steven Brust (Lanham, MD: Lexington Books, 2018), 8. For more on this debate, see the helpful volume by Brian M. McCall, *The Architecture of Law: Rebuilding Law in the Classical Tradition* (Notre Dame, IN: University of Notre Dame Press, 2018).

27 J. Budziszewski, *What We Can't Not Know: A Guide* (Dallas: Spence, 2004), 108.

regardless of the metaphysical underpinnings of natural law, natural law either retains its persuasive forcefulness, or it does not.

New natural law simply seeks to make those goods explicit so that those who reject the metaphysical presuppositions of classical natural law can still agree with them irrespective of metaphysical agreement. Classical natural law deems these goods as implicit in its conception of human nature *from the start*. In other words, the question about what is "good" to order one's life around is a matter of apologetical starting point more than it is substantively different in kind. Classical natural law theory infers moral norms from the starting point of human nature, whereas the new natural law tradition deduces moral norms as a result of reasoning about goods. It is not so much that new natural law rejects antecedent conceptions of "human nature" altogether as it is that it offers an apologetic that one need not begin at theoretical abstractions about human nature in order to arrive at moral norms and intelligible goods that could be shared by non-Christian and Christian alike.

A Protestant Evaluation of Robert P. George's New Natural Law Theory

Evangelical Protestants owe Robert P. George an immense debt of gratitude for the work he has done on natural law, for they stand as the recipients of a body of knowledge and a collection of arguments that many evangelical Protestant intellectuals and political activists have relied on for their own approach to public ethics. When one surveys the range of issues that attend to evangelical political witness in America—from abortion, euthanasia, human rights, justice, and religious liberty to gender, sexuality, and the definition of marriage—evangelicals have found themselves in common cause with George and indebted to his work.

Any critique of George's natural law theory has to do more with what it omits as an explicitly Christian moral theory than what the theory itself advances. Protestants may find themselves objecting to *how* NNL argues, not to *what* it argues, since Protestants find themselves aligned with the goals of NNL theorists in matters of public ethics.

The most important question we should consider in our assessment is whether George's NNL theory is *Christian* at all? There are two ways to answer this question. First, NNL arose in response to studying Thomas

Aquinas's work, which means the catalyst for the entire NNL question originates in, though is certainly not limited to, debates around medieval theology. The whole topic hovers over eminently theological categories. Second, though NNL proponents do not espouse a specific Christian theism or rely on an expressed doctrine of biblical revelation in their account, proponents do not believe they are operating in conflict with Christian theism or Christian revelation as much as they are operating alongside it. George is stalwartly Catholic himself. It should be made clear that George in no way sees his project as antithetical to biblical revelation. On the contrary, George insists that faith and reason are intertwined and complementary and that anyone who would forge a divide between Christianity and NNL is forging a false dichotomy.[28] George has, on numerous occasions, even lauded Protestantism's emphasis on the Bible as a guiding source for its doctrinal foundations and its role as an authoritative source in Christian public ethics. Absent is virtually any antagonism between Catholicism and Protestantism in George's rendering of NNL.[29]

But does this mean that natural law that is void of *immediate* and *explicit* reference to the triune God is illegitimate as a Christian approach to ethics? If NNL saw itself in opposition to Christian theology, that would be a problem. Yet that is not what is happening. In using NNL, George is ultimately speaking a different dialect from Christian theology, though both are of the same language.

One way to think about the project of natural law is to think about the discipline of physics. Can physics be an intelligible discipline apart from recognizing God's existence and ascribing to him the glory due to him?[30] Yes, of course. Much of modern scientific advancement has proceeded by those who are avowedly atheist. Professed atheism, however, does not invalidate the legitimacy of discoveries about the operations of the universe and its (literal) natural laws. Science cannot answer for an ultimate why, but it can offer hypotheses about what is. One need not be a Christian to make profound discoveries about the way God's world works. To state otherwise is to undermine the integrity of common grace. There can be physics apart

---

28 For more on this, see Walker and George, "Interview," 14.

29 Andrew T. Walker, "Protestants and Catholics in the Public Square: An Interview with Princeton's Robert P. George," *Light* 3, no. 1, Summer 2017, 43–45.

30 I'm indebted to my friend Ryan T. Anderson for this helpful metaphor.

from metaphysics in that physics seeks to explain the universe's physical laws mechanistically. Nevertheless, it cannot answer why there is a universe or what value it has.

In the same way, NNL seeks to posit a morality that one could, in theory, agree to without *immediately* adverting to God's existence as the foundation for morality. The question of God in NNL is one of timing: When does God's existence factor into the discussion? Perhaps to the frustration of evangelical Christians, God enters the equation later than may be desired; nonetheless, God ends up being the ultimate source for, well, *everything.*

The issue of God's place in NNL is understandably tense. Why not state where this is inevitably leading and confess the metaphysical prerequisites to natural law up front? I find this to be a legitimate criticism. While I appreciate George's complementary attitude to biblical revelation, NNL seems to smuggle in metaphysical presuppositions from the start without explicitly saying so. NNL would do well to be more explicit that the eternal law orders the universe that NNL inhabits.[31]

In many respects, the divide between classical and new natural law camps resembles a divide that some evangelicals may find themselves having with Robert P. George, and that is the wish for a more explicit biblical centrism. As the classical natural law tradition criticizes the new natural law tradition of attempting to furnish a natural law theory without immediately adverting to metaphysics and theology, evangelicals may register legitimate concern that an ethical theory without specific mention of Scripture or God is insufficient to claim a binding obligation. A desire for theocentric morality aside, George is either right or wrong that his views obtain the force of persuasion based on their own merits.

This raises the issue of whether an approach to natural law centered more on theism and revelation and one centered more on practical reason are not perhaps talking past one another.[32] I would propose that when Scripture

---

31 For a volume critical of George's theory of natural law, see McCall, *Architecture of Law.*

32 For more on this debate, see Sherif Girgis, "Subjectivity without Subjectivism: Revisiting the Is/Ought Gap," in *Subjectivity: Ancient and Modern,* ed. R. J. Snell and Steven F. McGuire (Lanham, MD: Lexington Books, 2016), 63–88; Steven A. Long, "Natural Law or Autonomous Practical Reason: Problems for the New Natural Law Theory," in *St. Thomas Aquinas and the Natural Law Tradition: Contemporary Perspectives,* ed. John Goyette, Mark S. Latkovic, and Richard S. Myers (Washington, DC: Catholic University of America Press, 2004), 165–96.

speaks in the categories of natural law, it does so through two domains: (1) natural law from *above* and (2) natural law from *below*. We might liken "natural law from above" to how Scripture posits a world ordered by God, as we see in Romans 1, where the focus is on the ontology of divine order. We may call this domain the approach based on more theoretical and speculative reasoning about how the universe is ordered according to eternal law. "Natural law from below" denotes how Scripture portrays the unfolding saga of moral action as it relates to individual agency and practical reasoning, as we see in Romans 2:15 with the law "written on their hearts." Romans 2 focuses on *how* the moral law is revealed, and that is by reasoned reflection. The evangelical would want to state that the explanation for reason, goods, and the intellect's ability to grasp is because of God's sovereign will for creation.

In other words, Scripture's foci for natural law encompass both theoretical and practical foundations. Evangelical Protestants are rightly concerned with anchoring truths supremely in Scripture. So the formal principle of the Reformation, *sola Scriptura*, is always controlling. Is NNL compatible with Protestant convictions about Scripture? Understood correctly, yes. This, however, is where we need to have an appreciable understanding of how theory can help supply (but never supplant) and explain the moral commands we see in Scripture. I believe that George's theory is the best rational explanation for the Bible's portrait of moral action.

The chasm between the two camps is not unbridgeable. The old and new may end up forming some type of complementary relationship in which the practical side needs to be more forthcoming about the metaphysical ordering of the "good," and the theoretical side needs to understand the value of basic goods deriving from practical reason's operation (which, I'll admit, seems to me to be the basis of how we understand that the "nature" we possess is intelligible). Even if we insist that practical knowledge can stand on its own without theoretical knowledge, that, to me, does not put the theoretical in opposition to the practical.

Affirmations

Protestants, I would argue, can affirm a number of elements of new natural law theory, including those described below.

Theory

A significant lacuna in evangelical ethics is a lack of overarching theory undergirding our theological commitments. What does that mean, practically speaking? While Protestant ethics reaches decisive conclusions on moral questions, the tendency is to locate these conclusions by biblical fiat *alone*. At the risk of being misunderstood, I wish to clarify that our ethics *ought* to be supremely biblical. As an evangelical Protestant within the Reformed tradition, I subscribe to *sola Scriptura*, but proof-texting ethical conclusions is not tantamount to advancing a theory of morality. Underneath an ethical conclusion, there must be a *rationale* for why the ethical conclusions are intelligible. If Scripture directs humanity to certain ends, apart from the obvious horizon of obedience to God, what about the directive makes sense on its own terms?

For example, Ephesians 4:15 states, "We are to grow up in every way into him who is the head, into Christ." Ephesians 4:28 instructs Christians to work hard and to do it honestly. No Christian disagrees with these commands. But *why* are we to grow up into Christ? *Why* are we to work faithfully and honestly? Underneath the text is an implicit directive guiding our actions. It assumes goods that NNL makes explicit, and we can see NNL ethics and biblical ethics as intertwined since the Bible's understanding of human nature is not at odds with NNL's own view of human nature.

This is chiefly the value of NNL and where evangelical Protestants stand to benefit from it. NNL as a *theory* offers an explanatory foundation for the moral directives of Scripture: NNL helps us understand that each of us acts to pursue an end we understand as beneficial. NNL is a powerful analytical tool to give rational explanations to Christian moral reflection. The Bible is full of moral obligations and moral prohibitions. NNL helps us understand why those obligations and prohibitions exist: obligations are informed by goods that our reason directs us to obtain out of a concern for God's glory and our personal well-being; prohibitions are informed by privations of those goods that reason directs us to avoid out of a concern for God's glory and our well-being.

Furthermore, NNL is a cognitivist and realist theory of ethics, as is Christian ethics. Both NNL and Christian ethics believe that moral norms are reasoned, objective, universal, and ultimately intelligible. This stands in contrast to ethical traditions that are voluntarist, subjective, relative, and emotive.

Human Dignity

The most profound contribution that NNL has offered on the public stage is its account of human dignity. NNL stands opposed to instrumentalizing the human person for some supposed greater good or leaving justice to convention, consensus, or majoritarianism. In one essay, George contrasts the natural law tradition with Friedrich Nietzsche's nihilism, in which "all things are permitted." In Nietzsche's system, George sees degradation and dehumanization as a feature, not a defect: "Where reason has no sway in practical affairs, the sole question is who has the power. And the powerful have no reason to spare the weak."[33] Elsewhere, George has argued for a doctrine of human rights on the premise that "if there are principles of practical reason directing us to act or abstain from acting in certain ways out of respect for the well-being and the dignity of persons whose legitimate interests may be affected by what we do," then rights obtain on the basis of enacting legal protections that protect a person's faculties to experience goods necessary to human flourishing.[34] A right to free speech exists, for example, because speaking truthfully as one grasps truth is necessary for ordering one's life as a self-constituting agent. From support for unborn life to the definition of marriage to religious liberty and more, the whole panoply of public ethics adopted by NNL theorists represents conclusions that evangelicals should sympathize with.

Delight in God's Creation

The "basic goods" thesis of NNL helps us understand the glory of God's creation and the teeming intelligibility of its goods. Let's use the concert illustration. Concerts are one of my favorite activities. After the concert ends, however, I sometimes feel genuine disappointment and sadness at the experience being over—as though something was left unfinished and some joy left untapped, and I wanted the show to continue. NNL helps explain

---

33   Robert P. George, "The 1993 St. Ives Lecture—Natural Law and Civil Rights: From Jefferson's 'Letter to Henry Lee' to Martin Luther King's 'Letter from Birmingham Jail,'" *Catholic University Law Review* 43, no. 1 (1993): 149.

34   George, "Natural Law," 174.

this situation. I so enjoy live concerts because it is how I respond to the intrinsic good of beauty.

Before familiarizing myself with NNL, I did not have the vocabulary to explain why I enjoyed an activity like a concert because the wonder and joy of a concert left me wanting *more*. I would constantly try to extract more meaning and joy out of the experience. Then it hit me: the reason I enjoy concerts so much is simply because the experience of aesthetic appreciation is thrilling and beneficial in itself. I cannot derive any greater benefit from the experience of the concert other than the concert itself. In turn, this brings me to my knees in thankfulness to God for designing us as beings who can respond to God's creation with such delight. God's provision of goods for us to grasp and experience is inexhaustible, meaning that the basic goods are always there for us to obtain (Ps. 16:11).

The same goes for the rewarding experience of having children. Everyone with children knows they are costly, are time-consuming, and can induce great disruption. But children are a source of unspeakable delight. I never tire of my children. I would lay down my life for them in an instant. Why is that? It's because the basic good of family life tells me that the presence of children is noninstrumentally valuable. I cannot derive any greater joy from being a father than simply being a father.

Criticisms

Despite the affirmations listed above, I would, nonetheless, offer a few criticisms of new natural law theory.

Admitting Metaphysical Assumptions

The universe we inhabit is a God-ordered universe. NNL theorists such as George are entirely in agreement with this proposition. Yet in reading NNL literature, one can easily detect a reticence about God's immediacy and necessity to the theory. Again, to avoid being uncharitable, NNL theorists are decidedly *not* antagonistic to God. The argument of NNL often comes across as though it is metaphysically neutral, as though its intricacies require no metaphysical groundings themselves.[35] But a closed system of

---

35 Phillip E. Johnson critiques the work of Robert P. George, John Finnis, and Germain Grisez along the same lines. See Phillip E. Johnson, "In Defense of Natural Law," *First Things*, November 1999, 70–74.

moral theory that appeals to its own internal reasonableness, without God, can easily be criticized by simply replying, "According to whose authority?" NNL needs greater grounding for its normativity. As a Protestant Christian, I wish that NNL theorists—who are predominantly Catholic—would be more forthright in stating their metaphysical assumptions about the theory.

Another criticism, perhaps, is the relative paucity of biblical interaction in George's work. In fairness, George does not see himself as a theologian or exegete, so he cannot be faulted for pursuing a theory on grounds outside his specific field. George cites Romans 2:15, the locus classicus for natural law, in various places throughout his work. Given that text, one might reasonably desire for George to insist that God has indeed instilled an innate knowledge of the moral law known not simply by use of reason but by divine endowment that undergirds the faculty of reason to begin with. Paucity of biblical interaction circles back to my criticism above that NNL is stubbornly committed to deriving a secular account of natural law while smuggling in metaphysical presuppositions. George and the NNL tradition are correct, however, to aver that we come to *know* the details of that endowment through our reasoned reflection.

Even here, there are tensions concerning the use of the Bible in George's thought. For example, George and the NNL tradition are opposed to capital punishment because NNL teaches that one may never intentionally kill. Owing to my belief in *sola Scriptura*, I must simply disagree and state my belief that capital punishment is permissible when justified on biblical grounds. When NNL takes norms to an absolute degree that eclipses the Bible's own moral insights, the Bible—and not philosophy—is the ultimate authority. But in fairness to George and the NNL tradition, they, too, believe that Scripture is inerrant and infallible. What the difference ultimately comes down to is a difference of interpretation. The NNL tradition would never see their morality as opposed to the teaching of Scripture.

God's Glory as the Ultimate Reason for Action

Robert P. George's approach to natural law could be neatly summarized as "reason for action." That, in short form, is what George and the NNL tradition are setting out to do—to articulate the reasons for why humans act and to formulate norms for respecting, protecting, and promoting the basic goods that fulfill human nature. In my estimation, they do so powerfully and convincingly yet with a focus toward *penultimate* reasons for action. My constructive criticism is to opportunistically use the NNL schema to consider how its formula could be expanded on with a view of *ultimate* reasons for actions. George is undoubtedly correct that humans act on the basis of reasons to pursue integral human fulfillment. A Christian account of NNL would then help us gain new insights about our "understanding of the human condition" considering sin and our ultimate destiny as persons.[36]

As Christians, our reason for action goes beyond merely earthly good(s) to the celestial good. Paul instructs his audience in 1 Corinthians 10:31 to perform all actions for the sake of God's glory. To borrow George's term, what is our *reason for action* as Christians? We understand our ultimate reason for action as pursuing God's glory. That is the ultimate end or telos of our being.

God's glory, strictly speaking, is the highest good that we can obtain as well. Therefore, it is to our benefit to act in accordance with the nature of God's holiness. For in rightful action, we learn what true happiness is—the creature's communion with God. Colonial American theologian Jonathan Edwards drives home this point in his sermon "Nothing upon Earth Can Represent the Glories of Heaven." It is an extraordinary sermon. In it Edwards makes one essential argument: God cannot act to obtain greater happiness because that would mean God is less than happy in himself, so in God creating the world, he did so to expand and enlarge the sweep of who could partake in that happiness. Man's end, therefore, is to experience God. When that occurs, man is happy. The sermon is worth quoting at some length:

> Natural reason tells us this, that God created man for nothing else but happiness. He created him only that he might communicate happiness to him. And therefore the happiness that God designed him [for] must be exceeding great. Let it not be an objection to this, that God created

---

36 Rufus Black, "Is the New Natural Law Theory Christian?," in *The Revival of Natural Law: Philosophical, Theological and Ethical Responses to the Finnis-Grisez School*, ed. Nigel Biggar and Rufus Black (Burlington, VT: Ashgate, 2001), 157.

man chiefly for his own glory. I answer, this is not different: for he created them that he might glorify himself this way, by making them blessed, and communicate his goodness to them.

'Tis evident that the end of man's creation must needs be, that he may be made happy, from the motive of God's creating the world; which could be nothing else but his goodness: for it was either because of his goodness, or inclination to make others happy, or for his own happiness. But it can't be for his own happiness; for it is impossible that an eternal, an infinite Being, should be capable of receiving more happiness than he has already.

Therefore the motive of God's creating the world must be his inclination to communicate his own happiness to something else. This reason tells us. If it be said that the end of man was that God might manifest his power and wisdom, holiness or justice, so I say too; but the question, "Why did God will to make known his power and wisdom, etc.? What could move [God] to will that his power and wisdom should be known? It would add nothing to God's happiness that those were known"—no, but the knowing of them makes us happy, and not God: and this is the end why God has showed his power and wisdom. . . .

Reason tells us that man was created to be happy in the beholding of God's own excellency, and therefore that the happiness of the saints will be exceeding great. The creation of the world is nothing but God's manifestation of his own perfection and excellency. 'Tis certain that God did not thus exert his excellencies for nothing, nor did he give man a capacity of perceiving these manifestations—and the glories and excellencies of God in them—for nothing; but it would be utterly in vain if there were none to behold and admire them. Wherefore it follows that man, or rational beings in general, was created to behold the manifestations of God's excellency, and to view them, and to be delighted with the sight of them. . . .

Wherefore, seeing God created man with so earnest a desire of very great happiness, and the better men are, the more earnestly do they desire, we may certainly conclude that good men enjoy as much as they desire: for God did not create in man so earnest a desire, when at the same time he did not create for so much as he should desire. This is a desire [that] is not an effect of the fall, [as] we have showed; but God created man with nothing that should torment him, as a desire that could never be satisfied would be an eternal torment. Therefore God has made it evident that good men shall obtain exceeding great happiness.[37]

The richness of this sermon is stunning. Notice how Edwards's argument is soaked with the themes of reason, teleology, and glory. For Edwards, reason, end, and glory all coordinate to formulate the ultimate reason for all things.

Evangelicals, on one level, should find George's theory compelling on its own terms as a rational explanation for obtaining moral goods while also wanting to see beyond the horizon of the rational to the divine. As evangelicals, we would want to insist that the true end of man is not basic human goods alone but God's glory.[38] For as the Westminster Shorter Catechism teaches, "Man's chief end is to glorify God, and to enjoy him forever."[39]

Conclusion

I refuse to choose between the view of natural law presented by Robert P. George and my Protestant convictions. In my view, the two are complementary, and if we look back to an earlier Protestant Reformer, Niels Hemmingsen, a protégé of Philipp Melanchthon, we see a remarkably similar argument accented with the Reformation's God-centered worldview. In Hemmingsen's remarkable volume, he uses categories later echoed in the work of George. As Hemmingsen states,

For if what is concluded is honorable or useful or pleasant, a man thereupon is carried along by a natural impulse to obtain it; but if reason

---

37 Jonathan Edwards, "Nothing upon Earth Can Represent the Glories of Heaven," in *Sermons and Discourses, 1723–1729*, ed. Kenneth P. Minkema, vol. 14 of *Works of Jonathan Edwards* (New Haven, CT: Yale University Press, 1997), 145–52, http://edwards.yale.edu/.

38 Again, the NNL tradition to which George subscribes does not see itself in opposition to theology. On this, see Germain Grisez, "Human Persons' True Ultimate End: The Continuity between the Natural End and the Supernatural End," in *Second International Conference on Thomistic Philosophy* (Santiago, Chile, 2014), 499–523; Grisez, "The Doctrine of God and the Ultimate Meaning of Human Life," in *The Doctrine of God and Theological Ethics*, ed. Alan J. Torrance and Michael Banner (London: T&T Clark, 2006), 125–34; Grisez, "The True Ultimate End of Human Beings: The Kingdom, Not God Alone," *Theological Studies* 69, no. 1 (February 2008): 38–61.

39 The Westminster Shorter Catechism is available online, for example, on the Orthodox Presbyterian Church website, https://www.opc.org/.

discovers that what is concluded is shameful, useless, or unpleasant, then just as the mind judges that that thing ought not to be embraced, so the will turns away from it in disgust. Consequently, one ought to be amazed at the workmanship of God, who created man in such a way that in him are both cognitive and appetitive faculties, that is, the faculties by which things are perceived and desired. It is fitting to gaze upon and wonder at these, so that we may be grateful to our creator, who has adorned this miniature world—that is, man—with gifts so wondrous.[40]

In his volume, Hemmingsen establishes a natural law theory without any reference to theology, and he expressly does so to demonstrate "how far reason is able to progress without the prophetic and apostolic word."[41] In many ways, Hemmingsen is a precursor to George, and the fact that a Protestant Reformer demonstrated similar insights ought to show us the possibility for compatibility between the Reformed tradition and George's views.

My first exposure to the work of Robert P. George came years ago. In his work, I understood that the ethical convictions espoused are not simply fideistic or sectarian. Rather, because we live in an ordered universe under the design of a triune God, all moral action within that ordered universe is eminently reasonable. As a younger evangelical at the time, I was searching for rational justification of why I held so dearly to my convictions. Why, for example, did I believe that abortion was wrong and that devaluing and redefining marriage would lead to further social harm? Why did a concept like human rights seem so important if one believes that religious liberty is necessary to human flourishing? I knew what the Bible said, but I wanted to plumb the depths further to understand this world that God created. Well, Robert P. George's explanations gave powerful clarity on so many of the ethical values I held dear as an evangelical Christian. That is ultimately why I find his work so valuable and why I think you should too.[42]

---

40 Niels Hemmingsen, *On the Law of Nature: A Demonstrative Method* (Grand Rapids, MI: CLP Academic, 2018), 49.

41 Hemmingsen, *On the Law of Nature*, 181.

42 I want to thank my friend and legal scholar Sherif Girgis for offering feedback on this essay.

5

Making Men Moral

Government, Public Morality, and Moral Ecology

Micah J. Watson

THREE DECADES AGO a young, pretenured Princeton professor published his first book with Oxford University Press, *Making Men Moral: Civil Liberties and Public Morality*.[1] Since the publication of that book in 1993, Robert P. George has authored scores of articles; written and edited several books; established the James Madison Program at Princeton University; advised presidents and popes; taught students who are themselves now senators, pundits, and professors; and played the banjo in venues well known and obscure. To describe his still ongoing career as illustrious is an understatement. Given the breadth of his intellectual interests and expertise—bioethics, philosophy of law, natural law, Catholic social thought, and jurisprudence—it is worth our time to revisit that first book. It is worth our time not merely because it is an introduction to George's thought and approach to the life of the mind, though it is that. Rather, as I suspect George himself would insist, we do well to read and wrestle with the arguments in this book because through that wrestling, we engage fundamental questions about human nature, law, and politics. In other words, we do well to grapple with this book because by doing so,

---

1 Robert P. George, *Making Men Moral: Civil Liberties and Public Morality* (Oxford: Oxford University Press, 1993).

we pursue the *truth* about these important matters that inform how we live well together.

This chapter acts as a sort of guide to George's book and an introduction to these consequential issues. The book, while clear and concise, does deal with some academic and technical jargon commonplace in moral and legal philosophy. In the first section, I consider the central thesis of George's argument and describe not only its substance but the deliberate approach he takes in framing what is at stake and in presenting his own arguments as well as those of his interlocutors. We can learn a good deal not only from *what* George argues but *how* he argues. In the next section, I move to the argumentative substance of the book itself, laying out George's articulation and critique of what he calls the "central tradition," briefly describing his treatment of competing theories and concluding this section with his positive argument for a perfectionist foundation for political goods such as freedom of speech and privacy. The final section highlights three takeaways from the book, whose relevance has only increased in the thirty years since its publication. Students of George's thought will find that *Making Men Moral* sets up much of his later work on specific issues like pornography and the more abstract but nevertheless crucial notion of a healthy moral ecology. We begin with George's central thesis, what it is and is not, and how he makes his case.

The Central Thesis of *Making Men Moral*

Someone once wisely said that we must "rise to the level of argument" rather than assume the conditions for a good argument are already there. We cannot really argue well about whether *Roe v. Wade* or *Obergefell v. Hodges* was rightly decided until we first determine what it means to properly interpret the Constitution. We will talk past each other arguing about abortion or gay marriage if we don't clarify our terms and identify the first principles that inform our view of human nature and human goods and how politics should promote and protect those goods.[2] Underneath every political argument lie oft-unstated assumptions about what counts as the criteria whereby an argument is successful in the first place. Sometimes we need to clear the ground on which we construct our arguments before we can

---

2   Alasdair MacIntyre, *After Virtue: A Study in Moral Theory*, 2nd ed. (Notre Dame, IN: Notre Dame University Press, 1984), 6–22.

meaningfully interact with and adjudicate between competing conclusions about specific norms and policies. *Making Men Moral* is a "clearing the ground" sort of book. While readers find controversial topics mentioned throughout the book, one must go elsewhere in George's corpus for arguments about abortion, gay marriage, cloning, and the like.[3] The success of these latter arguments, however, depends in part on the soundness of the ground clearing in *Making Men Moral*.

What sort of ground clearing is George up to? *Making Men Moral* challenges a particularly prominent understanding of what justice requires for the types of law we can rightly pass and enforce. That understanding is articulated and defended by several powerful thinkers who identify with the school of public philosophy known as liberalism, or sometimes political liberalism. "Liberalism" here is understood not in the partisan sense by which we would characterize Barack Obama or Alexandria Ocasio-Cortez as liberal but in the broader sense of a political philosophy based on ideas like the consent of the governed, government's role in protecting individual rights and liberties, and equal protection of the laws.[4] Most theorists in the particular school that George engages in this work are also "antiperfectionist," which means that they reject a "perfectionist" approach to law. A perfectionist approach to law holds that at least some of what governments legitimately do is pass and enforce laws and policies that restrict vice and promote virtue. In George's own words, "A central thesis of this book is that there is nothing in principle unjust about the legal enforcement of morals or the punishment of those who commit morals offenses."[5] The burden of George's book, then, is (1) to show that the arguments marshaled by critics of government's perfectionist role fail and (2) to sketch out the beginnings of an argument for why a perfectionist approach actually grounds liberalism's genuine achievements (freedom of speech, press, assembly, etc.) better than the attempts of the antiperfectionist liberals.

If antiperfectionist liberals are correct about the illegitimacy of governments "making men moral," then constructing arguments for policies that

---

3 See, e.g., Robert P. George, *In Defense of Natural Law* (Oxford: Oxford University Press, 1999); George, *The Clash of Orthodoxies: Law, Religion, and Morality in Crisis* (Wilmington, DE: ISI Books, 2001); George, *Conscience and Its Enemies: Confronting the Dogmas of Liberal Secularism* (Wilmington, DE: ISI Book, 2013).

4 Hence, on that partisan level, most Democrats and Republicans are "liberals" in this sense.

5 George, *Making Men Moral*, 1.

restrain certain vices like pornography or for laws that might promote certain virtues like self-reliance are quixotic. One must first establish that such policies can be legitimate before moving to specifics.[6] One must clear the ground first and then build the house of policy-specific arguments. While the next section describes George's ground-clearing argument in more detail, it's worth noting here George's approach to writing and argument. Readers of George's later works will find these observations familiar.

The first thing to note about George's writing is his clarity. A few months before he died, C. S. Lewis was asked in an interview about what made for good writing. "The reader . . . does not start knowing what we mean. If our words are ambiguous, our meaning will escape him," Lewis wrote. "Writing is like driving sheep down a road. If there is any gate to the left or the right the reader will most certainly go into it."[7] Christian readers in particular should not flinch at being compared to sheep, and the concepts and terminology involved in moral jurisprudence and political theory can create confusing gates that tempt us to go offtrack. George, however, does an outstanding job of writing such that we stay on the path. He preempts misunderstandings by beginning with clear definitions. He clarifies what he is up to (critiquing liberal scholars, arguing for perfectionist politics) and reminds readers what he's not doing (making prudential judgments about particular legislation). He anticipates questions and objections and builds in necessary qualifications and counterpoints. He distinguishes between when he is interpreting what a thinker means, on the one hand, and when he is charitably retrofitting a thinker's argument so that it can be as strong as possible, on the other.[8] Given the material, one cannot say that it's easy reading. But those who read with care and persistence are in good hands with George as a guide to not only his arguments but his critics' as well.

Speaking of critiques, the second virtue of George's approach is fairness. George writes in the same tradition as Aristotle and Thomas Aquinas, and naturally, his approach builds on the insights and arguments adduced

---

6   The "can be" language is important. As we see below, that it is part of government's role to promote virtue and restrain vice does not mean that *every* attempt to do so is just or prudent.

7   C. S. Lewis, "Cross-Examination," in *God in the Dock: Essays on Theology and Ethics*, ed. Walter Hooper (Grand Rapids, MI: Eerdmans, 1970), 263.

8   George, *Making Men Moral*, 65.

by those two thinkers, among others. But George also lives by the lesson Aristotle taught about his own teacher, Plato: "Plato is dear, but the truth is dearer still."[9] And thus, rather than treat Aristotle and Thomas as un-impeachable, George acknowledges shortcomings in each luminary's think-ing and offers a modified theory that builds on what works and addresses what doesn't. George also acknowledges the genuine accomplishments of the theory in his crosshairs, liberalism, as he begins his preface by noting that the natural law tradition has been "slow to appreciate the insights of liberalism when it comes to basic civil liberties such as freedom of religion, speech, press, assembly, and the right to privacy."[10]

Third, and finally, George has a superb knack for precisely represent-ing the arguments of his fellow scholars, distilling their various claims and evidence without diluting their strength or creating straw men that are easy to knock down. George explicitly rejects the practice of some to craft an amalgamated "liberalism" and take that apart. Rather, he devotes chapters to specific figures—Ronald Dworkin, John Rawls and David A. J. Richards, Jeremy Waldron, and Joseph Raz—and cites their work and words to represent their arguments in terms they themselves would recognize.[11]

These virtues of George's approach are not ancillary but central to the arguments and theories about political morality and cultivating a virtuous citizenry. A democratic culture depends on citizens who can not only en-gage in reason about what matters but engage reasonably with those with whom they disagree.[12] By inviting readers to think clearly, acknowledge weaknesses in their own tradition and strengths in rival traditions, and represent opposing figures with charity, the medium becomes part of the message, and the approach complements the substance. We turn now to the argumentative substance of *Making Men Moral*.

---

9   The Latin version of Aristotle's line in *Ethics* reads, literally, "While both are dear, piety requires us to honour truth above our friends." Aristotle, *The Complete Works of Aristotle: The Revised Oxford Translation*, vol. 2, ed. Jonathan Barnes (Princeton, NJ: Princeton University Press, 1984), 1732.

10 George, *Making Men Moral*, xii.

11 Granted, they would not necessarily agree with what George does after his descriptions.

12 At the same time, in his discussion of free speech, George notes that the value of giving and receiving of reasons through free speech is not uniquely tied to democracies. George, *Making Men Moral*, 207.

The Argumentative Substance of *Making Men Moral*

As mentioned, the burden of *Making Men Moral* is to show that anti-perfectionist arguments fail to demonstrate that laws aiming to cultivate virtues and restrict vice are unjust *in principle*. The book is divided roughly into three sections. In what follows I briefly describe each section and draw some conclusions from each about George's thought.

Introducing Morals Legislation and Perfectionist Politics

The first section is composed of the introduction and chapters 1 and 2. In the introduction, George first introduces the topic, defines his terms, lays out the scope and trajectory of the book, and very briefly describes the philosophical school he himself belongs to. In chapter 1, he draws from Aristotle and Thomas Aquinas to illustrate the "central tradition."[13] While a multitude of voices and varying emphases make up that tradition, one unifying thread is the belief that governments exist to do more than provide safety, promote comfort, and protect people from external threats.[14] They also exist to promote virtue, to help make people good. This is what is meant by "perfectionist," which does not imply an expectation that perfection is attainable but rather that moral improvement is desirable and that government can play a salutary role in cultivating it.

It is this aspect in particular that has fallen out of favor in modern times but that George nevertheless aims to refine and defend. He agrees with Aristotle that the purpose of the polis is to help shape our character but disagrees with Aristotle's elitism, his identification of the good as singular rather than plural, and his notion that the government is the primary player in inculcating virtue. He agrees with Thomas as well that the purpose of government is to lead its citizens to virtue, albeit guided by prudence and knowing government cannot legislate against every vice but only the most egregious.[15] But he disagrees with Thomas that the government should actively legislate in matters of faith in addition to matters of morality.

---

13 George belongs to what has become known as the new natural law school. See Andrew T. Walker's chapter in this book for more on this important aspect of George's thought.

14 George, *Making Men Moral*, 20.

15 Thomas Aquinas, *St. Thomas Aquinas on Politics and Ethics*, trans. and ed. Paul E. Sigmund (New York: W. W. Norton, 1988), 54–55.

In chapter 2, George takes us back to a lively British legal debate from the late 1950s precipitated by the Wolfenden Report, which recommended that British law should decriminalize homosexual behavior. The Wolfenden Report did not address whether homosexual behavior was in fact immoral but whether it was appropriate for the government to concern itself with personal, consensual matters. The report concluded that it was not in fact appropriate for the British government to concern itself with the "realm of private morality."[16] It is important to note that the report's conclusion rested not so much on rejecting the moral disapproval of consensual homosexual acts but rather the central tradition's holding that governments should be in the business of promoting virtue and restricting vice.[17]

The Wolfenden Report prompted a debate between legal philosopher and judge Patrick Devlin and H. L. A. Hart, a very prominent Oxford University philosopher of law. George takes us through the famous back-and-forth between these two thinkers, with Devlin defending the legislation of morals (and thus critiquing the Wolfenden Report) because of the necessity of social cohesion and with Hart objecting not so much to the traditional case for morals legislation but Devlin's contention that widespread moral disagreement threatens social order and thus the stability of society itself. George does more than just recount their debate, however, as he attempts to rehabilitate Devlin's position such that the case for morals legislation rests on firmer ground.

The contours of these different treatments and debates are too much for a detailed treatment here. What the introduction and first two chapters of George's book accomplish is an articulation of morals legislation and perfectionist politics that George then defends from the critiques of the scholars considered in chapters 3–6 (section 2 of the book). Nevertheless, without going into a detailed treatment, we can outline six key claims George believes accompany a sound understanding of morals legislation.

First, the government does have a role to play in actively encouraging virtue and discouraging vice. But the government is not the only nor even the primary actor in doing so.

---

16 Wolfenden Report, or, Report of the Committee on Homosexual Offences and Prostitution, United Kingdom Parliament, October 29, 1957, https://www.parliament.uk/.

17 Thus the question whether homosexual behavior is virtuous or vicious was not the issue at stake, at least on the surface.

Second, what constitutes the good life to be encouraged is variegated. That is, there are multiple human goods, and a virtuous life can take shape in an infinite number of legitimate though incommensurable ways. Contra Aristotle, the contemplative life of the philosopher is not the only way to achieve one's telos.

Third, contra Thomas, the government's proper role in fostering right moral behavior does not extend to coercing correct religious behavior and belief. In other words, though the government has an interest in protecting and fostering moral behavior, that interest does not necessarily extend into the religious foundations of morality, only the question of morality itself.

Fourth, Aristotle is correct to note that we become moral through our actively choosing the virtuous path; we are volitional creatures, and choice matters. Nevertheless, our environment shapes our perception of what we take to be morally choice worthy and how likely it is that we can actively *will* to make those choices.[18] Just as our individual choices about our health are constrained by how polluted our biological habitat is, so our moral choices are influenced by what George calls the "moral ecology" of our lives: the background assumptions, norms, and incentives that constitute our moral habitat.[19] Governments can and should act to preserve our moral as well as our physical ecological health.

Fifth, consistent with Thomas, believing in the reality of moral goods and morals legislation does not entail that governments must address every moral or immoral nook and cranny of human behavior. There are often strong, prudential reasons for governments to tolerate immoral behavior.

Sixth, and finally, contra Devlin, a sound perfectionist defense of morals legislation depends on the actual truth of one's judgment about what is virtuous and vicious for human character and flourishing. A concern for social order by itself does not justify government enforcement of this or that moral stance merely because it is popular or conducive to keeping people in line. Far from providing an overactive government with a blank check to interfere with its citizens' liberties, this insistence on the moral truth of any matter restricts a government's reach because its officials cannot rightly address any issue they please just for the sake of social order or cohesion.

18 That is, our environment affects our knowledge of what's good *and* our will to act on that knowledge.
19 George, *Making Men Moral*, 45.

In Defense of Morals Legislation

If the first section establishes the foil that antiperfectionist liberals engage, in the second section (chaps. 3–6) George works dialectically with several scholars—antiperfectionists *and* perfectionist liberals—to demonstrate that while the central tradition can and should be refined, we have no conclusive reason to doubt its core claim that morals legislation is a legitimate purpose of government. These chapters constitute the meatiest portions of the book and yet also the most rewarding for diligent readers. Here we see George faithfully presenting and astutely critiquing arguments from some of the biggest names in political and legal theory. Once again, a detailed walk-through is not feasible, but a brief word on each chapter is illuminating.

In the third chapter, George traces the various arguments of Ronald Dworkin purporting to establish that morals legislation runs afoul of a proper understanding of what "equal concern and respect" for citizens requires of any government.[20] Dworkin's arguments shifted over the course of his career, but the main thrust is that a commitment to human equality requires that we do not privilege collective interests over individual rights (this risks violating rights) and that we do not impose on citizens require-ments that they themselves cannot recognize as in their interests (this fails to show them respect). But there is no reason, George responds, to suppose that collective interests are necessarily at odds with individual rights. A proper understanding of the common good understands these rights "not as constraints on the pursuit of the common good, but as constitutive aspects thereof."[21] As for the claim that subjecting citizens to requirements they don't recognize as being in their self-interest, this principle is overbroad insofar as it makes problematic *any* law restricting human behavior that potential actors might find contrary to their interests. More important, it's just not true that a law restricting vicious behavior necessarily disrespects citizens. Paternalistic laws requiring, say, seatbelts or restricting pornography can be understood as in the best interests of the persons who live under such laws given an understanding of the value of such persons and the threat posed to their well-being by both drunk drivers and smut. Proponents of morals legislation see such laws as respecting actual persons and their

---

20 Ronald Dworkin, *Taking Rights Seriously* (Cambridge, MA: Harvard University Press, 1977), 198, quoted in George, *Making Men Moral*, 85.
21 George, *Making Men Moral*, 92.

well-being more so than merely their self-interests. Treating people with interests and free will but not reducible to those interests and volitional capacity means that good legislation falls between an all-encompassing, directive nanny state, on the one hand, and a free-for-all leaving people entirely unrestrained, on the other.[22]

In chapter 4, George draws from the Lincoln-Douglas debates to respond to the elegant arguments of Jeremy Waldron that there can be a strong moral right to do something wrong. This is a wonderfully complex chapter in which George gets into the weeds of rights and claims theory. The case for a moral right to do something wrong depends both on the good of protecting individual agency and on the potential for governmental overreach to damage the common good. That is, if Aristotle is right that moral improvement requires acts of the will, then any regime that attempts to police every moral act—and by so doing diminish the possibility of moral failure—damages the conditions needed for becoming virtuous. Moreover, government policies are often blunt instruments, and thus even well-intentioned attempts to guide moral behavior can have terrible, unintended consequences. Thus, Waldron argues, it is possible to say (1) that someone has a moral right to engage in such and such a behavior (such that this person should not be interfered with) and (2) that the behavior is nevertheless wrong.

George qualifies Waldron's conclusions by agreeing in part and disagreeing in part. He denies that there can be a *moral* right to engage in vicious behavior, but he agrees that there can be something of a weak or "shadow" right *not to be interfered with* by government. There is no strong moral right to engage in a wrong, but there can be a claim against some other party's authority to police or oversee that wrong. Consider the wrong of blasphemy.[23] People of faith or no faith at all can understand blasphemy to be a moral wrong and undermining of character.[24] At the same time, there are strong prudential reasons to doubt that government officials are well suited to both determine what counts as blasphemy and discourage

---

22 The critic may respond that governments can get these judgments wrong, both the substance of what conduces to human flourishing and the prudential wisdom needed to apply that substance to particular policies and social situations. This is, no doubt, true, but it is a liability that no approach to politics is immune from.

23 The example is mine, not George's.

24 People of faith and people of no faith, though, likely have very different accounts of why blasphemy is wrong.

or punish it. If this is true, then we would not speak of a positive right to blaspheme, because such behavior damages one's character. But we could speak of a right not to be policed in such matters by the state, a right that applies not so much to our action but rather implies a duty on the part of the state to refrain from making things worse by attempting to restrain this particular immoral behavior.

There is one final lesson to draw from this chapter. Waldron avers that denying his claim of a strong moral right to do wrong will lead to a rather pinched set of life choices for people living in a free society. George counters this claim in two ways. First, there are some choices that simply will not contribute to a genuinely free and flourishing society. The government may have strong prudential reasons not to interfere with the free choice of citizens to join the Nazi Party, but neither the common good of society nor the individual good of citizens is furthered by anyone actually joining the Nazi Party. We would all be better off if such choices were not made. Second, the plurality of genuine human goods and the infinitely diverse ways in which they can be realized contradicts the claim that some choices being left off the table necessarily leads to a drab, pinched, and boring society in which people's choices are reduced to various shades of gray.

Speaking of gray, in chapter 5 George first considers the shadowy figures of John Rawls's original position and Rawls's broader project before subjecting the Rawlsian-inspired philosopher David A. J. Richards's antiperfectionist and "autonomist" liberalism to severe scrutiny. Readers familiar with Rawls know that he purports to find fair principles of justice for a pluralistic society by deriving them from the deliberations of persons stripped of their knowledge not only of their place in society (race, class, situation in life) but also of their conceptions of the good.[25] There has been a good deal of development both in Rawls's work and among his critics since the early 1990s,[26] but two of George's points remain important. The first is that while Rawls does achieve some measure of impartiality in the original position by stripping decision makers of their self-knowledge, this comes at the cost of deliberating

---

25 John Rawls, *A Theory of Justice*, rev. ed. (Cambridge, MA: Belknap Press of Harvard University Press, 1999), 102–38. The idea is that people in the original position will come up with principles for a society that do not privilege their particular place in life but instead rest on the minimal basics of what any human being needs for a reasonably decent life.

26 For example, Anthony B. Bradley and Greg Forster, eds., *John Rawls and Christian Social Engagement: Justice as Unfairness* (Lanham, MD: Lexington Books, 2015).

about what is actually good for human beings. That is, unlike people in the real world, who, at their best, commit to principles and ways of life because of a judgment that those principles and practices are actually good, Rawls's deliberators in the original position value their positions merely because they happen to belong to them.[27] This may reduce the unfairness mixed in to any deliberative process, but it is not compelling to anyone who believes our political life should be informed by a vision of what is good for human beings.

The second takeaway here is that Rawls's approach is not actually neutral. There may be a semblance of neutrality *within* Rawls's theory, given the strictures of the original position, but for one standing outside the theory considering its merit, Rawls's construction based on neutrality cannot be justified without taking into account whether it is fair or good or just.[28] George illustrates this aspect of Rawls's thought by describing Richards's Rawlsian and putatively Kantian criticism of perfectionism. If Rawls can sometimes be coy about the practical political outcomes of his approach, Richards almost exults in defending the goods of a supposedly neutral liberal commitment to justice as fairness. George points out the tension, however, between Richards's criticism of perfectionism for favoring some ways of life over others and his praise of such practices as pornography, illicit drug use, prostitution, and sodomy as potentially or genuinely constitutive of human flourishing.[29] The question whether Richards is correct about such positive claims and his criticism of laws that restrict these practices is beside the point. For if he thinks such practices do contribute to human flourishing and favors policies and laws that reflect that understanding, then he actually favors morals legislation and must give up any pretended commitment to autonomy or neutrality as such. Richards's inconsistency here is one more indication that a foundational neutrality is impossible.

There is one final liability to Richards's particular appropriation of Rawls's theory, and that is his noncognitivism. That is, Richards rejects the possibility that reason can identify choice-worthy actions or ends and instead

---

27 We have then a subtle echo of the problem of Euthyphro, who debated with Socrates shortly before the latter philosopher died. Do citizens in Rawls's original position choose his political principles because they are good? Or are they good because Rawls's citizens choose them?

28 Rawls would later acknowledge this point, resulting in him writing *Political Liberalism* as an attempt to ground his theory differently, albeit still on a moral basis by his own admission. John Rawls, *Political Liberalism* (New York: Columbia University Press, 1996), 11.

29 George, *Making Men Moral*, 145–46.

believes all actions are motivated by subrational factors.[30] If Richards is right, then we should expect to find his case for his approach to appeal not to what we think is true but rather what we might feel or want. We return to this observation in the concluding section of the chapter.

George's final chapter in this second section considers the liberal perfectionism of the late Joseph Raz, one of George's graduate school mentors (along with John Finnis). Like George, Raz is a perfectionist. Unlike George, however, Raz is a perfectionist liberal. One does not defend liberalism because it leads to better consequences over time, nor because it protects the right to choose absent any consideration of what is chosen. Rather, Raz's liberal perfectionism means he thinks that autonomy is intrinsically good and that government intervention in supposedly "victimless" crimes violates that autonomy. Raz does not agree with Richards that morally vicious acts can be somehow valuable merely because they are chosen or because they coincide with desires or appetites we happen to have.

It is clear that George finds much to admire in Raz's dismantling of antiperfectionist liberalism and in his defense of liberal perfectionism and autonomy. Nevertheless, George presses Raz on how one can distinguish between how *morals* legislation supposedly violates autonomy and how *any* laws or policies violate human autonomy. If autonomy is an intrinsic good, and we should not act directly against any intrinsic good, then it is not clear how to distinguish a law restricting a solitary figure in harming his character through pornography[31] from a law restricting the same person in defrauding his neighbor through an internet scam. Both actions are immoral, and both laws impinge on his autonomy.

George's understanding of autonomy avoids this difficulty (and others) because he holds that while autonomy is valuable, it is instrumentally valuable rather than valuable in itself. Unlike intrinsically valuable human goods, such as art or friendship, autonomy is valuable insofar as it is a condition of what George calls "practical reasonableness."[32] This is an important but complex idea central to George's work as well as his natural law collaborators.

---

30 George, *Making Men Moral*, 157.

31 It should be noted, though, that even pornography is not a victimless crime. Even if the consumption of pornography can be solitary, the production of it is not. That said, by George's account, even if a crime is private and solitary, there is no reason why the outlawed behavior is *in principle* beyond the reach of a community's laws and policies. One can victimize oneself.

32 George, *Making Men Moral*, 177.

John Finnis defines practical reasonableness as "the basic good of being able to bring one's own intelligence to bear effectively (in practical reasoning that issues in action) on the problems of choosing one's action and lifestyle and shaping one's own character."[33] In other words, it is the very activity of using our knowledge to reason about how we should act externally, acting thus, and then harmonizing our internal emotions and dispositions with those right actions. This good is *reflexive*, which means we need to actively participate in it for the good to be realized. In this sense it is like friendship, which is certainly more than the mere choice to pursue a friendship but cannot exist without that choice. Volition is necessary but not sufficient for its realization. Just as the action of a forced apology is not an actual apology, so the goods of friendship and practical reasonableness are not actual goods unless we knowingly and willingly participate in them. No one else can be a friend for you, nor think for you about what actions are right and how to align one's character with those right actions. Hence the necessary but still instrumental role of autonomy. We need to freely choose some goods for them to actually be goods, but as we see with freely made choices to pursue wickedness, such as abortion or racial discrimination, autonomy by itself is not intrinsically valuable. It is good instrumentally insofar as it is a pre-condition for the realization of intrinsic goods. Thus understood, George's perfectionism can give autonomy its due without the troublesome moral implications that follow from thinking human autonomy is an end in itself.

The twists and turns of George's interactions with Dworkin, Waldron, Rawls, Richards, and Raz are far more complex than captured in the summary treatment afforded here. Yet the conclusion of these chapters is significant. George subjects his own refined version of the central tradition's commitment to the legitimacy of morals legislations in principle to the test of several robust thinkers and finds no conclusive reason to think that commitment violates justice or fairness, nor does it undermine the prospect of human flourishing. Indeed, far from it.

George's Alternative Proposal

The last section of George's book is a single concluding chapter titled "A Pluralistic Perfectionist Theory." George recognizes that it is not enough

---

33   John Finnis, *Natural Law and Natural Rights* (New York: Oxford University Press, 1980), 88–89.

to disarm arguments critical of his position. One must make a positive case, and here George offers a provocative conclusion to his book by claiming that his alternative approach better promotes and protects political goods than theories from antiperfectionist liberals.[34] Here George works his way through several crucial political values in the American political tradition: freedom of speech, freedom of the press, privacy, freedom of assembly, and freedom of religion. Unlike rival approaches to public morality, George grounds our political tradition's commitment to these civil liberties in an understanding of what is good for human beings as such and how that good can be realized in an infinite number of ways. While any approach has difficulties to overcome, and George's is no exception, his pluralistic perfectionism gives a principled account for the best features of liberalism without depending on the shaky consequentialism of weighing various harms, on the one hand, or the farcical prospect of respecting "neutrality," on the other.

Three Takeaways

Thirty years have passed since *Making Men Moral* hit the scene. Given the importance of the principles and ideas considered and the breadth and depth of George's treatment, one could draw any number of takeaways. I conclude this chapter by briefly highlighting three critical notions we find in George's work that remain vital for understanding the purpose of government and our own role as Christian citizens committed to the common good.

The first notion is the concept of moral ecology, which we encountered briefly above in discussing how the surrounding culture affects our personal attempts to live virtuously.[35] A family in 2023 may be just as committed to raising children free from the ill effects of pornography as a family living back in 1953, but the surrounding conditions in 2023 have made that task much more difficult. In his treatment of the Hart-Devlin debate in chapter 2, George distinguishes between social order and social cohesion. As Hart pointed out, a breakdown of a shared morality may not lead to a

---

34 I should note George's caveat here that this chapter is only a sketch. But it is nevertheless a very suggestive sketch, and students of George can see in his later work the fulfillment of the IOU stated here.

35 See p. 104.

breakdown of social order, and in fact, the relaxations of sexual mores in late 1950s Britain had not led to anarchy or the overthrow of the government. Yet such a moral sea change could result in the breakdown of social cohesion, such that something very valuable is lost even if social order is maintained. Writing in the early 1990s, George described this loss in a way that now seems almost prophetic, noting the phenomenon of a sort of "drifting apart" that can happen between friends but also within an entire society.[36] The debates about sexual controversies in the 1990s have only intensified in the three decades since then, as we have gone from arguing about laws penalizing intimate same-sex behavior to implementing laws and policies punishing opposition to same-sex marriage and policies protecting the self-understandings of some with gender dysphoria. Wherever one stands on the substance of those issues, the severe polarization—the drifting apart—that our culture has experienced over the last few decades seems inexplicable apart from the chasm between us on these fundamental moral issues and our disagreement about government's role in adjudicating them.[37] There is a sense that we have *lost* something intrinsically valuable, and George's articulation of the good of social cohesion, informed by tangible moral goods, helps us understand what has been lost.[38]

The second idea that was prescient when *Making Men Moral* was written and remains so today is George's critique of emotivism and his championing of reason. In his treatment of Richards, and to a lesser extent Devlin, George points out the problems that follow from rejecting the central tradition's claim that people can use their reason to identify choice-worthy ends and morally licit means for action. The *can* here is crucial. While George is more optimistic than some about humanity's capacity to reason well, he is not naive about what Isaiah Berlin called the "crooked timber of humanity," or the Christian doctrine of original sin. Moreover, George acknowledges that emotions are an important part of what it means to be human and that sound decision-making must take feelings into account.[39]

---

36 George, *Making Men Moral*, 68.

37 See Robert D. Putnam, *Our Kids: The American Dream in Crisis* (New York: Simon and Schuster, 2015); Charles Murray, *Coming Apart: The State of White America, 1960–2010* (New York: Crown Forum, 2013).

38 One way to understand George's work is as a way to resist that "drifting apart" while promoting the good wisely in light of deteriorating circumstances.

39 George, *Making Men Moral*, 203.

Whatever challenges there may be with the relationship between sin, reason, and emotion, the view espoused by Richards and earlier thinkers such as Thomas Hobbes[40] and David Hume[41] that reason is by definition instrumental and thus that all our decision-making is ultimately determined by subrational motives has profound and devastating consequences for a healthy moral ecology and a vibrant political pluralism. If human beings do not reason about their differences, then there is no such thing as an honest mistake or people coming to different conclusions in good faith. Our differences stem from our different desires and appetites, and thus when someone differs from us on an important matter, it is fruitless to reason with them, just as it would be fruitless for them to reason with us. As C. S. Lewis writes about the rejection of reason's role in determining what is right, "When all that says 'it is good' has been debunked, what says 'I want' remains."[42] Thus Richards characterizes opposition to his preferences as steeped in emotion or hatred and as not merely wrong but "brutal, callous, and inhumane."[43]

One need only peruse our national debate online and offline to see the bitter fruits of this rejection of the possibility of reason. Rather than appealing to the reason of those with whom we disagree on important matters, far too often we instead think to make progress for our side by unmasking the ulterior hidden motives of our opponents. If Richards and like-minded thinkers are correct, then there simply is nothing else but those ulterior motives, and thus we see champions and foot soldiers on both left and right flame each other's motives in a zero-sum rhetorical game rather than appeal to the better and more reasonable angels of our nature.

The third and final idea to highlight from George's work is the complete and utter demolition of the pretense to neutrality made by antiperfectionist political liberals in theory and a chorus of pundits and regular people in our public discourse. This pretense functions in two ways. On the one hand, advocates of inherently controversial positions resting on contestable claims

---

40 "For the thoughts are to the desires, as scouts, and spies, to range abroad, and find the way to the things desired." Thomas Hobbes, *Leviathan*, ed. J. C. A. Gaskin (Oxford: Oxford University Press, 1996), 48.

41 "Reason is, and ought only to be the slave of the passions, and can never pretend to any other office than to serve and obey them." David Hume, *A Treatise of Human Nature* (London: Penguin Books, 1985), 462.

42 C. S. Lewis, *Abolition of Man* (New York: HarperCollins, 2001), 65.

43 George, *Making Men Moral*, 157.

can frame their proposals as if they are not controversial at all but are the commonsensical conclusions drawn from what "everyone knows." Think, for example, of pro-choice advocates who claim to speak for "women," as if we don't find women on all sides of the abortion issue. On the other hand, pretensions to liberal neutrality lend themselves to those who want to rule out-of-bounds any position they disagree with without actually weighing the reasons for such a position. Here we might think of those who criticize school vouchers because they will be used by parents who prefer private religious schooling, as if public schools are somehow based on less controversial or contested ideas than private schools.

But if George's treatment of Dworkin, Rawls, and Richards is correct, then there is no such thing as a neutral approach. It's not unusual to hear in common discourse or the classroom that one "cannot legislate morality." But the reality is that one cannot *not* legislate morality insofar as every policy, law, regulation, and legal restriction is based on some conception of a good to be promoted or protected or on some ill to be prevented or remedied. One need only ask what the purpose of the law or regulation is, and at some point the answer has to boil down to something like "Life will be better with this law or policy than it would be without it."

This is a tremendously liberating truth about our roles as good neighbors and citizens. It does not absolve us from the challenge of thinking hard about moral principles and how to apply them in tangible ways conducive to the common good. But it frees us from the canard that we somehow are violating democratic principles of fairness when we advocate for government fulfilling its appropriate role in promoting virtue and restraining vice. After all, in a democracy we don't so much *impose* values on each other as we *propose* this or that policy through the democratic process and abide by the results. Given the success of George's ground-clearing work in *Making Men Moral*, we are free to contribute to what might be built on a common ground cleared from a false neutrality and awaiting our renewed efforts to cultivate a healthy moral ecology suitable for the flourishing of real human beings pursuing genuine human goods.

6

Robert P. George versus John Rawls

On Public Reason and Political Liberalism

Hunter Baker

JOHN RAWLS WILL ALMOST SURELY be remembered as the most consequential political philosopher of the twentieth century for his books *A Theory of Justice* and *Political Liberalism*. Indeed, it is possible to make a case that Rawls's work had such impact on the United States Supreme Court that he succeeded in changing the court's traditional "rational basis" standard into something more strongly resembling Rawls's own concept of "reasonableness," thus altering the course of American jurisprudence through the line of cases that eventuated in *Obergefell v. Hodges*.[1]

While a number of thinkers have taken aim at what they perceived to be vulnerabilities in Rawls's work, Robert P. George is one of the most effective. His critiques of Rawls go straight to the heart of the matter and raise questions that are not easily dismissed.

As an example, Rawls's most famous illustration and accompanying logic is his "veil of ignorance." The reader is invited to stand behind a veil that obscures whatever destiny he or she might face on planet earth upon being born. From the perspective of such a preexistent person, who recognizes that any possible future could potentially be his or her own, such an individual (indeed, all individuals) would choose a particular set of rules to govern life

---

1   Obergefell v. Hodges, 135 S. Ct. 2584 (2015).

in the society into which he or she would be born, and we naturally expect that these rules would involve nondiscrimination and the equal sharing of resources.[2] A great many readers have been strongly impressed by Rawls's veil and the clarification of social rules that appears to follow.

Robert George, however, notes important problems with A Theory of Justice that should not pass easily by. The one that is of special concern here is George's observation that individuals in the Rawlsian "original position" lack any concern about the worthiness of ends other than the fact that they are their ends.[3] To be still more specific, the individual standing behind the veil makes decisions with self-preservation in mind rather than considering the role of merit.[4] Robert Nozick, a very different philosopher from George, protests that Rawls's answer seems unsatisfying "unless we were sure that no adequate historical-entitlement theory" is available.[5] Both George and Nozick, then, sense that Rawls's theory of justice might end up avoiding important questions regarding justice. Nozick notes that Rawls's theory gives no real attention to the choices people make during their lives and how they develop their capabilities.[6] These questions—serious questions about human agency and life and how to live it—are precisely the kinds of inquiries that have occupied Robert George during his career.

It should perhaps be no surprise, then, that George finds problems with Rawls's later work Political Liberalism that parallel those in A Theory of Justice. While the problem with Rawls's view of justice has to do with its elimination of merit as a criterion of evaluation, Political Liberalism relativizes the category of truth. As merit is essentially irrelevant to the question of justice in Rawls's theory, so too is truth to his account of political liberalism. Getting away from a strong view of truth may, in fact, have been Rawls's point.

Rawls's theory is essentially an attempt to solve the problem of pluralism in modern societies. While some other efforts seek to slice through the Gordian knot by simply dividing the sacred from the secular, Rawls

---

2   See generally John Rawls, A Theory of Justice (Boston: Belknap Press of Harvard University Press, 1971).

3   Robert P. George, Making Men Moral: Civil Liberties and Public Morality (New York: Oxford University Press, 1993), 134.

4   George, Making Men Moral, 136.

5   Robert Nozick, Anarchy, State, and Utopia (New York: Basic Books, 1974), 201–3.

6   Nozick, Anarchy, State, and Utopia, 214.

correctly recognizes that excising religion from the public square is far from adequate. The challenge is bigger than religious difference. Rather, philosophical differences or differences in worldviews could prove equally threatening. The reality of the situation in his day was unavoidable given the rise of secular totalitarianism in the twentieth century.

While Jean-Jacques Rousseau sought a solution in a bland, ethical civic religion in which the only real sin was to think one's fellow citizen was going to hell, Rawls looks to rebuild a space for discourse in which participants commit themselves to a practice of self-consciously communicating across religious, ideological, and philosophical boundaries in accordance with his idea of public reason. The truth, in the classical liberal style, is something aspired to by various parties who meet in civic debate to test their ideas against one another. But for Rawls, the normal practice of simply speaking, writing, organizing, and voting in an unselfconscious way and hoping for the truth to emerge from the free interplay of ideas is essentially obsolete and should be replaced by the framework he proposes.

Before getting more deeply into Rawls's approach, it is worthwhile to consider that the standard public square, which is less regulated by political philosophers, has proved itself reasonably well. It is not crazy to ask whether we actually need the kind of reformation of motive and behavior Rawls suggested. One could argue, for example, that something like a classically liberal approach to civic participation carried the United States through the civil rights era and indeed that activists such as Martin Luther King Jr. achieved a great deal without any fine parsing of the religious, the secular, and "comprehensive doctrines" (discussed below). King's "Letter from Birmingham Jail," which is now read by a great many students in state colleges and public schools across the land, explicitly argues from Christian natural law premises and sources (thus invoking the authority of God). Given such a valuable historic precedent (and a more constructive one than the "wars of religion" to which Rawls briefly alludes),[7] one might find sympathy for Sanford Levinson's confusion as to why the test of simple persuasion is inadequate as the bar to be surmounted.[8]

---

7   John Rawls, *Political Liberalism* (New York: Columbia University Press, 1993), xxiii–xxiv.
8   Sanford Levinson, "Religious Language and the Public Square," *Harvard Law Review* 105, no. 8 (June 1992): 2077.

John Rawls's Framework[9]

Before discussing Robert George's critique, it is important to understand the framework John Rawls proposes. Rawls recognizes the artificiality and unfairness[10] of a simple sacred-secular divide that would disfavor, say, Catholicism, while freely welcoming Marxism, so he created a category he refers to as "comprehensive doctrines." They can be religious, philosophical, or moral, and they tend to proceed from a tradition of thought and doctrine.[11]

While they can be "reasonable," it is also the case that they operate under "burdens of judgment" and generally recognize that such burdens exist for everyone. What are burdens of judgment? They are the mass of things we sift through as we try to make sense of the physical and social world. How complex is the evidence? What weight should be given to it? How different are the experiences of people? To what degree is indeterminacy a problem—that is, are questions being asked for which we can't rationally determine an answer? How can goals be prioritized in a limited social space?[12] In other words, the burdens of judgment are part of our common experience as human beings. The reasonable adherents of common doctrines will understand and agree to a kind of political existence that holds comprehensive doctrines to one side while they interact with each other on the basis of what can be held in common.[13]

It is critical to understand that Rawls's version of the public square sets reasonableness at a premium. His reasonableness is not the same as rationality. And maybe that helps us understand the lack of ambition for and interest in the lofty concept of truth. Rationality is less important to Rawls than the fact that participants in the public square see themselves as highly concerned with mutuality and reciprocity. The focus, then, is not on rational

---

9   This summary cannot help but be informed by (though I have not drawn directly from) a previous essay I wrote dealing with similar subjects: Hunter Baker, "The Secularist Biases of Rawls' 'Neutral' Rules," in *John Rawls and Christian Social Engagement: Justice as Unfairness*, ed. Anthony B. Bradley and Greg Forster (Lanham, MD: Lexington Books, 2015), 91–104.

10   The reality is that government fundamentally operates through the exercise of coercion. Coercion is unpleasant whether the source of ideas driving the exercise is ideologically secular or religious.

11   Rawls, *Political Liberalism*, 59.

12   Rawls, *Political Liberalism*, 56–57.

13   Rawls, *Political Liberalism*, 60–61.

justification. Rather, the point is to successfully determine the ideas and courses of actions others would find it reasonable to accept.[14]

Jacques Maritain noted something similar in effect as he and others worked on the UN Declaration on the Rights of Man. Participants in the discussion and drafting of the document were able to agree on many of the rights as long as they did not inquire into the sources of their beliefs. It wasn't difficult to arrive at a list of rights, but it was incredibly difficult to agree on some kind of common, rational justification for them.[15] Rawlsian political liberalism leaves the rational justification behind because it finds the "basis of social unity" somewhere else.[16] (This is a point that figures significantly in Robert George's response, examined below.)

Properly schooled, the now reasonable adherents of comprehensive doctrines will agree with their need to restructure their participation in politics into a form palatable to other reasonable people differently situated. Keeping in mind something like the phenomenon Maritain noted, this political liberalism explicitly avoids the metaphysical. Instead, political liberalism seeks an "overlapping consensus" that emerges from a reasonable mix of political values to which we can all agree to be bound.[17] Critically, the state must restrain people from bringing their various comprehensive doctrines into political debates over "constitutional essentials" and "matters of basic justice." Evangelism, for example, could still occur but not political activism seeking to influence at least these fundamental laws. With regard to this most critical and essential subset—that is, constitutional essentials and matters of basic justice—only argumentation that comports with a "reasonable political conception of justice" may be employed. Accordingly, only "political values that others as free and equal" could be expected to endorse are permitted a deciding role within the system.[18] The type of reason that results from this kind of discipline is what Rawls calls "public reason," because it should be available to everyone.[19]

---

14 Rawls, *Political Liberalism*, 62–63.
15 Jacques Maritain, *Man and the State* (Washington, DC: Catholic University of America Press, 1998), 76–77.
16 Rawls, *Political Liberalism*, 63.
17 Rawls, *Political Liberalism*, 134–35.
18 Rawls, *Political Liberalism*, 137.
19 Rawls, *Political Liberalism*, 225.

Rawls does not hem in the comprehensive doctrines out of favoritism toward the skeptic, at least not on the face of things. The reason to restrain them is not a belief that they are the stuff of fantasy or fever dreams over against a more positivistic vision. They are kept out in service of the idea that such virtuous segregation of ideas fosters fairness and prudence.[20] In Rawls's view, the holders of comprehensive doctrines should be pleased to agree to this kind of system. It is true that they will have to hold back cherished convictions, but the restraint serves a good cause. They are not like late twentieth-century mainline Protestants losing confidence by the hour under the assault of science and enlightened social progress. They are, instead, people who see the prudential value of political liberalism and public reason. The formula is simple. Does one observe the fact of pluralism in modern society? Yes. Does one accept that it is important to figure out how to live together peaceably? Yes. If so, then the Rawlsian conclusion is to embrace a system of the type proposed and to live under its restrictions in the name of the common good.

Rawls's program has to be taken seriously. First, he is one of the most important political philosophers of his era, if not the most important. Those of us who teach political thought sometimes joke that he is the reason we are still employed. Second, his proposal is brilliant, in its own way. Rawlsian political liberalism is significantly more sophisticated than ham-handed secularism combined with an aggressive form of church-state separation and makes demands of ideological parties arguably similarly situated to religious ones. Third, it is likely that Rawls has significantly affected the jurisprudence of the United States Supreme Court. For most of its history, the court has shown tremendous deference to state legislatures when applying its "rational basis" level of scrutiny. One of my law professors (a card-carrying liberal from New York City) instructed our group of first-year students that the only way she could see legislation overturned on the "rational basis" standard (the absolute lowest standard) would be if a law dictated something like requiring everyone to wear one green shoe every Tuesday. Shockingly, the Supreme Court would eventually overturn a law criminalizing same-sex sexual contact without need of any higher standard than the "rational basis" test.[21] Whether or not one agrees with such a law,

---

20 Rawls, *Political Liberalism*, 150.
21 See Lawrence v. Texas, 539 US 558 (2003).

is it possible to come up with a rational account to support it and certainly one better than the "green shoe" law could have produced? Of course. So what happened? I would argue that John Rawls successfully convinced members of the court to adopt as its "rational basis" standard a standard much more like his "reasonableness" than like the old rationality.[22] Is it rational to ban homosexual acts? On some accounts, certainly. The biological complementarity of the sexes alone suggests as much. But is it reasonable according to Rawlsian lights? Almost definitely not. Thus, the result.

This way of thinking is counterintuitive to many people and thus requires further explication. To separate the rational from the reasonable is difficult for us to do. We tend to think of a rational person as a reasonable person and vice versa. But remember that Rawls is more concerned with something like social harmony than he is with getting the correct answer, so to speak. As a result, he separates the two concepts.

Rationality remains the thing we understand it to be. Can we produce some kind of justification for the course of action that we recommend? Now, this justification has to have some credibility. If I told you we need to allocate budget dollars to fly to the moon to gather a large quantity of green cheese that will be delicious, then I have offered a justification but one without credibility. In fact, men have gone to the moon and found it is made of rock, not aged dairy products. My proposal would be irrational. On the other hand, if I made any other argument that corresponded to facts and led to a course of action, I would honor the requirements of rationality.

We often use reasonableness as a synonym for rationality. If you tried to sell me the idea of traveling to the moon to get green cheese, I could just as easily tell you that you are being unreasonable as I could say that you are being irrational. Rawls means something else by *reasonableness*. His version of reasonableness can be thought of more in the way one might think of a dispute with a neighbor. Let's say that you have a dog that lives in your fenced-in backyard. If the dog barks all night, the neighbor might complain to you that the noise is disruptive. It would be reasonable for him to expect you to try to do something about the dog's bad habit, such as sending him to obedience school to curb the barking. It would perhaps be unreasonable of you to refuse to try to limit the barking. The nature of

22 Baker, "Secularist Biases," 98–99.

this reasonableness is focused on the relationship the two of you have as neighbors and what you might be able to expect from one another. Let's say his complaint is different, and he says that your dog stares into his backyard through the gaps in his fence, thus interfering with his privacy. At that point, you might say, "You aren't being reasonable." What you would primarily mean is that he expects too much of you in asking you to try to limit what a dog can perceive.

With regard to the debate over something like gay marriage, it is fairly easy to see the difference in how rationality and reasonableness are understood in the Rawlsian scheme. One can rationally argue that male and female bodies are complementary in nature and that reproduction of the human race (and thus the future of society) rests entirely on the male-female sexual relationship and consequent raising of children by those who sired and birthed them. Indeed, one could conclude that the experience of a mother and father gives children of the male or female sex a more well-rounded understanding of their fellow human beings as they mature. I could even make a kind of scientific argument that the interaction of the male and female sex organs—implied by their very design and structure— is required for human survival. Other uses of these sex organs, scientifically speaking, could represent something highly eccentric, useless, irrelevant, and even a distraction from an overriding goal of nature. One could agree or disagree with those statements, but there is clearly a rationality at work. Rawls would focus on how any argument restricting homosexuality would appear to homosexuals. They would find it unreasonable to abandon the gay lifestyle for any rational reason I could suggest unless I could prove that there was some great and pressing danger resulting from their activity. In fact, I would have to demonstrate to them that they are being unreasonable (in the Rawlsian sense) in maintaining their same-sex preferences. Thus, we can see the rational and the reasonable sitting on opposite sides of a question. If it seems as if such reasoning could preclude serious consideration of important moral questions, that is indeed the case.

Robert George's Critique of *Political Liberalism*

In his exploration and critique of Rawls's theory, Robert George highlights the very thing Rawls preferred to keep out of the main view. Appeals "to principles and propositions drawn from comprehensive doctrines" have to be "excluded as illegitimate" regardless of the likelihood that they are true. While it would be one thing to agree to such a restriction temporarily and as part of a modus vivendi (an unsettled way of living together as opposed to Rawls's more ambitious and virtuous "overlapping consensus"), George argues that it goes too far to demand that the strategy is somehow "morally required" because of the existence of reasonable pluralism.[23]

A great deal, according to George, depends on whether one interprets Rawls narrowly or broadly. In a narrow interpretation, the good citizen vindicates his responsibility simply by offering "sound reasons" accessible to "reasonable people of good will." If the exercise worked at that level, then public reason would be a fairly wide-ranging thing that would rule out "secret knowledge" and esoteric mysteries but would not restrict even controversial propositions offered in the course of a rational argument.[24]

George thinks, correctly in my view, that it is suitably virtuous for citizens to refrain from inhibiting the liberty of others unless doing so on the basis of claims that could be defended by rational argumentation. Indeed, one might draw a line connecting justice and justification. It is wrong to attempt to use the coercive power of government without offering a justification. George's friend and fellow scholar Hadley Arkes has characterized human beings as the kind of creature that gives and receives justifications.[25] Thus, it should be expected that justifications would accompany arguments for laws.

George argues, however, that Rawls is unsatisfied with the narrow interpretation of his vision for the public square. Instead, Rawls is looking for a version of political liberalism that restricts more discourse.

George interrogates Rawls's theory specifically with regard to how it would deal with the Catholic natural law tradition. Roman Catholic teaching regarding natural law addresses morality, justice, and human rights by making appeals to a common human reason possessed by essentially all. The natural law tradition, according to George, while nonliberal, comprehensive, and associated with a faith, possesses "its own principle of public reason" dealing with concepts such as "natural law, natural right, natural

---

23 Robert P. George, *The Clash of Orthodoxies: Law, Religion, and Morality in Crisis* (Wilmington, DE: ISI Books, 2001), 49–50.

24 George, *Clash of Orthodoxies*, 49–50.

25 Hadley Arkes, *First Things: An Inquiry into the First Principles of Morals and Justice* (Princeton, NJ: Princeton University Press, 1986), 13.

rights, and/or natural justice." The question, then, is whether it would be fair for Rawlsian political liberalism to exclude appeals to natural law. It makes sense to assume that Rawls is thinking of something like the natural law tradition when he criticizes the failure of "rationalist believers" to acknowledge "the fact of reasonable pluralism."[26]

This charge against "rationalist believers," however, is factually incorrect. Robert George and many others similarly situated readily acknowledge the existence of reasonable pluralism. They may spend their entire lives, as George has, engaging with the pluralism that exists in their societies and attempting to offer rational arguments for consideration by those with whom they disagree. Claiming that rationalist believers deny the fact of reasonable pluralism becomes a convenient way to avoid engaging with their arguments.[27]

At the heart of the matter is danger to Rawls's own vision of his theoretical position. If he were to argue that positions taken by rationalist believers were false or unsound in some way, then George concludes that Rawls's political liberalism would collapse into a kind of "comprehensive liberalism." That move, of course, would undermine the whole scheme, which is designed to act as an alternative to the tournament of comprehensive doctrines. So instead of engaging with the arguments of rationalist believers, Rawls denies that their claims can be "publicly and fully established by reason." George does not accept what he views as an evasion. The arguments offered by rationalist believers will be "sound or unsound." If they are sound, then why exclude them? If they are unsound, then exclude them on that basis. The soundness of the argument should be what counts, not whether they can be termed, in Rawls's view, "unpublic."[28]

George further argues, with the natural law tradition, that there are "uniquely correct answers" to political questions. Should human beings be liable to enslavement? Should they be coerced with regard to religious belief? These are questions that have right answers. If we consider something like abortion, while it is true that the debate has often been bedeviled by underdetermination (that natural law does not offer precise applications of morality to every legal question that arises) and (early on) the immaturity

26 George, *Clash of Orthodoxies*, 51–52.
27 George, *Clash of Orthodoxies*, 52–53.
28 George, *Clash of Orthodoxies*, 52–53.

of science, one could also argue that our knowledge of the unborn child will eventually overcome those problems and lead to another correct answer. If someone cannot arrive at a correct answer to some of these problems, George would argue that the cause is an error of reason.[29]

Does it make any sense to argue that rationalist believers (or natural law proponents) are unreasonable because they maintain the availability of some of these correct answers? The mere fact that people can be found on either side of a question does not render it unanswerable. Neither does it mean that both sides are equally reasonable. To the extent that rationalist believers argue that their reasonable opponents may be "less than fully reasonable (sometimes culpably, sometimes not)" in their judgments on certain issues, they are not unreasonable to do so.[30]

To some extent, George suggests, the problem may go all the way back to Rawls's original theory of justice. The conditions behind the veil of ignorance don't encourage participants to seek moral truth. They may not select them because they don't want to be hedged in by them in their new, unknown lives. In George's words, they are "risk averse." But just because those behind the veil might not choose such principles does not make them unjust.[31]

George's description of the people behind the veil as "risk averse" is extremely important. Rawls's theories regarding justice and political liberalism orient thought in the direction of a kind of social hedging. As I have written elsewhere, "If one has no idea whether he will be a coward, hero, inventor, or bum, then better to create a world that is kind to cowards and bums."[32] Likewise, Rawls's political liberalism positions participants in the public square to constrain truth claims of comprehensive doctrines so as to prevent conflict. If individual merit or virtue gets less than it might be due from behind the veil, so too does truth in the regulated tournament of comprehensive doctrines.

It is also critical here to recall George's narrow and wide interpretations of Rawlsian political liberalism. If the interpretation is narrow and his "comprehensive doctrines" principle covers merely a small number of

---

29 George, *Clash of Orthodoxies*, 54.
30 George, *Clash of Orthodoxies*, 54–55.
31 George, *Clash of Orthodoxies*, 55.
32 Baker, "Secularist Biases," 100.

critical protections for participants, then it may make sense to accept it. If the interpretation is broad, however, and the hedge covers almost everything really important (e.g., how to approach even life-and-death issues such as abortion and euthanasia), then the better path would be to reject the bargain.

In addition, it is important to note that holders of comprehensive doctrines may not be free to demonstrate the truth of their positions to the same degree. To return to George's discussion of "rationalist believers," it is clear that many of them have the idea that they can make their views convincing to large numbers of persons through strong arguments. They stand to lose much by accepting the straitjacket of political liberalism.[33] Perhaps more crucially, those who hold strongly (at least in political liberals' estimate) to comprehensive doctrines may find their position radically undercut by a referee who refuses to admit that it is actually another competitor.

In his examination of *Political Liberalism*, Robert George (as well as several others) notices a tell that may be considered revealing. It is important to the currency of the theory that the variety of areas not touching on constitutional essentials and basic justice be conceived of as quite broad. And even if such areas are touched on, citizens can make appeals to comprehensive doctrines if they can adduce suitably public reasons. Rawls then requires that they explain such appeals in terms of "a reasonable balance of political values."[34]

This is where the tell comes in. George highlights a footnote in *Political Liberalism* that has become infamous. The note addresses abortion, which is perhaps the single most contested political issue in the United States. (We can at least observe that it appears to be the question superseding all others when it comes to the process of confirming Supreme Court justices.)[35] Taking into account three political values—respect for human life, reproduction of political society, and the equality of women—Rawls breezily and somewhat inexplicably concludes, "Any reasonable balance of these three values will give a woman a duly qualified right to decide whether or not to end her pregnancy during the first trimester."[36]

33 There may be some echoes of this dynamic in the attention-getting debate between Sohrab Ahmari and David French.
34 George, *Clash of Orthodoxies*, 57.
35 Indeed, one might imagine that the travails of Robert Bork, Clarence Thomas, and Brett Kavanaugh during their confirmation hearings had much to do with the belief that each could provide a decisive vote on any revisitation of abortion as a constitutional issue.
36 Rawls, *Political Liberalism*, 243n32.

George, reflecting on the note, expresses his astonishment at the boldness of Rawls's conclusion. How could it be justified without appealing to "moral or metaphysical views" regarding the status of the unborn and the justice of terminating their lives? Still more bluntly, George asks this challenging question: "Why does the value of women's equality override the value of fetal life?"[37] Likewise unimpressed, Paul Campos has demonstrated the ease with which political values could be reformulated to compel the opposite result or at least a much modified one. He sees Rawls's footnote as an example of using "reason" as a "god term." Further, the invocation of reason becomes the equivalent of actually giving reasons.[38] According to George, the footnote demonstrates the potentially nefarious operation of political liberalism in a concrete controversy: "It seems plainly, if silently, to import into the analysis of the question a range of undefended beliefs of precisely the sort that 'political liberalism' is supposed to exclude."[39]

Very likely because of the force of the critiques lodged by George and others, Rawls ultimately backed off the footnote to some degree, although George notes that he pointed to Judith Jarvis Thomson's work in the process. George observes that her summation essentially echoes Rawlsian political liberalism. She does not assert that the pro-life claims regarding the embryo or the fetus are wrong or untrue but rather argues that opponents are not unreasonable in rejecting them.[40]

So while George acknowledges that it is certainly possible for reasonable people (especially in the Rawlsian sense) to reject the pro-life position, the fact that some people hold that view does not mean that "the human right of the unborn not to be killed" does not exist. The better approach would be to identify human rights where applicable and then to protect them. George's closing sentence in his critique of the Rawlsian-Thomsonian approach is worth quoting in full:

There is all the difference in the world between rebutting these arguments and ruling them out in advance on the ground that they implicate deep

---

37 George, *Clash of Orthodoxies*, 58.
38 Paul F. Campos, "Secular Fundamentalism," *Columbia Law Review* 94, no. 6 (October 1994), 1820n16.
39 George, *Clash of Orthodoxies*, 58.
40 George, *Clash of Orthodoxies*, 58–59.

moral and metaphysical questions in dispute among reasonable people subscribing to competing comprehensive doctrines.[41]

For Catholic and Protestant Consideration

Robert George's critique of Rawlsian liberalism should be both convincing and alarming to Catholics and Protestants alike, many of whom would embrace the "rationalist believer" label. If the interpretation of political liberalism is the broad one George warns of, then to accept the Rawlsian bargain means to lose far more than we gain. That would require us to significantly trim our sails in the public square in hopes of reducing the level of conflict inherent in pluralism, but it might end up forcing us to simply submit to a cynical rule-bounding process that grants everything to a left-liberal sensibility while consigning Christian views to a collapsing space. Indeed, if something like the dynamic apparent in the infamous footnote discussed above were to hold, Christians would essentially forfeit their ability to strongly contest fundamental issues concerning the sanctity of life. Thanks to the analysis provided by Robert George and others, it becomes fairly obvious that Christians of various stripes have good reason to decline the invitation to embrace the Rawlsian system.

It should also be understood that to take the Rawlsian route may have serious implications for democratic governance. For Rawls, the Supreme Court is the premier institution for enforcing public reason. To that end, the court employs judicial review of legislative acts. Rawls imagined a court that would use judicial review as a tool to block any violations of public reason by preventing the operation of "transient majorities" and "narrow interests."[42] On the one hand, the language Rawls uses is somewhat appealing, but on the other, it seems that he is basically talking about the frustration of democratic processes through the trump-card power of the court. Public reason becomes a new kind of authority in the system. Part of the problem is, as the title of one of George's books suggests (*The Clash of Orthodoxies*), that public reason may assume the status of a new orthodoxy, banishing all the others but ruling perhaps even more absolutely.

---

41 George, *Clash of Orthodoxies*, 61.
42 Rawls, *Political Liberalism*, 233.

Oliver Wendell Holmes favored doing away with natural law in favor of recognizing the authority of legislative power. John Rawls would bypass natural law too but would also bypass much of what legislatures might do in favor of building the edifice of public reason. Unsurprisingly, public reason appears to accord extremely well with the basic beliefs and preferences of secular elites. Sexual autonomy is in. The sanctity of life is out.

It should also be noted that the way a proper American court should function is to apply "black letter" law—meaning the Constitution, federal law, and so forth—in the exercise of its power of judicial review. Reliance on law maintains accountability for the court as it wields its power. But if the ability to strike down laws depends only on some unspecified public reason, then the court operates almost as an elite committee of mandarins who are the true rulers of a political community. That is not the nature of the court envisioned by the American Constitution. Neither is it wise in the eyes of Christians to leave so much to a group of judges with lifetime appointments and infected with the same fallen nature that applies to us all. The new political liberalism may take away substantially more than it gives.

Conclusion

Robert George's attack on Rawlsian liberalism is direct and unsparing. And as he notes, the critique of this form of liberalism is based on neither "private revelation" nor "esoteric information."[43] It is, rather, a critique that is bullish on the idea of truth and our ability to rationally discover it.

Having offered reasons to refuse the Rawlsian treaty (which one might uncharitably interpret as of a piece with those offered to Native Americans in terms of its effects and unacknowledged impact), George argues that rather than adhering to a new formulation of liberalism, we need only repair to an earlier model, an "old-fashioned liberalism." This would not be the liberalism of the sexual revolution but a broader liberalism of "the rule of law, democratic self-government, subsidiarity, social solidarity, private property, limited government, equal protection, and basic human freedoms, such as those of speech, press, assembly, and, above all, religion." This liberalism is one to refine, rather than replace, and one to conserve with exemplars such as Abraham Lincoln, G. K. Chesterton, John Paul II,

43 George, *Clash of Orthodoxies*, 56.

and the American founders who can serve as guides. This liberalism is, as George elegantly names it, "a liberalism of life."[44]

This liberalism of life is a liberalism of self-government and accountability for the whole body politic. Rather than leaning so strongly on a group largely detached from the public and possessing a strange, almost plenary power to alter the Constitution, Robert George's liberalism would depend on a citizenry that informs itself and learns to act virtuously so as to preserve both freedom and the commonwealth. It is a liberalism of reading, learning, gathering, debating, and voting. This liberalism is self-consciously about something Rawlsian liberalism abjures, which is the sometimes painful but also satisfying process of seeking the truth and conforming ourselves to it.

It is here, perhaps, that we should circle back to a point raised near the beginning of this chapter. I have little doubt that Robert George would easily include the Reverend Martin Luther King Jr. within his pantheon of those who promote "the liberalism of life." King's "Letter from Birmingham Jail" is not a statement that rests on some morally neutral public reason of the kind Rawls upholds in pursuit of social harmony. Rather, it is frankly religious, bluntly points to natural law, and seeks to convince his readers—actually, the kind of readers who are concerned more about dissension than fulfilling the demands of morality—that there is a real right and a real wrong. King wants the readers of his public letter to reconsider their priorities and to gain moral courage. The question isn't what is reasonable according to Rawlsian lights (though he could have pursued a different kind of analysis to establish something like that). Instead, he is determined to appeal to the consciences of his audience. He seeks to touch something inside of them, something that has to do with their souls and their Creator.

Consider the following statement from the famed letter, which sits atop the Western political tradition as a kind of crown:

> How does one determine whether a law is just or unjust? A just law is a man made code that squares with the moral law or the law of God. An unjust law is a code that is out of harmony with the moral law. To put it in the terms of St. Thomas Aquinas: An unjust law is a human law that is not rooted in eternal law and natural law. Any law that uplifts human

44 George, *Clash of Orthodoxies*, 56.

personality is just. Any law that degrades human personality is unjust. All segregation statutes are unjust because segregation distorts the soul and damages the personality.[45]

I would argue that the way King carried his prophetic grievance to the public fits far better with the kind of liberalism Robert George has defended and would have us adopt than it does with the more sterile Rawlsian alternative. We should hold on to the former and challenge ourselves to continue to plumb its depths for the sake of true human flourishing and should deny the latter as an example of making men without chests.[46]

---

45 Martin Luther King Jr., "Letter from Birmingham Jail," African Studies Center, University of Pennsylvania, accessed November 19, 2021, https://www.africa.upenn.edu/.
46 Men without chests, of course, refers back to the image so effectively deployed by C. S. Lewis in *The Abolition of Man* (New York: HarperOne, 2009).

7

Human Dignity and Natural Rights

Robert P. George's Work and Virtue

Adeline A. Allen

RARE IS A SCHOLAR'S LIFELONG WORK so comprehensively oriented toward virtue that it naturally fits to think of it in terms of, well, the seven virtues. But Robert P. George's work and life is one such delightful, worthy rarity. In this chapter, I consider George's work in human dignity and natural rights as oriented toward the four cardinal virtues of justice, prudence, courage, and temperance and the three theological virtues of faith, hope, and love.

Justice

Justice, Thomas Aquinas says, is the perpetual and constant willingness to render to each man what is due to him.[1] What is due to man, then, should start with what, or who, man is.

Man is a reasoning animal, as Robert P. George has written extensively. First, the "animal" part of that definition. A human being is a person who is a body-soul composite:[2] not existing as some sort of a spiritual self

---

1   Thomas Aquinas, *Summa Theologiae* 2a2ae.58.1.
2   I cite George's work extensively throughout, including his work with coauthors. Patrick Lee and Robert P. George, *Body-Self Dualism in Contemporary Ethics and Politics* (New York: Cambridge University Press, 2008), 15–19, 48; Robert P. George and Christopher Tollefsen, *Embryo: A Defense of Human Life*, 2nd ed. (Princeton, NJ: Witherspoon Institute, 2011), 70–76.

occupying a material vehicle, like a "ghost in a machine" would, but as a true unity.[3] Without the soul, the body is incomplete, *and it is also true that without the body, the soul is incomplete*—that is, less than fully human.[4] Thus, George says,

> The body is no mere extrinsic instrument of the human person (or "self"), but is an integral part of the personal reality of the human being. . . . We do not occupy or inhabit our bodies. The living body, far from being our vehicle or external instrument, is part of our personal reality. So while it cannot exist apart from the soul, it is not inferior. It shares in our personal dignity; it is the whole of which our soul is the substantial form.[5]

This is what the great Christian tradition has understood, explicated by Thomas, following Aristotelian thought—and *contra* the Platonists, Cartesians, and Gnostics, who would think of the person as a dualism of the body and the self.[6]

Now the "reasoning" part of the definition: Christians are well familiar with the Genesis account of how God made man in his very image and likeness. George explains what this means, that man is made in the *imago Dei*. We are endowed with reason and freedom, that capacity for "deliberation, judgment and choice."[7] Being image bearers, we partake in God's

3   Lee and George, *Body-Self Dualism*, 67; George and Tollefsen, *Embryo*, 111; Robert P. George, *The Clash of Orthodoxies: Law, Religion, and Morality in Crisis* (Wilmington, DE: ISI Books, 2001), 42, 327–30; Robert P. George, "Gnostic Liberalism," *First Things*, December 2016, https://www.firstthings.com/.

4   Lee and George, *Body-Self Dualism*, 15–19, 66–74; George, "Gnostic Liberalism." Cf. G. K. Chesterton on Thomas Aquinas's teaching: "It was a very special idea of St. Thomas that Man is to be studied in his whole manhood; that a man is not a man without his body, just as he is not a man without his soul. A corpse is not a man; but also a ghost is not a man. . . . St. Thomas stood up stoutly for the fact that a man's body is his body as his mind is his mind; and that *he* can only be a balance and union of the two." G. K. Chesterton, *St. Thomas Aquinas* ([Mansfield Centre, CT]: Martino, 2011), 27.

5   George, "Gnostic Liberalism."

6   Lee and George, *Body-Self Dualism*, 15–19; George and Tollefsen, *Embryo*, 64; George, *Clash of Orthodoxies*, 42; George, "Gnostic Liberalism."

7   Robert P. George, "Natural Law, God and Human Dignity," in *The Cambridge Companion to Natural Law Jurisprudence*, ed. George Duke and Robert P. George (New York: Cambridge University Press, 2017), 63, 67; see also Lee and George, *Body-Self Dualism*, 56–74; George and Tollefsen, *Embryo*, 60, 105; Robert P. George, *Conscience and Its Enemies: Confronting the*

creative power by sharing, though in a limited manner, in his power to be an uncaused cause:

> the power to envisage a possible reality or state of affairs that does not now exist or obtain; to grasp the intelligible point—the value—of bringing it into being, and then to act by choice (and not merely by impulse or instinct, as a brute animal might) to bring it into being. That state of affairs may be anything from the development of an intellectual skill, or the attainment of an item of knowledge, to the creation or critical appreciation of a work of art, to the establishment of marital communion.[8]

This capacity for reason and freedom is natural to—inherent in—*every* human being: an attribute that each of us has by virtue of simply being human.[9] Every human being, by definition, has this root capacity of reason; none does not.[10] What of babies in the womb, newborn babies, the cognitively disabled, or the aged and infirm who suffer from dementia? George's answer is astute and elegant: we are talking here of *root* capacity of reason, not only of *immediate* capacity. It matters not that some human beings (say, mature adults) have that capacity of reason immediately accessible relative to others (say, a newborn baby or an elderly person with severe dementia).[11] That is,

> The criterion for full moral worth is having a nature that entails the capacity (whether existing in root form or developed to the point at which it is immediately exercisable) for conceptual thought and free choice—and not the *development* of that natural basic capacity to some degree or other (and to what degree would necessarily be an arbitrary matter). The criterion for full moral worth and possession of basic rights is not having a

---

Dogmas of Liberal Secularism (Wilmington, DE: ISI Books, 2016), 84–85; Robert P. George, "Natural Law, God and Human Dignity," *Chautauqua Journal* 1, no. 8 (2016): 4.

8   George, "Human Dignity," in *Cambridge Companion*, 63; George, *Conscience and Its Enemies*, 85; George, "Human Dignity," *Chautauqua Journal*, 4.

9   George, "Human Dignity," in *Cambridge Companion*, 63; George and Tollefsen, *Embryo*, 79, 111; Robert P. George, "Natural Law," *Harvard Journal of Law and Public Policy* 31, no. 1 (Winter 2008): 173–74.

10 See George, "Human Dignity," in *Cambridge Companion*, 63; George and Tollefsen, *Embryo*, 79.

11 Lee and George, *Body-Self Dualism*, 82–83, 93, 152–55; George and Tollefsen, *Embryo*, 78–80, 111, 113, 116–31; George, "Human Dignity," *Chautauqua Journal*, 2; George, "Natural Law," 174.

capacity for conscious thought and choice which inheres in an entity, but being a certain kind of thing, that is, having a specific type of substantial nature. Thus, possession of full moral worth follows upon being a certain type of entity or substance, namely, a substance with a rational nature, despite the fact that some persons (substances with a rational nature) have a greater intelligence.[12]

Thus we see that in the very young, very old, very sick—as in the strong and accomplished and able-bodied—is the *imago Dei*, that rational and free nature. It is because of this rational nature and moral agency of human beings that each person possesses human dignity inherently and equally.[13] Each is properly accorded the full moral worth of "*being a person*, since a person is a rational and morally responsible subject."[14] The concern here is for the persons themselves, not for attributes they may or may not possess. Put another way, the concern is in the inherent nature or substance of man, not in some variable or accidental attributes.[15] Each person has that rational nature and moral agency, irrespective of size, age, degree of development, intelligence, or skin color.[16] If that's the case, then each person has "*inherent and equal fundamental dignity and basic rights.*"[17]

But notice what happens if this is not the case: If human dignity and rights were predicated not on the inherent nature of the person but on some *accidental* attribute instead—say, athletic ability, cognitive ability, size, or degree of development—then the person's moral worth would vary by degree from person to person depending on that accidental attribute. Some would have *more* worth than others.[18] So if measured by athletic ability, Kobe Bryant would have been worthier than the rest of us. If measured by cognitive ability, Albert Einstein would have been worthier than the rest of us—and those of us with a sound mind worthier than the aged with

12 Lee and George, *Body-Self Dualism*, 93–94.
13 Lee and George, *Body-Self Dualism*, 82–83, 152–55.
14 Lee and George, *Body-Self Dualism*, 83.
15 Lee and George, *Body-Self Dualism*, 133–40, 152–55; George and Tollefsen, *Embryo*, 111, 113, 116–31.
16 Lee and George, *Body-Self Dualism*, 93, 133–40, 152–55; George, *Clash of Orthodoxies*, 42; see George and Tollefsen, *Embryo*, 21, 111, 113, 116–31; George, "Natural Law," 173–74.
17 Lee and George, *Body-Self Dualism*, 93 (emphasis added); see also George, "Natural Law," 173–74.
18 Lee and George, *Body-Self Dualism*, 93; George, *Clash of Orthodoxies*, 133–40, 330–32.

Alzheimer's disease.[19] If measured by size or degree of development, a fully mature adult would be worthier than a toddler, a toddler than a newborn, and a newborn than the embryo in the womb.[20]

Here let us pause for a moment to consider an argument against George's position as centered on the following clever analogy: The embryo is to the adult human being like an acorn to an oak tree. Despite the continuity of development between the two, acorns and oak trees are *different* things, and we value oak trees but not acorns. Thus we value adult human beings but not embryos—so the argument goes.[21]

To this argument, George's clear-eyed response is that the choice of analogues is rather poor, making for a flawed analogy.[22] It is true that the oak tree does *not* differ *in kind* but only *in degree* from the acorn.[23] But the reason we value oak trees is *not* the same reason we value human beings. We value oak trees for their magnificence and grandeur, which comes with maturity and size. Now, that magnificence is an *accidental* property of the oak trees, because not all oak trees have it (e.g., when the tree is still a mere oak sapling). So we do not find all oak trees equally valuable precisely because we value them for their accidental attributes.[24]

But we value human beings *not* for any accidental properties, such as their achievements or any honor that has been conferred on them. Rather, we value human beings for their inherent, essential nature as rational and free beings.[25] That is, we value embryos as human beings *because* they do not differ in kind but merely in degree from adult human beings—and so human beings all, *by virtue of who they are in essence*, are inherently worthy.[26] George continues: If we were to go along with the earlier flawed analogy, we would end up with the shocking, terrible position of killing infants. Infants here would be like oak saplings, and oak saplings are regularly destroyed by

19 See George and Tollefsen, *Embryo*, 177; George, *Clash of Orthodoxies*, 330–32.
20 See Lee and George, *Body-Self Dualism*, 136, 138; George, *Clash of Orthodoxies*, 330–32.
21 Michael J. Sandel, "Embryo Ethics: The Moral Logic of Stem-Cell Research," *New England Journal of Medicine* 351, no. 3 (July 15, 2004): 207–9; see also George and Tollefsen, *Embryo*, 175.
22 George and Tollefsen, *Embryo*, 175–76. For other arguments against George's thought on embryos as human beings and their inherent dignity and for George's responses to these arguments, see George and Tollefsen, *Embryo*, 143–99; George, *Clash of Orthodoxies*, 323–36.
23 See George and Tollefsen, *Embryo*, 177–79.
24 George and Tollefsen, *Embryo*, 176.
25 George and Tollefsen, *Embryo*, 176–77.
26 George, *Clash of Orthodoxies*, 332.

managers of oak forests to manage the health of mature oak trees as deemed necessary. No one seems to feel a sense of loss or think anything of it, and that is, again, because "we simply do not value members of the oak species—as we value human beings—because of the *kind* of entity they are."[27] But the killing of infants is *not* tolerated for precisely the reason that we do, *and should*, value all members of human beings for their intrinsic nature.[28]

Notice what else has to be true if human dignity and rights are *not* predicated on the inherent rational nature and moral agency of man but instead on some "non-rational motivating factors, such as feeling, emotion or desire."[29] Then, chillingly, David Hume would be right that reason is no more than "the slave of the passions,"[30] and Thomas Hobbes that "the thoughts are to the desires as scouts and spies, to range abroad, and find the way to the things desired."[31] And if *that* subjectivist and noncognitivist view is right, George says, "then it seems to me that the entire business of ethics is a charade, and human dignity is a myth."[32]

So if justice, again, is the perpetual and constant willingness to render to each man what is due to him, and if man is by nature a possessor of inherent dignity and moral worth, what *would* be due to man? Certain duties would be owed to him, the flip side of which would be that he has rights. Of particular interest are rights that are man's by nature of who he is: *natural* rights.

Prudence

What do natural rights have to do with prudence? Prudence can be understood as practical reason in pursuit of the good and away from evil.[33] So if

27 George and Tollefsen, *Embryo*, 178.
28 George and Tollefsen, *Embryo*, 177–78. To the argument that people seem to mourn the death of an infant or a child more than they do the death of an embryo, George responds that it is reason, not emotion, that properly guides our ethical judgments. George, *Clash of Orthodoxies*, 332–33. To the argument that the high rate of natural miscarriages points to a justification of using embryos for research material, George responds that by the same token, the high rate—until very recently in history—of infant mortality would have pointed to a perversion like justifying infanticide. George, *Clash of Orthodoxies*, 333–34.
29 George, "Human Dignity," in *Cambridge Companion*, 65.
30 David Hume, *A Treatise of Human Nature* (1739; repr., Oxford: Clarendon, 1888), 2.3.3.415.
31 Thomas Hobbes, *Leviathan* (1651; repr., Indianapolis: Hackett, 1994), 41.
32 George, "Human Dignity," in *Cambridge Companion*, 65; George, *Conscience and Its Enemies*, 81, 87; George, "Human Dignity," *Chautauqua Journal*, 6.
33 See Thomas Aquinas, *Summa Theologiae* 1a2ae.94.2; see also John Finnis, "Aquinas and Natural Law Jurisprudence," in Duke and George, *Cambridge Companion to Natural Law Jurisprudence*,

each person has natural rights, here is a sketch of George's work in natural rights as applied to the pursuit of what is good and away from evil in four issues: abortion, stem-cell research, euthanasia, and marriage.

George has shown that each person has inherent and equal dignity and moral worth by virtue of his humanity, which is to say that he has natural rights, irrespective of size or degree of development. One of the absolute moral prohibitions is the prohibition against the intentional killing of innocent life, because each person has the right to life that is natural to the kind of being he is.[34] So it follows that the baby in the womb has a natural right to life that should not be violated; the baby possesses inherent dignity and moral worth—owing to that root capacity of reason and freedom mentioned above—though he is young in age and early in development.

18–19, 20; George, "Human Dignity," in *Cambridge Companion*, 59; Robert P. George, "Religious Liberty and the Human Good," *International Journal for Religious Freedom* 5, no. 1 (2012): 35.

34 See George and Tollefsen, *Embryo*, 98, 102, 104, 107; Robert P. George, "Natural Law and Positive Law," in *Common Truths: New Perspectives on Natural Law*, ed. Edward B. McLean (Wilmington, DE: ISI Books, 2000), 161; George, "Human Dignity," *Chautauqua Journal*, 3.

The basic goods of human life are the "most fundamental dimensions of our well-being": they are "basic" because they are intrinsic, and they are "goods" because they are good for us. George and Tollefsen, *Embryo*, 98; see also George, "Human Dignity," *Chautauqua Journal*, 35; George, "Religious Liberty," 35. Aquinas calls basic goods *indemonstrabile* and *per se notum*, that is, "known in themselves and not through the mediation of some further proposition." Finnis, "Aquinas and Natural Law Jurisprudence," 20; Christopher Tollefsen, "Natural Law, Basic Goods and Practical Reason," in Duke and George, *Cambridge Companion to Natural Law Jurisprudence*, 135. These goods reflect the reality of who the human being is as a bodily being, who is also a reasoning being that is made to be in community. George and Tollefsen, *Embryo*, 98–99; George, "Natural Law," 172. These basic goods include life, health, knowledge, art, skillful work, play, friendship, marriage, practical reasonableness, and religion. George, "Human Dignity," in *Cambridge Companion*, 59; George and Tollefsen, *Embryo*, 98–99. It is the basic good of life for man as a bodily being that is related to the right to life that each human being inherently possesses. George and Tollefsen, *Embryo*, 98, 104–5, 106–8.

When the basic goods of life are respected and promoted, human rights are well served. George and Tollefsen, *Embryo*, 105–8; see also George, "Natural Law," 173–74; George, "Human Dignity," *Chautauqua Journal*, 1–2. This is true precisely because basic goods are prior to rights. See George, "Religious Liberty," 37. Conversely, when the basic goods of life are damaged, human rights are violated. George and Tollefsen, *Embryo*, 105–8; also George, "Natural Law," 173–74. For a fuller treatment of the connection of basic goods, human dignity, and human rights, see George's work on natural law, e.g., George and Tollefsen, *Embryo*, 97–108; George, "Human Dignity," in *Cambridge Companion*, 59–65; George, *Conscience and Its Enemies*, 82–84; George, "Natural Law and Positive Law," 151–68; George, "Natural Law," 171–96; Robert P. George, "The 1993 St. Ives Lecture—Natural Law and Civil Rights: From Jefferson's 'Letter to Henry Lee' to Martin Luther King's 'Letter from Birmingham Jail,' " *Catholic University Law Review* 43, no. 1 (1993): 143–57; George, "Human Dignity," *Chautauqua Journal*, 1–14.

George has done tremendous work in the defense of life in his scholarship, advocacy, and work as a public intellectual.[35] His eloquence and moral clarity are unsurpassed.

He has worked tirelessly against the evil of abortion and its accompanying culture of death. Here, let us consider his work particularly against the abortion of babies diagnosed with Down syndrome. He has criticized the practice as sharing the same evil and ugly characteristics as eugenics, in vogue at the turn of the nineteenth century and into the Progressive Era.[36] Eugenics ultimately led to the Nazis' philosophy of *lebensunwertes leben*, or life unworthy of life. The elites of advanced nations subscribed to eugenics, and before they knew it, the very same philosophy led to the Nazis' extermination of Jews, the disabled, and others deemed defective.[37]

George's critique of our own in-vogue belief and practice of abortion, with our elites at the helm, is powerful. "The pressure on couples to 'terminate'—kill—their Down Syndrome offspring is utterly vile," he writes. "Having Down Syndrome is not a crime. It certainly should not be a capital offense—in utero or otherwise. People with Down Syndrome are not *lebensunwertes leben*. No human beings are."[38] When we abort these Down syndrome babies, how are we *any* different from the Nazis in deciding who lives and who dies or whose life is unworthy of life?

Consider also George's work in defending embryos from being used in stem-cell research. Human embryos, he writes, are *embryonic humans*; the fully mature adult has been the very same person—the very same living,

---

35 George's work on the defense of human rights has brought him to serve on the President's Council on Bioethics, as a presidential appointee to the US Commission on Civil Rights, as chairman of the US Commission on International Religious Freedom (USCIRF), and as the US member of UNESCO's World Commission on the Ethics of Scientific Knowledge and Technology (COMEST). "Robert P. George, Director," James Madison Program in American Ideals and Institutions, Princeton University, accessed July 15, 2021, https://jmp.princeton.edu/.

36 See generally Bessie Blackburn, "Cited at Nuremberg: The American Eugenics Movement, Its Influence Abroad, the Buck v. Bell Decision, and the Subsequent Bioethical Implications of the Holocaust," *Bound Away: The Liberty Journal of History* 4, no. 1 (2021).

37 See Adam S. Cohen, "Harvard's Eugenics Era," *Harvard Magazine*, March–April 2016, https://www.harvardmagazine.com/; Bradley Thomas, "The Progressive Ideas That Fueled America's Eugenics Movement," Foundation for Economic Education, March 7, 2019, https://fee.org/; Robert Jay Lifton, "German Doctors and the Final Solution," *New York Times Magazine*, September 21, 1986, 64.

38 Robert P. George (@McCormick Prof), Twitter, October 25, 2020, 1:42 p.m., https://twitter.com/McCormickProf/status/1320435660961026050.

bodily entity—ever since he was a tiny embryo in his mother's womb, "a unified, self-integrating human organism" (that body-soul unity he speaks of) as opposed to someone who came into being when some form of consciousness or higher cognitive ability inhabited the body (*contra* that popular belief of a ghost in a machine, as noted above).[39] Because of this, the same human dignity and natural rights are *theirs* just as much as they are *ours*.[40] Again, they are possessors of that root capacity of reason and freedom that is fundamental, natural, and inherent to every human being, no matter how small or embryonic. This natural attribute of human beings—these "apparently transcendent features"[41] of who people are—means that people are properly always ends in and of themselves, and they should never be treated as simply means.[42] They should never be used *as* means to an end, be the end good and noble, like the research using some humans (such as embryonic humans) to cure diseases for the good of health.[43]

What is true of embryonic humans is also true of the aged and infirm, however ravaged by disease.[44] George has worked tirelessly against the culture of death here as well. Perhaps the old man has now been suffering from dementia or Alzheimer's for many years. Perhaps there is no way for his mind to be restored before he dies. No matter: that root capacity of reason is still part of his inherent substance as a person, although no longer immediately accessible.[45] Euthanasia is as great an evil as abortion.[46] The embryo, the baby in the womb, the very aged and sick—all are worthy lives

39 George, *Clash of Orthodoxies*, 324–30; see also Lee and George, *Body-Self Dualism*, 130–40; George and Tollefsen, *Embryo*, 1–3, 27–55, 149–56, 220; Patrick Lee and Robert P. George, "The Wrong of Abortion," in *Contemporary Debates in Applied Ethics*, ed. Andrew I. Cohen and Christopher Heath Wellman (Malden, MA: Wiley-Blackwell, 2005), 13–24.

40 George and Tollefsen, *Embryo*, 20–21; George, *Clash of Orthodoxies*, 336.

41 George and Tollefsen, *Embryo*, 106.

42 George and Tollefsen, *Embryo*, 102, 106, 108, 199; George, "Human Dignity," *Chautauqua Journal*, 2. When we use people as means, as we do when we use embryos for research, we treat them not as ends, as they are properly worth. In other words, we treat them as less than they are worth as humans: a dehumanization. We treat them as things—we *commodify* them. See George, *Clash of Orthodoxies*, 322; Robert P. George, "What's Sex Got to Do with It? Marriage, Morality, and Rationality," *American Journal of Jurisprudence* 49, no. 1 (2004): 74–75, 82.

43 George and Tollefsen, *Embryo*, 93, 102, 104, 106, 108, 199; George, *Clash of Orthodoxies*, 332, 336.

44 Lee and George, *Body-Self Dualism*, 151–75.

45 Lee and George, *Body-Self Dualism*, 152–55; see also George, "Human Dignity," *Chautauqua Journal*, 2n1; George, "Natural Law," 174.

46 See Lee and George, *Body-Self Dualism*, 155–62; George and Tollefsen, *Embryo*, 104.

to be defended and protected because of the inherent and equal dignity and moral worth of each.[47]

If evangelicals are well familiar with the pro-life argument from the biblical truth that man is made in the image of God, George is, shall we say, *bilingual*. As a faithful Catholic, he holds to and is fluent in the *revelation* of the truth of the *imago Dei*, but he is also fluent in the truth accessible by *reason*—what it means that man is made in the image of God as explored, grasped at, and explained by reason (see above regarding the nature of man as a reasoning and free being). Saint Paul speaks of law that is "written on their hearts" while their "conscience also bears witness," meaning that it is knowable to the Gentiles apart from God's special revelation (Rom. 2:15).[48] The following quote from Pope John Paul II, which George is fond of, is worthy of attention and pondering: "Faith and reason are like two wings on which the human spirit rises to the contemplation of truth."[49] On *both* faith and reason, George is not only wonderfully bilingual and sophisticated,[50] but the evangelical tradition would do well to learn from him and from the riches of the tradition of which he is a son.

---

47 See George, "Human Dignity," *Chautauqua Journal*, 3; see also Lee and George, *Body-Self Dualism*, 169–75, for a particularly insightful discussion of dignity and human life in the face of suffering.

48 See also George, "Human Dignity," in *Cambridge Companion*, 67; George, *Conscience and Its Enemies*, 89–90; George, "Human Dignity," *Chautauqua Journal*, 7.

49 John Paul II, *Fides et Ratio* (encyclical letter), Vatican, September 14, 1998, https://www.vatican.va/; George, *Clash of Orthodoxies*, xiv, 303–16; Kevin Spinale, " 'Sustained by Faith': An Interview with Robert P. George," *America*, November 7, 2011, https://www.americamagazine.org/. Pope John Paul II says that faith and reason "are two orders of knowledge." George, *Clash of Orthodoxies*, 313. George elaborates, "But they are linked, and, to some extent, overlapping, orders. Some truths are known only by revelation; others only by philosophical, scientific, or historical inquiry. Those known by revelation are often, however, fully understandable, or their implications fully knowable, only by rational inquiry. And often the full human and cosmic significance of those knowable by philosophical, scientific, and historical inquiry only becomes evident in the light of faith. . . . If, as the Pope says, faith has nothing to fear, and much to gain from, reason, then it is also true that reason has nothing to fear, and much to gain from, faith." George, *Clash of Orthodoxies*, 313–14.

50 See, e.g., George, "Human Dignity," in *Cambridge Companion*, 57–74; Lee and George, *Body-Self Dualism*, 74–81, 169–75; George and Tollefsen, *Embryo*, 18–25, 203; George, *Clash of Orthodoxies*, xiv, 56, 273–316; George, *Conscience and Its Enemies*, 89–90; George, "Human Dignity," *Chautauqua Journal*, 7–10; George, "Religious Liberty," 38–43; Robert P. George and Kevin Spinale, "Attend to Your Spiritual Life," *First Things*, July 12, 2016, https://www.firstthings.com/; Robert P. George, "Courage: Speak Truth in Love!," filmed October 27, 2018, at Love and Fidelity Network Conference, Princeton, NJ, 14:20, https://www.youtube.com/.

Evangelicals rightly think of the word of God as the truth and seek to live accordingly with Scripture as central to their lives. Evangelicals are also a people who, central to their identity, feel keenly the calling to share their faith with unbelievers—that is, to be a witness for Jesus, to evangelize, to share the "good tidings" of great joy of Jesus Christ. But to the culture today, to the very people whom evangelicals are trying to reach, arguments with "The Bible says . . ." as speaking the truth, powerful to evangelicals themselves and even to the broader culture in earlier times, are deemed irrelevant at best and reviled at worst. So it seems that evangelicals can use a supplement to their use of Scripture to be more effective witnesses to Christ. Being able to speak to the culture using the *common currency* of reason[51]—something that everyone is capable of and has a natural hunger for—is a mighty and wonderful witness to truth and, ultimately, to Christ himself as *the* truth. All truth is God's truth after all.[52] It would be good for more evangelicals to follow in George's footsteps, bilingual in both revelation and reason, in the service of truth.

One more example of George's work on prudence, or practical reason, is his robust witness to truth in the area of marriage. His eloquent and influential exposition that marriage is a *comprehensive* union of man and wife—a conjugal, intellectual, dispositional, volitional, affective, and spiritual union, properly oriented to the begetting and nurturing of children[53]—is, like his work in the defense of life, an argument based on

51 George, "Human Dignity," *Cambridge Companion*, 66–68; George, *Conscience and Its Enemies*, 88–90; George, "Human Dignity," *Chautauqua Journal*, 10; George, "1993 St. Ives Lecture," 150; see also George, *Clash of Orthodoxies*, xiv, 316.

52 See n49 above. G. K. Chesterton, writing on the life of Thomas Aquinas, the exemplar of the study of reason and revelation, observes, "St. Thomas was willing to allow the one truth to be approached by two paths, precisely *because* he was sure there was only one truth. Because the Faith was the one truth, nothing discovered in nature could ultimately contradict the Faith. Because the Faith was the one truth, nothing really deduced from the Faith could ultimately contradict the facts. It was in truth a curiously daring confidence in the reality of his religion." Chesterton, *St. Thomas Aquinas*, 73. Thus Thomas—of the Dominican tradition, famous for its confidence and openness in exploring truth in reason—could declare boldly and without contradiction in "Adoro Te Devote," a eucharistic hymn that he composed, "Credo quidquid dixit Dei Filius," or "I believe, for God the Son has said it." Andrew Davison, interview by Ken Myers, *Mars Hill Audio Journal*, April 20, 2021, audio, 26:47, https://www.marshillaudio .org/; "Adoro Te Devote," Gregorian Chant Hymns, June 30, 2014, http://gregorian-chant -hymns.com/.

53 Lee and George, *Body-Self Dualism*, 179–85.

reason.[54] His work in defending marriage also leads to the natural rights of children as the *fruit* of marriage.[55] It is, additionally, his work and generous mentorship that has influenced a generation of scholars to fight for the right of children to be known, raised, and loved by the very parents who gave them life—within that marriage.[56] What is owed to children here has to do with what is conducive to their flourishing, toward a full measure of their humanity and away from what makes their life less than fulfilled.[57] From time to time, George's critics level against him the criticism that he ought to care about *other* ills in the world than, say, the redefinition of marriage—issues such as violence, gangs, or child poverty. George's response is right on: the best cure for all these ills is the recovery of a robust culture of marriage and family.[58] And the data from social science (no surprise) provide overwhelming support for George's position.[59]

So we see that George's excellent work in defending life and marriage through the currency of reason has been put to good use in the virtue of prudence: in pursuit of the good and away from evil, in pursuit of life and what makes life flourish, away from its privations.

54 Sherif Girgis, Ryan T. Anderson, and Robert P. George, *What Is Marriage? Man and Woman: A Defense* (New York: Encounter Books, 2012); George, *Clash of Orthodoxies*, xiv, 75–89, 310–11; George, "What's Sex Got to Do with It?," 63–85.

55 See Lee and George, *Body-Self Dualism*, 180–81.

56 See, e.g., Melissa Moschella, *To Whom Do Children Belong? Parental Rights, Civic Education, and Children's Autonomy* (Cambridge: Cambridge University Press, 2016); Ryan T. Anderson, *Truth Overruled: The Future of Marriage and Religious Freedom* (Washington, DC: Regnery, 2015); "Who We Are," CanaVox, accessed July 15, 2021, https://canavox.com/; Katy Faust and Stacy Manning, *Them before Us: Why We Need a Global Children's Rights Movement* (New York: Post Hill, 2021); Adeline A. Allen, "Surrogacy and Limitations to Freedom of Contract: Toward Being More Fully Human," *Harvard Journal of Law and Public Policy* 41, no. 3 (Summer 2018): 753–811.

57 See Lee and George, *Body-Self Dualism*, 180–81; see also George, "What's Sex Got to Do with It?," 74–75, 82; George, "Courage," 24:10.

58 George, "Courage," 25:45; see also Lee and George, *Body-Self Dualism*, 180.

59 See, e.g., W. Bradford Wilcox, Wendy Wang, and Ian Rowe, "Less Poverty, Less Prison, More College: What Two Parents Mean for Black and White Children," Institute for Family Studies, June 17, 2021, https://ifstudies.org/; Anderson, *Truth Overruled*, 48–52; Kristin Anderson Moore, Susan M. Jekielek, and Carol Emig, "Marriage from a Child's Perspective: How Does Family Structure Affect Children, and What Can We Do about It?," *Child Trends* (2002): 1–2, 6, https://www.childtrends.org/; Alysse ElHage, "How Marriage Makes Men Better Fathers," Institute for Family Studies, June 19, 2015, https://ifstudies.org/; David C. Ribar, "Children Raised within Marriage Do Better on Average. Why?," *Child and Family Blog*, October 2015, https://www.childandfamilyblog.com/; Ana Samuel, "The Kids Aren't All Right: New Family Structures and the 'No Differences' Claim," *Public Discourse*, June 14, 2012, https://www.thepublicdiscourse.com/.

Courage and Temperance

Courage is "that which binds the will firmly to the good of reason in face of the greatest evils," Thomas Aquinas says.[60] George is to be admired for his courage, for holding fast to the good of reason in his defense of human dignity and natural rights in the face of ugly opposition, rabid vehemence, and even a death threat.

George's defense of human rights brought him to serve as chairman of the US Commission on International Religious Freedom (USCIRF), among other positions. Among the many courageous stances he has taken, here is one. He and six other members of the USCIRF each offered to take one hundred lashes with a cane out of the one thousand lashes that Saudi Arabia imposed as a sentence on a Saudi blogger named Raif Badawi in protest against the Saudi government's crush on dissent and free speech.[61]

To state the obvious, many of the positions for which he stands (like the ones sketched in this chapter) are not the popular ones in our day. They are not positions that catapult one to glory in the eyes of our world's elites. So those who oppose George are legion: from Twitter trolls to hostile media to a pro-abortion extremist who advanced a death threat against him (and who subsequently went to prison for it).[62]

In spite of all this opposition, George teaches and writes and speaks with winsomeness. There is a self-control and a discipline at work in him— nothing other than temperance[63]—such that he is consistent, unwavering, and *cheerful* in advancing his arguments based on the elucidation and articulation of reason in the face of emotionally charged topics.

That disposition leads to his being not only a cheerful warrior but also a *leader* of a band of cheerful warriors. He is a beloved and generous teacher and mentor to a generation of younger scholars and thinkers, as mentioned above. He is also the patriarch, one might say, of the family of the James Madison Society, consisting of fellows and friends of the James Madison

---

60 Thomas Aquinas, *Summa Theologiae* 2a2ae.123.4.

61 B. C., "Lash Us Instead," *The Economist*, January 21, 2015, https://www.economist.com/. See n34 above for more on the relationship of basic goods and human rights.

62 "'Pro-Choice Terrorist' Sentenced for Death Threats against Pro-Lifers," *Catholic News Agency*, October 4, 2012, https://www.catholicnewsagency.com/; Sara Israelsen-Hartley, "'Most Influential Christian Conservative Thinker' Robert P. George Joins News Board," *Deseret News*, September 12, 2010, https://www.deseret.com/.

63 See Thomas Aquinas, *Summa Theologiae* 2a2ae.157.3.

Program in American Ideals and Institutions, a program that he founded in 2000 at Princeton University (and, full disclosure, a program at which I was a visiting fellow in the 2017–2018 academic year). Perhaps one reason his critics oppose him today is the same reason the Athenians opposed Socrates: he corrupts the youth in rejecting the worship of the local gods,[64] be it the local god of abortion or the redefinition of marriage. May George be spared the hemlock though. May this cheerful, courageous warrior of truth and reason be blessed continually in his work and leadership.

Faith, Hope, and Love

George is fond of recalling the following from the late Father Richard John Neuhaus: "We have to remember that we are not in charge of making things turn out all right. That's God's job. We are in charge of being faithful. We are just supposed to be faithful. The rest is God's part."[65] This seems to be a sustaining call on George's life. He considers his vocation in academia to be one of truth seeking and truth telling, no matter the cost—be it friends, influence, or prestige.[66] He exhibits constancy and steadfastness, over three decades now at his post as a professor at Princeton University, that is all the more admirable given the opposition to who he is and what he stands for. This kind of committed faithfulness is lovely, and it is rare.

And if faithfulness is something to which we are called in our vocation and something that George models so well, it also points to the caller, from whom may we hear the sweet words at the end of the ages, "Well done, good and faithful servant" (Matt. 25:21, 23). George's faithful witness to truth and reason is a testament to his steadfast *hope* in the truth itself. He is cheerfully confident in the truth because he believes that truth is inherently luminous.[67] George writes, "Hope exists because we really do possess the capacities for

---

64 See Robert P. George, "The creedal yard sign phenomenon is big in my neighborhood," Facebook, November 1, 2020, https://www.facebook.com/robert.p.george.39/posts/102220335141 19563.

65 Spinale, " 'Sustained by Faith.' "

66 See "Truth Seeking, Democracy, and Freedom of Thought and Expression—A Statement by Robert P. George and Cornel West," James Madison Program in American Ideals and Institutions, Princeton University, March 14, 2017, https://jmp.princeton.edu/; "Some Thoughts and Advice for Our Students and All Students," James Madison Program in American Ideals and Institutions, Princeton University, August 29, 2017, https://jmp.princeton.edu/; George, "Courage," 5:01, 10:50, 21:35; see also George and Spinale, "Attend to Your Spiritual Life."

67 George, "Courage," 14:10.

reasonableness and virtue; truth—including moral truth—is accessible to us and has its own splendor and powerful appeal."[68] His manifest security in the truth and witness of it is ultimately due to the intrinsic attractive quality about truth, being light itself.

This is no surprise, given that the truth is ultimately *the* truth in the person of Christ. "Truth is, in Christian teaching, both universal and universally longed for," George writes; "God *is* truth—Jesus Christ, as the Son of the living God, is 'the way, *the truth*, and the life'" (John 14:6 KJV).[69] And of course, as Scripture says, "Hope does not put us to shame" (Rom. 5:5). George is careful to distinguish hope—true hope—from flimsy optimism.[70] He is here standing on the sure foundation of hope as nothing short of a theological virtue.[71]

"So now faith, hope, and love abide, these three; but the greatest of these is love" (1 Cor. 13:13). George's work on human dignity and natural rights has been oriented to the virtue of love after all.[72] If love is willing the good of the person,[73] what is the good of man?

George has spent his professional life to point the way, to illuminate and articulate and defend what is good for man as a being who is made in the very image and likeness of God, what is due to him by virtue of his nature and so by virtue of his natural rights. If we are called to love our neighbor, and our neighbor is a human being who bears God's image, George helps us understand what that means—when the culture exerts tremendous pressure instead on the expediency of sacrificing our neighbors (little babies, children, the weak or infirm, our spouses and families) on the altar to the idol of self.

Ultimately, George's work points to the love of God himself, whose image stands in every neighbor we are called to love. It is, of course, love of God that we are commanded to first and foremost, with all our heart, soul, strength, and *mind*. George has been a faithful, hopeful exemplar in this way of love. Once, when asked what he would like to see written on his own epitaph, George responded simply, "He loved."[74] Indeed. His life's work attests to this.

---

68 George, "Human Dignity," *Chautauqua Journal*, 10.

69 George, *Clash of Orthodoxies*, 316 (emphasis original).

70 George, "Courage," 22:35.

71 George, "Courage," 23:10.

72 See George, "Courage," 23:42.

73 George and Spinale, "Attend to Your Spiritual Life."

74 Robert P. George, "Robert P. George on the Breakdown of the Family Unit, Family Law, Love Meaning and Much More," interview by Greg Ellis, *The Respondent*, June 13, 2021, video, 56:45, https://www.youtube.com/.

8

Bringing Body and Soul Together (Again)

*Robert P. George, Oliver O'Donovan, and
the Place of Resurrection in Body Ethics*

Matthew Lee Anderson

IN THE THIRTEENTH CANTO of his *Inferno*, Dante enters the forest of the suicides. The pilgrim hears howls of suffering but sees no one. At the behest of Virgil, Dante breaks off a branch of a nearby tree and is met by a cry of outraged pain. Only then does he discover that those who destroyed their bodies on earth have become trees in their torment. It is a memorable scene. Despite his extensive knowledge of Thomas Aquinas and his account of natural law, Dante instead emphasizes the inability of natural reason and poetic imagination to grasp the nature of the suicides' punishment. Virgil is both Dante's philosophical and poetical mentor. Yet the pagan thinker emphasizes how *incredible* the real punishment would be if one has only Virgil's writings: at the outset, he suggests that Dante will see a punishment that "would seem to strip my words of truth."[1] Dante underscores natural reason's limits by framing the punishment in explicitly theological terms. Just as "doubting Thomas" needed to touch Jesus to confirm his faith, so Dante the pilgrim must break a branch to discover the truth. Though they

---

1   Dante, *Inferno*, canto 13, line 50. The Italian is *la cost incredibile*. Dante, *Inferno*, trans. Robert Hollander (New York: Anchor Books, 2002), 239.

will receive their bodies back in the general resurrection, they are denied the dignity of being clothed with them again: in a parody of Christ's death on the cross, the suicides' bodies will hang limp, like Judas once did, from the trees that they have now become.[2] There is a sense here that suicide is so unique that natural reason can only dimly grasp the scope of its wrongness.

Dante's narrative rests on a deep commitment to the paramount importance of the body for the moral life—a vision shared by Robert P. George, who over the course of his career has been a prominent defender of the body's centrality to human flourishing.[3] On George's account, biological life is an "essential and intrinsic aspect of a human person."[4] Human beings are animals—sensing, bodily organisms who endure through time. While we are organisms, though, there is a "radical difference in kind" between us and other species, as humans are capable of "spiritual actions," such as the insight required for *modus tollens* or other logical inferences. Humans are animals and persons. That is, we are animals with a rational nature, which is constituted by having the "basic, natural capacities . . . for conceptual thought and deliberation and free choice."[5] This means that every substance of a rational nature—every human body, every human person—has moral worth. And it means that the "basic goods" that underwrite practical action perfect and fulfill the animal organisms who we are. Because the human body is the person, we should not regard it as an instrument for attaining a pleasure or end that does not genuinely perfect the body. On George's understanding, many contemporary moral controversies arise from the conflict between his hylomorphic account (that human persons are a body-soul composite) and a resurgent gnosticism that regards the "self as

2 Dante, *Inferno*, canto 13, lines 103–5.

3 My indebtedness to Professor George runs deep, as does my gratitude. I found my way into thinking about the body as an undergraduate by reading Plato and Saint Paul. I was guided through the latter by philosopher Dallas Willard's *Spirit of the Disciplines*. My thought on the subject was deepened by John Paul II's *Theology of the Body*. Yet it was George's work on the body that crystallized its importance for contemporary controversies and helped me grasp more clearly the often tacit—but sometimes overt—gnostic disregard for the body at work in liberal ethics.

4 George has developed his view both on his own and through collaborations with Patrick Lee, Christopher Tollefsen, and others. I hope they do not regard it as a slight if, for convenience's sake, I attribute coauthored pieces to George alone in the body of this essay. See Patrick Lee and Robert P. George, *Body-Self Dualism in Contemporary Ethics and Politics* (Cambridge: Cambridge University Press, 2008), 2.

5 Lee and George, *Body-Self Dualism*, 94.

a pure consciousness" and "the body as a mere extrinsic tool."[6] By dividing the person from the body, gnostic liberals have grounds to argue that some bodies (such as embryos) are not persons and to dismiss the centrality of biology for morally licit norms of life (as in gay marriage).[7]

George's diagnosis of the gnostic roots of contemporary liberalism might be new to many evangelicals, but it was shared by a variety of twentieth-century Protestant moral theologians. For instance, Paul Ramsey once wrote that the "acids of modern liberalism" have eaten away at the moral bonds of marriage, intergenerational piety, and the connection between "conscious life and nascent life."[8] Yet the dissolution of these bonds, he went on, has its roots within "the death of the bond of soul with body in the understanding of personal life in a dualistic age." Indeed, Ramsey saw such a dissolution as a unique threat to Protestantism. While the task of Roman Catholicism was to overcome the "rigidity and seeming 'naturalism'" of the moral bonds between conjugal love and procreation, the "task facing Protestantism is the often quite unacknowledged need to forge them again."[9] Ramsey's most important bioethical work was self-consciously founded on an unequivocal endorsement of the body: as "man is a sacredness in the social and political order, so he is a sacredness in the natural, biological order."[10] Channeling none other than Karl Barth, Ramsey went on to say, "He is a sacredness in bodily life. . . . He is an embodied soul or ensouled body."[11]

The question of the body's place within theological ethics poses something of a paradox. On the one side, the body has a unique and fundamental place for our knowledge of natural law: we have no more intimate or extensive knowledge of the human nature that moral norms are tied to than the knowledge of our flesh. As Saint Paul writes in Ephesians 5:29, "No one ever hated his own flesh, but nourishes it and cherishes it." Suicide is incoherent

---

6   Lee and George, *Body-Self Dualism*, 2.

7   Robert P. George, "Gnostic Liberalism," *First Things*, December 2016, 34–35.

8   Paul Ramsey, "Responsible Parenthood: An Essay in Ecumenical Ethics," *Religion in Life* 36, no. 3 (1967): 343.

9   Ramsey, "Responsible Parenthood," 343.

10 Paul Ramsey, *The Patient as Person: Explorations in Medical Ethics*, 2nd ed. (New Haven, CT: Yale University Press, 2002), xlvi.

11 Ramsey, *Patient as Person*, xlvi. In *Church Dogmatics*, Barth describes Jesus as "one whole man, embodied soul and ensouled body." See Karl Barth, *Church Dogmatics*, ed. Geoffrey W. Bromiley and Thomas F. Torrance, trans. Geoffrey W. Bromiley (Peabody, MA: Hendrickson, 2010), 3.2:327.

because it contradicts this principle, fundamentally severing a person from the basis for that individual's very self. On the other side, our knowledge of the body's inclinations can be distorted. We may not hate our flesh, but it can sometimes seem as though our flesh hates us. In sickness, in starvation, in depression that rewires our brain chemistry, in chronic pain—our bodies turn against us and disrupt the integration of self and body that we otherwise unreflectively enjoy. We are never more alienated from our flesh than when in pain. We shout, "*It* hurts," when we stub our toe precisely because in that moment our toe seems more like a broken instrument than part of ourselves. Temporary seasons of alienation are ordinary aspects of maturation and aging. Teenagers going through puberty must learn anew what it means to live within their bodies. Such a transition is disorienting: learning to love our flesh takes time. Our bodies often seem to have a will of their own, which rages against our will. The unity of body and soul must be learned and embraced.

Here I want to explore what an evangelical ethic might contribute to the task of keeping body and soul together in the face of the gnostic liberalism George has rightly critiqued. My exploration is sympathetic to George's hylomorphism; on the details of the metaphysics, I have no disagreement. Yet, like Dante, I worry that the philosophical resources that George's natural law theory provides may be an insufficiently potent prophylactic against the emerging challenges of our liberal regime—especially the efforts to extend life indefinitely and to rewrite the contents of human nature itself. Philosophy might not be able to sufficiently secure the "sacredness" of humanity's biological life on its own terms. Yet that is not to say that theology can dispense with nature or her laws. Indeed, an evangelical ethic that starts from the resurrection of Jesus Christ must acknowledge the immediacy and intimacy we have with our bodies and the centrality of that bodily experience for understanding the world. While Protestant theologians like Paul Ramsey have been averse to founding ethical norms on our apprehension of natural law outside the revelation of Christ, they have also struggled to integrate their doctrines into ethics—proving, paradoxically, the enduring power of natural law for moral reasoning.[12] To undertake this exploration,

---

12 At this point in his work, Ramsey gives a theological foundation for his endorsement of the body's "sacredness." At the outset of his preface, he includes the "sanctity of life" as among those "moral and religious premises" that he must make explicit. Ramsey, *Patient as Person*, xlv. Only

then, I first offer a few appreciative questions about Robert George's account before turning to Ramsey's student Oliver O'Donovan's effort to incorporate nature into a thoroughgoing evangelical ethics. Such a juxtaposition helps clarify, I hope, what beginning with the resurrection can and cannot do for an ethic of our flesh.

Robert George on the Body

George's "new" natural law theory unequivocally rejects any derivation of moral norms from theoretical descriptions of human nature, yet it does so without severing the link between the goods of human life and our nature. Our judgment of what is to be done is founded on our knowledge of "basic goods," which are "the intrinsic aspects of human fulfillment."[13] These goods—which include friendship, life, marriage, religion, and knowledge—are "genuinely *fulfilling* or *perfective* of us and others like us."[14] As such, they supply us with ultimate reasons for action: they are irreducible answers to why one is doing something, as they are sufficient on their own to motivate a person to act and are "intelligibly choiceworthy for their own sakes," rather than only intelligible for the sake of some other end.[15] Our knowledge of basic goods is grounded not on our experiences of enjoying life or marriage or on the intuitions that such experiences might give rise to. Rather, the basic goods are self-evident: their choiceworthiness is a practical insight, a "rational apprehension that being healthy [or being married or having knowledge] is an aspect of human flourishing, worthy of pursuit and protection."[16] Such a practical insight recognizes the unique opportunity that an individual has to perfect himself. Still, the basic goods are connected to human nature,

---

two years previously, in a substantive defense of a nondualistic anthropology, Ramsey introduced the same formulation with the qualification that it arises from the "religious outlooks and 'on-looks' that have been traditional to us." There, Ramsey is explicit that the sanctity of human life has an origin "alien to him," such that it matters little for the morality of abortion whether we think life begins at conception or no. Paul Ramsey, "The Morality of Abortion," in *Life or Death: Ethics and Options* (Portland, OR: Reed College, 1968), 72. Three years after *Patient as Person*, Ramsey moved the theological foundation to the center of the expression: "Human beings are a sacredness, under God, in the biological order." Ramsey, "Abortion: A Review Article," *The Thomist* 37, no. 1 (1973): 181.

13 Patrick Lee and Robert P. George, *Conjugal Union: What Marriage Is and Why It Matters* (New York: Cambridge University Press, 2014), 22.

14 Lee and George, *Conjugal Union*, 26 (emphasis original).

15 Lee and George, *Conjugal Union*, 24.

16 Lee and George, *Conjugal Union*, 27.

even if our knowledge of them is not derived from metaphysical speculation about human nature. However new George's view is, it is still a natural law account: as aspects of *human* flourishing, a full philosophical explication of basic goods and their role in ethics requires some discussion of what constitutes human nature.[17]

While our knowledge of basic goods is not derived from metaphysics, George employs metaphysics to dialectically defend basic goods against those who reject them.[18] On George's hylomorphic account, human persons are a body-soul composite, individuals whose animal bodies have a formal principle of unity and life, namely, a rational soul.[19] Where substance-dualist accounts would locate the person in the soul, and materialist accounts deny the soul altogether, George's hylomorphism argues that the human person *is* a living body *with* a rational soul. George builds his defense of humans' animality out of the mundane, quotidian reality of sensation, which he argues is a bodily phenomenon and thus incompatible with substance dualism. The human soul does not depend on the body for all its functions, such as willing or engaging in conceptual thought, and thus can survive the death of the body. At the same time, the soul is functionally dependent on the body: while it is conceivable that an immaterial entity (such as an angel)

---

17   As George and Lee acknowledge, the "naturalist approach is correct to hold that moral norms are in some way grounded in human nature." Lee and George, *Conjugal Union*, 36. Mark Murphy has distinguished between weak and strong natural law theories, and he thinks that natural law theories must be of the strong variety but that on such a theory, basic goods cannot be self-evident since they require human nature to explain them. Mark C. Murphy, *Natural Law and Practical Rationality*, Cambridge Studies in Philosophy and Law (Cambridge: Cambridge University Press, 2007), 16. What Murphy misses about George's teacher John Finnis—and I think George as well—is that the contents of "human nature" are known only through basic goods. Thus, practical reason has epistemic priority for understanding human nature—even if human nature is ontologically prior. John Finnis, *Reason in Action* (Oxford: Oxford University Press, 2011), 5–6.

18   George suggests that speculative arguments can cast doubt on self-evident practical truths but can also be "employed affirmatively in support of a self-evident practical truth, often with persuasive force." While there "can be no 'evidence' of 'self-evidence,'" George thinks that theoretical or metaphysical arguments can "remove doubts about their truth." See Robert P. George, *In Defense of Natural Law* (Oxford: Oxford University Press, 2001), 62–63. This dialectical approach is, I suspect, partially why George's natural law theory has been developed in rather limited and spectacular directions. That is, it has been invoked on questions of marriage, abortion, euthanasia, and transgender rights—rather than on questions of markets and the economy, environmentalism, or other questions of ethics that are not immediately tied to the nature of the body.

19   Lee and George, *Body-Self Dualism*, 66–67.

might reason without matter, the human soul is "naturally dependent upon sensation and thus is by nature incomplete."[20] As such, if a soul exists without the body, its functioning is impeded and "unnatural."[21] The subject of action is, properly speaking, the *whole human being*—a body-soul composite.

Such a position enables George to escape two interrelated threats. First, the fact that human persons are animals means we are not constituted by our experiences of the world, which are preserved for us in the form of psychological continuity.[22] Persons come into being when the living organism that is one's body is conceived and go out of existence when that same organism has died. As such, the person enjoys numerically identical continuity across time within the body one has—even if that individual does not experience psychological or biological continuity. What matters, on this view, is achieving the goods that really are fulfilling of this organism, rather than having experiences or sensations or pleasures that might be (temporarily) satisfactory but offer no real perfective value.

The ethical upshot of this is that bodies cannot be instrumentalized for the sake of pursuing pleasures or experiences that would attract us but not be genuinely fulfilling or perfective of our persons. In his rejoinder to Robert Nozick's vaunted "experience machine" thought experiment, George argues that the body must not be regarded as fungible for the sake of a satisfaction or enjoyment that might be had without it. As the thought experiment goes, we can imagine a machine that would give users the pleasure of engaging in an activity like playing a piano sonata without actually doing so. One plausible conclusion from the thought experiment is that we should care about *doing* things, rather than simply *experiencing* them. But George goes a step further, arguing that choices to pursue a pleasure or satisfaction apart from a genuinely perfective end reduce real goods to experiences of pleasure and so always involve some "retreat from reality into fantasy." If the "experience" could be had in some way besides undertaking a fulfilling activity in the body, then the body becomes "a mere external means to one's end—a state existing in consciousness."[23] As a moral theory, hedonism

20 Lee and George, *Body-Self Dualism*, 68.
21 Lee and George, *Body-Self Dualism*, 73.
22 Lee and George, *Body-Self Dualism*, 34–37. George and Lee bring together Derek Parfit's account of personal identity with Robert Nozick's "experience machine" and demonstrate how both have an account of personal identity that is founded on psychological states.
23 Lee and George, *Body-Self Dualism*, 112.

rests on a dualism that regards the source of the pleasurable sensations or feelings as immaterial to our evaluation of what one is doing: every hedonistic choice, "by its nature, involves reducing the real world—including our bodies and others—to the level of replaceable and dispensable means of obtaining an effect in one's consciousness."[24]

Second, George's hylomorphism and its endorsement of a rational soul preserves the uniqueness of human dignity against views that would ascribe the equivalent moral value to every species by attaching it to characteristics that come in degrees, like sentience, consciousness, self-awareness, and rationality. For George, "being a substance *with a rational nature* is the criterion for moral worth."[25] This nature expresses itself through activities particular to the species, which George argues include conceptual thought and free will.[26] Yet the criterion for moral worth is only *having* this nature, not actualizing it.[27] And possession of a nature is not a matter of degree. For George, *persons* themselves are valuable for themselves, not as "vehicles for what is intrinsically valuable."[28] Even if persons are not in a position to actualize their nature, we must regard them as ends in themselves and not damage their pursuit of a basic good in seeking basic goods for ourselves because they possess a rational nature that has full moral worth.[29]

George's metaphysics and affirmation of the unique value of human beings make the basic good of human organic life inviolable.[30] George's claim

---

24 Lee and George, *Body-Self Dualism*, 107.

25 Lee and George, *Body-Self Dualism*, 86 (emphasis original).

26 Lee and George, *Body-Self Dualism*, 52–65.

27 Lee and George, *Body-Self Dualism*, 82–83.

28 Lee and George, *Body-Self Dualism*, 86.

29 On the "radical" capacity, see Lee and George, *Body-Self Dualism*, 82–83, 119–30. The basic goods are not just for an individual, but for *everyone like me*. Moreover, communion with others is itself a basic human good. As such, it would be inconsistent for us to pursue fulfillment for ourselves while not respecting others' pursuit of fulfillment. As a result, the "thought of the golden rule, basic fairness, occurs early on in moral reflection." Lee and George, *Body-Self Dualism*, 93.

30 This is part of the difficulty of articulating and defending the claim that organic, bodily human life is a good in itself that must be respected. For John Finnis, the basic good of life can be more or less perfectly instantiated: "One may well be overwhelmed by the distance between [the vegetative existence of a person in irreversible coma] and the integral good of a flourishing person. Nobody wants to be in such a condition, and no decent person wants to see anyone else living like that. The good of human life is indeed very inadequately instantiated in such a person's life. Still, the life of a person in irreversible coma remains human life; *it is a good, however deprived.* True, life of such a deprived and unhealthy kind has little appeal. . . . No

that persons are intrinsically valuable in themselves, rather than as vectors for other valuable qualities or attributes, might seem incommensurate with the notion that basic goods are themselves intrinsically choiceworthy and that, as such, they are the final reasons for action. After all, knowledge, marriage, friendship, and so on are not *persons*. Yet there are two important caveats to this claim.

First, basic goods *perfect* persons, so that to choose them in some practical context affirms and seeks to bring into being a dimension or aspect of a particular individual's life. In that way, basic goods are transparent for persons. We might say that while human beings are intrinsically *valuable*, basic goods are intrinsically *choiceworthy*—where the latter names their role in guiding concrete decisions.

Second, biological life is one of the basic goods and, in a sense, a presupposition to our attainment of the other basic goods. As George notes, it is odd to think that "the fulfillment of an entity is intrinsically valuable, and yet the entity itself is not." Viewing one's biological organism as valuable only instrumentally or conditionally (because one values consciousness or the activities that are possible to mature, healthy human beings) implicitly identifies oneself with something besides that bodily entity and thus engages in a dualism that denigrates one's bodily life and demeans the person. On George's account, it is impossible to regard one's *whole self* as instrumentally or conditionally valuable: "One must value, at least implicitly, one's own being or preservation as in itself good."[31] In that way, organic life functions as a presupposition for one's freedom to pursue other basic goods. Crucially, this entails that death is an assault on the good of the person, as it both impedes the individual's opportunity to pursue other valuable basic goods and attacks one's participation in the basic good of (organic) life. As George writes, death "itself is never a dignity—it is, in a way, the supreme indignity." This supplies a reason *against* "hastening death," rather than a reason for choosing it.[32]

There is much to commend this account of the body. Yet I wonder whether it can bear the moral weight that George asks of it or whether

---

human good, considered apart from integral human fulfilment, has the appeal which each of the components of that ideal enjoys when all of them are considered together." John Finnis, Joseph M. Boyle, and Germain Grisez, *Nuclear Deterrence, Morality, and Realism* (Oxford: Oxford University Press, 1987), 305–6.

31 Lee and George, *Body-Self Dualism*, 161.

32 Lee and George, *Body-Self Dualism*, 173.

the body's centrality to the moral life ultimately relies on our knowledge of Christ's resurrection. One challenge arises from efforts to indefinitely postpone death or render it unnecessary through the development of anti-aging therapies. If the good of human (bodily) life is intrinsically choice worthy, then we always have reason to extend it, regardless of the costs of doing so. Such a worry arises, I think, if body and soul are kept together *only* on the basis of nature and philosophical reason, as within those terms death remains a potent enemy—rather than the defeated, disarmed enemy of 1 Corinthians 15.[33]

To be clear, the good of life is not the only reason for action we have in the face of death: its positive, directive force is not obligatory in the way that the prohibition against taking human life is obligatory.[34] Yet that means opposing indefinite life-extension projects can only be prudential, rather than principled: the possibility of damaging other basic goods in seeking to live forever might stop us from making the attempt. But we might also conclude that because the basic good of life is necessary for *any* participation in the basic goods, such damage would be permissible to accept (on grounds of double effect).[35] New natural law proponents' position that the basic goods are incommensurable in practical situations cuts a variety of ways. It prohibits aggregating the damages to basic goods in order to know what one should do, which would effectively be a form of consequentialism. But it also might entail that one could reasonably accept such damages (provided one does not choose them) while pursuing, to the bitter end,

33 Throughout 1 Cor. 15, Paul refers to those who have died in Christ as those who "sleep" (15:6, 18, 20, 51). Such imagery does not sanction choosing death, but it also might preclude choosing against death in perpetuity.

34 Crucially, new natural law proponents affirm an asymmetry between positive and negative norms, in which the directive force of positive reasons is only suggestive but the force of prohibitions is absolute. Finnis argues that the "reasons *for* my choosing are infinite in number." Our finitude means we cannot pursue every good option, and so there is not a single right decision in every situation. But we can also "refrain from doing anything." That is, we can respect the negative, exceptionless norms that the "reasons against" supply for us. In that sense, reasons for and reasons against are asymmetrical in their force and normative power. See Finnis, *Reason in Action*, 226–30.

35 The "doctrine of double effect" allows that causing harm as a side effect of pursuing a good is acceptable, even though directly causing that harm to pursue a good would not be. The account of intention and double effect is a crucial part of the new natural law proponents' view. Among other places, see Finnis's critique of proportionalism in John Finnis, *Fundamentals of Ethics* (Washington, DC: Georgetown University Press, 1983), 85.

a single basic good. When that basic good makes all the others possible, as life does, such a choice seems especially reasonable.

We might invoke related challenges from the desolate lands of techno-futurist fantasies, where the aim of technological development is to make ourselves post- or transhuman. For such views, the charge of dualism is not an objection, and the defense of bodies on the basis of human nature is a nonstarter. If the pursuit of indefinite life extension has sacralized nature, post- and transhuman fantasies have turned against her outright. Yet it is just such a blatant rejection of nature that undercuts appeals to it as a philosophical source: the unavailability of empirical evidence (of any kind) of the badness of such projects leaves philosophical critiques rather shorthanded.

Such possibilities may not trouble George's account of abortion, euthanasia, and marriage as resting on the affirmation of the dignity of the human body, but they do raise questions about the extent to which the body and soul can be kept together without appealing to the resurrection of Jesus Christ. Consider the place of the postmortem self in George's argument. George suggests that philosophy "can provide strong evidence for the conclusion that the soul, in fact, does survive death." Yet if the body transfers to the soul some of its powers, and the soul subsists beyond the life of the body, then we might wonder whether the person *becomes* the soul. As George recognizes, the soul that subsists beyond the life of the body "is not, strictly speaking, the same substance that understands and wills before death and after death."[36] Such a conclusion would be unhappy for George's animalism, to be sure. But why is the soul not the same substance after death? Without the Christian doctrine of the resurrection of the body somewhere in the background, it seems plausible to think that the soul persisting after death is the same substance that understood and willed prior to death. Such a position would come near to the view of Aristotle, whose hylomorphism seems to be commensurate with the ongoing subsistence of *something* beyond the death of the body but that also seems to regard personal immortality as an impossibility.[37] Like George, Thomas Aquinas sees his account of the

---

36 Lee and George, *Body-Self Dualism*, 73.
37 See Aristotle, *Nicomachean Ethics* 1111b19–30. "How does an element which is divine, eternal, impassive find lodgement in and association with the mortal organism which has in it nothing that can survive the death of the material body? To this question Aristotle has no answer."

soul's inclination toward the body as a reason to accept the resurrection of Christ, but we might wonder whether the resurrection supplies grounds for Thomas to read Aristotle in the manner he does, since it is a unique event that expands humanity's imagination and opens up new lines of argument about the relationship between body and soul.

The question about the resurrection's role in determining the body's place in ethics also has a practical dimension, which arises when we reflect on what we should do when human nature turns against itself through sin. Those who pursue experiences based on "feelings" rather than goods diminish their ability to grasp the goodness of the goods they have rejected. Though the body recalcitrantly inclines toward its flourishing even when we reject such inclinations, destructive choices eventually turn our flesh against itself. People using illicit recreational drugs might have accepted a tacit dualism, out of which they pursue the "experiences" of satisfaction without the underlying goods. Yet their alienation from their nature in this respect makes appeals to their nature dissatisfactory, for they have in practice already rejected the principle to which one is appealing.[38] Alienation from the body is a closed circle, from which there is no escape—except by that which comes to the body (in a sense) from beyond it, as in the resurrection from the dead.

There is a puzzle here, then, about whether the metaphysical principle of the soul's union with the body is sufficient to keep body and soul together,

---

Patrick Duncan, "Immortality of the Soul in the Platonic Dialogues and Aristotle," *Philosophy* 17, no. 68 (November 1942): 319.

38 In "Marriage and the Liberal Imagination," George observes that those who fail to grasp the intrinsic value of basic goods "ordinarily do not judge them to be valueless." They might still see a point to marrying, even if they do not recognize its basic goodness. He goes on to suggest, however, that they "cannot imagine . . . why spouses would perform marital acts, not (or not merely) as a means to, or of, procreation, pleasure, expressing feeling and the like, but above all, and decisively, for the sake of marriage itself, understood as actualized in such acts." He observes that the practical insights that marriage has its own intelligible point and that marriage is consummated in the union of male and female cannot be attained "except with strenuous efforts of imagination, by people who, due to personal or cultural circumstances, have little acquaintance with marriage thus understood." As such, whatever undermines the "sound understanding and practice of marriage in a culture . . . makes it difficult for people to grasp the intrinsic value of marriage and marital intercourse." Such a discrepancy indicates that George is ambivalent about how optimistic we should be that "imagination" can secure our perception of the basic goods when our knowledge of them has become corrupted. See George, *In Defense of Natural Law*, 143.

when the value of doing so is precisely what is in question. There may be something to Dante's own evangelically mediated construal of the body in *Inferno*, canto 13. If Virgil is incapable of demonstrating the true depths of the suicide's violation of the body, other attempts are surely in trouble. An ethic that is founded on the resurrection offers a surety to the metaphysical principle of the soul's union with the body, but it does so by vindicating the body over and against the forces of death and sin that would tempt us to spurn it. The resurrection gives us grounds to affirm the body's inviolability and centrality to our person with a force not available to natural reason.

Oliver O'Donovan on the Body

Still, matters are not so simple for evangelical ethicists. Even when they claim to found ethics on the resurrection of Jesus, they often revert to nontheological frameworks in wrestling with moral questions that the body gives rise to. Oliver O'Donovan, for instance, once raised worries similar to those offered here against his teacher Paul Ramsey. Despite Ramsey's unequivocal criticism of the bifurcation of body and soul, O'Donovan contends that Ramsey fails to ground body-soul unity *theologically*. Ramsey rejected the Platonic and Aristotelian accounts of the soul, since the former reduces bodily life "to an acceptable level of indifference" and the latter "reduces the stature, the worth, and the irreplaceable uniqueness of the individual person (long before his dying) to a level of acceptable transiency or interchangeability."[39] Yet on O'Donovan's reading, the "principle of body-soul unity . . . is not strong enough to bear the weight that Ramsey puts on it."[40] The resurrection binds body and soul together *without* reifying biological life in such a way that we are committed to the project of indefinite life extension, and it does so by relativizing the goodness of organic human life and revealing its fundamental determination by God. Moreover, the resurrection plays more than a "merely limiting role" in the relationship of body and soul; it is "the intellectual foundation of [body-soul unity] in Christian thought."[41]

---

39 Paul Ramsey, "The Indignity of 'Death with Dignity,'" *Hastings Center Studies* 2, no. 2 (May 1974): 60–61.

40 Oliver O'Donovan, "Keeping Body and Soul Together," in *Covenants of Life: Contemporary Medical Ethics in Light of the Thought of Paul Ramsey*, ed. Kenneth L Vaux and Mark Stenberg, Philosophy and Medicine 77 (London: Springer, 2011), 42.

41 O'Donovan, "Keeping Body and Soul Together," 43.

O'Donovan's assertion that the resurrection grounds our understanding of the body is commensurate with his broader concern to articulate an ethics that arises from the gospel of Jesus Christ, especially from the "resurrection of Jesus Christ from the dead."[42] On O'Donovan's account, humanity's rebellion against God "has not succeeded in destroying the natural order to which he belongs." But that can be said only on the basis of God's vindication of that order in the resurrection of Christ. While the ontological grounds for this order are resilient, our epistemological access to it is also limited by sin, such that "any certainty we may have about the order which God has made depends upon God's own disclosure of himself and of his works."[43] The upshot of this view is that the knowledge of the natural order and its implications for ethics remains "in part," so that the unbeliever "does not have to be ignorant about the structure of the family, the virtue of mercy, the vice of cowardice or the duty of justice."[44] Yet the knowledge of that order is intrinsically incomplete—and *because* it is incomplete, it cannot properly be said to be known at all. Just as adding different endings to Schubert's *Unfinished Symphony* would transform our understanding of its meaning and significance, so the disclosure of the completion of history and the moral order in Christ transforms our grasp of them. As O'Donovan writes, "Knowledge of the moral order is a grasp of the total shape in which, if anything is lacking, everything is lacking."[45] As such, the resurrection of Jesus Christ not only secures or grounds more deeply what is naturally known but provides distinct or unique ethical content itself.

---

42 Oliver O'Donovan, *Resurrection and Moral Order: An Outline for Evangelical Ethics* (Grand Rapids, MI: Eerdmans, 1986), 11, 13.

43 O'Donovan, *Resurrection and Moral Order*, 19. O'Donovan contends that considerable confusion has arisen in theology from not properly ordering the ontological and epistemological dimensions of ethics, which has led to a polarized choice "between an ethic that is revealed and has no ontological grounding and an ethic that is based on creation and so is naturally known." On the one hand, then, O'Donovan follows Barth in asserting the epistemological challenge to "natural law" moral reasoning. Yet on his reading, Barth himself failed to properly differentiate the ontological and epistemological issues and so repudiated dimensions of the doctrine of creation "which ought never to have fallen under suspicion." On the other hand, though, Emil Brunner's political work discloses that he "understood the theological task as a discrete exercise in cultural accommodation," which renders it incapable of responding to those liberation theologies that subject theology to the "sectional perceptions of a single cultural group ('black' theology, 'feminist' theology, *etc.*)." O'Donovan, *Resurrection and Moral Order*, 86, 91.

44 O'Donovan, *Resurrection and Moral Order*, 88.

45 O'Donovan, *Resurrection and Moral Order*, 89.

Christian ethics means that "certain ethical and moral judgments belong to the gospel itself," that the "church can be committed to ethics without moderating the tone of its voice as the bearer of glad tidings."[46]

Yet if O'Donovan seeks to ground ethics in the resurrection of Jesus, he also attends to the fact that our unique intimacy with our bodies poses a challenge to doing so. O'Donovan speaks freely of the "natural order" and seems to give its deliverances something near to a free-standing authority for moral judgments. As he notes nearby, the "relation of human beings to their own bodies is . . . the last frontier of nature." While we might banish birds, trees, and every other mark of nature from our world, we cannot escape the natural: when we take off our clothes to bathe, "we confront our own bodily existence." Such an encounter means that freedom must be one of conformity to "its immanent laws" and that we plan "our activities in co-operation with them." Citing Saint Paul's dictum in Ephesians 5:29 that "no one ever hated his own flesh, but nourishes it and cherishes it," O'Donovan argues that hating one's own flesh is the "limit of self-contradiction to which our freedom tends." Indeed, warring against our bodies is the terminus to which our self-hatred is drawn, as the worshipers of Baal on Mount Carmel "were impelled to cut themselves with knives."[47]

It is telling for the difficulties of developing a thoroughgoing evangelical ethic that O'Donovan fails to carry through his theological program of grounding ethics in the resurrection in his otherwise astonishingly prescient discussion of transsexualism (or what today has come to be known as transgenderism).[48] Though much of the chapter is philosophical in its approach, his final observation is "of a more confessionally Christian kind." "The sex," he writes, "into which we have been born . . . is given to us to be welcomed as a gift of God." He goes on, "The task of psychological maturity—for it is a moral task, and not merely an event which may or may not transpire—involves accepting this gift and learning to love it, even though we may have to acknowledge that it does not come to us without problems." It is our responsibility to develop our vocation in accordance with the possibilities given to us in our biological sex. There is no room on

---

46 O'Donovan, *Resurrection and Moral Order*, 12. See also xi.

47 Oliver O'Donovan, *Begotten or Made?* (Oxford: Oxford University Press, 1984), 6.

48 Forty years later, his discussion remains the single most profound treatment of the subject by a Christian theologian.

this view for hastily dismissing those who find such a task difficult as psychologically disturbed, for the gap between "bodily form as such" and the "problems it poses to us personally in our individual experience" applies well beyond questions of transgenderism. Yet O'Donovan does not reach for the resurrection and the hope for our bodies' repair that such a doctrine gives rise to. Instead, he writes that "responsibility in sexual development implies a responsibility to nature."[49] That is true, but when it comes to the question of gender dysphoria, the gift of God in creation is precisely what one has been alienated from. The impotence and frustration that one feels in the face of such fragmentation is real, but the final remedy is only possible when our flesh is raised with Christ's through the Spirit. Those who suffer wait—and by God's grace, they can wait with hope. As we are released from the task of anxiously subduing our flesh, we can be set free to merely live within it—the flawed, and ultimately fatal, flesh that will someday shine with a radiance and glory we cannot begin now to even imagine. Starting from the resurrection generates a very different moral atmosphere (one that, I think, sounds like good news!) than nature ever can.

O'Donovan, then, is willing to appeal to nature when addressing contested moral questions, even while he thinks that nature is insufficient on its own to resolve them. In responding to Robert Adams's rejection of nature as a category for sexual ethics, O'Donovan observes that *natural* and *unnatural* are "terms that come into play when questions arise about how we shall conduct ourselves as embodied souls and ensouled bodies."[50] It is possible, he argues, to be too skeptical about what nature can supply for the moral life; if nothing else, nature "knows that life is better than death!" While we need Genesis and the Gospels to understand "life and death theologically as the imprint of our creation and fall," we do not need them to "tell us that there *is* an order of value in which life is preferable to death."[51] The "range of features in human existence" that we describe as nature can "clearly ground some moral discernments." And these can then "point the way to the understanding that a doctrine of creation can supply." The step from a "philosophy of nature to a theology of creation" does not mean abandoning "one set of

---

49 O'Donovan, *Begotten or Made?*, 29.

50 Oliver O'Donovan, *Church in Crisis : The Gay Controversy and the Anglican Communion* (Eugene, OR: Cascade Books, 2008), 91.

51 O'Donovan, *Church in Crisis*, 96.

interests for another," then, but rather being directed back to the world to see what intelligibility the goods of nature have in light of their redemption. The "language of 'nature' and its concerns for the body-soul relation must be framed within a fully theological account of creation and redemption."[52]

At most, then, the goods of nature can "point" the way practical reasoning must go, but they are not so transparent that we can rely on them, especially when nature herself has been called into question. What we need is nearer to what Virgil requires of Dante, namely, *participation* in nature through the Spirit so that we can recognize the goods of nature as they are. Nature can only point the way toward a doctrine of creation; it cannot answer for itself. Such a limit is crucial, since it supplies dialectical resources for responding to moral positions that call the *contents of (human) nature themselves into question*, as in the case of transhumanism, posthumanism, or indefinite life extensions. When human nature itself becomes an object of artifice, no nonviciously circular defense of it can be made. One can only turn outside nature, to the disclosure of Jesus Christ, whose person sanctions human nature even within the limits of death.[53]

Conclusion

The body's place in the moral life is a deep puzzle that has animated the very best of moral and philosophical reflection since Plato. George's Thomistic

---

52 O'Donovan, *Church in Crisis*, 95.

53 O'Donovan makes his Christological resources more explicit in his discussion of embryo research—and for good reason, as such research raises the fundamental question of *who* is a person. See *Begotten or Made?*, 65–66. See also O'Donovan's discussion of the risks of in vitro fertilization and the mastery of the tools of divine providence (including death) that is involved in it. *Begotten or Made?*, 82–83. Gerald McKenny has argued that O'Donovan's acceptance of some sort of variation and change within the realm of nature means that O'Donovan is not able to definitively rule out certain biotechnological interventions. McKenny himself, however, notes that O'Donovan might block such a move by arguing that medicine "should be restricted to the treatment of pathologies (that is, to therapy as opposed to enhancement)." Gerald McKenny, *Biotechnology, Human Nature, and Christian Ethics*, New Studies in Christian Ethics 37 (Oxford: Oxford University Press, 2018), 46. This, however, is more or less what I take O'Donovan to do in his opening chapter of *Begotten or Made?* For instance, he notes, "A medicine which differentiated sharply between interfering in a healthy body and curing a sick one, as Western Christian medicine used to do, preserved an understanding of freedom which respected the constraints of health. But now the challenge is explicit." *Begotten or Made?*, 6. O'Donovan also has other resources for blocking such a move. Specifically, the natural order is secured and vindicated *by Christ*. What blocks technological interventions is, ultimately, a willingness to respect the uniqueness of divine action in affirming the created order of nature as such.

hylomorphism is among the best contemporary accounts of our corporeal lives. It offers a compelling antidote to the incipient and pervasive neo-gnosticism of liberal ethics. Although George mainly develops his view by addressing controversial moral questions, his defense of the body begins in a much more quotidian fashion—with sensation, our basic experience in our bodies of the world around us. There is perhaps a hint here of the therapeutic value of George's view: the moral task of keeping body and soul together might require us to look beyond the arenas of spectacular disagreement, where the war over the body is most apparent, to the hidden and mundane arenas, where our intuitions about the body are constantly being formed.

The above inquiry is not about whether George's metaphysics are right but whether they can bear the weight that is being asked of them. My worry arises from a deep appreciation for George's work and my own ongoing puzzlement over how Christians should navigate ethical controversies. The self-evidence of the basic goods that George defends seems to leave discursive reflection on their metaphysical underpinnings morally inert: if such arguments cannot supply *evidence for* the goodness of life or marriage or any other basic good, then it is not clear on what basis they can defeat objections to them. While some readers of new natural law have regarded it merely as a covert form of accommodating Catholic moral teaching to the canons of public reason, I worry that there is (paradoxically) a logical impasse built into the view: What does it mean to persuade someone of the goodness of a basic good when that goodness is self-evident and underived?[54]

This is not simply a question of political or public tactics or strategy. Rather, it is a question about how we can secure an account of the body and the moral life in the midst of disagreement. If a liberal ethic severs body from soul, then it is best understood as a disagreement about the content and meaning (and even existence!) of nature itself. The rational instability of defending nature on its own terms is endemic: there is no amount of

---

54 George writes that dialectical arguments "may be employed affirmatively in support of a self-evident practical truth, often with persuasive force." He suggests that the compatibility of the basic goods with anthropological evidence places "something of a burden on anyone who would deny the proposition stating this practical judgment to account for the universality of phenomena such as friendship, intellectual inquiry and worship." Perhaps. Yet in situations where one person does not grasp an opportunity as intrinsically valuable, it is not clear what "persuasion" means *except* supplying them reasons *on the basis of which* they might affirm the practical conclusion. See George, *In Defense of Natural Law*, 62–63.

metaphysics that can resolve the deep disagreement about nature's meaning with those who reject it at the outset. George's account might have resources to deal with that problem: religion is one of the basic goods, and without it the whole system may be less stable than it appears.[55] But it is a crucial reminder that even within the terms of new natural law, we cannot ask more of metaphysics for ethics and political controversies than it can supply.

That is not to say that an evangelical ethic can dispense with metaphysics: while the consecration and inviolability of bodily life offered by the incarnation and resurrection of Jesus Christ is irreplaceable, these truths also lack practical specificity for our moral lives. The unwillingness of evangelicals to fully incorporate metaphysics into our moral deliberations has led to our widespread accommodation of practices that distort the character of bodily life by blocking or violating its natural rhythms—like contraception, in vitro fertilization, vasectomies, and milder forms of nontherapeutic, mood-enhancing drugs such as caffeine, marijuana, and so on. Evangelicals' emphasis on the cross has eclipsed our doctrine of creation, preventing us from fully appropriating the moral implications of the fact that Christ's resurrection is the confirmation and validation of creation, a validation that transcends creation's intrinsic possibilities without violating or denigrating them. O'Donovan's evangelical ethics rightly sees within nature "pointers" to the flourishing of the creature, even if those pointers are too epistemically limited to develop an ethic that would effectively answer a world ordered by rejecting them. Evangelicals must affirm nature and her laws.

At the same time, an evangelical ethic's affirmation of nature must be founded on the witness of Christ, which means it offers us something more

---

55 Finnis grants that if theistic explanations for morality fail, they introduce a "rational instability" into the system itself. The *necessity* of the basic goods that grounds their obligatoriness is "the necessity of our given nature," which "is a necessity only because the divine creative (and unnecessitated) choice opted for this world rather than none and rather than a world containing beings of radically other nature." The source of the instability if this further explanation is denied would come from the "perishability of [the basic goods'] instantiations in fleeting lives," rather than from their content itself. Still, Finnis unequivocally agrees with Mark Murphy's judgment that once the possibility of a theistic explanation for the basic goods is raised, "adherence to the natural law [becomes] rationally unstable in the absence of a certain sort of theistic stance." While a natural law *jurisprudence* might be feasible without such theological underpinnings, a natural law *ethic* is not. John Finnis, "Grounds of Law and Legal Theory: A Response," *Legal Theory* 13, nos. 3–4 (2007): 341. Citing Mark Murphy, "Finnis on Nature, Reason, God," *Legal Theory* 13, nos. 3–4 (2007): 193.

than the confirmation of what is already known. An evangelical engaging George's metaphysics can offer more than a half-hearted two cheers: embracing hylomorphism means following the "pointers" of the body as far as they can go, while recognizing the limitations of building a moral system—much less a persuasive moral system—out of them. Yet the revelation of nature's meaning and end in Christ means saying a forceful *no* to the broader systemic, institutional, and cultural movements that would overturn nature itself. To that extent, an evangelical ethic is more comprehensive: it can say a strange *yes* to death and a *no* to the attempt to prolong life precisely because it looks beyond death toward a life that the eye cannot see nor can the mind imagine. Its *no* is founded on the basis of that *yes*, and as such, it can remain fully good news to those who would initially reject it. To that extent, its persuasive power remains—untapped and unrealized.[56]

---

56 I'm indebted to Michael Baldwin and Gary Hartenburg for their feedback on this chapter. I am especially grateful to Beth Butler for discussion and for her editorial assistance, which saved me from a great number of infelicities.

9

A Person Is a Person,
No Matter How Small

Robert P. George and the Pro-Life Movement

Scott Klusendorf

ROBERT P. GEORGE'S IMPACT on pro-life apologetics, from which evangelicals can benefit tremendously, can be summed up in a sentence: he equipped battle-weary pro-life advocates to engage critics on hostile turf.[1] His body of work helped transform pro-life advocacy from a movement of short-sighted activists convinced that victory was one Supreme Court pick away to a movement of thinkers intellectually equipped to dig in for the long haul. To understand the significance of that transformation, readers need to understand the fallout from 1992. For many pro-life advocates, what happened that year was unthinkable.

Shell-Shocked Pro-Lifers

First, in 1992 the Supreme Court dashed the hopes of pro-lifers convinced that *Roe v. Wade* was on life support. Not only did the court fail to overturn *Roe*, it reaffirmed its "essential holding"—namely, "the right of the woman

---

1 Parts of this chapter are adapted from Scott Klusendorf, "You Can Hate Abortion and Love Women: What's under the Debate over Life," *DesiringGod*, June 6, 2019, https://www.desiring god.org/; Klusendorf, "A Bad Faith Argument," *World*, January 18, 2022, https://wng.org/; Klusendorf, "A Brief History of the Pro-Life Movement: What Can We Learn Moving Forward?," *BreakPoint*, 2012, https://www.breakpoint.org/. Used by permission.

to choose to have an abortion before viability and to obtain it without undue interference from the state."[2] True, the justices in *Planned Parenthood v. Casey* tossed a bone to pro-life advocates by ditching *Roe*'s trimester framework and allowing modest abortion-control legislation, but *Roe* itself wasn't going anywhere. To make matters worse, three Republican-nominated justices—Sandra Day O'Connor, Anthony M. Kennedy, and David Souter—engineered the pro-life defeat. Pro-lifers not only lost a crucial decision; they lost confidence that judges appointed by pro-life presidents could save them.

Second, pro-lifers feared losing the only political party sympathetic to their views.[3] Their fears were not unfounded given the political realignment of the late 1980s.[4] Prior to that realignment, the early pro-life movement had defenders in both major parties. For example, Democrat Senator Ted Kennedy wrote in 1971 that while he sympathized with women facing crisis pregnancies, abortion on demand conflicted with the value our civilization places on human life: "Wanted or unwanted, I believe that human life, even at its earliest stages, has certain rights which must be recognized—the right to be born, the right to love, the right to grow old."[5] On the House side, Democrat Dick Gephardt was a cosponsor of a proposed 1977 human life amendment aimed at undermining *Roe*.[6] That same year, Democrat Jesse Jackson penned an op-ed for *National Right to Life News* in which he pointedly asked, "What happens to the mind of a person, and the moral fabric of a nation, that accepts the abortion of the life of a baby without a pang of conscience?"[7] As late as 1982, Democrat Senator Joe Biden voted for a human life amendment specifically designed to give states freedom to reverse *Roe*.[8] Two years later, Tennessee Senator Al Gore voted for an

2   Roe v. Wade, 410 U.S. 113 (1973).

3   Robert Pear, "G.O.P. Faces Fight on Abortion Issue," *New York Times*, May 26, 1992.

4   For more on this realignment, see Ramesh Ponnuru, *The Party of Death: The Democrats, the Media, the Courts, and the Disregard for Human Life* (Washington, DC: Regnery, 2006), 21–32.

5   Ted Kennedy to Catholic League member Tom Dennelly, August 3, 1971, in Robert P. George, *The Clash of Orthodoxies: Law, Religion, and Morality in Crisis* (Wilmington, DE: ISI Books, 2001), 276–77.

6   Adam Nagourney, "In Turn, 6 Presidential Hopefuls Back Abortion Rights," *New York Times*, January 22, 2003.

7   Jesse Jackson, "How We Respect Life Is the Over-Riding Moral Issue," *Right to Life News*, January 1977.

8   Lisa Lerer, "When Joe Biden Voted to Let States Overturn *Roe v. Wade*," *New York Times*, March 29, 2019.

amendment to the Civil Rights Act of 1984 that would have protected unborn humans at conception.[9]

Every one of these legislative attempts to gut *Roe* failed, and by the mid-1980s, the bipartisan pro-life coalition was in free fall. Democrats like Gephardt, Biden, Kennedy, and Jackson flipped their positions once they aspired for higher office. New York governor Mario Cuomo framed the Democrats' new talking points in a 1984 speech in which he claimed that although he "personally opposed" abortion, he would not force his views on those who disagreed.[10] Meanwhile, left-leaning Catholics and evangelicals justified voting for these newly minted pro-choice (Democrat) candidates with an appeal to moral equivalency. True, the candidates in question were mistaken on abortion, but they were right on other important "whole of life" issues such as opposition to war, concern for the poor, and care for the environment. The political strategy in play was simple: shrink the significance of abortion so it was more or less equal with other issues, thus providing political cover for candidates sympathetic to abortion.

By 1992, pro-life Democrats were homeless. Their party was fully committed to the abortion license. That year, Pennsylvania governor Bob Casey Sr.—a pro-life Democrat—was not allowed to speak at his party's national convention because he intended to give a pro-life speech. The Republican Party alone offered political hope to pro-life exiles, but now some of its leaders were pressuring the platform committee to weaken the party's pro-life stance. The platform held, but after Bill Clinton's victory, a number of high-ranking Republicans caved. "I am pro-life, and I intend to remain pro-life," said William Kristol, chief of staff to Vice President Dan Quayle. But, he added, "I think the party is better off if it makes some adjustment."[11] Meanwhile, the Republican Majority for Choice promised a primary challenge to every pro-life candidate up for election.

Third, pro-lifers faced an emerging threat of silence from clergy worried that opposition to abortion was harming evangelism. During the late 1980s and early 1990s, Operation Rescue organized direct, nonviolent blockades

---

9   Douglas Johnson, "Gore Can't Get His Story Straight on 1984 Vote to Define Unborn Children as 'Persons' from Conception," *Right to Life News*, November, 1999.

10   George, *Clash of Orthodoxies*, 277.

11   Robert Shogan, "Republicans Pressed to Ease Up on Anti-Abortion Stance," *Los Angeles Times*, December 20, 1992.

outside abortion clinics across the country, resulting in over seventy-five thousand arrests. The protests reached their zenith in the summer of 1991, when thousands of pro-life advocates assembled in Wichita, Kansas, over a six-week period, temporarily shutting down the city's three major abortion clinics. The media, of course, conveyed a different narrative. Pro-life advocates were violent agitators assaulting desperate women. The claim was false, but the storyline stuck with a growing number of evangelical pastors who fretted that pro-life advocacy was turning off prospective converts. Acting on the advice of church-growth consultants armed with marketing surveys, many pastors retooled their primary worship services. Sunday mornings were no longer about biblical proclamation aimed at equipping believers to be salt and light in the culture. They were about addressing the felt needs of unchurched seekers. True, securing courageous pastoral leadership on abortion was always a challenge, but now pro-lifers heard that their advocacy for the unborn was sabotaging the Great Commission aims of the local church. As Gregg Cunningham points out, a large number of evangelical congregations "became so seeker-sensitive they were believer worthless."[12]

And just when pro-lifers thought it couldn't get worse, the evening of November 3, 1992, decisively put to rest any hope of victory before the new century. A pro-abortion candidate won the presidency of the United States in an electoral landslide. Abortion advocates not only controlled the federal courts; they now commanded the executive and legislative branches of government. Conservative pundits said this would never happen. The American people, so the argument went, were more or less pro-life, and if pollsters would only ask fair questions, we'd see that. Our primary problem was activist judges and a biased press, not the voting public.

The political winds of 1992 suggested otherwise. Bill Clinton's bifurcated stance on abortion—"It should be safe, legal, and rare"—resonated with many voters who wanted to have their cake and eat it too. As journalist Christopher Caldwell pointed out, Americans like to condemn abortion with words but keep the option legally available:

Even where Americans claim to disapprove most strongly of abortion, they booby-trap their disapproval so that it never results in the actual

12 Cunningham said this often during his pro-life training seminars in the 1990s.

curtailment of abortion rights. A pro-life regime is not really something Americans want—it's just something they feel they ought to want.[13]

Indeed, a citizenry that was truly pro-life would press Clinton to explain *why* abortion should be rare. After all, if it does not intentionally kill an innocent human being, why care about making it rare? But if it does intentionally kill an innocent human being, isn't that reason enough to legislate against it? A majority of Clinton voters didn't care to ask. It was enough that their candidate personally opposed the practice. Later, when Clinton proved to be anything but moderate on abortion—twice vetoing legislation that said you cannot pierce the skulls of partially born fetuses and vacuum out their brains—they shrugged their shoulders and supported him anyway.

By Clinton's second term, pro-life messaging was itself conflicted. Should pro-life advocates focus on the grisly reality of late-term abortion or on the felt needs of abortion-minded women? For many pro-life leaders, the verdict was in. Focusing on abortion was a mistake. We'd won the moral debate over the humanity of the unborn and the evil of abortion, so they claimed, but had failed to convince women that abortion was not in their own best interest. The pro-life movement as a whole, not just pregnancy centers, needed to focus less on babies and more on the felt needs of women.[14] Our problem was practical, not moral.

But was it? If women opting for abortion truly agreed with pro-lifers on the moral question, why did they consider it conceivable to kill their fetuses for practical problems but never their born children?[15] A mother who tells you, "I truly believe my unborn offspring is a human being with a right to life, but I will kill him anyway to solve my practical problem," has a deeply flawed, utilitarian worldview completely at odds with pro-life ethics. She may convey pro-life sentiment, but she doesn't agree with pro-lifers that unborn humans share a profound and equal dignity with born ones. That is a moral problem, not a practical one. Likewise, a man who says, "I personally oppose abortion but want it to be legal," may not like

---

13 Christopher Caldwell, "Why Abortion Is Here to Stay," *The New Republic*, April 15, 1999.

14 Paul F. Swope, "Abortion: A Failure to Communicate," *First Things*, April 1998.

15 Francis J. Beckwith, "Taking Abortion Seriously: A Philosophical Critique of the New Prolife Rhetorical Shift," in *Life and Learning X: Proceedings of the Tenth University Faculty for Life Conference, June 2000 at Georgetown University*, ed. Joseph W. Koterski (Washington, DC: University Faculty for Life, 2002), 119–40.

abortion, but he doesn't truly oppose it. Nor does he grasp the nature of moral reasoning.[16] After all, is there any morally serious person in America today who argues that while he personally opposes spousal abuse, he won't oppose you beating your wife? Meanwhile, polling data suggested that the public had indeed settled the moral question of abortion but not in a manner favorable to pro-lifers. A whopping 62 percent supported its continued legality in the first trimester.[17] This was not a practical problem but a deeply moral and intellectual one.

The Arrival of a Pro-Life Intellectual

Put simply, pro-lifers in the 1990s had problems much worse than activist judges and biased pollsters. We had idea problems. The worldview assumptions that made abortion plausible to many of our fellow citizens were deeply entrenched in the culture and weren't going away anytime soon. A bigger March for Life was not going to fix that problem. To position ourselves for eventual victory, we had to reengage the public with a persuasive case for life that could compete at the highest levels of academia and government.

But that was a tall order. The abortion controversy was rigged in favor of cultural elites who did not take us seriously. Instead of refuting pro-life arguments, they dismissed them as articles of faith with no standing in the public square. To compete in the marketplace of ideas, pro-life advocates needed Ivy League talent to put their arguments on equal footing with pro-abortion ones. They needed someone within academia to rebuild their movement into a formidable intellectual force to be reckoned with, despite political headwinds.

Robert P. George gave marginalized pro-life advocates a good dose of intellectual toughness. First, he reset the ground rules of the abortion debate, giving pro-life arguments a fighting chance to be heard. Second, he confronted a destructive view of the human person that made abortion plausible to millions of Americans. Third, he helped restructure the face

16 Carl E. Olson, "The Case against Abortion: An Interview with Dr. Francis Beckwith, Author of *Defending Life*," *Ignatius Insight*, December 5, 2007.

17 Susan Yoachum, "California Pro-Choice—Early-on Poll Says Late-Term Abortions Opposed," *San Francisco Chronicle*, March 10, 1997; CBS News and *The New York Times*, CBS News / *New York Times* Monthly Poll #1, January 1998. Support for early abortion has held at 61 percent in a June 25, 2021, AP poll. David Crary and Hannah Fingerhut, "AP-NORC Poll: Most Say Restrict Abortion after 1st Trimester," *AP*, June 25, 2021, https://apnews.com/.

of pro-life advocacy, elevating rank-and-file activists into a movement of thinkers equipped to engage at the level of ideas.

Resetting the Terms of Engagement

George began by challenging the ground rules that prevented pro-life arguments from getting a hearing in the first place. Chief among them was the secularist demand for strict metaphysical neutrality. George argued that such a demand was utterly fallacious.

First, abortion advocacy, he claimed, is driven not by pure empirical reasoning but by an aggressive secular orthodoxy that was anything but neutral in its fundamental assumptions of truth and human value. On the contrary, secularism affirms that it alone should be the standard for public affairs. Since the final ethical standard is the individual, secularism claims to make prudential pronouncements, not moral ones, about public policy. In fact, the ideology of "public reason," advocated by figures such as John Rawls, holds that any belief system asserting transcendent moral authority is unable to provide guidance for public life. Individuals who hold such convictions should keep them private.[18] As George has countered, however, secular-neutralist orthodoxy pushed a set of comprehensive doctrines in its own right about the nature of reality and thus was not entitled to privileged standing in the public square.

Second, metaphysical neutrality is impossible. Everyone in the abortion debate does metaphysics. Either you believe that each and every human being has an equal right to life, or you don't. Pro-life advocates, following the Declaration of Independence and Abraham Lincoln, hold to an intrinsic view of human value. That is, all humans are equally valuable in virtue of the kind of thing they are, not some function they perform. Although they differ immensely with respect to talents, accomplishments, and degrees of development, they are nonetheless equal in their fundamental dignity because they share a common human nature. Their right to life comes to be when they come to be (at fertilization). Conversely, abortion-choice advocates espouse a functionalist view of human value. Being human is nothing special. What matters is your ability to immediately exercise an acquired property like self-awareness, desires, or sentience. Given that

18 George, *Clash of Orthodoxies*, 4–7, 42–43.

embryos and fetuses cannot immediately exercise these acquired properties, they have no right to life.

Notice that both positions—the intrinsic view and the functionalist view—use philosophical reflection to answer the same metaphysical question: What makes humans valuable in the first place? If the pro-life view is disqualified for asking metaphysical questions, the pro-choice view is as well.

Third, George argued, state neutrality is impossible. Either the state recognizes the humanity of the unborn and thus protects them, or it doesn't and thus permits killing them. Suppose it's 1860, and the Supreme Court takes no position on the humanity of slaves but affirms the legal right to own them as property. Would anyone with a functioning conscience consider this neutral?

Fourth, opposition to abortion is not an article of blind faith, as secularists allege. To the contrary, pro-life advocates present arguments for their position and defend them with reasons that are rationally superior to those offered by abortion advocates. Rather than relying merely on scriptural injunctions or ideological rallying cries, pro-life advocates began to adopt George's use of natural law to make their points. Asserting that there are moral truths accessible to all people in creation, pro-life advocates developed a new line of argument more persuasive in the public square. In this case, natural law leads us to the science of embryology, demonstrating that the unborn are distinct, living, and whole human beings.

In advancing the argument that the human embryo is deserving of the status of personhood, George supplanted the pro-choice line of argumentation, which relied on its own interpretation of the science surrounding human embryology to justify the unmitigated killing of life in the womb. Throughout the corpus of his work, George has dismantled the notion that killing human embryos and fetuses in later stages of human development is merely good health care. He notes, "The opinion that abortion is good medicine is a philosophical, ethical, and political opinion; its judgement is brought to medicine, not a judgement derived from it."[19] Thus, to expose the false narratives and pseudoscience of the pro-choice orthodoxy, George laid out the biological facts that accord with the personhood of the human

---

19   Robert P. George, *Conscience and Its Enemies: Confronting the Dogmas of Liberal Secularism* (Wilmington, DE: ISI Books, 2013), 190.

embryo and then constructed the ethical and political implications that appropriately account for the personhood of the embryo.

Unlike somatic cells that are mere parts of larger human beings, human embryos are whole living organisms that direct their own internal development. Since *Roe*, scientific research has conclusively demonstrated that the human embryo is a new organism completely separate from the mother at conception.[20] There is no rational basis for affirming that an embryo is simply a part of another body; it is itself a body. Apart from any intervention or medical deficiency, the embryo will mature through different stages of development, and when he or she matures into adulthood, that individual will be the same organism as the embryo in the mother's uterus.

Philosophically, pro-life advocates contend that you are identical to your former embryonic self. You didn't come from an embryo. You once were an embryo. George has emphasized that the embryo, which is genetically distinct from both the father and the mother, is a distinct human being, a new individual. The growth of an embryonic person into an adult is continuous, but it does not involve a change in substance.[21] Pro-life advocates rightly insist that this new human shares an essential quality with all others: personhood. Thus, if you are intrinsically valuable now, you were intrinsically valuable back then. George formally presents the pro-life argument as follows:

- Proposition 1: Human beings are valuable (as subjects of rights) in virtue of what they are.
- Proposition 2: Human beings are human physical organisms.
- Proposition 3: Human physical organisms come to be at conception.
- Therefore, what is intrinsically valuable (as a subject of rights) comes to be at conception.[22]

Rational judgment objectively leads us from scientific facts to moral reasoning. From this it follows that if it is wrong to discriminate on the

20 Dobbs v. Jackson Women's Health Organization, 597 US __ (2022).
21 George, *Clash of Orthodoxies*, 72–73.
22 Patrick Lee and Robert P. George, "The Wrong of Abortion," in *Contemporary Debates in Applied Ethics*, ed. Andrew I. Cohen and Christopher Heath Wellman, Contemporary Debates in Philosophy 4 (Malden, MA: Blackwell, 2005), 17–18.

basis of skin color and gender, it is wrong to do so on the basis of size, stage of development, location, or degree of dependency. People of good will do not need special revelation to recognize these truths. They are accessible through reason. Dismissing them with phony appeals to religion is a dodge, not a refutation, one that pro-lifers should call out.

That's precisely what George did in a 1998 exchange with Stanley Fish of Duke University. Two years prior, Fish published an article in *First Things* arguing that rational discourse on abortion was near-impossible because the two sides have radically different starting points. Pro-life advocates begin with religion: abortion is a sin against God, who infuses life at conception. Pro-choice advocates begin with science: the decision to abort should be made according to the best scientific opinion about when life begins. There was no way to bridge the two given that they can't even agree on what the conversation is about.[23] George replied with equal vigor that the question of when life begins is not a theological inquiry (or even a metaphysical one) but an empirical one. To answer it, we go to the science of embryology, not religion. True, pro-life Christians see abortion as a sin against God, but they do so precisely because it is the unjust taking of human life.[24] Indeed, nothing would please pro-life advocates more than to have the issue of abortion resolved precisely in accordance with the best scientific evidence as to when a new human being comes into existence as a self-integrating organism whose unity, distinctness, and identity remain intact as it develops. Later, when both men were panelists at the 1998 American Political Science Association Convention, Fish publicly conceded George's point.[25] For battle-weary pro-lifers, it was a defining moment. George demonstrated that pro-life arguments could prevail in a skeptical public square.

At bottom, for George, the claim that unborn humans have value and a right to life is no more religious than saying they don't. Either they do, self-evidently, or they do not. It's also no more religious than saying that toddlers have value and a right to life. The inherent dignity of human life has been recognized across cultural and historical boundaries because it is

---

23 Stanley Fish, "Why We Can't All Just Get Along," *First Things*, February 1996.

24 George, *Clash of Orthodoxies*, 67.

25 Charles Colson and Nancy Pearcey, *How Now Shall We Live?* (Carol Stream, IL: Tyndale, 1999), 130–31.

evidently reasonable. It is written into the fabric of the universe itself; our conscience testifies to this. As embryology has discovered, this life, worthy of respect and protection, does not begin at birth or self-awareness; it begins at conception. The pro-life position is not only grounded in divine revelation; all claims for human value rest on prior metaphysical commitments that one has toward the view of life's innate dignity.

As a professor of jurisprudence, George's pro-life scholarship has not been limited to philosophical debates. His work has proved crucial in formulating pro-life implications in public policy. In addition to demonstrating that the case against abortion is reasonable, he has shown that it is appropriate and crucial that those moral convictions be implemented in legislation and court cases. From its beginning, our nation has respected natural law as a basis for its positive law. George has explained that "the common good of public morality, that is, the good of a healthy moral ecology, generates obligations in justice for all of us, just as do the common goods of public health and safety."[26] It is from that law that our "inalienable rights" in the Declaration of Independence come. Legislating morality is not a violation of religious disestablishment when it aligns with what all rational agents know to be good by virtue of their practical reasoning skills.

Applied to the issue of abortion, natural law clearly recognizes the personhood of the unborn beginning at conception. As a precept of natural law, the sanctity of human life should be held sacred by every person and every nation. For George and other natural law proponents, the unjust nature of abortion transcends what is codified into a written code. The value and dignity of the unborn is a right that precedes its codification into a written text of law. Simultaneously, the American legal tradition before *Roe* upheld one's right to not be deprived of the intrinsic right to life from those who would impinge on it. Even when one branch of government failed to apply the natural right to life acknowledged by the Declaration, other Americans recognized the need for a fresh defense of human dignity. As the Supreme Court dehumanized slaves in *Dred Scott v. Sandford*, rejecting their citizenship, Abraham Lincoln decried the court's decision as unconstitutional and, more importantly, in violation of universal moral precepts. George rightly makes the case that our

26 George, *Clash of Orthodoxies*, 94.

relationship with *Roe* is the same: we as human beings and as republican citizens ought to uphold the value of human life and defy unjust legislation that violates natural law.[27]

Furthermore, constitutional democracy is most effective when it desires to promote the common good. It presumes both the dignity and equality of every individual. When democracy ceases defending its weakest members, the unborn, it fundamentally fails as a project.[28] Protecting the unborn is consistent with the fundamental right to life that is already secured in our nation's law. It is on this basis that George's advocacy for the pro-life cause has been so effective. The defense of the unborn is both rational and completely consistent with America's legal tradition. In the present-day abortion debate, the enemies of the unborn have attempted to castigate the aims of the pro-life movement by calling *Roe* settled law. Through advocating for a natural law jurisprudence, Robert George has not only demonstrated that the so-called right to terminate life in the womb is an unsettled point in American jurisprudence, but he has also proved it to be completely opposed to the aims of the American legal project. The Bill of Rights and subsequent amendments to the Constitution were not enshrined to dispense unfettered liberties to the citizenry to constitute their lives in any manner they desire, even at the expense of others. Rather, ordered liberty as promoted by the Constitution ought to give all members of society the freedom to contemplate, pursue, and achieve the goods that are known through natural law.

It is precisely for this reason that abortion is a heinous evil. Far from being a fine point of debate in the American legal system and the broader American culture, abortion deprives the most vulnerable members of society from pursuing the goods that the Constitution gives them the freedom to pursue through the unjust termination of their lives. Through the natural law jurisprudence advocated by Robert George, the pro-life legal movement in the United States has a reinvigorated and sustained effort to reverse the trajectory of abortion law of the last fifty years so that every life in the womb may be protected by law to come to fruition and pursue meaningful lives.

27   Robert P. George, "'A Republic ... If You Can Keep It': Why Lincoln Defied *Dred Scott* and We Must Defy *Roe*," *First Things*, January 22, 2016, https://www.firstthings.com/.
28   George, *Clash of Orthodoxies*, 133–34, 142.

Exposing a Destructive and Dehumanizing Worldview

In their zeal to defend unborn life, early pro-life advocates often ignored the underlying worldview assumptions that made abortion plausible to their fellow citizens. As a result, they were talking right past their critics.

In particular, they failed to address questions of philosophical anthropology—namely, what people ultimately believed about the nature and purpose of human life. Philosophical anthropology answers questions like What does it mean to be human? and What makes us valuable in the first place? How you answer largely determines your position on abortion. Nevertheless, almost no one in evangelicalism was addressing these questions in the 1990s, especially in seeker-driven churches. It took a Catholic scholar like George to demonstrate their vital importance in defending life.

Consider the claim "The unborn are human, but they are not persons." Idling behind that claim is a philosophical anthropology known as body-self dualism. According to this thinking, the real you has nothing to do with your body, which is mere subpersonal matter in motion. The real you is your thoughts, aims, desires, capacity for relationships, and other traits associated with higher cognitive function.[29] Before you gain (or after you lose) these traits, your physical body exists, but you do not. True, at fertilization a physical human organism came to be, but the real you showed up later.

Personhood theory applies body-self dualism to law and ethics. Personhood theory says that being human isn't enough to ground your right to life. For example, embryos and fetuses may be human, but they are potential persons, not actual ones. Only actual persons—that is, those with a selected level of cognitive function—have value and a right to life. Lose that function, and you forfeit your right to life. In short, we are left with two classes of human beings: human nonpersons we can legally kill and human persons we can't. If you don't make the grade, actual persons can override your interests, including your right to life.

As George points out, body-self dualism is counterintuitive. You are forced to say things like "My body existed before I did" or "I was mere matter until my conscious self showed up." You also must admit that you've never hugged your mother, since one cannot hug desires, thoughts, and

---

29 Robert George, *Clash of Orthodoxies*, 34–36. See also Patrick Lee and Robert P. George, *Body-Self Dualism in Contemporary Ethics and Politics* (Cambridge: Cambridge University Press, 2008).

aims. It also cannot explain simple statements like "You see." Sensory acts like seeing involve bodily acts (via the eyes) and intellectual acts (via the mind). Both are inextricably wound up in human nature.[30]

Meanwhile, personhood theory grounded in body-self dualism cannot account for fundamental human equality. Does each and every human being have an equal right to life, or do only some have it in virtue of some characteristic that none of us share equally and may come and go within the course of our lifetimes? If an arbitrarily selected trait like self-awareness (or any other cognitive function) grounds fundamental human value, and we don't share that trait equally, those with more of it have a greater right to life than those with less. Human equality is a myth.

Worse still, personhood theory justifies and perhaps requires intentional killing outside the womb. Fetuses and newborns are not self-aware. Can we kill both? Meanwhile, we're left with a philosophical foundation for involuntary euthanasia and involuntary organ donation. Put simply, if the interests of actual persons override the rights of potential ones, what's wrong with intentionally killing cognitively disabled patients to benefit others? On personhood theory, cognitively disabled humans not only *could* be but *should* be used for organ harvesting that benefits actual persons. Suppose a tornado destroys an elementary school for intellectually gifted children, leaving dozens of young victims in dire need of organ transplants. Around the corner, a daycare facility for kids with severe cognitive disabilities is spared. Why can't we procure organs from the cognitively disabled kids to save the gifted ones? After all, the interests of actual persons always override those of potential ones.

Body-self dualism is profoundly destructive to a Christian view of the human person. It undermines the fundamental equality of all image bearers and divides us along arbitrary lines. Why does cognitive function confer value in the first place? And why *that* trait and not something else?

Restructuring Pro-Life Advocacy

Imagine introducing yourself as a pro-life apologist at an evangelical philosophical conference in 1992. You'd likely be met with puzzled looks.

---

30 Robert George and Christopher Tollefsen, *Embryo: A Defense of Human Life*, 2nd ed. (Princeton, NJ: Witherspoon Institute, 2011), 72.

If you introduce yourself that way today, you might be asked to present a paper. What's changed?

What's changed is that because of men like Robert P. George—and those influenced by him—pro-life advocates take their intellectual commitments far more seriously than they did in 1992. For example, at Life Training Institute, where I serve as president, we're seeing a growing number of aspiring pro-life apologists eager to engage at the idea level. They're reading substantial defenses of the pro-life position by Francis J. Beckwith, Christopher Kaczor, Patrick Lee, and Hadley Arkes and using what they've learned to enthusiastically engage arguments from critics such as Michael Tooley, Jeff McMahan, David Boonin, and Judith Jarvis Thomson.

The transformation of pro-lifers into thinkers has not been lost on our opponents. As early as 2008, abortion-choice advocates Kate Michelman and Frances Kissling lamented that a new generation of pro-life advocates present "a sophisticated philosophical and political challenge" to what was once considered a settled debate.[31]

It's only going to get worse for Michelman and Kissling. Pro-life apologists are now keynoting major worldview conferences sponsored by Alliance Defending Freedom, the Colson Center, Focus on the Family, Stand to Reason, and Summit Ministries—to name a few. They're also equipping students at Catholic and Protestant high schools. Thirty years ago, a pro-life assembly at one of these schools consisted of an abstinence talk or perhaps a postabortion testimony. While both topics are vital to character formation, they do not persuade students that the pro-life position is true and reasonable to believe. Now Christian schools increasingly recognize the need to equip their students intellectually before sending them off to the secular university.

Admittedly, abortion is not going away tomorrow. Now that *Roe* has been reversed, the conflict will intensify. Already, an aggressive woke culture defines pro-life advocates as oppressors and seeks to cancel their arguments. But pro-life advocates aren't going to budge. Thanks to men like Robert George, we're a much tougher bunch than we were in 1992.[32]

---

31 Frances Kissling and Kate Michelman, "Abortion's Battle of Messages," *Los Angeles Times*, January 22, 2008.

32 I want to thank Christopher Parr and Caleb Newsom for their assistance with this chapter.

10

Taking Courage in the
Truth about Marriage

Robert P. George and the Defense of the Family

Jennifer Marshall Patterson

LAW IS A MORAL TEACHER. Even the campaign to make law "neutral" between competing conceptions of marriage reveals as much.[1] "There is no neutral marriage policy," Robert P. George has stated.[2] Law inevitably teaches a view of marriage.

What the law has taught for the last half century is what George refers to as a "revisionist view" of marriage. Since the first no-fault divorce law in the United States in 1969, marriage has become increasingly associated with adults' private pleasure and dissociated from the well-being of children and the common good of society. "The institutions of marriage and the family have plainly been weakened in cultures in which large numbers of people have come to understand themselves as 'satisfaction seekers,'" wrote George in 1993.[3]

When George entered the academic arena in 1985, the United States was in the midst of a decades-long upheaval in marriage habits. The marriage

---

1 Robert P. George, *The Clash of Orthodoxies: Law, Religion, and Morality in Crisis* (Wilmington, DE: ISI Books, 2001), 75.
2 Sherif Girgis, Ryan T. Anderson, and Robert P. George, *What Is Marriage? Man and Woman: A Defense* (New York: Encounter Books, 2012), 96.
3 Robert P. George, *Making Men Moral: Civil Liberties and Public Morality* (New York: Oxford University Press, 1993), 37.

rate had declined for decades. Divorce, cohabitation, and unwed childbearing had risen sharply for more than a decade. This erosion of the institution of marriage had debilitating consequences for individuals, especially
children, and for society as a whole. Social science researchers were only
beginning to assess the extent of these negative outcomes in the late 1980s
and early 1990s.

Meanwhile, political philosophy was in the thrall of John Rawls's theory
of justice as fairness.[4] Rawls argued that fairness required government to be
neutral with respect to competing worldviews concerning the good. Civic
discourse, he insisted, should be conducted in terms of "public reason."
Arguments should be based on the kinds of justification with which all
reasonable citizens could agree. Rawls's "public reason" standard explicitly
ruled out arguments derived from comprehensive worldviews, including
religion and natural law.[5] This revisionist account of what constitutes reason
for public purposes shaped the dynamics of discourse even as the revisionist
account of marriage was taking hold in the public mind.

For more than three decades, George's work has resisted this revisionism
in marriage and the restriction of moral reasoning about it. Evangelicals
can learn much from his efforts to recover the understanding of marriage
as a comprehensive, monogamous, and permanent relationship of husband
and wife in public policy, private initiatives, and practice. In good evangelical fashion, this chapter makes three alliterative points about George's
work on marriage, noting his coalition efforts, his case for marriage, and
his call to courage.

Coalition Efforts

Everyone involved in publicly making the case for marriage in recent
decades can point to ways their efforts have benefited from the work of
Robby George. Sometimes this has been through his direct, personal ef-

---

4   John Rawls's A Theory of Justice was published in 1971. He developed these ideas further in
    Political Liberalism, published in 1993.
5   Rawls made adjustments to the idea of public reason during the course of his career but never
    to the point that religious argument could be more than superfluous to the kind of justification
    he insisted was needed for civic discourse. His last formulation allowed for arguments to be
    made on the basis of comprehensive worldviews but required that proponents provide "in due
    course" justification under the strictures of public reason. See John Rawls, Justice as Fairness:
    A Restatement (Cambridge, MA: Belknap Press of Harvard University Press, 2001).

forts, in other cases through the network of institutions and projects he has helped launch. For as much as George stands out for his singular example in making the case for marriage, a significant feature of his influence has been working to expand public leadership on marriage. This he has done through developing coalitions; teaching, mentoring, and partnerships; and encouraging diverse initiatives that go beyond the intellectual to shape habits and culture.

Building Coalitions: Marriage, the Public Good,
and the Manhattan Declaration

Two examples, one among academic scholars and one among Christian leaders, illustrate coalition building to respond to particular challenges. In 2006, *Marriage and the Public Good: Ten Principles* was published by the Witherspoon Institute, an organization founded by George and Luis Tellez. The book emerged from a colloquium on marriage with experts in law, philosophy, psychiatry, economics, sociology, and history. The colloquium and monograph sought to address the conceptual challenge to marriage from changes in law and culture over several decades. Marriage was "losing its preeminent status as the social institution that directs and organizes reproduction, childrearing, and adult life."[6]

Marriage and the Public Good sought to show "why the public has a deep interest in a socially supported normative understanding of marriage."[7] Drawing on science and philosophy, it argued that marriage is the lifelong union of husband and wife that promotes their welfare and that of any children they might bear. Cultural recognition of this reality strengthens civil society, political liberty, limited government, and the common good. Public policy either supports or detracts from such an understanding of marriage. To support it, the document proposed policies to preserve the institution of marriage as one man and one woman, reform divorce law, end marriage penalties in welfare programs, expand family tax relief, and attend to the interests of children conceived through fertility treatments with anonymous donors.[8]

---

6   Witherspoon Institute, *Marriage and the Public Good: Ten Principles* (Princeton, NJ: Witherspoon Institute, 2006), 10.
7   Witherspoon Institute, *Marriage and the Public Good*, 11.
8   Witherspoon Institute, *Marriage and the Public Good*, 7.

A second major coalition example is the Manhattan Declaration, a statement of Christian solidarity on the issues of life, marriage, and religious liberty.[9] Drafted by George in conjunction with Timothy George of Beeson Divinity School and Charles Colson, the document was signed by 150 evangelical, Catholic, and Eastern Orthodox leaders at the time of its release in fall 2009.[10] More than half a million others have signed it since.

Claiming the mantle of historic Christian witness against injustice and social ills, the Manhattan Declaration challenged the revisionist view of marriage with a biblically reasoned account in the interest of the common good. Citing Genesis 2:23–24 and Ephesians 5:32–33, the statement explained that marriage is ordained by God, central to his covenant at creation, and reflective of the union of Christ and the church. Yet the church has not lived up to this high view of marriage:

> We confess with sadness that Christians and our institutions have too often scandalously failed to uphold the institution of marriage and to model for the world the true meaning of marriage. Insofar as we have too easily embraced the culture of divorce and remained silent about social practices that undermine the dignity of marriage we repent, and call upon all Christians to do the same.[11]

Throughout history, Christian believers and unbelievers have understood the marriage union of man and woman to be the basic social institution: "Marriage is an objective reality . . . that it is the duty of the law to recognize and support for the sake of justice and the common good."[12] When law fails to do so, it leads to religious-liberty conflicts for those who dissent from the government-endorsed view of marriage and to an undermining of parental authority as schools teach children contrary to parents' beliefs. It also harms the common good "when the law itself, in its critical pedagogical function, becomes a tool for eroding a sound un-

9   "Manhattan Declaration: A Call of Christian Conscience," November 20, 2009, https://www.manhattandeclaration.org/.
10   Original signatories included, among others, Timothy Keller, Albert Mohler, and Joni Eareckson Tada.
11   "Manhattan Declaration," https://www.manhattandeclaration.org/.
12   "Manhattan Declaration," https://www.manhattandeclaration.org/.

derstanding of marriage on which the flourishing of the marriage culture in any society vitally depends."[13]

In the face of these challenges, the Manhattan Declaration is a pledge among Christians to uphold the biblical truth about marriage. Motivated by love of neighbor, the declaration commits to advocate for the definition of marriage in law as one man and one woman and to seek to renew a culture supportive of the institution as a lifelong union. It calls for Christians to take courage in their confession.

Building Leadership: What Is Marriage?

George's teaching, mentoring, and partnerships on intellectual projects have cultivated emerging leaders who continue to take a public stand for marriage. A prime example is his coauthorship of a 2012 treatise on the meaning of marriage with two former students, Sherif Girgis, now associate professor of law at the University of Notre Dame, and Ryan T. Anderson, currently president of the Ethics and Public Policy Center. Their book, *What Is Marriage? Man and Woman: A Defense,* began with an article published by the *Harvard Journal of Law and Public Policy* in 2010.[14]

What Is Marriage? was the most significant scholarly contribution upholding the nature and meaning of marriage during the decade prior to the Supreme Court–mandated legal recognition of same-sex marriage in 2015. The book was cited twice by US Supreme Court Justice Samuel Alito in his dissenting opinion in the 2013 *United States v. Windsor* case, in which the majority struck down the federal Defense of Marriage Act. *What Is Marriage?* generated many derivative publications, media appearances, academic speeches, and presentations to policy makers. The authors' case for marriage, discussed below, provided public officials and concerned citizens with an important framework for engaging the marriage debate at a critical moment.

Building a Bridge from Head to Heart

What Is Marriage? is characteristic of the philosophical, legal, and moral arguments George has made on behalf of the institution of marriage

---

13 "Manhattan Declaration," https://www.manhattandeclaration.org/.
14 Sherif Girgis, Robert P. George, and Ryan T. Anderson, "What Is Marriage?," *Harvard Journal of Law and Public Policy* 34, no. 1 (Winter 2010): 245–87.

throughout his career. His example and encouragement have also fostered initiatives on a range of other domains.

The truth about marriage must reach not only the mind but also the heart and habits. George was a catalyst behind a major multifaith conference held at the Vatican in 2014,[15] from which a series of documentary films emerged.[16] Upholding the truth about marriage is above all a matter of practice, which requires formation to cultivate the virtues needed both before and after wedding vows. In 2005, Princeton students started the Anscombe Society to build community around an alternate view of marriage and sexuality to that of the campus hook-up environment. Chapters soon formed at other schools, and the Love and Fidelity Network was launched to support their efforts.[17] George has been a frequent speaker at the network's conferences.

Even as he has encouraged many voices to tell the truth about marriage, George's particular contribution has been a robust philosophical case for marriage, with special attention to its legal implications. His work especially addresses public confusion about the institution as it has been expressed most potently in the challenge to the legal definition of marriage.

This brings us to George's case for marriage.

The Case for Marriage

Over the course of decades, widespread divorce, cohabitation, and unwed childbearing changed how people thought about marriage. The purpose of marriage grew less clear as the practice of marriage became more associated with adults' emotions than children's needs. As the logic of permanence and the link to childbearing loosened, the historic norms of marriage began to appear like just that—outdated traditions that were evolving for modernity or antiquated religious ideals that were fading away in a less reverent society.

At the same time, the perceived rules of public engagement had changed. The Rawlsian notion of public reason had taken hold, allowing cultural gatekeepers in the media, the academy, and the law to give the general impression that religious and moral perspectives were inappropriate justifications in debates over a fundamental issue like marriage. Moreover, the

---

15 "Vatican Hosts International 'Humanum' Colloquium on the Complementarity of Man and Woman," *Inside the Vatican*, December 1, 2014, https://insidethevatican.com/.

16 *The Humanum Series*, Ecce! Films, 2016, http://www.eccefilms.com/.

17 Love and Fidelity Network, https://www.loveandfidelity.org.

argument that government policy defining marriage should be neutral with respect to rival views held considerable sway.[18]

Appeals to experience, religious belief, or moral tradition on behalf of marriage seemed to avail little. Where the practice of marriage should have made its purposes plain within the context of family, fractured households only compounded confusion about the institution. Where religious teaching and social tradition should have inspired explanation of the public significance of this union, the meaning of marriage had been for some time more assumed than argued.

This was the context in which the effort to change marriage law to recognize same-sex relationships emerged. Marriage had come to be seen by many—even some who continued to view it as the union of a man and a woman—as an emotional-sexual relationship set apart by its intensity and priority over other relationships. On such grounds, what objection could be made to allowing same-sex couples to get marriage licenses? Advocates charged that those who resisted could be motivated only by prejudice or by personal beliefs that held no standing in public debate. They argued that there was no rational basis for marriage as it had historically been recognized in law. In their view, the understanding of marriage as the union of husband and wife was irrational bigotry.

Such was the charge as the revisionist movement sharpened its focus to overturn the legal definition of marriage. Rebutting this challenge would require addressing more fundamental questions. What sets marriage apart from other human relationships? Why should the law particularly recognize this type of bond? What, fundamentally, is marriage? These are the questions George and his coauthors Girgis and Anderson undertook to answer in their 2012 book *What Is Marriage?* What follows is a summary of their case for marriage.

The Case for Marriage: A Summary[19]

Marriage is a comprehensive, permanent, monogamous relationship rooted in the biological complementarity of man and woman. It is an

---

18 Robert P. George, *Conscience and Its Enemies: Confronting the Dogmas of Liberal Secularism* (Wilmington, DE: ISI Books, 2016), 300, Kindle. George cites the example of Stephen Macedo, who, on the basis of Rawls, "claim[s] that law and policy must be neutral with regard to competing understandings of marriage and sexual morality."

19 This section summarizes arguments made in Girgis, Anderson, and George, *What Is Marriage?*

emotional and bodily union ordered to procreation, spousal unity, and shared family life. Marriage unites a man and a woman in the only type of relationship that brings about new human life and joins mother and father to structure a new family.[20]

Marriage is a distinct form of human relationship with a particular structure. This is true apart from any individual preference or social recognition. Marriage has an objective reality independent of spouses' inclinations or society's esteem for a particular type of relationship. Marriage is a basic good that actualizes human flourishing, both individually and in community.

The institution of marriage has public significance because its structure and purpose have implications for the ordering of civil society. The reality that a new human being may come to exist as a result of the bodily union of a man and a woman makes this relationship unique among all others. The fact that a child enters the world highly dependent, needing years of nurture from his mother and father in order to reach independence, makes these parents' comprehensive, permanent sharing in family life of particular consequence to society. No other social arrangement can provide as holistically and effectively for the all-encompassing needs of children—nor, for that matter, for the needs of mothers and fathers. Civil law acknowledged these unique realities of our human existence and government's interest in them. It did so by recognizing marriage as the comprehensive, permanent, monogamous union of man and woman.

Sexual complementarity explains why the other features have historically been part of the legal tradition of marriage. Recognizing the institution of marriage as one man and one woman—who join to form the only type of bodily union that can bring forth children and provide them with a mother and a father—makes the norms of permanence and monogamy nonarbitrary. These norms are rationally linked to the sexual complementarity on which marriage is based.

This pervasive understanding of the reality of marriage throughout human history has recently been challenged by a "revisionist" account,

---

20 Even childless marriages of husband and wife participate in the form of this comprehensive union: "Acts that fulfill the behavioral conditions of reproduction are acts of the reproductive-type even where the nonbehavioral conditions of reproduction do not happen to obtain." George, *Clash of Orthodoxies*, 85.

as Girgis, Anderson, and George call it. This account makes the desires of adults, not the needs of children, the central basis of the public recognition of marriage.

The revisionist account of marriage made its public policy debut in 1969 with no-fault divorce undermining permanency. The norm of sexual complementarity was targeted as early as 1993 by a Hawaii state supreme court decision that marriage licenses could not be denied to same-sex couples. This served as a wake-up call that the assumed definition of marriage as the union of a man and a woman could no longer be taken for granted and would need to be explicitly stated in law. Over the next two decades, Hawaii and a number of other states made this explicit in their state law or constitution. Voters or their elected officials in a total of forty-four states affirmed this understanding of marriage.[21]

Yet courts began to overrule citizens. Rulings by the United States Supreme Court in 2013 and 2015 struck down federal and state laws recognizing marriage as the union of one man and one woman. As a result of these decisions, all levels of government were required to recognize same-sex unions as marriage.

These developments severed the public institution of marriage from the norm of sexual complementarity of husband and wife. Instead, the distinguishing feature of such a reconfigured legal bond is the emotional weight one attaches to it.[22] As one advocate characterized it, this vision of marriage designates a relationship with your "Number One Person."[23] Monogamy, which logically proceeded from sexual complementarity, has subsequently been challenged by some.[24]

Revisionists described their project as expanding marriage by making more couples eligible for it. They appealed to fairness, arguing that marriage law should be neutral with respect to competing visions of it. George argues that the revisionist proposal is not an enlargement but a wholesale substitution. Sexual difference is the objective reality of marriage; without it, the essence, meaning, and purpose of the institution are altered. What

---

21 Girgis, Anderson, and George, *What Is Marriage?*, 5.

22 George, *Conscience and Its Enemies*, 273.

23 John Corvino and Maggie Gallagher, *Debating Same-Sex Marriage* (New York: Oxford University Press), 15.

24 Ryan T. Anderson, "How the Media Are Promoting Polyamory: The New 'Marriage Equality'?," *Daily Signal*, July 24, 2015, https://www.dailysignal.com/.

many have called the "redefinition" of marriage would be better described as the "abolition of marriage" in law.[25]

Public Impact of the Revisionist Account of Marriage

Replacing the meaning of marriage is not neutral in its effect. The law historically expressed the norms inherent in the reality of marriage. Participating in the institution of marriage actualized its norms even if spouses could not articulate its theory. Today, if a marriage license merely designates the intensity of emotional commitment around a sexual relationship, the law fails to teach the reality of marriage. This makes it harder to discern the objective meaning of marriage.[26]

The revisionist account of marriage delinks it from childbearing. Historically, marriage norms particularly provided stability and security for children. The more marriage is detached from the bearing and raising of children, the more it jeopardizes children's well-being. In recent decades, as the institution of family has weakened in its capacity to provide for the needs of children, government has expanded to provide for their welfare. The evidence is clear that this substitution has been far from adequate. In addition, the more that marriage is disconnected from children, the more that family courts must step in to address disputes over custody, financial support, and care arrangements.[27]

That the revisionist account is not neutral in its effects has been most immediately apparent with respect to religious liberty. Creative professionals providing wedding-related services have been sued for declining to use their talents to celebrate same-sex weddings. Christian adoption agencies whose convictions prevent them from placing children with same-sex couples have been forced out of child welfare services in several cities and states. Those who continue to speak and to act consistent with the truth about marriage and sexuality are increasingly facing religious liberty challenges in a number of areas of everyday life.

Rather than debating the reasons for which the law recognized marriage as one man and one woman, revisionists simply claimed that it was unjust for the law to do so. Such law was based, they argued, on the type of

---

25 George, *Conscience and Its Enemies*, 273.
26 Girgis, Anderson, and George, *What Is Marriage?*, 8–9.
27 Girgis, Anderson, and George, *What Is Marriage?*, 8–9.

contested moral worldview barred by Rawlsian public reason. The appeal to moral neutrality avoided having to debate the merits of the actual view of marriage to which it objected.[28]

The revisionists' purported neutrality does not stand up to scrutiny. As George explains, to argue that the law must be morally neutral about marriage is to make a moral argument. Neither the claim nor its justification are morally neutral.[29] This assertion with respect to marriage is an example of a broader problem with secularist claims generally. Despite revisionists' pretensions, "there can be no legitimate claim for secularism to be a 'neutral' doctrine that deserves privileged status as the national public philosophy."[30]

This is at the heart of what George has described as "the clash of orthodoxies" between secularists, on the one hand, and religious believers, on the other. The conflict arises over the "source and nature of morality and the proper relationship of moral judgment to law and public policy."[31] Orthodox secularism claims a monopoly on reason, narrowly defined in Rawlsian terms and therefore suitable to the neutrality it prescribes for the public square. But George faults secularism for being *inadequately* reasonable and aims to show that Christian morality is more rationally compelling.[32] A central argument of George's work is that we can reason about morality and that this should be a part of public discourse.

The New Natural Law Account of Marriage

This account of marriage is located in a larger moral-philosophy project known as new natural law theory. Following philosophers Germain Grisez and John Finnis, Robert George has been a leader in applying the theory to public moral questions of our day, such as life, marriage, and religious liberty. New natural law is a system of ethical reflection on certain basic human goods that are grasped by practical reason, that is, reason ordered toward action. As identified in this theory, basic human goods are intrinsic aspects of human flourishing and fulfillment, such as life and knowledge.

28 George, *Clash of Orthodoxies*, 77.
29 George, *Clash of Orthodoxies*, 75.
30 George, *Clash of Orthodoxies*, 20.
31 George, *Clash of Orthodoxies*, xiii.
32 George, *Clash of Orthodoxies*, 4.

These basic goods are noninstrumental. They are not means to further ends but ends in themselves—ends of human action. They are the particular objectives for which one acts, stated in terms that cannot be reduced to any further purpose for action. Because they constitute fundamental aspects of human well-being, these basic goods provide practical reason with opportunities to act. Choices toward these ends are intelligible: they have a discernible point in relation to human well-being and fulfillment (e.g., health is a good for which to act). These ends—these basic human goods—are the first principles of practical reason; they direct all rational reflection with respect to action. Basic human goods are reasons for action.

Thus far, the theory describes how any coherent practical reasoning works; it does not yet supply moral guidance.[33] Moral norms arise from the basic practical principles working together to guide choice.[34] Because these basic human goods constitute human well-being, when considered as a whole they direct action toward "integral human flourishing." "Morally good choices," George explains, "are choices that are in line with the various fundamental aspects of human well-being and fulfillment integrally conceived."[35]

Marriage is one of the several basic human goods, as is friendship. But on this account, marriage is distinct from friendship, not merely a more intense version of the same good.[36] Marriage is the one-flesh union of a man and a woman that is oriented to procreation and shared family life.[37] The relationship is an intrinsic good, not simply a means to the end of procreation.[38] By contrast, the revisionist view of marriage amounts to friendship (in which a spouse is your "Number One Person"), which is not inherently related to procreation.[39] The new natural law account also differs from accounts in which marriage is instrumentally related to procreation.[40]

---

33 Human acts can be intelligible and morally wrong. In describing the first principles of practical reason, new natural law theorists are simply showing how any end of human action is chosen under the aspect of the good, that is, as something that brings about an aspect of human flourishing, even if that conception is mistaken.

34 Robert P. George, *In Defense of Natural Law* (New York: Oxford University Press, 1999), 49.

35 George, *Conscience and Its Enemies*, 247.

36 Girgis, Anderson, and George, *What Is Marriage?*, 14.

37 Patrick Lee and Robert P. George, *Body-Self Dualism in Contemporary Ethics and Politics* (New York: Cambridge University Press, 2008), 179–80.

38 George, *Clash of Orthodoxies*, 78.

39 Lee and George, *Body-Self Dualism*, 179.

40 Lee and George, *Body-Self Dualism*, 179.

Call to Courage

George's arguments have contended with opposing viewpoints in the academy, legislatures, and courts. But perhaps even more important is what his argument and example have communicated to those who *share* his view of marriage. To these, his message has been to speak and to act boldly on the truth about marriage for the good of all.

When George began writing about the meaning of marriage, the vast majority of Americans agreed with the law's recognition of marriage as the union of one man and one woman. Yet the reasons for which the law had recognized this understanding of marriage were largely assumed and rarely articulated. At the same time, defending marriage on the basis of religious and moral worldviews was deemed inappropriate by the increasingly prevalent standards of Rawlsian public reason. These factors had a dampening effect on the public defense of marriage.[41]

George's efforts have had an important purpose in equipping and emboldening those who believe the truth about marriage to take a public stand. His case for marriage has provided a way to articulate the reasoning that was long implicit in marriage law. His larger philosophical argument has shown the restrictions of Rawlsian public reason to be arbitrary and incoherent. To claim that the law must be neutral between two competing moral visions of marriage is not morally neutral.

Citizens should be free to make religious and moral arguments in public discourse. They should also be equipped to reason well about the public significance of the truth about marriage. Most critically, they need the courage to do so.

Some commentators have suggested that the campaign to salvage marriage in law was doomed from the start because of the overwhelming cultural dynamics against it. George challenged one such writer's view in a January 2020 piece reflecting on the previous decade of developments in marriage law. "What has been missing . . . is not something that was unavailable to us," wrote George. "People could have mustered it, but too many didn't. I am referring, of course, to *courage*."[42]

---

41 Of course, many other cultural factors also contributed, but these are outside the scope of this chapter.

42 Robert P. George, "Courage, Love, and Sacrifice in the Fight for Marriage Reality," *Public Discourse*, January 5, 2020, https://www.thepublicdiscourse.com/.

Courage through solidarity has been a major aim of George's coalition-building efforts. The Manhattan Declaration, for example, sought to strengthen resolve among Christians to stand for marriage in the midst of cultural opposition, costly though that might be. It pledged to do so for the good of all.

Courage is bolstered by the confidence of taking a stand on sound reason. George's case for marriage has served this end. It shows the connection between the truth about marriage and human flourishing.[43] It has helped many articulate aspects of what they have long believed but have been unable to express adequately.

A failure of courage to stand for what is right is ultimately a failure of love, George has argued. To love our neighbor as we ought, we need to witness to this fundamental aspect of the reality God has designed:

> We seek to preserve marriage—the real thing—because of the profound respects in which a flourishing marriage culture serves and benefits all members of the community, beginning with children. We need courage, we need to *muster the courage*, to love as we should—self-sacrificially.[44]

The call to sacrificial love brings us to the foundation on which our witness to marriage must ultimately be grounded: the Bible's account of marriage and its relation to Christ's self-sacrifice for the church.

A Biblical Account of Marriage

The Bible's history of the human race begins and ends with a wedding.[45] Its opening scene is the union of Adam and Eve. It closes with the marriage feast of Christ and the church.

Genesis 1–2 communicates the fundamental aspects of marriage and its historical significance. Marriage is basic to the creation order and to human culture. It is the beginning of human society and the foundation on which God's image bearers can pursue the cultural mandate to fill and govern the earth (Gen. 1:27–28).

---

43 George, "Courage, Love, and Sacrifice."
44 George, "Courage, Love, and Sacrifice."
45 Herman Bavinck, *The Christian Family*, trans. Nelson D. Kloosterman, ed. Stephen J. Grabill (Grand Rapids, MI: Christian's Library, 2012), 1, 162, Kindle.

The institution of marriage was ordained by God from the very beginning. Genesis 2:23–25 establishes marriage as a relationship that is grounded in the sexual complementarity of a man and a woman, comprehensive, permanent, and monogamous. Marriage is the basis of family and essential to the pattern and formation of society (Gen. 2:24).[46]

Established at creation, the institution of marriage was reaffirmed after the fall. The covenant with Noah reiterated the cultural mandate to be fruitful and multiply (Gen. 9:1, 7), which depends on the marriage relationship. Yet the curse of sin has had devastating effects for the marriage relationship (Gen. 3:16). The Ten Commandments reinforced the norms of marriage by prohibiting adultery (Ex. 20:14).

Jesus confirmed the creation account and the law's teaching about marriage (Matt. 19:4–9). The New Testament writers returned to and amplified the ethical implications of the one-flesh union established by God (e.g., 1 Cor. 7:1–11; Eph. 5:31–33). Paul made explicit that marriage reflects the union of Christ and the church (Eph. 5:32), building on Old Testament descriptions of the relationship of God and his covenant people in terms of marriage (e.g., Isa. 54:5–6; 62:5; Jer. 2:2) and of the people's unfaithfulness to God in terms of adultery (e.g., Jer. 3:1; Hos. 1:2).

Ordained at creation, the pattern of marriage has remained a norm of ethics throughout human history.[47] It is central to divine image bearers' pursuit of their purpose in the midst of creation. As Herman Bavinck notes, "Husband and wife receive the assignment to help each other in the calling entrusted to the human race: to multiply and thus to subdue the earth."[48] Marriage is a covenant made publicly before God and fellow human beings, signifying the natural and spiritual importance of the institution. Marriage is a temporal reality that points to eternal realities (Eph. 5:32).

---

46 Herman Bavinck, *Essays on Religion, Science, and Society*, trans. Harry Boonstra and Gerrit Sheeres (Grand Rapids, MI: Baker Academic, 2008), 122. Bavinck writes, "Implied in marriage is the family; in the family [is implied] society; in society [is implied] unity, community, and cooperation of the human race. . . . Marriage and family contain the point of departure and principles of all kinds of relationships that will later develop in society."

47 John M. Frame, *Systematic Theology: An Introduction to Christian Belief* (Phillipsburg, NJ: P&R, 2013), 63, 789.

48 Bavinck, *Essays*, 122.

How should these biblical teachings shape an evangelical public witness about marriage?

First, marriage has an objective reality rooted in creation. It is permanently normative for human ethics. Evangelicals should confess and live by this truth about marriage.

Second, an evangelical account should communicate the public significance of marriage as the essential building block of human society. Marriage brings together the two halves of humanity for the future of humanity. Its structure and norms have consequences for the good of our neighbors. It is a natural institution that "acquires a richer and deeper significance through special revelation," as Bavinck writes. "Marriage is therefore not a Christian institution in the sense that it owes its origin and its arrangement to Christianity. For it dates from the creation, having received at that time its rule and law."[49] Christianity does not alter the essence or external purpose of the created institution of marriage, but it reforms its internal practice in the wake of sin and opens our eyes to the wider spiritual significance of the institution.

Third, an evangelical public witness to marriage can start the conversation on marriage anywhere. Our common experience of the created world gives us many points of contact to do so. The God who created the world formed the human intellect and established ethical norms. Scripture testifies to the coherence of a morally inscribed cosmos. Wisdom is woven into creation. Every discipline—from philosophy to social science to art—can help us glimpse that wisdom. Provided that Scripture is our ultimate grounding, Christians can draw on any observation or argument consistent with it to engage others.[50] Sin will have frustrating effects on our capacity to reason together, particularly given the dominance of emotivism in our day. Even so, a belief in God's common grace that restrains sin should cause us to call on others to reason well about life together in community, including about the institution of marriage. We should have confidence that such appeals can bear fruit with God's blessing.

Finally, evangelicals should confess and live by the transcendent truth about marriage. As a temporal institution, marriage points far beyond its earthly meaning. Paul tells us that marriage directs our attention to the

49 Bavinck, *Christian Family*, 44.
50 William Edgar, "The Reformed Tradition and Natural Law: A Response," in *A Preserving Grace: Protestants, Catholics, and Natural Law*, ed. Michael Cromartie (Grand Rapids, MI: Eerdmans, 1997), 129.

mystery of Christ and the church (Eph. 5:32). This truth—Christ's sacrifice for the church—is the pattern and the power for believers' sacrificial love for one another in marriage, in the church, and in our communities. A witness to this self-sacrificial truth to which marriage points is essential in Christians' conduct within marriage. The perennial propensity to fall from such witness means we must not take it lightly. Finally, this transcendent truth about marriage is an even more profound reason for us to stand for the truth about marriage in public life, especially when such a stand requires courage and self-sacrificial love.

Gleaning from George's Leadership on Marriage

George's leadership on marriage provides a number of examples that should inform evangelicals' public witness on marriage. To stand on the truth about marriage in dissent from official policy calls for pursuing solidarity in community and taking formation seriously. Forming coalitions within and beyond confessional boundaries to rebuild a marriage culture is a worthy model to follow. Likewise, George's case for marriage helps us better express reasons for the enduring public significance of marriage that are implicit in the institution inaugurated by God at creation. As such, it offers important insights for public discourse about marriage.

New natural law's epistemic justification of this case opens up a wider set of questions. Similarly, use of the theory as a normative system for all ethical reflection invites further scrutiny.[51] A full critique of these issues is outside the scope of this essay, but a few preliminary comments are relevant here.

In responding to questions about the priority of practical reason and the perceived neglect of metaphysics in their theory, new natural law proponents "affirm that basic goods and moral norms *are* what they are because human nature *is* what it is."[52] A fuller statement would acknowledge that moral norms and human nature *are* what they are because God *is* who he is. In other words, God's being and character are ultimately determinative of metaphysical reality and ethics.

---

51 George, *Conscience*, 247. For evangelicals, differing assumptions about the noetic effects of original sin and the relationship of nature and grace are relevant here.

52 Robert P. George, ed., *Natural Law Theory: Contemporary Essays* (Oxford: Oxford University Press, 1992), 33. See also Robert P. George, "Natural Law, God, and Human Dignity," in *Natural Law and Evangelical Political Thought*, ed. Jesse Covington, Bryan McGraw, and Micah Watson (New York: Lexington Books, 2013).

George acknowledges elsewhere that most natural law theorists do, in fact, "believe that the moral order, like every other order in human experience, is what it is because God creates and sustains it as such." At the same time, he explains, "natural law theorists also affirm that many moral truths, including some that are revealed, can also be grasped by ethical reflection apart from revelation."[53] Presumably this refers to special revelation, but it is worth clarifying—to avoid implying that reason has an independent sphere of jurisdiction—that we are never "apart from revelation." Because we are created in the image of God, endowed with conscience, and surrounded by general revelation, everything about us as humans and the world around us reveals aspects of God to us.

This understanding of revelation should shape our interactions with others. As theologian William Edgar has observed, when we engage with someone with whom we have fundamental disagreements, "we are facing not a *tabula rasa* but someone who is receiving God's revelation, whether acknowledged or not."[54] Because that person is made in the image of God, has a conscience, and possesses knowledge of God, our interactions should reach for these realities in the other. This should make us more assured of appealing to general revelation on behalf of any truth of creation. All this is encumbered with sin, but we trust in God's common grace to let glimpses of truth shine through.

Conclusion

Revisiting George's leadership on marriage is not an exercise in hindsight. It is a guide to the current, ongoing debate over the freedom to live according to the truth about marriage.

While the United States Supreme Court mandated in 2015 that the government must recognize same-sex marriage, it did not require churches, other private organizations, or individuals to affirm such relationships as marriage—nor should any court do so in the future. Christians and other citizens must continue to speak and to act consistent with the truth that marriage is the union of one man and one woman.

Immediately following the Court's decision in 2015, the debate shifted to whether we will be free to dissent from the government's new view of

53 George, "Natural Law, God, and Human Dignity," 116.
54 Edgar, "Response," 129.

marriage in our workplaces, schools, and public discourse. The debate also expanded to challenge the recognition that sex is a fixed biological reality—that we are created male and female.

Preserving the freedom to speak and to act in accord with the truth about marriage and created sexuality will require Christians and other concerned citizens to engage in public debate about these issues. We need to explain what marriage is and why it matters to society as a whole. Because we image God, our speech and action should testify to the way that God has made the world.

There is much more to be said about marriage. Telling the truth about marriage with its many facets is a multidisciplinary endeavor that needs the contributions of theologians, social scientists, artists, and educators. There are many more ways to witness to that truth than philosophical argument. But evangelicals can state clearly with Robert George that marriage is a comprehensive, monogamous, permanent relationship built on the complementarity of man and woman that provides for a child's need of a mother and a father. We should learn from his example the importance of solidarity in coalition and reasoning well in public debate. Above all, we should heed the call to take courage and to speak and to act in a manner that is consistent with the truth about marriage.

11

For Such a Time as This

Robert P. George on Religious Freedom

J. Daryl Charles

TRACING ANY ONE THEME in Robert P. George's wider repertoire of work, on the one hand, is akin to tracing yeast in dough, given how integrated his thinking is and the degree to which philosophy, law, history, religion, and public affairs intersect in his writings. On the other hand, based on my own reading of his work, three broader themes—or, more accurately, clusters of issues—tend to stand out. These are (1) broader "life" issues (which encompass abortion, marriage, bioethics, health care, and human sexuality); (2) law, religion, and public morality; and (3) religious freedom.[1]

Robert P. George's Work on Religious Freedom

The list of publications—whether journal essays, book chapters, or op-ed pieces—as well as presentations, public lectures, and personal testimony that George has devoted to the subject of religious freedom would seem almost endless. His work in defending religious freedom, for example, appears in publications as diverse as the *American Journal of Jurisprudence*, *First Things*, *Foreign Policy*, *Georgetown Journal of International Affairs*, *International Journal for Religious Freedom*, *Journal of International Affairs*, *Loyola of Los*

---

1 While it is true that all these issues, eventually, bear on religious freedom, as florists, bakers, photographers, and others can testify in our day and as is intimated in this chapter, for the sake of categorizing George's work, I will allow these distinctions to stand.

Angeles Law Review, National Affairs, National Review, Orbis, Public Discourse, Touchstone, Wall Street Journal, Washington Post, Weekly Standard, and *West Virginia Law Review.* All this (and more) is evidence that, for George, religious freedom has *priority* among our most basic civil liberties—a view that he makes explicit elsewhere: "There is a special sense in which freedom of religion has priority or at least a pride of place"; the reason for this is that "it protects an aspect of our flourishing as human persons that is architectonic to the way we lead our lives."[2]

Perhaps most instrumental in this regard was George's appointment in June 2013 as chair of the US Commission on International Religious Freedom (USCIRF).[3] The commission was established through the International Religious Freedom Act of 1998 as an independent, bipartisan federal government agency, working in conjunction with the State Department to respond with sanctions in cases of international human rights violation. Among the commission's responsibilities is publication of an annual report on religious freedom around the globe, paying particular attention to those countries of concern that consistently demonstrate a pattern of violating religious freedom.[4]

Upon assuming chairmanship of the commission, George summarized his perspective on religious freedom as a matter of basic human rights.[5] A common assumption, he noted, is that religious freedom is about compromise or negotiation. That is, we respect the other's freedom for reasons of political expediency or with a view to avoid strife and eliminate tensions. This mode of thinking, however, misses the very essence of religious freedom properly understood, George insisted. Religious freedom is not first and foremost a matter of compromise or political bartering; rather, it is an essential component of human dignity. We therefore honor and respect people in matters of personal conscience, and it is for this reason that we

---

2   Robert P. George, *Conscience and Its Enemies: Confronting the Dogmas of Liberal Secularism* (Wilmington, DE: ISI Books, 2013), 113.

3   USCIRF commissioners are appointed by the US president and the leadership of both political parties in the Senate and House of Representatives. George would serve as vice-chairman of the commission in 2014 and as chairman again in 2015.

4   The reports are accessible at https://www.uscirf.gov/.

5   See Robert P. George and Katrina Lantos Swett, "Religious Freedom Is about More than Religion," *Wall Street Journal,* July 25, 2013, https://www.wsj.com/. Swett was the outgoing USCIRF Commissioner.

promote religious freedom. Human flourishing, George maintained, is only possible under such conditions. Coerced belief—or coerced nonbelief, for that matter—is *no belief* at all.[6] America's founders and framers understood the distinction between mere tolerance and respect for matters of conscience, hence the broad-based commitment to religious freedom in their "experiment in ordered liberty." Today, with religious freedom collapsing and disappearing both in the Western context and around the globe, George argued, it needs to be advanced both at home and as a central element in US foreign policy.[7]

In testimony before the US House of Representatives' Committee on Foreign Affairs in May 2014, George stressed the need to hold countries around the globe accountable for basic human rights violations and denying religious freedom. This need, he insisted, should be extended to all people, "whether they are Ahmadis, Baha'is, Jews, my fellow Christians, Rohingya Muslims or other minority Muslims in various places, Tibetan and other Buddhists, Hindus, atheists, people of all faiths and people who profess no faith." "By any measure," he noted,

> religious freedom remains under serious assault across the globe. Our report reveals that a very substantial proportion of the world's population live in circumstances in which they are either victimized by their own governments, or by mobs or terrorists who operate with impunity because of a government's unwillingness or inability to do anything about it, including bringing perpetrators to justice—much less deterring the atrocities that are committed against them.[8]

The general structure of George's argument for religious freedom consists of three principal elements: (1) what it is, (2) why it matters, and (3) what our responsibilities and duties, in this light, should be. In its essence, George

---

6 In this vein, George writes, "To compel an atheist to perform acts that are premised on theistic beliefs that he cannot, in good conscience, share is to deny him the fundamental bit of the good of religion that is his. . . . Coercing him to perform religious acts does him no good, since faith really must be free, and dishonors his dignity as a free and rational person. The violation of liberty is worse than futile." George, *Conscience and Its Enemies*, 124.

7 George and Swett, "Religious Freedom."

8 Robert P. George, *Protecting Religious Freedom: U.S. Efforts to Hold Accountable Countries of Particular Concern*, May 22, 2014, https://www.govinfo.gov/.

understands religious freedom as an expression of human dignity. It mirrors what this nation's founders described as "the sacred rights of conscience."[9] Because it is rooted in human dignity and our awareness of living in a moral universe, in character it is universal as opposed to particular, intrinsic as opposed to extrinsic, public as opposed to private, and not preferential or favoring any particular faith group. Religious freedom, then, can be understood as a fundamental human right, an individual right, an institutional right, a public right, and indeed a fleeting right.[10]

Why does religious freedom matter, and why should it be a priority for both individuals and governments? A current assessment of our own society and the world yields the tragic conclusion, as noted in George's 2014 testimony before the House of Representatives, that "religious freedom remains under serious assault across the globe." Domestic as well as international challenges confront us at every turn. In Western culture, those obstacles tend to be legal-historical, philosophical, and moral in nature. In terms of foreign policy, despite lessons of recent history,[11] it has become increasingly difficult for Western nations, including the United States, to understand violations of religious freedom as (1) a fundamentally inhumane treatment by nations and governments of their own peoples and therefore (2) a central element in responsible foreign policy. Added to this is the fact that Western nations increasingly suffer from "fatigue" in terms of their involvement in humanitarian affairs. Yet it is a fact that terrorism, genocide, and egregious human rights violations are on the increase on a global level.

A central question with which we must be confronted, therefore, is this: What responsibilities and duties do relatively free nations have toward their international neighbors? That is, what particular responsibilities do nations like the United States (or coalitions of nations) have in respond-

---

9   James Madison, "July 23, 1813: Proclamation on Day of Public Humiliation and Prayer," University of Virginia, Miller Center, accessed May 15, 2022, https://millercenter.org/.

10 So Thomas Farr, "What in the World Is Religious Freedom?," Religious Freedom Institute, November 1, 2019, https://www.religiousfreedominstitute.org/.

11 Consider the important post–World War II charter documents such as the 1948 Universal Declaration of Human Rights (UDHR) and the 1966 International Covenant on Civil and Political Rights (ICCPR). For example, article 18 of the UDHR states, "Everyone has the right to freedom of thought, conscience, and religion; this right includes freedom to change his religion or belief, and freedom either alone or in community with others and in public or private, to manifest his religion or belief in teaching, practice, worship and observance."

ing to egregious human rights violations, at the center of which stands religious freedom?

Two volumes published by George are exceedingly helpful in acquainting the thoughtful lay (i.e., nontechnical) reader not only with the width and breadth of George's work but also with his understanding of religious freedom. *The Clash of Orthodoxies: Law, Religion, and Morality in Crisis* (2001) examines many of the pressing broader "life" issues in our time—among them, abortion, infanticide, no-fault divorce, euthanasia and physician-assisted suicide, and homosexuality and sexual disorder. Underlying these sociocultural disputes, as George argues, are competing views of the source and nature of morality and the essential relationship between moral judgment and law and public policy. It is George's commitment to expose the underlying nature of inherently ethical issues and to demolish the "orthodoxies" of a militant secularism that makes *The Clash of Orthodoxies* particularly useful.

Conscience and Its Enemies: Confronting the Dogmas of Liberal Secularism (2013) brings together in one volume previously published essays on sociocultural and legal issues that extend over a wide range of topics and contemporary controversies, including natural law, bioethics, marriage, abortion, political liberty, immigration, the abuse of judicial power, and religious liberty. Responding to the frequent claims by cultural gatekeepers that disagreement in the public sphere constitutes "hatred," "bigotry," and "intolerance," George marshals a counterattack on the basis of reason and moral principle—a counterattack that is relentless yet eminently reasonable, patient yet powerfully persuasive. As suggested by the volume's title, the rights and duties of conscience are indeed "sacred."

The Structure of George's Argument for Religious Freedom: A Closer Look

A hallmark of virtually all George's work—and particularly his work on religious freedom—is the central conviction that not religious faith per se but principled reason can guide human beings in their intuition of human dignity and moral reality. Public arguments—and religious freedom is an *inherently* public matter—require that religious believers set forth their convictions in a manner that is publicly accessible. Here we may cite support from the Catechism of the Catholic Church:

In defending the ability of human reason to know God, the Church is expressing her confidence in the possibility of speaking about him to all men and with all men, and therefore of dialogue with other religions, with philosophy and science, as well as with unbelievers and atheists.[12]

The catechism is explicit in its defense of the use of human reason: moral truths "are not beyond the grasp of human reason, so that even in the present condition of the human race, they can be known by all men."[13] Conscience has a rational basis that is capable of being communicated to fellow human beings.

This, of course, is not to deny the mutually supportive relationship between faith and reason. For in the words of John Paul II, "Faith and reason are like two wings on which the human spirit rises to the contemplation of truth; and God has placed in the human heart a desire to know the truth."[14] Reason, as George depicts it, is "a spiritual capacity" that is "capable of guiding choices that are truly free."[15] Deprived of reason, faith is inclined to rely on feeling and subjective experience; in this way it runs the risk of no longer being universal in its expression and in its accessibility.[16] Reason, moreover, is what challenges both the inquisitive as well as those with whom we disagree. In fact, George wishes to demonstrate that Christians "are right to defend their positions on key moral issues as *rationally superior* to the alternatives" proposed by their militantly secular critics.[17] George's criticism of the secular mindset is not that it is contrary to faith; after all, a secular worldview assumes, *in faith*, that certain things are nonnegotiable and that everyone has a personal view of ultimate reality. Rather, it fails *the test of reason* properly understood.

Appeals to religious authority, of course, have their place, as George is well aware. That place, however, is not in the context of philosophical,

---

12 *Catechism of the Catholic Church* (Washington, DC: United States Catholic Conference, 1994), no. 39 (p. 17).

13 *Catechism of the Catholic Church*, no. 39 (p. 17).

14 John Paul II, *Fides et Ratio* (encyclical letter), preface, Vatican, September 14, 1998, https://www.vatican.va/.

15 George, *Conscience and Its Enemies*, 246–47.

16 So John Paul II, *Fides et Ratio*, no. 48.

17 Robert P. George, *The Clash of Orthodoxies: Law, Religion, and Morality in Crisis* (Wilmington, DE: ISI Books, 2001), xiv (emphasis added). On George's personal understanding and assessment of John Paul II's important encyclical *Fides et Ratio*, see *Clash of Orthodoxies*, chap. 15, "On *Fides et Ratio*."

legal, or political debates that bear on public policy and that need public accessibility. Public policy should be predicated on *public reasons*. Perhaps, however, religious believers will chafe under this conviction of George's. Perhaps they are convinced that God's revelation through Scripture is adequate as the chief means by which to argue in the public sphere. But the problem with this view is that most people whom we need to engage in public will *not* share this basic starting point. Scripture for them will hold no authority. Thus, it behooves us to ask how we might get to "first base," as it were, in our public arguments.[18] In George's view, this necessitates a reliance on natural law moral reasoning.[19] Here we may illustrate. Arguments in support of traditional marriage or normative sexuality or against abortion—arguments that are increasingly being excluded from the public arena in our own cultural environment, thereby impinging more and more on the matter of religious freedom—have both merit and authority not only because "God has said so" but also because they are patent to all, logically reasonable and observable based on human perception of scientific, biological, social-psychological, and moral reality.[20] When moral laws, for example,

18 Our goal in public witness, of course, is faithfulness and not "success." The degree to which we are found faithful in our stewardship of creation has nothing to do with earthly measurements of how "successful" we might be in those varied endeavors.

19 Here I am in full agreement with George, having devoted a recent volume to the natural law underpinnings of religious freedom; see J. Daryl Charles, *Natural Law and Religious Freedom: The Role of Moral First Things in Grounding and Protecting the First Freedom* (New York: Routledge, 2018). On the importance of natural law moral reasoning more broadly, see as well J. Daryl Charles, "Returning to Moral 'First Things': The Natural-Law Tradition and Its Contemporary Application," *Philosophia Christi* 6, no. 1 (2004): 59–76; Charles, *Retrieving the Natural Law: A Return to Moral First Things* (Grand Rapids, MI: Eerdmans, 2008); Charles, "Saving a Bad Marriage: Liberalism and the Natural Law," *Modern Age* 52, no. 1 (Winter 2010): 71–75; Charles, "Burying the Wrong Corpse: Second Thoughts on the Protestant Prejudice toward Natural Law Thinking," in *Natural Law and Evangelical Political Thought*, ed. Jesse Covington, Brian McGraw, and Micah Watson (Lanham, MD: Lexington Books, 2012), 3–34; Charles, "The Kuyperian Option: Cultural Engagement and Natural Law Ecumenism," *Touchstone* (May/June 2018): 22–28; Jordan J. Ballor and J. Daryl Charles, "Common Grace, Natural Law, and the Social Order," *Public Discourse*, September 11, 2018, https://www.thepublicdiscourse.com/.

20 The "apostle to the Gentiles" assumes the natural moral law in his dealings with both Jew and Gentile. Because of the law "written on [the human] heart" (Rom. 2:14–15), all are said to be "without excuse" (Rom. 1:20). Human beings know of moral reality through both creation and conscience (Rom. 1:18–21). In fact, Paul demonstrates natural law reasoning in Athens in the first part of his Areopagus speech (Acts 17:16–34), appealing to what is known and observed by all, even by the Epicureans and Stoics who constitute his audience. See, in this regard, J. Daryl Charles, "Engaging the (Neo)Pagan Mind: Paul's Encounter with Athenian Culture as a Model for Cultural Apologetics (Acts 17:16–34)," *Trinity Journal*, n.s., 16, no. 1 (1995): 47–62.

are broken in the human experience, those decisions are accompanied by repercussions that can be observed and explained in human biological, social-psychological, spiritual, and ethical terms.[21] The idea of "public morality," alas, collapses when and where society refuses to preserve a social environment—the "common good"—in which moral reality is affirmed, virtuous behavior rewarded, and vice discouraged.

At bottom, our disagreements in the public square are disagreements not over the role of faith or reason per se but over differing values and principles that issue out of differing worldviews. These moral-philosophical assumptions and differences, often unstated, have a profound effect on law and public policy and therefore must be debated rationally in public discourse, hard as that is in the current cultural climate. And as it affects religious freedom, people must be free to pursue rational inquiry, uncoerced in the formation and formulation of their most deeply held beliefs—beliefs that mirror their perception of ultimate reality.

A second, related element that forms the basis of George's understanding of religious freedom is the fact of human dignity. The uniqueness of the human person gives rise to the sacred rights of conscience, which in turn respond to moral reality and natural law.[22] The intrinsic human capacities for reason and freedom are foundational to any definition of human dignity; we are designed as rational, moral agents. These capacities, in theological terms, mirror in human beings the *imago Dei*, God's likeness, though in finite ways. This likeness, it needs emphasizing, is not dependent on whether a person believes in a personal God. The divine image is intrinsic to being human. Whatever people's view of ultimate reality, the *imago Dei* attests to humans' *worth* and hence their dignity as creatures. It is in this very dignity that human rights (and particularly religious freedom) are grounded. Such rights are not positive or legal or even merely civil in nature; they are *human* rights and hence inviolable, given the fact of human dignity. The person is prior to the state.

21 The truth is that, in the present cultural battles, the ideological left—and especially sexual activists—would love to frame moral issues as if they pitted reason and "science" against religious faith and superstition. It does not require religious faith, or Scripture, to acknowledge that an unborn child is a child or that a confused and disordered male is still male and not female.

22 George cites as authoritative the natural law argument for religious freedom as developed in *Dignitatis Humanae*, which was part of the work of the Catholic Church's Vatican II Council. George, *Conscience and Its Enemies*, 121–25.

The right to religious freedom, then, issues out of human dignity and the search for what is meaningful and true, regardless of how imperfect, unreasonable, and immoral that search may be. This right, tragically, is routinely violated today, and ideological justification for this violation or denial can be either religious—for example, in some Islamic cultures—or secular—as evidenced by virtually all of Europe and North America—in nature. Nevertheless, religious freedom is intrinsic and not merely extrinsic; it is universal and not merely personal, perspectival, or parochial; and it is inalienable rather than malleable, anchored in the dictates—and thus rights—of conscience rather than in mere preference, bias, or utility.[23]

But how shall we understand the "rights of conscience" in our day? The Christian view of freedom of conscience could not be more at odds with the understanding that prevails in contemporary secular society. Consider the following assessment:

> Conscience has rights because it has duties; but in this age, with a large portion of the public, it is the very right and freedom of conscience to dispense with conscience. Conscience is a stern monitor, but in this century it has been superseded by a counterfeit, which the . . . centuries prior . . . never heard of, and could not have mistaken for it if they had. It is the right of *self-will*.[24]

Self-will, it goes without saying, characterizes our own day in unmistakable ways. And yet the above citation comes from John Henry Newman over a century removed. Conscience, properly understood, conveys the very opposite of the self-will and autonomy that are so important to contemporary secular culture. It "identifies one's *duties* under the moral law."[25] Conscience has rights precisely *because* it has duties. The right to follow one's conscience in terms of religious freedom and respecting communities

---

23 George has written voluminously on how matters of conscience in our day are being increasingly violated by the ideological commitments of militantly secular culture. At least half the essays gathered in *Conscience and Its Enemies* are devoted to this development in one way or another.

24 John Henry Newman, *Certain Difficulties Felt by Anglicans in Catholic Teaching Considered . . . A Letter Addressed to the Duke of Norfolk* (London: Longmans, Green, 1897), 250 (emphasis added), cited in George, *Conscience and Its Enemies*, 111.

25 George, *Conscience and Its Enemies*, 112 (emphasis original).

of faith exists not because of self-will or autonomy but because of human dignity and moral reality. Rights, then, issue out of social obligations and duties; they do not precede them. Conscience suggests an immutable law of moral obligation.

Hence, it is accurate to insist, both historically and philosophically, that religious freedom has pride of place—and therefore priority—among our basic liberties. For this reason, it has been properly described as "the first freedom." Historically, that right was viewed by the American founders as central to civil society and thus needing constitutional protecting. Philosophically, it was understood as anchoring free societies and contributing to human flourishing. Religion concerns ultimate things; it translates into sources of meaning and value that are transcendent. In addition to its constitutive role allowing human beings and society to flourish, religion also serves as a buffer between the individual and the state as well as between social groups and the state.[26] Religious belief is prepolitical. Where that buffer is not found or where it degenerates, the result is either a "soft" or "hard" form of totalitarianism. Freedom of religion thrives in a just society; it disappears in a totalitarian setting.

A third important theme in George's work that bears significantly on religious freedom is the public nature of morality. Because moral truth matters and all human beings everywhere are subject to the moral laws of the universe, the purposes of law and the duties of government are weighty. Public morality is much like public health in that it goes beyond mere law and public policy, aiming at the wider common good.[27] Notice the perennial human pattern: private acts invariably become public, as pornography well illustrates.[28] Government and law exist to protect and promote the common good, a social environment that may be accurately defined as "the sum total of social conditions which allow people, either as groups or as individuals, to reach their fulfillment more fully."[29] This environment of general social welfare includes first and foremost the protection of people's religious

---

26 See in this regard George, *Conscience and Its Enemies*, chaps. 10 and 11.

27 George, *Clash of Orthodoxies*, 91.

28 George, *Clash of Orthodoxies*, 91–92.

29 *Catechism of the Catholic Church*, no. 1906 (p. 465). The Catholic Catechism succinctly identifies three elements constituting the common good: it presupposes (1) respect for the human person, (2) the social well-being and development of the citizenry, and (3) the stability and security of a just order (nos. 1906–1909).

freedom. That the government respects and protects both the individual's essential freedoms and nongovernmental spheres of society is not merely a political issue but foremost a moral issue.[30] If and where there is no ultimate truth to guide and direct human affairs, political activity, or the affairs of the state, then ideas and convictions can easily be manipulated for reasons of power.[31] As history demonstrates, a democracy without values easily turns into open or thinly disguised totalitarianism.[32]

Given the role of reason in witnessing to human freedom, the fact of human dignity giving rise to the sacred rights of conscience, and the expressly public nature of morality, religious freedom as George perceives it can be characterized by five elements:

1. It is universal and not merely domestic, applying to all people.
2. It is nonpreferential and not subject to favored social or cultural status.
3. It is a public and no mere private domain.
4. It entails duties and obligations rather than mere rights and privileges.
5. It is concerned for the health of the common good and not mere individualism.

Obstacles to Religious Freedom: An Assessment

In this light, it is necessary to probe, as George does in assorted writings, what major obstacles inhibit the advancement of religious freedom. In the American context, these obstacles are historical, constitutional, and moral in nature. On the matter of religious freedom and religiously informed moral judgment

---

30 Catholics speak of this relative autonomy in terms of "subsidiary," while Reformed Protestants refer to it as "sphere sovereignty."

31 In every generation it needs reiterating that democracy as such is instrumental; it needs virtuous citizens to work.

32 So John Paul II, *Centesimus Annus*, no. 46, Vatican, May 1, 1991, https://www.vatican.va/. Alexis de Tocqueville, it will be remembered, on his visit to America spoke of a tyranny of both the minority and the majority. He observed, with remarkable insight, "In America, the majority draws a formidable circle around thought. Inside those limits, the writer is free; but unhappiness awaits him if he dares to leave them. . . . If ever freedom is lost in America, one will have to blame the omnipotence of the majority," the end result being that "unpopular truths" will "no longer be spoken," while "popular untruths" will be "reiterated incessantly." Alexis de Tocqueville, *Democracy in America*, ed. and trans. Harvey C. Mansfield and Delba Winthrop (Chicago: University of Chicago Press, 2000), lvii, 244, 249. Tocqueville's broader discussion of a "tyranny of the majority" is found in part 2, chaps. 7 and 8.

in public life, what George calls "orthodox secularism" (and what I prefer to call "militant secularism") insists on the *strict and absolute* separation of not only church and state but religious faith and public life. What this entails has become fairly familiar: "no prayer, not even an opportunity for silent prayer, in schools; no aid to parochial schools; no displays of religious symbols in the public square; no legislation based on the religiously informed moral convictions of legislators or voters."[33] Here, of course, militant secularism shows its true colors, manifesting itself as fundamentally coercive. People are not free to express publicly their religious convictions (in any context), and they are discriminated against when and where they wish to give expression to those sentiments. Religious belief, hence, becomes privatized, preventing any religiously informed moral judgments from entering public affairs.

Another obstacle to a proper understanding of religious freedom, perennial in nature as George sees it, is to interpret respect for others, based on their inherent dignity and the sacredness of conscience, as mere "tolerance" or a sort of "nonaggression pact," with a view to avoid strife and eliminate controversy. But to tolerate dissent is mere prudence at best and is unprincipled at worst. To respect a person's conscience, however, is noble. Tolerance, if it is virtuous, must be oriented toward the truth, not merely tolerating or enduring what we reject or find offensive. It is morally wrong to tolerate what is wrong or evil in order to avoid another supposed wrong or evil. It is possible, as our own culture demonstrates with regularity, to tolerate the actions of others out of an indifference—even a hostility—toward what is true. By contrast, humility acknowledges that no one possesses all or even most truth and that people are "on their way" toward a fuller grasp of the truth. The result of this attitude is a voluntary and noncoercive posture toward religious belief and the public expression of that belief. The common good is realized (relatively speaking) not because we compromise truth or moral reality but because we wish to align ourselves, as far as it is possible, with it.[34] If truth is the aim, religious freedom may be seen as the societal *means*.

In this regard, the language of this nation's founders and framers was that of "accommodation," not "tolerance." They understood religious freedom to

---

33 George, *Clash of Orthodoxies*, 6.

34 See in this regard J. Daryl Charles, "Truth, Tolerance, and Christian Conviction: Reflections on a Perennial Question," *Christian Scholar's Review* 36, no. 2 (Winter 2007): 185–218.

encompass two jurisdictions—God and *Caesar*—even as they understood the one to transcend the other. We render to God what is his, and we render to Caesar what is his (Matt. 22:20–21).[35] Accommodating religion as the founders and our charter documents sought to do is not the expression of mere tolerance. Accommodation, properly conceived, has a conspicuously Christian character; that is, it presupposes the transcendent and a moral universe.[36]

Remarkably, in the West today, an intolerant "tolerance" is epidemic—or should we say pandemic. It informs all avenues of public discourse, imbuing law and legislation, permeating all discussion of human sexuality and the moral life, and demanding that society embrace pagan principles and lifestyles.[37] This brand of "tolerance" will not tolerate the "intolerable"; it will censor and exclude not only actions and behavior but attitudes. These "tolerant" inclusivists, alas, are not interested in facilitating debate and discussion or tolerating the presence of another outlook.[38] Their aim is to drive the traditional religious person and the moral viewpoint *out of the public arena*.[39] While it is true that as Christians we have no "abiding city," owing to our ultimate allegiance to God, it is also the case, as George challenges us again and again, that we are stewards of the created order and culture we are part of. The steward's challenge takes the following shape: we are to be oriented toward truth and the Master's transcendent authority (see Matt. 25:14–30). There is no guarantee or sense of programmatic timing in terms of our service. Talents and abilities have been given to us as stewards that vary greatly. We give joy to the Master in being creative and obedient with those talents. And we do not "bury our talents," which is to say, we do not hide, retreat, or isolate ourselves from the cultural context to which we are called.

George is especially attentive to the legal distortions that, in our own more recent history, have undermined a commitment to religious freedom. Both legal scholarship and legal precedent, he argues, can go awry, based on

---

35 This, of course, forms the basis for Augustine's concept of the "two cities."

36 The thinking of James Madison, Thomas Jefferson, and the founders, regardless of their personal faith commitments, recognized transcendent reality and two jurisdictions.

37 While George adopts this view, it has been set forth as well, with particular force and clarity, by Steven D. Smith, in *Pagans and Christians in the City: Culture Wars from the Tiber to the Potomac* (Grand Rapids, MI: Eerdmans, 2018).

38 After all, people who truly are interested in truth do not resort to coercion or squelching dissent.

39 What is interesting, however, is that secular fear of religion is aimed *only* at orthodox Christians and *not*, for example, at Islamists, for whom a strict separation of "church and state" is blasphemous. Surely, this double standard, this bald hypocrisy, needs an accounting.

faulty assumptions and a resultant faulty interpretation. Wrong interpretations, if not held in check or rebutted, can obscure the truth much faster
than ivy grows around a building.[40] Both interpretation and precedent must
accord with the Constitution, just as, by analogy, any dissenting theologian
of the Catholic Church must be constrained by the church's magisterium.[41]

Of course, the religion clause of the First Amendment has been a source
of abiding controversy for the better part of the last century. But what is the
plain meaning of the establishment clause of the First Amendment? What is
abundantly clear to George is that religious freedom is a basic human right
and *not* a mere "constitutional right" and that the establishment clause does
not forbid religion in any state of the union, even when government cannot
favor or sanction a particular religious group. The "free exercise" clause of the
Constitution makes little sense if religious freedom is not *prior to* the state
in terms of human moral and social obligation. Thus, we may conclude, the
establishment clause is advancing nonpreferentialism.[42] A key word in interpreting the clause is "respecting": "Congress shall make no law respecting an
establishment of religion." Against the militant-secularist interpretation of
the establishment clause, which presumes a strict or absolute separation of
church and state, the Constitution both "prohibits" and "respects." It prohibits
preferential treatment or an established church—a "Church of England," as
it were. At the same time, it respects its citizens by allowing them to have
any belief, even *no* belief, alongside the existence of "comprehensive" beliefs
such as Christian faith, by which "self-evident truths" are precisely that—
self-evident—and thus by their very nature needing public expression.[43] In
any case, the founders believed that the sacredness of conscience could and
would be defended at the bar of public reason. Neither indifference nor hostility characterized the founders' understanding of church-state relations.[44]

---

40 This forms the basis for George's argument in William C. Porth and Robert P. George, "Trimming the Ivy: A Bicentennial Re-Examination of the Establishment Clause," *West Virginia Law
Review* 90 (1987): 109–69.

41 Porth and George, "Trimming the Ivy," 110.

42 As to what precisely constitutes "religion," George identifies four elements: (1) the existence
of transcendent reality, (2) the nature of the human person, (3) an ultimate purpose of human
existence, and (4) the purpose and nature of the universe. Porth and George, "Trimming the
Ivy," 149n117.

43 The founders respected "any" belief provided that that belief not undermine the common good.

44 On the framers' commitment to religious freedom in the "American experiment," see Charles,
Natural Law and Religious Freedom, chap. 3.

At bottom, George would seem to understand the "wall of separation" between church and state, to use Jefferson's well-worn phrase, not as "high and impregnable," as contemporary rulings have asserted, but "low and permeable," as most of the founders seemed to understand it.[45] Perhaps rather than a "wall" of separation, it is more accurate to speak of a "fence," with gates that allow discourse, discussion, and debate when and where needed.[46] Church-state separation was originally envisioned as a means toward achieving religious freedom, by which freedom of religious belief and religious expression might flourish. Thus, it behooves us in the third decade of the twenty-first century to revisit the founders' intent, whose convictions were that the state should ensure a "tempered liberty."[47] Religious freedom, in the end, is both a moral imperative and practical necessity for any civil society. In the words of Alexis de Tocqueville, "Despotism may govern without faith, but liberty cannot."[48]

The Current State of Religious Freedom Worldwide and the Task before Us

As outlined in the previous section, religious freedom is a—if not *the*—central contemporary battleground in the wider cultural skirmishes engulfing the Western world.[49] And despite significant human rights developments

---

45 Also advancing this view are Daniel L. Dreisbach, Mark D. Hall, and Jeffry H. Morrison, eds., *The Founders on God and Government* (Lanham, MD: Rowman and Littlefield, 2004).

46 George would likely agree with the view of another constitutional scholar who maintains that the founders (with some exceptions) generally preferred the metaphor of a "line of separation" and not a "wall," inasmuch as the latter connotes antagonism or suspicion, whereas the former, like a "fence," suggests a fluidity and adaptability. So Daniel L. Dreisbach, *Religion and Politics in the Early Republic: Jasper Adams and the Church-State Debate* (Lexington: University of Kentucky Press, 1996), 157. And in fact, James Madison preferred the "line" metaphor as evidenced by his personal correspondence; see, e.g., "Letter from James Madison to Jasper Adams" (September 1833), reproduced in James Madison, *The Writings of James Madison*, ed. Gaillard Hunt (New York: G. P. Putnam's Sons, 1900), 9:484–88, esp. 487. In addition, Robert L. Cord argues that "there is no evidence that Jefferson ever sought an absolute barrier between religion and government," whether as a Virginia lawmaker, as US president, or as foreign minister to France. Cord, "Mr. Jefferson's 'Nonabsolute' Wall of Separation between Church and State," in *Religion and Political Culture in Jefferson's Virginia*, ed. Garrett Ward Sheldon and Daniel L. Dreisbach (Oxford: Rowman and Littlefield, 2000), 167.

47 So John Witte Jr., "One Public Religion, Many Private Religions," in Dreisbach, Hall, and Morrison, *Founders on God and Government*, 37.

48 Tocqueville, *Democracy in America*, 282.

49 Smith is inclined to view religious freedom as *the* major battle. *Pagans and Christians*, 302.

and documents forged since World War II (e.g., the 1948 Universal Declaration of Human Rights and the 1966 International Covenant on Civil and Political Rights), around the globe egregious human rights violations seem to be on the increase. Little progress in responding to these violations is being made in the twenty-first century. From forbidding public expression of religious belief to punishing those who dare inject the moral viewpoint into the public arena; from imprisoning or killing those who publicly express religious belief to killing those who have a conversion of belief; from mass murder and atrocity to torture, enslavement, and other crimes against humanity, abusers continue to operate with impunity.

Positively, February 2020 marked the official launch of the International Religious Freedom or Belief Alliance, a coalition of like-minded nations that are committed to opposing religious persecution and advancing religious freedom. As of June 2022, thirty-five nations belonged to this network.[50] And in addition to the USCIRF, noted earlier in this chapter, there are various organizations—for example, the Religious Freedom Institute, the International Rescue Committee, and International Christian Concern— that exist solely for the purpose of advancing the cause of religious freedom or tracking egregious human rights violations worldwide and encouraging those in political authority and public office to respond in appropriate ways.[51]

In addition to the above-noted positive developments, the United Nations Human Rights Council meets three times each year to examine global situations of concern and pass resolutions on various human rights issues. The degree to which the United Nations is actually committed to—and capable of—protecting religious freedom and addressing egregious human rights violations remains in question, for the same reason that the United Nations has been largely ineffective in preventing atrocity, mass murder, and other severe human rights violations. Additionally, voting members of the United Nations may be among those nations that are the most consistent offenders.

Two noteworthy annual reports are among those documenting the state of religious freedom worldwide. A primary feature of these reports is to identify those nations that demonstrate a pattern of severe human rights

---

50 International Religious Freedom or Belief Alliance, accessed June 8, 2022, https://www.state.gov/.

51 On the domestic front, organizations such as Alliance Defending Freedom and First Liberty Institute are doing yeoman's service in terms of legally protecting religious freedom.

violations. The USCIRF *Annual Report 2021* identifies fourteen nations that are "recommended for designation as countries of particular concern" (CPCs). These are Burma, China, Eritrea, India, Iran, Nigeria, North Korea, Pakistan, Russia, Saudi Arabia, Syria, Tajikistan, Turkmenistan, and Vietnam.[52] The report further makes recommendations in the light of these CPCs: (1) designating violators, (2) utilizing sanctions in response to violations, (3) prioritizing religious freedom, (4) advocating for prisoners of conscience, and (5) increasing aid to religious minorities. *Religious Freedom in the World Report 2021*, published by Aid to the Church in Need International, reports that religious freedom is violated in almost one-third of the world's nations (31.6 percent), where roughly two-thirds of the world's population is located (5.2 billion people). The worst persecution is located in twenty-six countries, home to 3.9 billion people (51 percent of the world's population). The report concludes that severe religiously motivated persecution is on the increase.[53]

As we are confronted with increasing threats to religious freedom, the needs both at home and abroad are great.[54] There is a job to do. From the standpoint of Christian faith, there is great responsibility to assist those who are persecuted for their faith, whatever that faith may be, and this is one of the noblest parts of our social witness. We are constrained and impelled by the Golden Rule to help those who are helpless. This, too, is a correlate of natural law, which requires of us that we do good and avoid doing harm. While Golden Rule ethics has a positive and a negative application—*do to others* as you would have them do to you, and *don't do to others* as you would not have them do to you—a third corollary applies in the case of religious freedom and human rights violations: *do not allow to be done to others* what you would not want done to you.

To the extent that we are still relatively free, we must act in good conscience. This entails, among other things, reminding those in public office and political authority of the high priority of religious freedom and doing so in the spirit of the founders. After all, "self-evident truths" are just that—

52 US Commission on International Religious Freedom, *Annual Report 2021*, April 2021, https://www.uscirf.gov/.

53 Aid to the Church in Need International, *Religious Freedom in the World Report 2021*, April 2021, https://acninternational.org/.

54 For extended commentary on contemporary threats to religious freedom, see esp. Charles, *Natural Law and Religious Freedom*, chap. 1.

self-evident and timeless; hence, again and again we need to contend for them. In the case of the West, this means confronting in fresh ways an aggressive (and intolerant) secularism that wishes to remove both the religious person and the moral viewpoint from the public sphere. Around the globe, this means marshaling any and all resources—political, economic, religious, and institutional—to aid the oppressed, applying political pressure where possible to those who violate basic human rights and religious freedom.

For the task at hand, then, let us in peculiarly Georgian terms (1) reappropriate public reason, (2) reaffirm natural law arguments in the public sphere, (3) expose secularist assumptions and reassert truth telling, and (4) work ecumenically.[55] Only in this way can we hope to make any progress on the front of religious freedom.

Ancient wisdom beckons us today, as it did in the past, to the task at hand. May we respond accordingly:

Rescue those being led away to death;
Hold back those staggering toward slaughter.
If you say, "But we knew nothing about this,"
Does not he who weighs the heart perceive it?
Does not he who guards your life know it?
Will he not repay everyone according to what they have done?
(Prov. 24:11–12 NIV)

---

55 One of the remarkable—and exceedingly encouraging—developments of the last generation is the degree to which Catholics and orthodox Protestants have been cooperating in common cause as we encounter a myriad of pressing sociocultural battles.

12

Robert P. George on Justice and Democracy

Natural Law, Classical Liberalism, and Prospects for a Protestant Political Theory

Mark Tooley

WHAT DOES A JUST SOCIETY require according to Robert P. George? How does he view American democracy and its ability to approximate justice? These questions seem especially pressing now amid increasing doubts about the classical form of "liberal" democracy and advocacy for illiberal alternatives. Evangelicals, like the rest of America, are confused, divided, and rancorous about the best course for our republic and about the nature of Christian political witness.

As George noted twenty years ago, Wilfred McClay has cited critics of American liberal democracy who imagine a "straight line leading from the 'shot heard round the world' to endemic divorce, gangsta rap, and the North American Man-Boy Love Association." Belief in such a straight line is increasingly common among postliberals who believe American democracy was built on false premises. George rightly rejects this conjectured "straight line" and, with caveats, affirms the best of the American experiment as in sync with natural law and Catholic teaching.[1]

---

1 Robert George, *The Clash of Orthodoxies: Law, Religion, and Morality in Crisis* (Wilmington, DE: ISI Books, 2001), 238–39.

Evangelicals in increasingly postdenominational America have never been in more need of a firm Christian tradition to guide them in thinking about democracy and politics. Can a great Catholic philosopher like George help evangelicals understand and articulate a smart and faithful political theology? Or are George's premises too rooted in specifically Catholic assumptions and their stance on natural law to gain wide acceptance by evangelicals? If so, can evangelicals respond to his teaching with their own Protestant understanding of statecraft in ways relevant to our current historical moment? Can evangelicals address justice in society based on a rich Christian architecture, or are we too captive to contemporary American ideological divisions and assumptions? At the very least, George's insights offer an intelligent perspective faithful to the teachings of his church that can inspire and motivate evangelicals when addressing justice in society.

Social justice is a phrase irritating to the ears of some conservative Christians, especially certain evangelicals. But Christians are called to promote justice in earthly society to the extent possible among fallen humanity. George, as a public intellectual, has devoted three decades on the public stage in America to advocacy for justice in society from a Catholic and natural law perspective. He has prioritized protection for natural marriage, the unborn, and other vulnerable persons who cannot speak for themselves and also for religious liberty domestically and internationally. But more broadly, he is concerned that sustaining democracy requires adherence to natural and moral law, absent of which regimes risk reverting to illegitimacy. He responds to increasing doubts about democracy across the ideological spectrum, both within and outside Christianity, with his own perspective on "liberalism." Protestants and evangelicals rightly resonate with most of his assumptions and goals for a democracy operating within a Christian understanding of moral law. But Protestants and evangelicals should also reflect on the failure of their communities to generate public thinkers equal in stature to George. And Protestants and evangelicals should work to contribute to George's themes with contributions from their own respective traditions.

I'm honored to have known George across two decades, thanks initially to his service on the board of the Institute on Religion and Democracy, of which I am now president. My predecessor, the late Diane Knippers, sought his service, rightly believing he represented the best of the then next generation of formidable Catholic public thinkers, in the tradition of Richard Neuhaus, Michael Novak, and George Weigel, who had helped found the Institute on Religion and Democracy in 1981. George, when he attended our board meetings, brought a blast of intellectual energy and enthusiasm. But he was often in the hallway, on the phone, sometimes participating in the board meetings of other organizations that were equally and understandably anxious for his counsel. George is a rare academic intellectual who is an effective networker and focused on disseminating his views for maximum societal impact. He's a public intellectual who speaks beyond a niche community thanks to the breadth of his knowledge, his capacity for clear communication, his ability to speak forcefully and quickly to unfolding events, and his talent for ecumenical and interfaith coalitions.

During those years of the early 2000s when I first knew him, George was especially focused on not just crafting public arguments in defense of natural marriage but also mobilizing for state referenda defining marriage as between one man and one woman. His intellect, drive, organizing skills, charisma, and fundraising contributed to a string of nearly unbroken state electoral victories until defeat in three states in 2012, indicative of shifting public opinion and foreshadowing the Supreme Court's 2015 federal imposition of same-sex marriage.

George's Call to Persist in Shaping American Democracy

This shift was evident when George delivered the Institute on Religion and Democracy's Annual Diane Knippers Lecture in 2014, and the pernicious impact on religious freedom was already obvious, as he noted. Ironically and even amusingly, his lecture was in the sanctuary of a very liberal Methodist church in Washington, DC, that proudly waved rainbow flags. They rented to us begrudgingly, and not long after George's speech, they refused to rent to us again, despite their signage insisting that all were welcome. Before George finished his remarks from the pulpit, the sound system was abruptly turned off. I never knew if the turnoff was prescheduled based on our rental agreement or if an irritable listening church staffer, unable to stomach George's eloquence on behalf of traditional Christian beliefs any further, angrily flipped the switch. It made no difference. George, without amplified sound, continued disclaiming for some time, more emphatic than ever and clearly heard by all who raptly listened.

The speech that evening revealed much about George's perspective on justice in society and about his expectations of American democracy.[2] Much of what George said was a robust "I told you so" regarding the unfolding social impact of same-sex marriage:

> It was only yesterday, was it not, that we were being assured that the re-definition of marriage to include same-sex partnerships would have no impact on persons and institutions that hold to the traditional view of marriage as a conjugal union? Such persons and institutions would simply be untouched by the change. It won't affect your marriage or your life, we were told, if the law recognizes Henry and Herman or Sally and Sheila as "married." It's all just a matter of "live and let live."[3]

We in the audience readily agreed and listened intently. "Those offering these assurances," George recalled, "were also claiming that the redefinition of marriage would have no impact on the public understanding of marriage as a monogamous and sexually exclusive partnership." Instead, these norms would supposedly spread more broadly. Warnings of conscience threats to traditional religionists by same-sex marriage and by "sexual orientation" antidiscrimination statutes were derided as "scaremongering." George cited assurances that no one would coerce Christian adoption services or religiously affiliated schools or business owners into betraying their conscience and religious convictions. And supposedly no one was proposing to recognize polyamorous relationships or normalize "open marriages," he sardonically noted. "That was then; this is now."[4]

George insisted that nobody should be surprised since, according to same-sex-marriage advocates, their whole "argument was and is that the idea of marriage as the union of husband and wife lacks a rational basis and

---

2   This essay draws heavily on three of George's publications: Robert George, "2014 Diane Knippers Memorial Lecture by Robert George on Marriage and Religious Liberty," *Juicy Ecumenism* (blog), Institute on Religion and Democracy, October 14, 2014, https://juicyecumenism.com/; Robert P. George, "The End of Democracy? The Tyrant State," *First Things*, November 1996, https://www.firstthings.com/; Ryan T. Anderson and Robert P. George, "The Baby and the Bathwater," *National Affairs* 41 (Fall 2019), https://nationalaffairs.com/. Used by permission of the publishers.

3   George, "Knippers Memorial Lecture."

4   George, "Knippers Memorial Lecture."

amounts to nothing more than 'bigotry,' " akin to racial segregation. Most don't understand that marriage is a conjugal relationship and not a sexual-romantic companionship or domestic partnership. So it is no shock that polyamory, open marriage, group marriages, throuples, and "temporary" marriages are now increasingly in parlance, he noted.

Disputes about sex and marriage are no longer seen as "honest disagreements among reasonable people of goodwill," George observed, but "battles between the forces of reason, enlightenment, and equality" and those of "ignorance, bigotry, and discrimination." The "excluders" are to be treated just as racists are treated, legally tolerated but socially stigmatized. Traditionalists who imagined some grand compromise accepting same-sex marriage but protecting conscience rights for dissenters were deluded, he said. George explained the reason:

> Liberal secularism never was and never will be what the late John Rawls depicted it as being and hoped it would be, namely, a purely political doctrine, as opposed to what he called a comprehensive view—a view of human nature, meaning, dignity, and destiny—that competes with other comprehensive views. Nowhere is the reality of contemporary liberalism as a comprehensive doctrine—a secularist religion—more plainly on display than in the moral-cultural struggle over marriage and sexual morality. Liberal secularism will tolerate other comprehensive views so long as they present no challenge or serious threat to its own most cherished values. But when they do, they must be smashed—in the name, for example, of "equality" or preventing "dignitarian harm"—and their faithful must be reduced to a dhimmi-like status in respect of opportunities (in employment, contracting, and other areas) that, from the point of view of liberal secularist doctrine, cannot be made available to them if they refuse to conform themselves to the demands of liberal ideology.[5]

George insisted that there "is no alternative to winning the battle in the public square over the legal definition of marriage—however dark and even hopeless the cause looks, and even if the time horizon is fifty or a hundred years." Some view the defense of marriage as a lost cause, he lamented, while

5 George, "Knippers Memorial Lecture."

admitting that defeatism is understandable given the formidable cultural obstacles. But he cited the turnaround in views on abortion since the 1970s when abortion rights were seen as permanent. And he recalled in the early twentieth century that "when eugenics was embraced by the elite institutions of American society—from the wealthy philanthropic foundations, to the mainline Protestant denominations, to the Supreme Court of the United States," "affluent, sophisticated, 'right-minded' people were all on board with the eugenics program."[6]

Citing "the left-wing—but anti-Hegelian—Brazilian legal theorist Roberto Unger [who] used to preach to us in courses at Harvard Law School, the future will be the fruit of human deliberation, judgment, and choice," George said,

> It is not subject to fixed laws of history and forces of social determinism. As the Marxists learned the hard way, the reality of human freedom is the permanent foiler of "inevitability" theses. Same-sex marriage and the assaults on liberty and equality that follow in its wake are "inevitable" only if defenders of marriage make their adversaries' prophecies self-fulfilling ones, by buying into them.[7]

George concluded his peroration by urging supporters of marriage and religious liberty to "stand up, speak out, fight back, resist! Do not be demoralized. Refuse to be intimidated. Speak moral truth to cultural, political, and economic power. Openly love what is good and defy and resist whatever opposes and threatens it." He implored cobelligerents to

> be prepared, if it comes to it, to pay the cost of discipleship. Stand together with anyone of any faith—Catholic, Protestant, Orthodox, Jewish, Mormon, Muslim, Hindu, Buddhist, Sikh, Jain—who will stand with you to uphold marriage and defend freedom. Be gentle as doves, to be sure, but cunning as serpents. Be relentless in your determination to defend what is right in the courts and in the streets, on the blogs and in the legislative chambers.[8]

6   George, "Knippers Memorial Lecture."
7   George, "Knippers Memorial Lecture."
8   George, "Knippers Memorial Lecture."

Importantly, George stressed working through all the available channels of American democracy in defense of traditional morality:

Pray ceaselessly. Work to elect champions of life, marriage, and religious liberty. Fight to keep the Republican Party faithful to the moral principles that have drawn so many former Democrats into it over the past three decades. Remember that our adversaries, having now won a complete lock on the Democratic Party, will now devote their attention and formidable resources to making inroads among Republicans. We must defeat those efforts, making clear to the Republican establishment that our loyalty to the Party is conditional on the Party's fidelity to its principles.[9]

Just as Republicans and others in the nineteenth century fought slavery, polygamy, and barbarism, George concluded, "we must stand . . . today with Lincolnian conviction and determination to prevail—no matter the cost, no matter how long it takes. It will not be easy. And, to worldly eyes, the horizon looks bleak. But 'mine eyes have seen the glory, of the coming of the Lord.'"[10]

George's citation of Lincoln, abolitionism, resistance to Mormon polygamy, and Julia Ward Howe's "Battle Hymn of the Republic" in his summons to multigenerational political warfare in defense of traditional morality was itself a robust expression of confidence in the ultimate viability and justice of American democracy. It recognized that variances between natural law (with Christian teaching) and American culture are not new but have always existed. In some sense, every generation has its battles over this gulf. In 2014, before the 2015 Supreme Court ruling for same-sex marriage and with state electoral victories still in recent memory, George was maybe in a more optimistic mode about American democracy's ability to deliver justice in sync with natural law.

George's Chastened Optimism about Democracy's Future

George has, at times, been considerably less optimistic, as in his 1996 article "The End of Democracy? The Tyrant State" for Richard John Neuhaus's *First*

---

9 George, "Knippers Memorial Lecture."
10 George, "Knippers Memorial Lecture."

Things, which hosted a grim symposium called "The End of Democracy?," provocatively asking if the American regime no longer merited support.[11] This conversation was organized when Neuhaus himself was uncharacteristically doubtful about America during the Clinton-era tide of cultural and sexual liberalism. Some longtime Neuhaus supporters denounced and even dissociated from *First Things* over the symposium. But decidedly not George.

Instead, George gave "two cheers" for American democracy but explained lengthily why he could not give three. "America's democratic experiment has been remarkably successful," he wrote, having "survived a civil war, a great depression, and two world wars, . . . assimilating into the mainstream of American life generations of immigrants," making "tremendous strides towards overcoming a tragic legacy of slavery and racial segregation," securing "safer conditions for working people and a meaningful social safety net for the most disadvantaged among us," demonstrating that "citizens of different religious faiths can live and work together in peace and mutual respect," and achieving economic prosperity that's "the envy of the world." The Declaration of Independence and our Constitution offer models of free government inspiring oppressed people globally, helping "American ideals of personal, political, and economic freedom" triumph over fascist and communist tyranny.[12]

As a faithful Catholic, George obviously esteems the teaching authority of his church and judges American democracy by it. He quoted Pope John Paul II's 1995 encyclical *Evangelium Vitae*, saying, "Fundamentally democracy is a 'system' and as such is a means and not an end. Its 'moral value' is not automatic, but depends on conformity to the moral law to which it, like every other form of human behavior, must be subject." George noted that this expectation of civil law conforming to moral truth predates modern democracy, articulated by Plato and Aristotle and further systematized by Thomas Aquinas.[13]

Laws and public policies are not morally legitimate merely because they are democratic, George asserted, as evangelicals certainly would agree. Paraphrasing Pope John Paul II, he noted that democracy is "uniquely valuable"

11 George, "Tyrant State."
12 George, "Tyrant State."
13 George, "Tyrant State."

for embodying "more fully than any alternative system the principle of the fundamental moral equality of citizens." So the "almost universal consensus with regard to the value of democracy . . . is to be considered a positive 'sign of the times,' as the Church's magisterium has frequently noted." But George warned that even democracy "may compromise its legitimacy and forfeit its right to the allegiance of its citizens" when its institutions "are manipulated" so that, in Pope John Paul II's words, "'right' ceases to be such, because it is no longer firmly founded on the inviolable dignity of the person. . . . In this way, democracy, contradicting its own principles, effectively moves towards a form of totalitarianism." For George, democratic institutions then become "mechanisms of injustice and oppression, thus defying the moral law to which they, like all human institutions and actions, are subject." He quoted Pope John XXIII in his 1963 encyclical *Pacem in Terris*: "Any government which refused to recognize human rights, or acted in violation of them, would not only fail in its duty; its decrees would be wholly lacking in binding force."[14]

George said that this presumption that democracy loses legitimacy when degraded and immoral is not just Catholic teaching. That laws and regimes "must be evaluated by reference to universal standards of justice is shared by people of different faiths and of no particular faith," he wrote, and is the "premise of any serious conception of human rights."[15] Judicial review of laws is intended to safeguard against democratic abuse of civil law rooted in moral law.

Sadly, George lamented, courts have themselves trampled on moral law by subverting "fundamental rights" often in the defense of other purported rights, such as in the *Dred Scott* decision invalidating citizenship for Black people and in *Roe v. Wade*, overturning laws protecting the unborn. These rulings subverted legislative authority and moral law. George also implicitly chided Justice Antonin Scalia, who, although Catholic and pro-life, insisted that democracies could permit abortion and euthanasia, because the majority rules, a position that George and Catholicism reject. For George, as with Pope John Paul II in *Evangelium Vitae*, abandoning the unborn betrays the "substantive principle of equal worth and dignity that is the moral

14 George, "Tyrant State."
15 George, "Tyrant State."

linchpin of democracy." Any regime, including democracies, can become a "tyrant state" when exposing "those most in need of the law's protection" to violence and oppression. George wrote that the "dark irony of American constitutional democracy" is that our judges who are specifically called to uphold legal equality are betraying this special trust. *Roe v. Wade*, by defying popular will and moral law, is especially "undemocratic."[16]

Institutions of American democracy, especially the courts, have made themselves the enemy of moral law, particularly as conceived by Christians and Jews, George declared. Quoting Mary Ann Glendon, George noted, "No other democracy is so careless of the value of human life," on abortion and ultimately on euthanasia and assisted suicide. Again quoting Pope John Paul II in *Evangelium Vitae*, George declared, "Laws which authorize and promote abortion and euthanasia are radically opposed not only to the good of the individual but also to the common good; as such they are completely lacking in juridical validity." For Pope John Paul II, "A civil law authorizing abortion or euthanasia ceases by that very fact to be a true, morally binding law." They are "crimes which no human law can claim to legitimize. There is no obligation in conscience to obey such laws; instead there is a *grave and clear obligation to oppose them by conscientious objection*." Pope John Paul II warned, "It is . . . never licit to obey it, or to take part in a propaganda campaign in favor of such a law, or vote for it." For him, in the ongoing conflict between "the culture of life" and "the culture of death," "we are all involved and we all share in it, with the inescapable responsibility of choosing to be unconditionally pro-life."[17]

Heeding this papal call to a culture of life, George said, entails making financial sacrifices; volunteering in pro-life pregnancy centers and hospices; working in the educational, legal, and political realms; praying constantly; and defending the family, which is, in Pope John Paul II's words, "the basis and driving force of all social policies." This work includes resisting "the trivialization of sexuality," which is "among the principal factors which has led to contempt for new life." George commended military doctors who refuse abortions, nonviolent protesters at abortion clinics, and even taxpayers who withhold partial payments to states with abortion funding.[18]

16 George, "Tyrant State."
17 George, "Tyrant State" (emphasis original).
18 George, "Tyrant State."

George recalled the 1992 *Planned Parenthood v. Casey* ruling in which the Supreme Court majority implored pro-life Americans to stop their resistance to legalized abortion and accept "a common mandate rooted in the Constitution." In their "ludicrous" demand, George said, they ignored constitutional democracy's mandate to seek the common good and protect fundamental human rights. "If the Constitution really did abandon the vulnerable to private acts of lethal violence, and, indeed, positively disempowered citizens from working through the democratic process to correct these injustices, then it would utterly lack the capacity to bind the consciences of citizens," he insisted. "Our duty would not be to 'accept a common mandate,' but to resist."[19]

So, George asked, in light of judicial usurpations of civil law rooted in moral law, has American democracy "forfeited its legitimacy?" Congress, presidents, and public opinion have not strongly resisted the courts and sometimes have abetted them, contributing further to the "crisis of democratic legitimacy" and illustrating a wider "failure of American democracy." Regime legitimacy depends on adherence to the common good, he reiterated. George concluded that anyone "prepared to consider seriously Pope John Paul II's teaching in *Evangelium Vitae* cannot now avoid asking themselves, soberly and unblinkingly, whether our regime is becoming the democratic 'tyrant state' about which he warns." Note that George used the word "becoming" and declined to declare that America has become tyrannical. Subsequent commentary across a quarter century indicates that he still does not regard our democracy as despotic and unworthy of support. But his warning of the possibility remains strong.[20]

George's Steady Plodding in Support of Classic Liberalism

In 2019, in a *National Affairs* piece coauthored with Ryan T. Anderson, George revealed more deeply his views of American democracy and its conflicts with moral law. He was seemingly less pessimistic than 1996 and, at least stylistically, less peppery than in his 2014 Institute on Religion and Democracy speech. Having digested the 2015 Supreme Court *Obergefell v. Hodges* ruling for same-sex marriage, he was rigorously methodical in

19 George, "Tyrant State."
20 George, "Tyrant State."

reviewing the merits and failures of American democracy. Specifically, he addressed the growing critique of "liberalism" as "incompatible with preliberal ideals of human flourishing," since it was increasingly defined by progressives as "unlimited choice," especially on abortion and sexuality. Against this critique, George and Anderson defended liberal democracy from an Aristotelian-Thomistic perspective, without accepting Lockean, Kantian, or Rawlsian liberalism, believing many "'liberal' political ideals and institutions predate liberal philosophy and . . . have proven effective at promoting the common good."[21]

This preliberal liberalism rejects "neutrality about the human good" but affirms "representative government, separation of powers, constitutional-ism, limited government and respect for the autonomy and integrity of institutions of civil society (beginning with the marriage-based family), jury trial, freedom of speech, freedom of religion, and other basic civil liberties," which "all pre-date John Locke" and "are more than defensible (and are indeed better defended) without invoking Lockean philosophical ideas." These "political ideals and institutions, . . . compared to the alternatives, best promote and protect the common good—even when we conceive of the common good in a manner quite alien to some central principles of Enlightenment or contemporary progressive liberalism."[22] George is not prepared to jettison the project of liberal democracy even as an increasing number of conservative Catholics, among others, are inclined to do. For George, liberal democracy is best sustained by a commitment to preliberal traditions that honor the natural moral law and the dignity of the rights-bearing person. Thus, George's vision for liberal democracy is decidedly Aristotelian-Thomistic, rather than Lockean-Rawlsian.

George and Anderson described Lockean-Rawlsian liberalism as neutral about the public good and "sidelining" religion from public life. The alter-native of illiberalism devalues freedoms of speech and religion since "error has no rights" and since "political authority should be subordinated . . . to spiritual authority." They admitted that these debates often oversimplify and fail to appreciate that societies aren't organized around theories and instead depend on "circumstances, experience, prudence, and technical expertise."

---

21 Anderson and George, "The Baby and the Bathwater."
22 Anderson and George, "The Baby and the Bathwater."

Thomas Aquinas, after all, said that rulers "must often choose between or among reasonable options, none of which is excluded by absolute moral principles." George and Anderson cited a "spectrum of options between the extremes." Identifying as "perfectionists" in the political-theory sense, they denied that liberty is ultimate but affirmed its instrumentality while insisting on limits. They rejected coercion on behalf of or against religion but affirmed that "some forms of religious establishment can be permissible—though not required," while rejecting religious establishment in America for historical and sociological reasons.[23]

There is no single best political regime, George and Anderson surmised. And regimes must be structured to guard against abuse by fallen humanity, which precludes extremes of "strict libertarianism" and "genuine socialism." "Thomas Aquinas famously taught that the law should not command every virtue or prohibit every vice," they recalled. "Attempts—in the name of the human good—to penalize every form or instance of immorality would actually undermine the human good" by allowing rulers too much power. So Thomas taught that "the state should limit itself to punishing the graver forms of immorality," which is a "preliberal" limit on government power. George and Anderson credited Thomas and not Locke for modern civil liberty. Civil liberties are not abstract absolutes from human nature but political rights justified and limited by the common good, determined by context and prudence.[24]

George's preference for Thomas Aquinas as natural law exponent and a father of civil liberty is understandable. Thomas was a Catholic saint to whom all Christendom owes profound intellectual and spiritual debt. But it's also important not to devalue Locke, who has become the chief *bête noire* for contemporary postliberals, especially for Catholic thinkers like Patrick Deneen. Interestingly, in his 2001 book *The Clash of Orthodoxies*, George wrote favorably of Locke as a vigorous exponent of natural law. If Thomas was the "classic premodern thinker of natural law," then the "modern *par excellence* is John Locke." As George noted, Locke wrote that the "State of Nature has a Law of Nature to govern it, which obliges everyone. And Reason, which is that Law, teaches all Mankind, who will but consult it,

---

23 Anderson and George, "The Baby and the Bathwater."
24 Anderson and George, "The Baby and the Bathwater."

that being all equal and independent, no one ought to harm another in his Life, Health, Liberty, or possessions."[25]

It's notable that George in *The Clash of Orthodoxies* also cited Locke's contemporary and cofounder of Anglo-liberalism Algernon Sidney, "whose defense of liberty, like any plausible defense of liberty, is a natural law defense." George quoted him at length about the duty to resist tyrants. As a fervent anti-Royalist and defender of liberty, Sidney opposed both the Stuart monarchs and the Cromwell Protectorate. He was executed for his exertions under King Charles II. George observed, "Both Sidney and Locke maintained that a sound account of natural law provides the most persuasive bulwark against oppression."[26]

Sidney, in his final speech before execution, decried tyranny, declaring that "none comes into the world with a saddle on his back, neither any booted and spurred to ride him."[27] Thomas Jefferson, whom George called Sidney's "disciple in the White House," famously echoed this quote in an 1825 letter to Henry Lee IV regarding the nation's founding principles.[28] Jefferson described the Declaration of Independence as deriving from the "harmonizing sentiments of the day," which included the "elementary books of public right, as Aristotle, Locke, Sidney, etc." Jefferson cited natural law as "common sense" that is accessible to all, George noted. Interestingly, although unremarked by George, Jefferson did not cite Thomas Aquinas.[29]

In *The Clash of Orthodoxies*, George also credited Jefferson's disciple James Madison for hailing the "transcendent law of nature and of nature's God" in *Federalist Papers* no. 43. George wrote, "The foundation of America's regime of freedom and equality, the world's first liberal democracy, would be incomprehensible in terms that reject the idea of natural law and natural rights." George described Jefferson, Madison, Abraham Lincoln, and Martin Luther King Jr. as advocates for American freedom and equality based on natural law. King declared, as George recalled, "I would agree with St. Augustine that 'an unjust law is no law at all.'"[30]

25 George, *Clash of Orthodoxies*, 162.

26 George, *Clash of Orthodoxies*, 163.

27 David B. Kopel, "Algernon Sidney: A Father of the Declaration of Independence," Cato Institute, July 3, 2016, https://www.cato.org/.

28 George, *Clash of Orthodoxies*, 163.

29 George, *Clash of Orthodoxies*, 157.

30 George, *Clash of Orthodoxies*, 164–65.

The credit George gave in 2001 to Locke, Sidney, Madison, Lincoln, King, and the American system is largely missing from his 2019 article with Anderson. In 2001, he observed that Pope John Paul II charted a "course fully in line with the 'liberalism' of the American Founding and constitutional tradition."[31] In 2019, George wrote nothing that contradicted his 2001 book, but the change in emphases perhaps reflected a shifting intuition about which principles most needed emphasis in the face of new challenges.

In 2019, George and Anderson emphasized the need to affirm free speech for ideas but with traditional restrictions on "slander, libel, conspiracy, false advertising, and incitement to violence," plus pornography, which they reject as "speech." From the natural law perspective, they said there is no single uniquely correct economic system, though the common good precludes both complete laissez-faire and collectivism. Government regulation of the market should be decided on the merits. Nor is there a "single uniquely correct way of structuring the relationship between church and state." Claims that "theology requires a specific political arrangement or proposes an 'ideal' arrangement is claiming too much." Hence "Pope Francis today and Pope Leo XIII more than a century ago were both articulating necessarily contingent judgments when they made claims about confessional states." The former is critical, and the latter was more affirming. "It's a contingent, prudential judgment—not a timeless truth of philosophy or theology." George and Anderson noted that "the political common good [as addressed by government] does not directly concern personal holiness or heavenly beatitude." They cited the Second Vatican Council:

> The religious acts whereby people, by their personal judgments, privately or publicly direct their lives to God transcend by their very nature the order of earthly and temporal affairs. The civil power therefore, whose proper responsibility is to attend to the temporal common good, ought indeed to recognize and favor the religious life of the citizenry, but must be said to exceed its limits if it presume to direct or inhibit religious acts.[32]

---

31 George, *Clash of Orthodoxies*, 235.
32 Anderson and George, "The Baby and the Bathwater."

George and Anderson summarized Catholic teaching by saying,

> The political community should foster the religious lives of its citizens (provided their way of life does not violate the rights of persons, public morality, or public peace), [but] it must not "direct or inhibit" religious acts because its jurisdiction is limited, as the council fathers teach, to the "temporal common good."[33]

Chief among common goods is public order. George and Anderson asserted that a "people might without injustice or political impropriety record their solemn belief about the identity and name of the true religious faith and community" through their constitutional order, by which they presumably meant a confessional state or some approximation. They rejected a "strict wall of separation at one extreme, and throne-and-altar unity at the other," in favor of an "in-between position" that "best fosters and favors the religious life of the citizens." And they paraphrased Richard John Neuhaus that the "alternative to the naked public square isn't the sacred public square but the civil public square in which citizens of all religious persuasions . . . can deliberate together about how we should order the life of the community we constitute."[34]

Ending with a qualified and measured endorsement of the American political order, George and Anderson reiterated their Thomist understanding of liberal institutions. "We should be aware of the demons in democracy," they warned, citing philosopher Ryszard Legutko, "and be sensitive to negative trajectories built into the logic of Lockean and other forms of Enlightenment liberalism, as Patrick Deneen argues." But they rejected Deneen's thesis, as described by Rod Dreher, that "classical liberalism strikes out." While "classical liberalism (or important elements of it) may not have hit a home run, it certainly hasn't struck out," they wrote. Examining the "philosophical defects of liberalism (as we ourselves have done) and recognizing the limitations of even morally defensible and desirable 'liberal' institutions is important" but "does not tell us what in effect will best promote the common good of any particular community."[35]

33 Anderson and George, "The Baby and the Bathwater."
34 Anderson and George, "The Baby and the Bathwater."
35 Anderson and George, "The Baby and the Bathwater."

George and Anderson concluded that "our 'liberal' institutions deserve better than to be dismissed a priori based on abstractions." And they "deserve to be admired when they enable the common good, and improved (or in some cases replaced) when they don't."[36]

Classical Liberalism and Protestantism

It would be fascinating to hear what liberal institutions George and Anderson think should be replaced. Their overall assessment that liberal democracy with its freedoms for religion and speech alongside protections against state coercion can sync with Catholic teaching and natural law is welcome news. A growing but still fortunately small, if formidable, chorus of Catholic integralists argue otherwise, some of them preferring a unity of throne and altar and all of them agreeing with Patrick Deneen about liberal democracy's intrinsic and irredeemable defects. Most orthodox and thoughtful Protestants and evangelicals would agree with George that Christianity does not directly dictate a specific form of governance. Instead, Christians are called to help build and sustain governments that best pursue justice, order, and liberty. Among the options so far realized among fallen humanity, liberal democracy has been the arrangement best able to facilitate at least approximate justice and human dignity.

Some evangelicals might wince at George not precluding a Catholic confessional state for some contexts. Perhaps at most, evangelicals would admit that such arrangements were maybe the best option available for much of Christendom's history. Moreover, one should hesitate to accuse George of adopting the idea of the confessional Catholic state as preferential and rather see it as one permutation of a host of possible church-state frameworks that could foreseeably allow for the common good among diverse peoples. But post-Reformation, few if any evangelicals could countenance this suggestion. A new but so far thankfully small resurgence of Christian reconstructionism would advocate the equivalent of a Calvinist confessional state, which most evangelicals would reject and on which George's thoughts would be most interesting.

George's rooting his preferred form of liberal democracy in Thomas Aquinas is neither surprising nor objectionable. It recalls Michael Novak's

---

36 Anderson and George, "The Baby and the Bathwater."

assertion that Thomas was the first Whig and essentially a founding grand-father, if not a direct father, of liberal democracy.[37] Evangelicals should vigorously affirm this insight while also pressing for elaboration on the very bumpy path across many centuries to freedom of religion and speech. Thomas favored civil government executing heretics as determined by church teaching.[38] Thomist premises built a potential foundation but did not construct the house, which required centuries more of lived experience. As historian Tom Holland describes, Christian ideas about human dignity and equality, ultimately developing into rights theory, unfolded slowly, gradually, but steadily across two millennia.[39] They are still unfolding today, as they will tomorrow. From this perspective, Thomas Aquinas and Locke, among others, are important chapters in a still unfolding story.

As Holland notes, the Protestant Reformation and subsequent events flowing from it were especially imperative for the development of mod-ern freedoms protected by liberal democracy.[40] As George recalls, the Protestant Reformers affirmed natural law, although they stressed that human sin had distorted it. This amplified distrust of human nature and consequent wariness of centralized authorities, including the church, ulti-mately enhanced Protestantism's trajectory toward liberal democracy. The Bible stresses that God is no respecter of persons. God deploys maidens and shepherd-boys to dethrone kings. He speaks his word to all who are willing to listen. Often it is the lowly who are most receptive to his mes-sage, while established religious authorities are resistant. All Christianity appreciates this divine economy in which the first become last and the last become first. But Protestantism relies especially on resistance to author-ity, tradition, and hierarchy, which is central to its role as the incubator of liberal democracy.

All Christianity appreciates the importance of the human individual, who is made in God's image, who is invited to communicate directly with him, who is judged by him and is offered redemption by him. As George, in his defense of "old fashioned liberalism," notes, "A central tenet of the

---

37 Michael Novak, "Thomas Aquinas, the First Whig: What Our Liberties Owe to a Neapolitan Mendicant," *Crisis Magazine*, October 1, 1990, https://www.crisismagazine.com/.

38 Thomas Aquinas, *Summa Theologiae* 2a2ae.11.3, https://www.newadvent.org/summa/.

39 Tom Holland, *Dominion: How the Christian Revolution Remade the World* (New York: Basic Books, 2019).

40 Holland, *Dominion*, 314–37.

Christian faith is that men are saved or damned as individuals."[41] But Protestantism, by stressing the priesthood of all believers and by often prioritizing personal over ecclesial interpretation, excels in individualism. Critics of contemporary and classical liberalism like Patrick Deneen rightly lament extreme autonomous individualism, which subjectivizes and personalizes all truth. Postliberals, especially integralists, in their critique of liberal democracy usually prefer to target the Enlightenment, perhaps because specifically naming Protestantism might discomfit potential allies. As Max Weber noted, the Enlightenment is the "laughing heir" of Protestantism, which can accept credit and blame for the Enlightenment's political fruits.[42] Catholic friends of American democracy and other liberal regimes should feel free to cite the providential role Protestantism played in advancing liberties and protections that benefit Catholics and millions of others around the world today.

Part of that Protestant story is John Locke, who was arguably the single most important political interpreter of the Reformation. Integralists and postliberals demonize Locke as the founder of liberalism, which they equate with all that is corrupt in the modern world. George, in his piece with Anderson, conflates Locke with John Rawls, although separated by three centuries. Locke, a believing Anglican who, as George has cited, believed in natural law, would not identify with Rawls, and Rawls, the once pious Episcopalian who became an atheist, would reject much of Locke. Perhaps it's better to let Locke stand on his own and to see him as a chief theorist behind the unfolding story of liberal democracy, especially for America, a long narrative including Thomas Aquinas but starting with the ancient Hebrews. In such histories it's best to avoid sweeping caricatures. For example, the evangelical thinker Francis Schaeffer in his historiography demonized Thomas for importing pagan classical philosophy, confusing a generation of evangelicals influenced by Schaeffer's apologetics.[43] History, including the development of liberal democracy, is ecumenical and complex.

---

41 George, *Clash of Orthodoxies*, 239.

42 Max Weber, *The Protestant Ethic and the "Spirit" of Capitalism; and Other Writings*, chap. 5, "Asceticism and the Spirit of Capitalism," trans. Peter Baehr and Gordon C. Wells (New York: Penguin, 2002).

43 Martin Cothran, "Where Francis Schaeffer Goes Wrong: Is the Belief in Natural Theology the Beginning of the End of Western Culture?," *Vital Remnants* (blog), January 15, 2009, http://vereloqui.blogspot.com/.

But at least Schaeffer offered an architecture for an evangelical understanding of history and political theory often lacking now. Robert George is a brilliant and tireless public thinker who spotlights the best insights of his Catholic tradition about justice, politics, and democracy when all are threatened by corrosive cultural trends. In *The Clash of Orthodoxies*, George extolled an "old-fashioned liberalism" that included "religious freedom, political equality, constitutional democracy, the rule of law, limited government, private property, the market economy, and human rights." He noted that many people who are today described as conservatives are actually old-fashioned liberals, himself included. So too, he noted, was Pope John Paul II, who labored for human rights, democracy, and especially religious freedom for all but especially the imprisoned nations behind the Iron Curtain.[44]

Evangelicals and Protestants should heed and esteem George, the "old-fashioned liberal" who believes in human rights and dignity for all, while also working to cultivate their own public thinkers, attached to the best of their traditions. Catholicism deeply appreciates the unfolding of church teaching and wisdom across time—and usually does so better than historic Protestantism and certainly than modern evangelicalism. Relying on George and others, evangelicals should reflect on the providential, centuries-long development and maturation of liberal democracy. That story is a complex zigzag that includes not just theorists but also conflict and compromise with unintended consequences that uplifted humanity. Liberal democracy's contemporary flaws cannot be corrected unless its background is recalled and its strengths reappropriated.

In *The Clash of Orthodoxies*, George concluded that "every Catholic should be, as Pope John Paul II himself certainly is, an old-fashioned liberal," supporting "religious freedom and other basic human rights," "limited government, the rule of law, private property, and at least some significant sharing by all citizens in the process of political decision making."[45] This counsel is relevant for Protestants and evangelicals too.

---

44 George, *Clash of Orthodoxies*, 232–33.
45 George, *Clash of Orthodoxies*, 257.

13

To Caesar (Only) What Is Caesar's

The Jurisprudence of Robert P. George

Adam J. MacLeod

"RENDER TO CAESAR the things that are Caesar's," our Lord told the lawyers who tried to embarrass him, "and to God the things that are God's" (Mark 12:17). Upon a first reading, this seems like one of Christ's simpler teachings. But sorting out *what* belongs to *whom* can be tricky. Caesar has a well-known tendency to claim that which does not belong to him. And though God's sustaining Logos is imprinted on all creation, it is not always easy to discern his face on the currency of his heavenly realm. But there we find his instruction in red letters. So we must scrutinize the oft-competing claims, partition the things in our possession, and allocate them to their lawful owners.

The stakes of the allocation are particularly high when Caesar claims not our money but our obedience to his laws. This claim does not always cause problems. Most of Caesar's laws agree with the great laws of our Lord. When Caesar declares, for example, that copyright infringement is a form of theft and instructs his judges to provide a remedy against those who appropriate literary and artistic expressions created by others, we find this law easy to reconcile with the eighth commandment[1] and all the other laws of God.

---

1 "You shall not steal" (Ex. 20:15). I recognize that different religious traditions number the commandments differently. Throughout this chapter, I refer to Anglican conventions as a via media. See the Anglican Church in North America, *To Be a Christian: An Anglican Catechism,*

We remember that all good laws can be summed up under the injunctions to love God and to love our neighbors as ourselves. And upon reflection, we can recognize that I fail to act in love toward my neighbor when I appropriate the benefits of his intellectual creation without his permission.

By obeying laws such as copyright statutes (and prohibitions against homicide, defamation, trafficking, and many other wrongs), we can render what is due to God and Caesar simultaneously. But some of Caesar's laws seem to have little to do with loving our neighbors. He might require us to refrain from preaching the gospel. He forbids compulsory prayer in his schools. He allows powerful companies to publish false and defamatory communications in our communities and even to carry harmful messages into our homes.

History is full of rulers, both imperial and petty, whose laws have favored the corrupt and well connected over the meek and the honest, liars over truth tellers, slave owners over slaves, and members of one race or tribe over others. We need not reach too far back in American history to remember the efforts of civil rights leaders such as Martin Luther King Jr., a Christian minister, to abrogate laws mandating racial segregation. A century earlier, Christian intellectuals such as Harriet Beecher Stowe and Frederick Douglass made a powerful case for the abolition of slavery, an institution that did not exist in our fundamental common law but was sustained by the laws of several states well into the nineteenth century.

Sometimes Christians have even disobeyed such laws. Christians operated the Underground Railroad to enable escaped slaves to evade the reach of the Fugitive Slave Act. And King famously defied a judicial order enjoining him from leading a peaceful protest against segregation in Birmingham, Alabama.

Sometimes Caesar raises the stakes quite high, as when he commands that we fight in unjust wars or that we teach our children important falsehoods. Does it belong to Caesar to demand that we deny the rights of children to be raised by their mother and father or that we participate in the deliberate killing of innocent human beings? These questions demand answers. But two contradictory answers both seem plausible. On the one hand, the

---

approved ed. (Wheaton, IL: Crossway, 2020), 106–8; *The Book of Common Prayer* (Huntington Beach, CA: Anglican Liturgy Press, 2019), 100–101.

apostle Paul tells us in his letter to the Romans that we have an obligation as a matter of conscience to obey Caesar's laws, for God has delegated authority to Caesar to make and enforce the law. On the other hand, all the Law and the Prophets are summed up in the injunction to love God and love our neighbors. And many of Caesar's commands seem unloving to both God and neighbor. So they would seem to be no laws at all.

It turns out that in order to render to each his own, we need to know what a law is. Fortunately, there exists an entire field of academic study devoted to that question: jurisprudence. Unhappily, many of the great jurisprudence scholars of the last century or so are dogmatically committed to statist ideologies, determinist worldviews, and overspecialization that deflects them from meaningful knowledge of law and legal justice. Unable or unwilling to perceive the universal human capacity to make and obey law, they have fashioned theories that hold no place for most human law—common law, civil law, and the *jus gentium* (that body of international law that is shared in common by all civilized nations). And they are quite bigoted against the moral law that everyone knows by reason, the law that, in Paul's words, all people have "written on their hearts" (Rom. 2:15).

That law written on the hearts of all human beings is known among Christian thinkers by the name that Cicero and other Roman jurists gave to it, "natural law," or by Aristotle's term, "natural justice." Human beings, in contrast to plants and animals, are beings capable of reasoned deliberation and choice as we decide what to do and what not to do. Though natural law is "natural" in the sense of being fitted to our nature, we do not derive it from general or special knowledge of human nature.[2] Instead, we know natural law as self-evidently true, we obey it, and we give it specific content in our lives as we reason and decide to do what is good and right.[3]

---

2 John M. Finnis, *Natural Law and Natural Rights*, 2nd ed. (Oxford: Oxford University Press, 2011), 33–36; Robert P. George, "Kelsen and Aquinas on the Natural Law Doctrine," in *Saint Thomas Aquinas and the Natural Law Tradition: Contemporary Perspectives*, ed. John Goyette, Mark S. Latkovic, and Richard S. Myers (Washington, DC: Catholic University of America Press, 2004), 237–59.

3 Thomas Aquinas, *Summa Theologia* 1a2ae.71.2; George, "Kelsen and Aquinas," 239, 241. For many centuries, jurists followed the Roman convention of distinguishing between two meanings or senses of "natural law." R. H. Helmholz, *Natural Law in Court: A History of Legal Theory in Practice* (Cambridge, MA: Harvard University Press, 2015), 2–3. The first sense recognizes that humans have an animal nature and that we share with other animals instincts for self-preservation and procreation, which instincts are "natural" laws governing our conduct.

Our agreements, conventions, habits, statutes, regulations, and judicial opinions do not determine the validity of natural law. To the contrary, natural law supplies the objective criteria by which all other laws are evaluated. Natural law does not depend for its existence on our assent or recognition. We can ignore natural law, we can efface it from our institutions and practices, even to some extent from our deliberations and character, but we have no power to eradicate it or to erase it entirely from our understanding.

The dominant jurisprudential theories that shaped the views of the last several generations of legal scholars, judges, and public servants admit only one criterion of legal validity: law is essentially power. All law is law insofar as it emanates from the will of Caesar, cultural elites, or some other powerful person or group. The criteria of legal justice that contemporary jurists employ are equally reductionist. They think that law can be assessed according to its economic efficiency or perhaps its facility for advancing the interests of historically oppressed groups. But of natural justice and righteousness they have little to say.

Robert George on Caesar's Laws

Enter the man who holds the McCormick Chair of Jurisprudence at Princeton University, Robert P. George. As the other chapters in this book make abundantly clear, jurisprudence is not Professor George's only area of interest, nor the only subject matter in which he has achieved mastery. But jurisprudence is his day job. And George's jurisprudence is an integral aspect of his entire academic project, informing and shaping his views on constitutionalism, human rights, and civil liberties.

George identifies law by its place within what he alternatively calls (following analytical philosophers with whom he studied jurisprudence at the University of Oxford) a "legal system" or "legal order."[4] Laws serve a role or

---

The Institutes of Justinian 1.2. Second, and more significantly for the purposes of this chapter, humans also have a rational nature and can assess our own actions and the actions of others for congruence with "natural" reason, a law that jurists call the *jus commune,* from which all just human laws derive either by addition or deduction. *The Digest of Justinian,* trans. Charles Henry Monro, ed. Theodor Mommsen (Cambridge: Cambridge University Press, 1904), 1:4. Human law is made and obeyed by the exercise of reason. Therefore, this chapter is concerned with natural law that is "natural" in the second sense of being consistent with human reason.

4   Robert P. George, "One Hundred Years of Legal Philosophy," *Notre Dame Law Review* 74, no. 5 (1999): 1533, 1542. The idea of a legal "system" is a recent, foreign import into Anglo-American jurisprudence. Common law jurists have always thought in terms of remedies and institutions

function within a legal order, and by understanding that function from the perspective of those who live and act within the order, one can understand the laws. As George explains,

> The central or focal case of a legal system, to borrow a principle of Aristotle's method in social study, is one in which legal rules and principles function as practical reasons for citizens, as well as judges and other officials, because of people's apprehension of their moral value.[5]

A lot is packed into that sentence. All of it stands at some distance from now-dominant conventions among legal academics in the United States. And all of it yields insight. The sentence is well worth unpacking.

It is worthwhile first to observe George's method of inquiry. He understands law better than most scholars today because he goes about acquiring understanding of the law in a more comprehensive, productive way. For the last century, American legal scholars have generally approached the study of law in one of two ways. George's approach improves on both.

Some scholars, known as legal realists or pragmatists, conceive of human law as deterministic, much like the motions of bodies in space, the conservation and loss of energy, and other subjects of study in the physical sciences. They treat jurisprudence as a predictive enterprise, wherein one can predict judicial outcomes given certain data about judicial decision-making, just as, after understanding the laws of gravity and thermodynamics, one can predict the motion and entropy of physical bodies given certain data. On this approach, the job of the jurisprudential scholar is to collect as much data as possible from prior judicial decisions and then to predict future judicial behavior in a scientific fashion.[6] So we hear a lot these days about "liberal" and "conservative" judges, and many law professors attempt to

---

that deliver legal justice in order to vindicate rights, sanction wrongs, and keep the peace. Most common law rights are customary in origin and not products of comprehensive, systemic, legal design. Historical jurists thus tend to think in terms of norms and institutions that sustain order or ordered liberty. Though analytical jurists such as George often use the term "systems," this essay employs the more ecumenical term "orders," a term that George also uses.

5 George, "One Hundred Years," 1547.

6 See generally George C. Christie, Patrick H. Martin, and Adam J. MacLeod, *Jurisprudence: Text and Readings on the Philosophy of Law*, 4th ed. (St. Paul, MN: West Academic, 2020), 820–99, 1187–1220.

correlate judicial decisions with various causal factors that have little to do with the law, such as economic conditions and cultural assumptions.

The other dominant approach in jurisprudence is shared by some nineteenth-century English scholars and American proponents of critical legal studies, critical race theory, and other poststructuralist approaches to law. These theorists all treat law as essentially the exercise of power. The power may be cultural, religious, or social. Or it might be more directly coercive, like the official command or prohibition of a state sovereign, backed by threat of sanction or injury. Whatever the source of power, what is interesting and important about law is not its content or its relation to justice but rather that it reflects an inequality of power.[7]

George does not deny that social sciences such as psychology and economics can teach us important truths about the law. Nor does he deny that power is a fact within human society or that it often plays a role in enforcing legal norms. Indeed, he affirms the necessity of legal authority and acknowledges that authority must sometimes be exercised coercively.[8] But he denies that efficiency, judicial habits, power, coercion, and inequality are everything that is worth knowing about the law. Indeed, they are not even what is *most* worth knowing. No theorist can adequately understand law "until he understands the practical point of the law from the perspective of actors within the system who do not perceive their own deliberations, choices, and actions to be 'caused,' but rather understand themselves to be making laws for reasons and acting on reasons provided by the laws."[9] Thus, to stand entirely outside all legal orders as an external scientific observer is to miss most of what is interesting and important about the law.

What is most important about law from the perspective of those who live within legal orders is not whether law predicts how judges might rule in future cases, nor that people who make laws have more power than other people, nor that inequalities of power will motivate people to act in compliance with the expressed will of the powerful. What is most important about the law—what is most central to the reality of law—is that it gives a person a reason to obey it, an obligation to act or refrain from acting in a certain way.

7   See generally Christie, Martin, and MacLeod, *Jurisprudence*, 495–684, 1067–1180.

8   Robert P. George, *In Defense of Natural Law* (Oxford: Oxford University Press, 1999), 107.

9   George, "One Hundred Years," 1542–43. Compare Finnis, *Natural Law and Natural Rights*, 11–18; Christie, Martin, and MacLeod, *Jurisprudence*, 1235–37, 1262–73.

George argues that a law provides a sufficient reason when it functions as part of a legal order that conduces to the common good of the community as a whole. People perceive law's validity as a function of law's ability to sustain the conditions necessary for the common good. So, George insists, a good descriptive theory of law ultimately comes to the "famous *practical* definition of law as an ordinance of reason directed to the common good," which the Christian philosopher Thomas Aquinas offered many centuries ago.[10]

To see *that*, George uses a method of inquiry known as focal-meaning analysis. Employed by Aristotle and then revived in the twentieth century by George's Oxford mentors, H. L. A. Hart and John Finnis, the practice identifies what is most salient or important about the thing being studied—what is central to the thing's identity and most focal to the meaning of the concept that we use to describe and think about the thing—and distinguishes what is peripheral or incidental. To borrow an example from Aristotle, the focal meaning of friendship is that each person in the friendship cares about the well-being of the other. One sees this fact about friendship when one considers a central case of friendship, a relationship in which each person desires what is good for the other and desires the friend's good for its own sake, and this desire for the good of the other is reciprocal.[11] That central case can be understood better in contrast to weaker or lesser instances of friendship, which partake less of what is most important about friendship. In peripheral or derivative friendships, the friends do not love each other for themselves but only for what each can get from the other.[12] An example is people engaged in a commercial transaction, where each desires the good of the other only instrumentally as a means to provide the service or item that the other wants and thus to complete the transaction.

Applying the focal-meaning method to the study of law, George sees (as Hart and Finnis saw) that what is most central to the identity of law from the perspective of those who inhabit legal orders is not that it has predictive efficacy, nor that its enforcement often requires the assertion of power. Like friendships of utility, prediction and power are incidental to law. A rule that *only* allows us to predict judicial behavior is peripheral to law; it is

10 George, "One Hundred Years," 1547.
11 Aristotle, *Ethics* 8.2.
12 Aristotle, *Ethics* 8.3.

contingent and parasitical on the prior existence of a real legal order in which parties and judges understand themselves to have legal obligations. And a command that *only* obliges us to act for fear of another's superior power is not a central instance of a law (i.e., not a good law) but rather is a defective law. A gunman who offers the choice, "Your money or your life," is neither giving us law nor supplying us with legal obligation, though he is certainly exercising power.[13]

By contrast, the central case of a law is a thing that carries a special kind of moral obligation that is intelligible within a legal order. Examples include a will, a contract, and a statute. Each of these supplies reasons for people to do something they might not have done otherwise or to refrain from doing something they might have done but for the existence of the law. To distribute a deceased person's things according to his or her last will and testament, to do what one promised to do in a contractual agreement, and to refrain from doing some act that is prohibited by statute are all examples of acting according to the law.

From those examples, the jurisprudence scholar can discern the focal meaning of a law. It is a reason that people have for acting or refraining from acting in a particular way. When people encounter a norm or institution and perceive that they have good practical reasons to submit to the authority of that norm or institution because of the function that it serves within a legal order that sustains the common good, then we can say that they have encountered a law.

Such things as wills, contracts, and statutes do not make themselves. Humans make them. So, as Thomas Aquinas recognized, law is not only oriented toward the common good; it is also promulgated. It can be promulgated either by conduct or by words.[14] Promulgation by conduct is how we get customary laws such as the jury trial, the estates of property ownership, and the laws of the high seas. Promulgation by words is how we get legislation and administrative regulations, known in jurisprudence as "positive" laws, so called because they are made by the positing and acceptance of a proposition or set of propositions.[15]

---

13 H. L. A. Hart, *The Concept of Law*, 3rd ed. (Oxford: Oxford University Press, 2012), 82–91.

14 Thomas Aquinas, *Summa Theologiae* 1a2ae.97.3.

15 See generally Richard Ekins, *The Nature of Legislative Intent*, Oxford Legal Philosophy (Oxford: Oxford University Press, 2012).

The promulgation of law is a creative act. And the creation of law is a human achievement. That we make laws is one way that we reflect the image of God, ordering creation within time in a way that resembles God's ordering of all creation across time and space.

Most human law is not *just* divine law or natural law applied directly to human activities by logical deduction. Choices must be made in the selection of law's features, just as an architect must make certain choices in the design of a house.[16] George has explained,

> Aquinas, following up a lead from Aristotle, observed that the positive law is derived from the natural law in two different ways. In the case of certain principles, the legislator translates the natural law into the positive [human] law more or less directly. So, for example, a conscientious legislator will prohibit grave injustices such as murder, rape and theft by moving by a process akin to deduction from the moral proposition that, say, the killing of innocent persons is intrinsically unjust to the conclusion that the positive law must prohibit (and punish) such killing. In a great many cases, however, the movement from the natural law to the positive law in the practical thinking of the conscientious legislator cannot be so direct. . . . [For example, the legislator] cannot identify a uniquely correct scheme of traffic regulation which can be translated from the natural law to the positive law.[17]

Natural law determines the just content of human law in part but not in whole. This partial indeterminacy is true even though natural law teaches that health is a human good and that coordinating vehicular traffic is necessary to preserve health. The moral fact that health is good and worth preserving and the empirical fact that traffic accidents injure people in respect of their physical health are both objectively true, and no just legal order could deny or ignore them. But there nevertheless remain open questions about how to coordinate traffic, whether to drive on the left or right, whether to use stoplights or roundabouts, and so on.

That much of natural law is indeterminate and that humans need to make choices about how to specify human law places law within the realm of

---

16 See Thomas Aquinas, *Summa Theologiae* 1a2ae.95.2.
17 George, *In Defense of Natural Law*, 108.

human creations, in what Aristotle called the order of making (as distinguished from the order of doing). Human law is an artifact or product of the practical reasoning in which people are always engaged while coordinating their actions to solve practical problems in community. George thus argues, "The natural law is in no sense a human creation. The positive law (of any community), however, *is* a human creation. It is an object—a vast cultural object composed of sometimes very complicated rules and principles, but an object nonetheless."[18] It has a moral purpose—the ordering of communities for a common good—but it exists as its own thing.

Legal reasoning is distinct from moral reasoning because human law is distinct from natural law.[19] This explains why legal obligation and moral obligation—what we owe to Caesar and to God—can come apart. It also explains why we may have obligations to submit to both Caesar and God, even when our obligation to obey God's higher law trumps Caesar's unjust demands.

What we owe to Caesar is the recognition that his laws are what they purport to be and that they oblige our submission even when they do not deserve our rational obedience. George affirms the teachings of earlier natural law thinkers such as Augustine, Thomas Aquinas, and Martin Luther King Jr. that an unjust law may be disobeyed in some cases, though the person disobeying the law must submit to the sanction and other consequences of disobedience to demonstrate respect for the authority of the persons and institutions that made the law.[20] This is why, for example, King marched to protest against racial segregation laws in defiance of a judicial order, then willingly sat in a Birmingham jail as punishment for his civil disobedience. The first act demonstrated King's obedience to natural law; the second demonstrated his submission to human law, which is indispensable to the ordering of the political community toward the common good.

A Conservative-Liberal Jurisprudence

Some may find other implications of George's jurisprudence surprising. For one, while he affirms natural law, George does not identify law with

---

18 George, *In Defense of Natural Law*, 109.

19 George, "One Hundred Years," 1548–49.

20 Robert P. George, "The 1993 St. Ives Lecture—Natural Law and Civil Rights: From Jefferson's 'Letter to Henry Lee' to Martin Luther King's 'Letter from Birmingham Jail,'" *Catholic University Law Review* 43, no. 1 (1993): 143, 154–56.

morality, nor even *good* law with morality. Law and morality occupy distinct normative domains. That an action should be done does not entail that the law requires it. That an act should not be done does not entail that the law forbids it. And human law often requires or forbids actions that natural law and divine law leave undetermined. To identify the rules and rights of the law, it is necessary to look at law as it is, rather than to identify law with moral or religious norms.

Because law and morality are distinct, the law can leave some moral questions unaddressed. George thinks that the law *should* refrain from enforcing every moral obligation. There are sound reasons for law to leave people at liberty to make moral and intellectual errors, as long as those errors are not grave and do not by themselves threaten the political community. Thus, though George is socially and culturally conservative, when it comes to the identification and competence of law, he is a liberal, in the classical sense of the word *liberal*, meaning someone who finds value in ordered liberty and the civil liberties that make it possible.

George's moral and political philosophy generally leads him to conclusions that today are described as "conservative" and "religious." The conviction that all human beings are bearers of equal rights, the conception of marriage as a comprehensive union of man and woman, and a theory of politics that recognizes a role for political society to play in promoting virtue and repressing vice are all hallmarks of a traditional approach to political questions. Many religious Americans share those convictions, and most nonbelievers reject them. For this reason (and for this reason alone, really), George is sometimes characterized as a moralist who wants to use the law to impose his own views on others. But that characterization misses the mark.

To be sure, George's philosophical inquiries often lead him to conclusions that political conservatives and religious citizens affirm. And George does not hold the view that government and public law can be neutral regarding competing conceptions of the good, the just, the true, and the beautiful. But none of that is sufficient to justify coercive moralism. George is not a coercive moralist. He supports civil liberties, including freedoms of speech and conscience and other rights to believe and say things that turn out to be untrue or wrong. And he believes that those liberties belong to everyone: the virtuous and the vicious, the wise and the foolish, the religious and the materialist alike.

George can be a social and political conservative while also being a civil libertarian in part because he understands that law and morality are not the same thing. As explained above, natural law is not human law, and human law is not just the logical entailments of natural law. Natural law and natural rights are enduring and are not contingent on human choice and action. Human law and civil rights are contingent on human choice and action; they can be otherwise than what they are, and they can change over time.[21] The separability of human law from natural and divine law entails that the law can leave people at liberty to decide certain moral questions for themselves.

At the same time, George's attention to both natural law and human law enables him to critique laws according to their proper ends, the extent of their orientation toward legal and natural justice. "If there are objective or true principles of justice (such as the principle of equality) that constitute a higher standard," George argues, "then legislative action may be rationally guided and criticized in the light of those principles; and legal rights, or the absence of certain legal rights, can be judged morally good or bad."[22]

Whether the law *should* enshrine any particular civil liberty is a different question from whether a right is recognized as a legal right within a society's legal institutions—indeed, it is a different kind of question—and the fact that civil liberties are possible does not mean that any particular liberty is justified. No society can justly recognize liberties to commit murder, mayhem, or enslavement, to take three obvious examples. There is, George argues, a relation between "the *time-bound historicity* and the *timeless rationality* of the principle of equal rights."[23]

More generally, the justice of a law is a question that neither legal scholarship nor legal philosophy can alone address. If some traditionalists have mistakenly identified the validity of a law with the justice of that law, many liberals and progressives have erroneously assumed that the power standing behind a command is a sufficient reason to oblige a person to obey. George avoids both errors.

Room for Difference

In other respects also, George's jurisprudence is less dogmatic than one might expect a natural law theory to be. His theory of law is consistent with a wide

21 George, "Civil Rights," 144.

22 George, "Civil Rights," 144–45.

23 George, "Civil Rights," 144.

array of legal concepts and with a variety of legal norms and institutions. It contains no principled grounds to reject: customary law in favor of legislation, or vice versa; legislative supremacy in favor of judicial review, or vice versa; or a wide latitude for voluntary arrangements in international law.[24] In all those areas (and more), George argues that natural law is indeterminate and that selecting one legal solution over other possible solutions is the job of human law itself. For example, natural law does not by itself entail that judges should have the power to review legislation for reasonableness, nor to strike down or refuse to enforce laws that judges find unreasonable.[25]

George does not argue that every feature of a just legal order is a matter of indifference. No just order may tolerate official actions and judgments that are arbitrary, retroactive, or confounding. The rule of law is a moral duty incumbent on all who hold public office, owed to their fellow citizens out of respect for their dignity as human beings, the kind of beings who act for legal reasons. The acts of making law and of obeying law are distinctly human acts, exercises of a uniquely human capacity. George calls this capacity "fitness for the rule of law."[26] Unlike inanimate objects and even animals, human beings are capable of governing themselves, acting for *reasons* rather than merely because of passions, appetites, desires, and vicious dispositions. The reasons according to which people govern their actions can include laws.

Unjust Law as Laws

Nevertheless, George's conception of the rule of law is a modest conception as compared to the conception employed by early American jurists, such as John Adams and Joseph Story. Following a standard convention in analytical jurisprudence, George equates the rule of law with the formal or procedural attributes articulated by an earlier jurist, Lon Fuller,[27] certain nonsubstantive characteristics of due process of law such as clarity, publicity, prospectivity, coherence, and consistent administration.[28]

---

24 George, *In Defense of Natural Law*, 228–45.

25 Robert P. George, "Natural Law, the Constitution, and the Theory and Practice of Judicial Review," *Fordham Law Review* 69, no. 6 (2001): 2269, 2279–81; George, *In Defense of Natural Law*, 110–11.

26 George, *In Defense of Natural Law*, 120.

27 George, *In Defense of Natural Law*, 113; George, "One Hundred Years," 1544–46.

28 Lon L. Fuller, *The Morality of Law* (New Haven, CT: Yale University Press, 1964).

By comparison, early American jurists thought that due process was a necessary, but not sufficient, condition for achieving the rule of law. They viewed the rule of law as the opposite of the rule of men, and they understood certain rights to be beyond the competence of officials to alter retrospectively. Such unalterable rights include both inalienable rights, such as the sanctity of life and conscience, and certain vested rights, such as noncontingent property estates and trust benefits, contracts and leases whose subject matter is not inherently wrong, and the rights of children to have the support of their natural parents.

George does not assign to the rule of law the task of placing substantive limits on legislators and administrators. But neither does he claim that the rule of law is the only constraint on official actions. The work performed in American law by prepositive, inalienable, and vested rights is performed in George's jurisprudence by the general, prepositive requirements of justice, that is, natural law. He insists that "even the most scrupulous adherence to the rule of law does not exhaust the debt owed by rulers to the ruled," for the "rule of law is not all that political morality requires. Beings that are fit for the rule of law deserve, moreover, to be ruled by laws that are just."[29]

George's jurisprudence has resources for evaluating law. Those resources are located outside human law, in natural law. George explains,

> Authoritative actors in a legal system may fail to secure or enforce a right that, morally speaking, ought to be secured and enforced; or they may posit and enforce a right that ought not to be posited and enforced. For example, the law might unjustly fail to give a certain class of human beings a legal right not to be enslaved or arbitrarily killed; that is, it might unjustly confer upon another class a legal right to enslave or kill them. The justice or injustice of such acts of positive law is measured by reference to standards of the higher law, i.e., the moral law, that are objective or true eternally and universally.[30]

On this account, the injustice of a law goes to its character rather than to its status as a law. An unjust law is a law, though defective. Indeed, an unjust law is all the more unjust for being backed by legal authority.

29 George, *In Defense of Natural Law*, 121.
30 George, "Civil Rights," 145.

The differences between George and earlier natural law jurists such as Adams and Story are insignificant in the grand sweep of American jurisprudence. But they do have some practical consequences. In particular, they affect how lawyers and judges are obligated to fulfill their oaths to uphold and defend the law, and they affect the extent to which those oaths can be reconciled with higher duties to obey the natural and divine law.

For example, consider the legal status of children. Because common law considers parental duties to be inalienable and the correlative rights of children to be vested, common law has no category for adoption but instead makes provision for neglected children by the offices of guardian and ward. In common law jurisdictions such as the United States (except Louisiana, which as a former French holding is governed by Continental civil law), termination of parental rights and legal adoption are not part of the fundamental law. State legislatures have created adoption privileges by statute in derogation of common law. Those legal innovations were soon followed by other legal changes that further weakened the bonds of the natural family, such as surrogacy enforcement and no-fault divorce. Following the lead of great English common law jurists, such as William Blackstone, American jurists throughout most of American history would have considered many of those innovations unreasonable and therefore beyond the competence of human lawmakers. Under canons of charitable construction, they would have gone to great lengths to avoid imputing to legislators any intention to disrupt the legal bonds of a natural family unless expressly mandated in particular detail by competent legislatures.

Like common law jurists, George stands opposed in principle to legal innovations that break the bonds of the natural family (though he might not go as far as common law in rejecting adoption). For him, the normative work is performed not by legal concepts and canons of judicial interpretation but by principles of natural law. Thus, he might say that a particular judgment terminating parental rights or enforcing a surrogacy contract over the objections of the natural mother is unjust, but whether it is a lawful judgment in the sense of being correctly derived from human law is a question to be answered by reference to the positive law of the jurisdiction in which the judgment is rendered. In George's jurisprudence, that a statute or judgment deprives a person of an established right does not by itself affect the legal status of the statute or judgment; it may be a law while being an unjust law.

Another example of a possible difference between George and earlier American jurists concerns the legal status of slavery laws. In American jurisprudence, the reasons for abolishing slavery without paying compensation to slave owners are found within the law itself. Slavery has no place in common law first and foremost because it is not among the immemorial customs of England, whence common law came. Furthermore, slave owning is inherently wrongful—*malum in se*, in the words used by common law jurists—and common law recognizes no right to commit an inherent wrong. Each statute or contract authorizing a relation of slavery is, as one jurist expressed it, "an antichristian law, and one which violates the rights of nature."[31] Common law thus includes both a conventional element—immemorial custom—and a natural law element—inherent wrongs—that count against slavery's recognition in law and legal judgment.

Because slavery has no place in common law, slave laws have no status as legal reasons but are only enactments backed by force: naked power. A slave statute or contract therefore cannot reach beyond the place where its maker has power to enforce it, and its power ceases the moment a slave gets beyond the lawmaker's jurisdiction. This is known as the English doctrine of free soil. Blackstone counted the right of emancipation secured by the doctrine among the "absolute rights" of common law.[32] As another jurist explained it,

> The law of slavery is, however, a law *in invitum* [by force of law contrary to consent]; and when a party gets out of the territory where it prevails, and out of the power of his master, and gets under the protection of another power, without any wrongful act done by the party giving that protection, the right of the master, which is founded on the municipal law of the particular place only, does not continue, and there is no right of action against a party who merely receives the slave in that country, without doing any wrongful act.[33]

It follows that any privileges of slave owning or trading cannot be vested rights but continue only so long as supported by positive enactments backed

31 . Forbes v. Cochrane, 107 Eng. Rep. 450, 460 (1824).
32 William Blackstone, *Commentaries on the Laws of England* (n.p., 1765), 1:*122.
33 Forbes v. Cochrane, 107 Eng. Rep. 456.

by necessity or force. As stated in an 1835 English decision, "It is therefore by virtue of the arbitrary institutions of society, and by those alone, that one man has an interest in the services of another: property, strictly speaking, in the person of a human being cannot exist."[34] By contrast, the right of the runaway slave to remain emancipated after escaping the slave-tolerating jurisdiction *is* vested, and no one may lawfully return him to the custody of his previous master.[35] From these legal reasons, American jurists derived the judgment that the Thirteenth Amendment and other laws abolishing slavery did not deprive slavers of any legal rights and that slave masters were therefore not entitled to compensation as a matter of law.[36]

By comparison, for George, the normative resources for limiting or terminating slavery are external to the law. He quotes with approval Justice Clarence Thomas's judgment, "Those who deny natural law cannot get me out of slavery."[37] Anyone who insists that rights of free soil and emancipation are historically contingent has no ground to insist that freedom is rationally superior to enslavement, and, as George explains, "Neither history nor convention could provide an adequate rational defense against the return in the future of some form of slavery."[38] This does not commit George to the view that slavery was compatible with common law, nor that the Fugitive Slave Act was constitutional, nor that the right to own slaves was entailed in the laws of any particular state. His legal theory simply commits him to no position on the question whether slavery was consistent with the laws of the United States prior to ratification of the Thirteenth Amendment, though his moral philosophy insists that slavery is incompatible with natural law and the inherent dignity of all human beings.

As George frequently points out, those same natural law principles that led to the conclusion that slavery is unjust find expression as political ideals in landmark instruments such as the Declaration of Independence and in the speeches and writings of prominent Americans such as Thomas Jefferson, Abraham Lincoln, and Martin Luther King Jr. And for most purposes, it may not matter whether we find the intellectual resources needed

34 Griffin v. Potter, 14 Wend. 209, 212 (N.Y. Sup. Ct. 1835).
35 Somerset v. Stewart, 98 Eng. Rep. 499 (1772).
36 See, e.g., Buckner v. Street, 4 F. Cas. 578 (E.D. Ark. 1871).
37 George, "Civil Rights," 145.
38 George, "Civil Rights," 146.

to abolish slavery and rehabilitate the family in our laws or in our political ideals and traditions. On the other hand, the extent to which injustice has pervaded our fundamental law does affect how we understand ourselves as Americans. On that question, George's jurisprudence is open to a wider variety of interpretations than that of earlier American jurists.

Caesar's to Caesar, God's to God

On George's account, consistency with natural law is not a criterion of a law's status as a law, understood as an artifact promulgated by one in lawful authority. It is instead a criterion of a law's normative force, understood as a reason for action. Some laws can be described accurately as laws insofar as they satisfy formal criteria of legal validity, especially authority and promulgation, but they are defective laws insofar as they are contrary to the common good, and therefore people do not always have sufficient reason to obey them.

Human laws that violate natural law fail to perform the function that law is supposed to perform. Just as a broken clock can be understood as a clock though it does not accurately tell the time, an unjust law can be understood as a law even though it does not obligate one to obey. The unjust law can intelligibly be understood as a law in one sense, though it fails to function as a law in the focal sense because by itself it does not supply a sufficient reason to act or refrain from acting in the way that the law dictates.

Caesar may demand our submission, though he may not always demand our obedience. Christians such as King who have used civil disobedience to call attention to grievously unjust laws demonstrated respect for the law both by refusing to obey the laws *and* by submitting to the penalty or liability for disobeying them. To obey Christ's admonition to render to God and Caesar what is respectively theirs is first to distinguish between law as an artifact of authoritative promulgation and law as a reason to direct our actions. Robert P. George's jurisprudence helps us see the difference.

14

Partners in Truth Seeking

Robert P. George and Cornel West

Paul D. Miller

THIS BOOK IS ABOUT engaging the work of Robert P. George—meaning, in other chapters, primarily his written work. But there are other kinds of work that contribute to George's legacy, the sort to which the apostle Paul was referring when he reminded us that we are God's "workmanship, created in Christ Jesus *for good works*, which God prepared beforehand, that we should walk in them" (Eph. 2:10). Most of George's good works of this sort are, presumably, not public, so as not to practice righteousness before others, as Matthew warned against (Matt. 6:1). But George in recent years has become public about one particular work: the work of friendship, especially friendship with one particular person. George's friendship with Cornel West—his fellow scholar, Christian, public intellectual, activist, and sparring partner—may stand among his most enduring, instructive, and inspiring public good works.

West and George's friendship piques interest because the two are, on the surface, almost comedically different, an odd couple ordered up from central casting. Only two years apart in age, born in the mid-Boomer generation, the two grew up on opposite sides of Jim Crow. West once referred to another White theologian as a "vanilla Texas brother, and I'm a chocolate California brother," which would be as apt in reference to George.[1] George is from West Virginia,

---

1 Cornel West and Robert George, "Kenan Distinguished Lecture in Ethics," Duke University, February 11, 2019, video, 1:34:11, https://www.youtube.com/.

the grandson of coal miners of Italian and Syrian background; West grew up in Sacramento, an African American son of a teacher and general contractor. Both scholars are more than scholars but in different ways: George is an accomplished guitarist and bluegrass banjo player; West has published three spoken-word albums and appeared in Hollywood blockbusters.[2] George speaks with the genteel, hyperliterate cadence of an Ivy League don; West speaks the earthy, rhythmic idiom of the Black Baptist tradition that forms part of his religious background. George is Roman Catholic; West claims Blaise Pascal, Søren Kierkegaard, and Dietrich Bonhoeffer on top of his Baptist roots. George is the second coming of Thomas Aquinas; West, of Frederick Douglass.

The two disagree on almost every major political issue of our time. George defends the free market and entrepreneurialism; West is a fierce critic of capitalism and what he calls imperialism. George is one of the foremost spokesmen for the pro-life movement and in defense of a traditional understanding of gender and marriage (he helped draft the Manhattan Declaration on life, marriage, and religious liberty); West holds typically progressive views on social issues. In the 2016 presidential primary elections, George endorsed Ted Cruz, a Republican senator from Texas; West favored Bernie Sanders, the democratic socialist senator from Vermont. Until the 2016 general election, the two could reliably be found on different sides of the partisan aisle.

But "love is never reducible to politics," West explains, "just as friendship is never reducible to agreement on public policy."[3] George, reflecting on their friendship and their disagreements, preached a short homily in 2021 on the meaning of friendship, inquiry, and truth:

> When I see a guy as smart as Cornel and he's well intentioned, with a good heart and spirit of Christian love like Cornel, who disagrees with me about something, my first reaction isn't to get angry. My first reaction is, "Wait a minute, I've got to rethink this. [There's a] possibility to be wrong about this; if somebody as smart and kind and compassionate as Cornel disagrees with me about this, it's time to think. . . . I know he's not a bigot

---

2   Cornel West played Councillor West in *The Matrix Reloaded* and *The Matrix Revolutions*, directed by the Wachowski brothers, admirers of West's work.

3   Cornel West, interview by the author over videoconference call, August 31, 2021.

and I know he's not a hater, I know he's not a libertine, I know he's not a fool, and so I better think about this more carefully and think it through again." And when that's your attitude, what you find is that you are never really adversaries, you're never really opponents, you are partners in the project of truth seeking. You have different views at the moment, you might end up with different views, but you're working together toward a common good, a common goal. Your goal isn't to defeat the other guy, or show the superiority of your arguments—that's not how we argue. It's to get at the truth.[4]

To those who might wonder how friendship could work across the political aisle, George and West might respond that if politics interferes with friendship, we do not understand true friendship at all.

Origins of a Friendship

George and West met while serving on the faculty of Princeton University. George has taught there since 1985, and West had an initial stint from 1988 to 1994, but the two did not interact substantively in those years. George sees in retrospect the seeds of their future friendship. "Before we ever formally became friends, I would sit in on faculty seminars at Princeton, and I would hear Cornel asking what I thought were exactly the right questions and then giving exactly the wrong answers—but interesting, provocative, compelling answers," George told an audience at Duke in 2019.[5]

West seems to have had a similar impression. In 2005, a student named Andrew Perlmutter asked West for help launching a new student magazine, *The Green Light*. West had returned to Princeton in 2002 after a time at Harvard. Both he and George were now more established scholars with widening name recognition. Perlmutter had a vision for a section in his magazine in which one faculty member would interview another. He asked West to pick someone to interview. "I told him I'd like to have a dialogue with Professor George because he's viewed as such a conservative," West replied.[6] West was already famous for being, in his words, a "revolutionary

---

4 Robert George, interview by the author over videoconference call, August 25, 2021.
5 West and George, "Kenan Distinguished Lecture."
6 Merrell Noden, "What's the Big Idea?," *Princeton Alumni Weekly*, June 6, 2007, https://paw .princeton.edu/.

Christian" and an outspoken activist for the left, and George's reputation for being a strong Christian voice on the opposite side of the political spectrum drew them together.

George immediately recognized the potential but thought a one-way conversation would be a waste. When Perlmutter conveyed the invitation to George, he answered, "Tell Professor West that Professor George says: 'But it is I who should be seeking baptism from you.'"[7] The two met and talked—in George's recollection—for four hours, including thirty minutes while standing at his car with his hand on the door handle. "It was almost love at first sight," George later described. "You do, despite some rather obvious differences, sometimes just find another person interesting. Someone who is saying things that are compelling and need to be said—whether one agrees with them or not—someone who is making you think."[8] "It was very clear that we had very kindred spirits," West recalled, "He had a sincerity and integrity and humility that I had a great attraction to, and so it was a simultaneously intellectual as well as spiritual coming together."[9]

When later that year or next George learned that the university leadership was trying to persuade senior faculty to teach undergraduate freshmen seminars in order to give younger students access to its most distinguished and practiced scholars, he invited West to develop and coteach a great books course. The result was "Humanities 414: Adventures in Ideas," which they cotaught roughly every other year for most of the next decade. The course description is short, simple, yet breathtakingly ambitious, the sort of thing that repels the casual student and commands the attention of those drawn to the core purpose of a university: "In this seminar, we will consider writings by influential ancient and modern thinkers who have reflected on the meaning of human existence and the terms of social and political life."[10]

The course became a running dialogue between the two as they riffed on a rotating selection of the greatest works of world literature significant in their own intellectual and spiritual formation—Plato, Sophocles, Augustine, Martin Luther, Niccolò Machiavelli, Karl Marx, Fyodor Dostoyevsky,

---

7   George, interview by the author.
8   West and George, "Kenan Distinguished Lecture."
9   West, interview by author.
10 Robert George and Cornel West, "Humanities 414: Adventures in Ideas," syllabus, Princeton University, no date.

John Henry Newman, John Dewey, Leo Strauss, C. S. Lewis, Martin Buber, Martin Luther King Jr., and others—while a dozen or so undergraduates listened, queried, and joined battle. "This is not just an academic discussion to be cute and smart," West explained, "but this is a heartfelt, life-centered wrestling with the quest for wisdom and compassion."[11]

"It was teaching together" that cemented their growing friendship, George later recalled. "It was that experience of pursuing understanding, pursuing knowledge, pursuing truth together that was the bond that united us."[12] The shared mission of liberal education, at which they individually excel, became a joint project in which they played off one another to powerful effect. "It was a magical experience," George noted. "You don't know what nirvana is until you've taught with this brother."[13] Similarly, West reflected that "Brother Robby's a masterful teacher." He elaborated, "He believes in Socratic energy, Socratic sensibility, so that he has some of the most power-ful critiques of the so-called conservative figures, just like I had some of the most powerful critiques of the leftist figures. That surprised the students."[14] George lamented that so few students could attend their discussions.

Their seminar worked because they have enough commonality to make discussion intelligible and enough disagreement to make it interesting. "We're fundamentally committed to the humanity of the outcasts and the marginalized and subjugated and the oppressed," according to West, but "it's just that we have very different analysis. My analysis of what it means looks at the world through the lens of the cross, . . . begins with empire, predatory capitalism, white supremacy, homophobia, anti-Jewish, anti-Arab, anti-Muslim [oppression]." George does not deny the reality of many such forms of oppression but approaches them differently. "Robby accepts significant slices of that, but his understanding of empire, his understanding of predatory capitalism is going to be very different than mine." George, for example, might raise questions about the way progres-sives have defined and diagnosed our social and political ills. West explains, "We have debates about institutional racism and structural racism—what

11 West, interview by the author.
12 Cornel West and Robert George "Cornel West and Robert George ('77) Hold Collection on Campus," Swarthmore College, February 10, 2014, video, 1:32:20, https://www.youtube.com/.
13 George, interview by the author.
14 West, interview by the author.

do we mean by these terms, how are these terms being used or abused in the public discourse?" Or to take another example, both George and West look to Frederick Hayek's work *The Road to Serfdom* (1944) as an important warning against the potential for authoritarianism implicit in socialism and economic planning, but West adds that there can be a "road to serfdom of a different sort if private [companies] and monopolies have absolutely no collective accountability to the public good."[15]

Their friendship is more than intellectual companionship. George recounts how, when teaching about the musical background to Robert Duvall's film *The Apostle* (1997), he broke out into song, singing the 1866 hymn "I Love to Tell the Story." West spontaneously joined in. The duo sang all four verses to applause from their students and inaugurated a tradition of musical appreciation they would carry on during their seminar break times and other areas of their lives (e.g., see a video of the two singing "This Little Light of Mine" to George's guitar accompaniment).[16] This vignette suggests the broader dimensions of their friendship. What started in a shared love of inquiry grew from deeper roots of spiritual commonality, watered with emotional resonance and shared experience. As George explains,

> The best part of the friendship is when we're not on camera, not in front of an audience. We may be at my house, where Cornel's come over for dinner, [or] it's late at night after one of our joint appearances—we're back at the hotel, I've got a glass of red wine, and he's got a glass of cognac. And we're sitting there and we're reflecting and we're talking about the things that are important to us and pushing each other a little bit and probing an issue. It's when we might be attending each other's family events: I might be attending his daughter's play, he might be attending something for one of my kids. That's where the best part of the friendship is.[17]

"We teach together, we talk together, we write together, . . . we pray together, we sing together," George recalls. "We always pray together before

---

15 West, interview by the author.

16 "Robert George and Cornel West Singing 'This Little Light of Mine,'" August 26, 2020, video, 3:39, https://www.youtube.com/.

17 George, interview by the author.

our appearance together, we pray for each other, we pray for each other's families."[18] West recalls George praying with him when West's mother passed away in early 2021. West, for his part, praises George's sense of humor and "artistic sensibility," because "he's got this wonderful way of connecting his artistic creativity and sensibility with a sense of humor, and for me that sense of humor goes hand in hand with humility. It's a fruit of the humility, it's an acknowledgment of incongruity, it's an acknowledgment of limitation, and therefore, all you can do is just laugh."[19]

In the years since they first taught together, the two have appeared at dozens of public events, giving wider audiences a taste of their repartee, their companionship, and their disagreements. A cursory search turns up joint talks at Swarthmore College (February 2014), the Hauenstein Center for Presidential Studies at Grand Valley State University (April 2015), Biola University (May 2015), Furman University (October 2015), Villanova University (February 2018), the Air Force Academy (March 2018), Arizona State University (April 2018), Brandeis University (October 2018), American University (December 2018), the Sheen Center for Thought and Culture (December 2018), Duke University (February 2019), Washington University in St. Louis (April 2019), Liberty University (August 2019), the Trinity Forum (August 2019), Baylor University (November 2019), the Federalist Society (August 2020), the St. Thomas Aquinas Catholic Center (January 2021), the University of Richmond (March 2021), and Florida State University (April 2021), as well as a dozen or more appearances on the Firing Line show, on C-SPAN, and at the American Enterprise Institute.

Joint Statements

Despite their partisan differences and because of their friendship, their common faith, and their shared commitment to democratic values, George and West have occasionally made common cause. In March 2017, Charles Murray, a conservative scholar and fellow with the American Enterprise Institute, was scheduled to speak at Middlebury College in Vermont. Murray's writings on race, class, gender, and intelligence are controversial and unpopular on the left. Middlebury students took control of the event and

---

18   George, interview by the author.
19   West, interview by the author.

prevented Murray from speaking by protesting, shouting, and chanting over him. When he tried to leave, someone physically assaulted the group and injured Middlebury professor Allison Stanger, who was scheduled to speak alongside Murray.

George believed the attack at Middlebury in 2017 "revealed there was a terrible intolerance of dissenting opinions in academic life and more broadly in the culture." George wanted to make a statement but not alone. He knew that, whatever their disagreements on other political issues, "Cornel fully shared [his] civil libertarian convictions about freedom of speech, freedom of thought, freedom of inquiry, freedom of discussion"—and he knew their agreement was not merely on the surface. Neither supported academic freedom as a narrowly prudential matter but because "free speech, free inquiry, [and] free thought all serve the cause of truth seeking," close to the core of their shared convictions and shared faith. George and West both believed that "we should respect freedom of speech and freedom of thought, not because there is no truth but because we need to be able to speak our minds and think for ourselves to get at the truth and truly appropriate the truth."[20]

The result was a March 2017 coauthored open letter titled "Truth Seeking, Democracy, and Freedom of Thought and Expression." George and West wrote, "The pursuit of knowledge and the maintenance of a free and democratic society require the cultivation and practice of the virtues of intellectual humility, openness of mind, and, above all, love of truth." They continued, "Even if one happens to be right about this or that disputed matter, seriously and respectfully engaging people who disagree will deepen one's understanding of the truth and sharpen one's ability to defend it."[21] Some five thousand other professors, teachers, educational staff, and others signed the statement. "We wanted it to be not only about truth seeking, but also about the maintenance of democracy," George later explained. "Freedom of thought, freedom of speech are essential not only for the truth-seeking mission of universities, the truth-seeking vocation of scholars and teachers, but also essential for the functioning of republican

20 George, interview by the author.
21 "Truth Seeking, Democracy, and Freedom of Thought and Expression—A Statement by Robert P. George and Cornel West," James Madison Program in American Ideals and Institutions, Princeton University, March 14, 2017, https://jmp.princeton.edu/.

democracy."[22] Both George and West later commented that they could recall no disagreements drafting the statement, West highlighting how the statement builds on arguments John Stuart Mill had made in his 1859 classic, *On Liberty.*

Similarly, George and West coauthored an op-ed in July 2020, a month and a half after the murder of George Floyd by a White police officer in Minneapolis and the eruption of protests and some violent riots across the nation in the aftermath. "Honesty and courage alone can save our wounded, disunited country now," they wrote. Some riots had targeted statues of American founders as symbols of racial oppression. "We need the honesty and courage to honor the contributions of the great men and women who have come before us," George and West responded, "[and] we need the honesty and courage to recognize the faults, flaws, and failings of even the greatest of our heroes."[23] George later suggested that their position reflects an "appropriate balance of concerns: . . . you see both the need to honor heroes—George Washington, Abraham Lincoln—but also to recognize that our heroes, like ourselves, are flawed."[24]

The debate over the place of historic figures in American life was close to home for George and West. Princeton University had, years before, considered and rejected the idea of removing Woodrow Wilson's name from its school of public policy (Wilson was an unapologetic racist and segregationist). But within weeks of Floyd's murder, Princeton abruptly changed course and removed Wilson's name with no public process or deliberation. West, though he agreed with the decision (he originally proposed the change while a doctoral student at Princeton in 1975), opposed the lack of public consultation. "The process has no legitimacy," West later said. "You can't just as a president dictate and pontificate that kind of policy without going through the channels of having a discussion with faculty and your largest community."[25] George concurred. "It just looks like the university was pressured into doing this," he explained, criticizing the university for "just capitulating to pressure like this."[26] The episode captures well the

22 George, interview by the author.
23 Robert P. George and Cornel West, "To Unite the Country, We Need Honesty and Courage," *Boston Globe*, July 15, 2020, https://www.bostonglobe.com/.
24 George, interview by the author.
25 West, interview by the author.
26 George, interview by the author.

duo's shared commitment to transparency, public deliberation, and the democratic process.

The Nature of Friendship

Why does their friendship work? Aristotle wrote that there are three kinds of friendship—friendships of pleasure, utility, and virtue—all of which play a role in George and West's friendship. We form friendships because they are fun, because they are useful, and because they are good. The types of friendship can blur and overlap, but Aristotle argued that friendships solely of pleasure or utility are fragile: "Such friendships are easily dissolved when the partners do not remain unchanged: the affection ceases as soon as one partner is no longer pleasant or useful to the other."[27] By contrast, friendships of virtue are the best and longest lasting:

> The perfect form of friendship is that between good men who are alike in excellence or virtue. For these friends wish alike for one another's good because they are good men. . . . Those who wish for their friends' good for their friends' sake are friends in the truest sense, since their attitude is determined by what their friends are and not by incidental considerations. Hence their friendship lasts as long as they are good.[28]

Aristotle believed that such friendships are possible only between good men because they require virtue; one can hardly imagine West and George's friendship if one or the other were not the man of integrity and conviction in private that he appears to be in public. "The friendship of good men implies mutual trust, the assurance that neither partner will ever wrong the other," Aristotle wrote. "Such friendships are of course rare, since such men are few."[29] These friendships take time and investment, and it is hard to form many of these kinds of friendship at once. This kind of friendship is easiest between equals. (Could George and West have been friends during Jim Crow? Surely yes, but at greater cost and effort, with more work to recognize and reaffirm their equality that the

---

27 Aristotle, *Nichomachean Ethics*, Library of Liberal Arts (Englewood, NJ: Prentice Hall, 1962), 218–19.

28 Aristotle, *Nichomachean Ethics*, 219–20.

29 Aristotle, *Nichomachean Ethics*, 220.

law then denied.) In Aristotle's words, "The friendship of brothers is like friendship among bosom companions. For they are equal and belong to the same age group."[30]

Though George and West's friendship is often treated as an oddity or described as unlikely because of their surface differences, their friendship looks different in an Aristotelian light. Given their shared profession of Christian faith, commitment to democratic ideals, and devotion to scholarship, it might be more surprising if they were *not* friends. Treating their friendship as surprising and countercultural is a damning indictment of the culture that tells us to let surface dissimilarities get in the way of deeper commonalities. George rejects their characterization as an "odd couple." "We're not," he insists. "We're united to each other in love, in true fraternal affection, . . . and above all in a devotion to the cause of liberal learning. It was that that brought us together."[31]

George echoes Aristotle's vision of friendship when he explains, "Friendship is fundamentally volitional. It is willing the good of the other for the sake of the other." For George, engaging in this kind of friendship redounds to our own benefit. "When we get to know a person because of our willingness to will the good of the person, then we can see the humanity in there," a vision of humanity that educates, shapes, and sanctifies us. "Where we fail is when we lose track of the humanity of the other person. Doesn't mean we have to agree with them, . . . but it means to understand their humanity, the thing that's common between us and them."[32] Understanding humanity is not the point of the friendship, not what started the friendship, but it is one of the ultimate fruits of the friendship.

Solomon shared Aristotle's admiration for a certain kind of friendship, reflected in some of the most famous aphorisms about friendship:

A friend loves at all times,
and a brother is born for adversity. (Prov. 17:17)

Perhaps reflecting on his father David's friendship with Jonathan, Solomon observed,

---

30 Aristotle, *Nichomachean Ethics*, 222.
31 West and George, "Collection on Campus."
32 West and George, "Kenan Distinguished Lecture."

A man of many companions may come to ruin,
> but there is a friend who sticks closer than a brother. (Prov. 18:24)

Friendships of pleasure and utility avoid hard things, but friendships founded on virtue or the pursuit of God cannot avoid them. That is why Solomon wrote,

Faithful are the wounds of a friend;
> profuse are the kisses of an enemy. (Prov. 27:6)

The company and wisdom of a true friend can be among the best joys of life:

Oil and perfume make the heart glad,
> and the sweetness of a friend comes from his earnest counsel.
> (Prov. 27:9)

With some parallels, C. S. Lewis wrote about the four loves: affection, friendship, erotic love, and charity. Friendship is "that luminous, tranquil, rational world of relationships freely chosen" that arises when people find "that they have in common some insight or interest or even taste which the others do not share and which, till that moment, each believed to be his own unique treasure."[33] Lewis noted that our modern age is taken with eros in ways the ancient world was not. "To the Ancients, Friendship seemed the happiest and most fully human of all loves; the crown of life and the school of virtue. The modern world, in comparison, ignores it."[34] Friendship has no root in passion, instinct, or biological need. Modern culture is almost suspicious of close friends with no tie of passion or blood. Because of the modern preoccupation with eros, Lewis noted—in 1960—the need "to rebut the theory that every firm and serious friendship is really homosexual."[35] Scholars have noted a "friendship deficit" among men in the twenty-first century.[36] It may

---

33 C. S. Lewis, *The Four Loves* (1960; repr., New York: Harvest, 1991), 89, 96.

34 Lewis, *Four Loves*, 87.

35 Lewis, *Four Loves*, 90.

36 Daniel Cox, "American Men Suffer a Friendship Recession," *National Review*, July 6, 2021, https://www.nationalreview.com/.

be in part because our culture no longer has a category for asexual intimacy among men.

In fact, Lewis thinks there is something uniquely masculine about the friendship of shared tasks: "We Braves, we hunters, all bound together by shared skill, shared dangers and hardships, esoteric jokes."[37] This closeness is perhaps seen in George and West's shared project of truth seeking against the mutually recognized danger of opprobrium from one's tribe. The notion that friendship is rooted in a shared mission explains why friendship is possible across social and cultural barriers, including the barriers of race and partisan preference. "In a circle of true Friends each man is simply what he is: stands for nothing but himself," Lewis writes. "No one cares twopence about any one else's family, profession, class, income, race, or previous history."[38] They come to care but not as the foundation of their friendship.

Aristotle believed this kind of friendship only possible among men of virtue. Lewis recognized that men could unite behind a wicked cause and that every form of love can become a rival to the true God and mistake itself for the highest love. The highest love is something more: "This primal love is Gift-love. In God there is no hunger that needs to be filled, only plenteousness that desires to give. . . . Divine Gift-love—Love himself working in a man—is wholly disinterested and desires what is simply best for the beloved."[39] Without "Gift-love" to complete and sanctify friendship, even friendships of common purpose can deteriorate into selfish quests to remake the other into our image or, worse, quests to advance a wicked purpose. We see a description of our highest ambition as Christians in Moses when we read, "The LORD used to speak to Moses face to face, as a man speaks to his friend" (Ex. 33:11); in James's description of Abraham, who was called "a friend of God" (James 2:23); and in Jesus's Farewell Discourse, in which he calls the disciples his "friends" (John 15:14–15). Aristotle was right that the highest form of friendship is between men (and, we might add, between women) who are united in virtue and who wish each other's good; he did not know the true ground of that friendship.

West summarizes the connection well. "Love is never reducible to politics, just as friendship is never reducible to political agreement. [In true

---

37 Lewis, *Four Loves*, 95.
38 Lewis, *Four Loves*, 103.
39 Lewis, *Four Loves*, 175, 177.

friendship] you learn how to revel in somebody's humanity, their laughter, their subtlety. [You] give them the benefit of being wrong and pointing it out." West sees a parallel with elements of the Black tradition: "Follow the anthem of Black people, you lift your voice, every voice, take that voice seriously, bounce off against other voices in order to enhance the quality of your voice." That explains, for him, his friendship with George: "And so, anytime I get a chance to spend time with my dear brother Robby, . . . it's really a matter of trying to simply bear witness to a love and trying to stay on that love train."[40] That friendship in turn both bolsters his religious commitment and reinforces his intellectual humility and sharpness. West puts it this way:

> You're Socratic because you're suspicious of dogma but there's certain dogma you're willing to live and die for, like love thy God and love thy neighbor. And for [George] and I, we love our enemies and we get in a lot of trouble. . . . It's a brotherhood, it really is, a sense of just enjoying each other and learning so much from each other in so many different ways.[41]

Deeper Commonalities

Their joint statements point toward George and West's deeper shared commitments and the foundations of their friendship. Theirs is a friendship of shared virtue and a shared mission. They are professing Christians, seeking to understand the life and teaching of Jesus Christ; they are Americans, dedicated to the ideals of freedom and equality that animate our shared experiment in free government; and they are educators, committed to free inquiry, a classically liberal education, and the pursuit of truth. Importantly, these three commitments—to the kingdom of God, to the articulation and defense of American ideals, and to the truth-seeking mission of education—blur together, interlock, and reinforce one another. Common to all is the necessity of mutual love and respect among all people, because that is the second greatest commandment in Jesus's kingdom, the implication of political equality in the United States, and the condition of pursuing truth together in the academy. As George and West state, "We need the honesty

---

40 West and George, "Kenan Distinguished Lecture."
41 West and George, "Kenan Distinguished Lecture."

and courage to treat decent and honest people with whom we disagree—even on the most consequential questions—as partners in truth-seeking and fellow citizens of our republican order, not as enemies to be destroyed."[42]

In other words, the two agree on the preeminent need to follow Jesus, to guard the American experiment, and to be a truth-seeking human. The meaning of the American experiment is rooted in the ideals of the US Constitution and the Declaration of Independence—as well as in the history of our striving to live up to those ideals. George reflects that he and West share an "understanding of what I call American ideals and institutions," such as "the fundamental civil liberties: religion, press, assembly, the right to petition for redress of grievances, due process," but also an understanding of "our failure, too often, in our national history to live up to those ideals and those principles." Though they disagree on particular policies, they agree on the foundation of classical liberalism, or civic republicanism—and they recognize threats to it from both sides of the political spectrum.[43]

The two are also "old fashioned humanists," because, as George states, "we're believers in human freedom and human dignity." That is, they are students who believe "in the need to study man not simply and exclusively from a scientific perspective, where we study the things in which human freedom figures. And that's what literature is about, that's what philosophy is about, and that's what religion is about."[44] The humanities and social sciences exist to study "the meaning of human existence and the terms of social and political life," in the words of their undergraduate seminar syllabus. These fields of study are premised on a certain view of humanity—that we are not mere biomechanical machines, that there is something more to us unaccounted for by the hard sciences—and thus on the idea that the investigation into humanity may be more art than science but is no less valuable and insightful for it. A crucial aspect of this investigation is that, most often, it yields the best results as a joint effort, in conversation, and in community, which is why classrooms and universities exist but also why these institutions succeed best when they rest on and foster mutual respect and dignity among their communities of truth seekers.

---

42 George and West, "To Unite the Country."
43 George, interview by the author.
44 George, interview by the author.

Community, however, does not trump the truth. George and West are united as well on the priority of truth over tribe. Being a true humanist, pursuing truth with integrity, requires that we have "the honesty and courage to be willing to change our beliefs and stances if evidence, reason, and compelling argument persuade us that they are in need of revision," they argued in their 2020 joint statement, "even at the cost of alienating us from communities in which we are comfortable and rely on for personal affirmation, solidarity, and support."[45]

These virtues—humility, honesty, courage, truth seeking, mutual respect, equality, liberty—are prerequisites for either democracy or the academy to work. Where do they come from? George and West both believe that Christianity is not the sole possible source of such virtues and that common projects like democracy and scholarship are possible in other contexts—but Christianity is certainly the foundation for them. West insists that the basic virtues of integrity, honesty, and decency are "possible anywhere around the world." But he says, "[While] I don't think that we Christians in any way have a monopoly on getting at the limitations of who we are, as human beings, we just have a conception of it that connects it to grace."[46] That unique Christian grounding is what the two share in common.

"My conception of what it means to be human is to be a follower of Jesus of Nazareth," West says,

> which means you pick up your cross and deny yourself and follow him
> in terms of trying to cultivate forms of character and virtues that have to
> do with *kenosis*, with emptying yourself and giving yourself and learn-
> ing how to serve others and putting the kingdom as the major priority in
> regard to how you live.[47]

This, in turn, has implications for how we live, including how we live as citizens, learners, and friends. It fosters "this whole sense of acknowledging our dependence [on God], knowledge in our finitude, but also the gratitude, the sense of wonder," that characterizes the Christian life. It also means, according to West, that "in our quest for truth, beauty, goodness, and the holy

---

45 George and West, "To Unite the Country."
46 West, interview by the author.
47 West, interview by the author.

we start with our finitude and fallenness, no doubt about that. So it means, then, that we're always listening, open, trying to learn, because we know we'll never ever have a possession of the truth."[48] Being a Christian means knowing one is imperfect, thus always in need of learning, thus always in need of others—especially others who seem to see things we do not. As West puts it, "So me and Robby would say quite explicitly we both were gangstas before we met Jesus, and now we're redeemed sinners with gangsta proclivities."[49]

Their shared Christianity is the site of more differences, preeminently between George's Catholicism and West's Protestantism. "Our disagreements go back to Kierkegaard versus Aquinas," according to West. "Robby has a commitment to reason . . . whereas I have a stronger critique of the human capacity for rationality, so that reason itself is part of the fall. . . . I have a thicker conception of the fall and evil than he does."[50] George concurs: "Our shared Christian faith is one of the anchors of our relationship. He has a deep respect for Catholicism; I deeply respect the Protestant traditions," he explains. "We both believe in the harmony of faith and reason, but he, being a Kierkegaardian, is a bit more skeptical of the power of reason than I, as a Thomist, am. My critique of his position is that it's a little too fideist. His critique of mine is that it's a little too rationalist."[51]

The depth of West's commitment to speaking the truth in love, respecting those he disagrees with, was illustrated in 2017. He traveled to Charlottesville to participate in the counterprotests against the Unite the Right rally. He confronted one of the White supremacists face-to-face:

I said to the brother in Charlottesville when I was with the sick White brothers in the Klan and the neo-Nazis, "Jesus loves you just like he loves me." He said, "Are you losing your mind?" I said "It's true! That's Jesus! He loves you just as much; he ain't selected me like I'm so special." But I said, "But you've got to make a different choice, man." I said, "You're a Christian?" He said, "Yeah." I said, "Well okay, I'm a Christian too! How is it you wanna kill me?"[52]

48 West, interview by the author.
49 West and George, "Kenan Distinguished Lecture."
50 West, interview by the author.
51 Robert George, email to author, October 24, 2021.
52 West, interview by the author.

West probably did not make a new friend that day, but his courage to remind an American Nazi that Jesus loves him is a powerful testament to a life of integrity—an integrity core to his friendship with George.

Antitribalism

The two come together in a posture of both intellectual and epistemological humility—and courageous, uncompromising defenses of the institutions that they believe embody that humility in our social and political life. What does this look like in practice? It often looks like a conscious rejection of tribalism and a deliberate seeking out of partnerships with those who think differently. George cites as an example West's advocacy to save the Classics Department at Howard University. Howard announced in April 2021 that it would dissolve the department, reflecting long-standing criticism from the left that the classics were racist, ethnocentric, irrelevant, or outdated. West, despite his progressive sympathies, publicly disagreed. "Academia's continual campaign to disregard or neglect the classics is a sign of spiritual decay, moral decline and a deep intellectual narrowness running amok in American culture," he wrote in a *Washington Post* op-ed with Jeremy Tate. "Students must be challenged: Can they face texts from the greatest thinkers that force them to radically call into question their presuppositions?"[53]

West defended the classics as a necessary part of a full education, even flipping the script and arguing that the classics, rightly understood, re-inforced key aspects of the Black tradition. "This classical approach is united to the Black experience," he wrote. "It recognizes that the end and aim of education is really the anthem of Black people, which is to lift every voice. That means to find *your* voice, not an echo or an imitation of others." And so, engaging the classics does not mean parroting them, "but you can't find your voice without being grounded in tradition, grounded in legacies, grounded in heritages."[54] West later reflected that "people want to trash Shakespeare, trash Dante, and say that's a leftist position. No, it's just wrong. It's got nothing to do with ideology and so forth; it's just wrong." West's humanism is grounded in a subtle but important philosophical commitment that he shares with George but not with his fellow progressives: "I do

---

53 Cornel West and Jeremy Tate, "Howard University's Removal of Classics Is a Spiritual Catastrophe," *Washington Post*, April 19, 2021, https://www.washingtonpost.com/.

54 West and Tate, "Removal of Classics."

make a distinction between deeper human identity and a sexual identity, a gender identity, . . . a racial identity."[55] Our common humanity is prior to and more important than our differences.

George, reflecting on West's willingness to go against the prevailing views of his political allies, comments, "If you want to know why Cornel and I are bosom buddies and brothers, there that explains it."[56] West's courage to put principle and conviction about truth seeking over tribal loyalty captures, in a nutshell, West and George's commonality. George takes the same approach to his camp: "If the right-wing playbook is supposed to be x and I don't think x is right, I'm not going to go along with it just because it's our tribe's playbook."[57]

George and West both bucked their tribes in 2016. George did not endorse the Republican presidential nominee, Donald Trump, and West did not endorse the Democratic presidential nominee, Hillary Clinton. Their refusals surprised and scandalized their respective political camps—but not each other. "The fact of the matter is, Cornel understands me and understands what makes me tick in a way that most of my conservative friends don't. . . . Not very many of my conservative friends have the depth of understanding of me, of what makes me tick, that Cornel [has]," and vice versa, George explains.

> So when he refused to endorse Hillary Clinton in 2016 and his friends on the left went ballistic and just accused him of everything, every terrible thing, and called him names, the least surprised person in the world was me. I knew he wasn't going to endorse Hillary Clinton. Because Cornel is a man of principle.[58]

The same held true in the other direction:

> When I refused to endorse Donald Trump, a lot of people on the conservative side said, "You're going to elect Hillary Clinton, this is going to be your fault, it's going to be a disaster." . . . However disappointed a lot

55 West, interview by the author.
56 George, interview by the author.
57 George, interview by the author.
58 George, interview by the author.

of my other friends were, Cornel just assumed that I wouldn't endorse Trump, and he was right. He was the least surprised person in the world.[59]

West, for his part, is often criticized from the left because, as he recalls, his critics tell him, "You are using your legitimacy to provide a platform for someone who you know attacks our identity."[60]

Friendship, Character, and Politics

What should we learn from the public friendship between Robert George and Cornel West? In what sense is it a good work *for us*? Their friendship and their increasing willingness to speak publicly about it teach us about the nature of friendship—which, if Aristotle, Lewis, and Solomon are right, is no small matter. If friendship helps us practice love, become virtuous, and give and receive images of God to one another, then holding up a model of successful friendship across lines of political disagreement and cultural difference would be an extraordinarily valuable work for us all.

There is a small tension here: neither man is given to boasting about good works, nor would they want to trivialize their friendship by turning it into a Sunday school lesson. When asked why they have allowed their friendship to become the subject of public comment, both can be elliptical. My sense is that, having seen and enjoyed the good of a friendship rooted in virtue, Christian love, and shared mission, they recognize how rare it is and how helpful it might be for others who have little experience of it. Perhaps they know, even if they are too modest to say, that this kind of friendship is especially needful given the interlocking crises of American democracy, American Christianity, and the American academy (and, I might add, American masculinity). True friendship is a spiritual discipline, an antidote to what ails our democracy and our universities, and an answer to the plight of loneliness that many people experience in contemporary culture. George and West did not become friends for these purposes, but their friendship shows a path forward for our spiritual, cultural, and political good.

George drew the connection between friendship, character, and politics in 2019. As he put it, Christianity teaches humility, including intellectual

---

59 George, interview by the author.
60 West, interview by the author.

humility. If we don't have that humility, "then the only explanation for someone disagreeing with me is that they must either be stupid or malicious, and either one is no good. And of course, then we're not going to learn anything." That arrogant refusal to learn has ripple effects on one's character, intellect, and relationships: "We will choose as our friends only people who are going to reinforce what we already think. That will be our circle of friends. . . . We will not challenge ourselves; we will be the opposite of Socratic. Dogmatic is the opposite of Socratic." The solution is to open oneself to friendship—not the echo chamber of like-minded people but the iron-sharpening challenge of those who are different. "That is why it's so important," George says, "to cultivate friendships with people who don't see things just the way you do, people who have had different sorts of experiences in life, come from different sorts of backgrounds, but also have different sorts of convictions."[61]

This has political implications because friendship across lines of difference is a microcosm of the challenges facing the United States, among the most pluralistic societies in the world and one that is in the midst of profound cultural and demographic changes. Some observers wonder if Americans have much in common anymore, especially across the partisan divide, and if a country that lacks a sense of commonality can hold together. Or, in George's terms, he wonders how thin our similarities can be and still allow us to find commonality and friendship. That is a special problem for the diverse patchwork and melting pot of America. Citing Jonathan Haidt, George reminds us, "Social science tells us that success in social life correlates very heavily with people being like each other, that pluralistic cultures tend over time to be less successful and more fragile." Cultural homogeneity bolsters social cohesion and stability (except for minorities excluded from that homogeneity). We need to consciously work against the lure of homogenization because pluralism is not natural and takes effort: "It takes courage, because it means you're putting stuff at risk, like friendships with people who don't agree with you. It means not knowing who you might turn out to be. You think you're this person, but on reflection you change your views—you might be a different person than you recognize."[62]

61 West and George, "Kenan Distinguished Lecture."
62 West and George, "Kenan Distinguished Lecture."

George's language about friendship here—not knowing how friendship might change who you are—is strikingly similar to language he used to describe a true liberal arts education five years previously:

> When we enter the liberal arts enterprise in its dimension of critical think-ing and therefore of self-criticism, we are boarding a train not knowing the destination to which we're headed. We may board the train believing one thing passionately, powerfully, emotionally attached to it, knowing that we might leave the train thinking something very different. We might board the train as one kind of person with one kind of self-understanding, and leave the train as a person quite unlike anything we would have wished to be like when we boarded the train. That vulnerability, rooted in intel-lectual humility, a sense of one's own fallibility, is vital to the self-critical component of liberal arts education.[63]

For George, a true friendship is a liberal education: your friend is your teacher—and you are his—and you do not know in advance what the lessons might be or how you might change. In turn, to pursue a liberal education rightly, we must be true friends: friends to our teachers, to fellow students, and, above all, to the truth itself. Both friendship and truth seeking require humility, the recognition that we have things to learn, curiosity, a belief that there is a truth we must pursue, and the virtues of truth telling, faithfulness, and courage. Being a true friend and being a good truth seeker are, for George, parallel enterprises, both rooted in and outgrowths of his Christian faith.

It is easy to see the broader social and political implications. Both this kind of friendship and truth seeking are essential for the mission of the university and for the fate of the American experiment. Truth seeking and true friendship require mutual respect, equality, free speech, and more: they depend on, and reinforce, the ideals that undergird a free society. It is not surprising that George and West's friendship is founded on both their mutual Christianity and also on their love for the American experiment and academic inquiry, in both of which equality is a necessary component. Their friendship is, in microcosm, a living embodiment of Christian love, democratic equality, and scholarly truth seeking.

---

63   West and George, "Collection on Campus."

Afterword

Seeking the Truth, Speaking the Truth

A Dialogue between Robert P. George and Andrew T. Walker

ANDREW T. WALKER.[1] Professor George, this is a book primarily for conservative, evangelical Protestants. What do you think is important for that readership to know about you and why you think your work is important to their concerns? What do you want evangelicals to know about you, effectively?

ROBERT P. GEORGE. I'd like evangelical Protestants, as well as Catholics, to understand as deeply as possible the relationship between faith and reason. I'd like people across the spectrum of Christian belief to appreciate the profound sense in which faith and reason really are the "two wings on which the human spirit rises to the contemplation of truth."[2] We, as Christians, whether we are Protestant or Catholic, should not denigrate reason, just as we should not denigrate faith. We should certainly not treat faith and reason as if they are enemies or suppose that our faith commitments—our belief in Jesus Christ, our belief in God's revelation, our belief in the authority of Scripture—require us to abandon reason as a faculty for grasping and understanding important truths.

Now, we as Christians across the spectrum and across the Reformation divide recognize that we human beings are fallen. We are frail and fallible

---

1 This dialogue took place on January 31, 2022, over videoconference call. It has been retained in full but has been lightly edited for print.
2 John Paul II, *Fides et Ratio* (encyclical letter), Vatican, September 14, 1998, https://www.vatican.va/.

creatures. Our fallenness pertains not only to our will but also to our intellect. The fall not only weakens the will to do good, to do right, but it also darkens the intellect. It means we must not deify reason or suppose that it's infallible. It's not. It's quite the opposite. It's fallible. We're fallible. We certainly shouldn't suppose we can get along without faith or God's self-revelation in the person of Jesus Christ. All that is true.

At the same time, we need to recognize that reason is capable of helping us understand, among other things, right and wrong, to understand profound moral truths, including moral truths revealed in Scripture. Just as faith illuminates the truths that reason can identify, reason can help us understand the meaning of what is revealed. You see this most clearly at the very beginning of Scripture in the second chapter of the book of Genesis, where we're told that a man shall leave his father and mother and cleave unto his wife, and the two will become one flesh (Gen. 2:24). We need reason to go to work to understand what that could possibly mean: two human beings, two distinct organisms, become one flesh. We might be tempted to believe that it is only some kind of metaphor. A man and a woman united in marriage become so emotionally close to each other that, metaphorically speaking, they are like one flesh, but by the application of the philosophical method, of reason, we can see that what is being revealed by Scripture is not that the one-flesh union of husband and wife is a metaphor but that it is literally true. In my work on marriage, especially the books I've written on marriage with Sherif Girgis and Ryan Anderson in one case, *What Is Marriage? Man and Woman: A Defense* (2012), and Patrick Lee, *Conjugal Union: What Marriage Is and Why It Matters* (2014), I use philosophical methods of inquiry and analysis to show that husband and wife in consummating their marriage literally become one flesh. The two unite as a single reproductive principle and in a certain sense—that is, for this purpose—become a single organism.

I'll very briefly explain—the full explanation is in the books (where, in addition, possible lines of counterargument to the position are anticipated and addressed). In the case of some human activities, such as locomotion (walking, for example) or eating, the organism performing the act is the individual human being. If I get up and walk across the room, I do that as an individual. In digesting a meal, I do that as an individual. With respect to a different human activity and function, reproduction, however, we do not perform the act or function as a single individual or organism, but rather the unit performing the reproductive act is the male-female unit. They become one flesh and, as such, a single principle and complete organism with respect to the reproductive process. There's a whole lot more to be said about that, but I hope it enables you to begin to see the way it relates to understanding—grasping the meaning—of what is revealed in Scripture.

Rationally inquiring, using your intellect, thinking, and reasoning are not only helpful but essential. Despite our fallibility, they can prevent us from veering off into a profound misunderstanding of the Bible, say, with respect to marriage. It would be very easy to misinterpret the Bible as proposing the one-flesh union as a mere metaphor, but we would have it completely wrong to leave it only at the level of metaphor.

WALKER. So you might say, and I often say this to my students, "If we jettison the Bible, we're not just jettisoning revealed religion; we're actually jettisoning objective, coherent accounts of reality itself." When secular progressivism sees itself as working against revealed religion, we would reply that it's really not merely revealed religion that they're rejecting; they're rejecting all rational concepts related to morality, concepts such as, for example, human dignity. I'm assuming you would agree with that.

GEORGE. I would want to talk to the individual, the secular progressive, to see what he actually thinks. Saint Paul tells us in the letter to the Romans that there is a law written on the hearts even of the Gentiles, that is, the people who don't have the law of Moses, God's special revelation. And that law is sufficient for them to be held accountable for their actions and ultimately judged. What that tells us is that there are truths knowable by reason, even for those who do not know—or recognize the authority of—Scripture.

Throughout history, there have been people who have no knowledge of the Hebrew revelation, such as Socrates, Plato, and Aristotle, who have been great truth seekers and have attained certain profound truths. Some of this made early Christian thinkers wonder, especially in the case of Plato, whether Plato might have had some access to the Hebrew Scripture or whether God might have given him some private revelation. I think there's no reason to believe either of those things actually happened. He had used the power of his intellect in an extraordinary way to get a hold of, admittedly in an incomplete and imperfect way, certain profound truths. Now, Plato understood that there was objective truth. Aristotle understood that there was an objective truth. They didn't need Scripture to get that. They got that. They used what was available to them, their intellects, to understand it as deeply as possible. It is remarkable to consider how brilliantly they did. Of course, once we have the revelation, we see so much more clearly. I like to use an analogy to the 1939 movie *The Wizard of Oz*. We move from drab black-and-white scenes of Kansas, the Kansas farmland, to suddenly see the land over the rainbow, where everything is bright and clear and in color. Then, we finally get to the land of Oz itself and see its astonishingly magnificent beauty.

WALKER. What I teach my students is that nonbelievers see the world in black and white and that Christians see it in color, as far as the fullness of what revelation reveals. Non-Christians have genuine insights into moral realities and moral principles but only according to one epistemological domain—reason. Christians, on the other hand, gain access to an additional epistemological domain, namely, divine revelation, which parallels with and illuminates what we know about basic moral principles.

GEORGE. I think that's right. Beginning with the ancient revelation to the Jewish people, you now have a spotlight on what is by the light of fallen reason visible but in black and white—as if "through a glass darkly" (1 Cor. 13:12 KJV).

WALKER. Now that you've read the manuscript, what were your reactions and your impressions? What did authors get right and wrong?

GEORGE. Well, Andrew, I would thank you for the honor you did me by organizing this volume, even if I didn't think it was a high-quality volume. It was just a lovely thing for you to do for me. I appreciate your effort to bring my work to greater prominence in the evangelical world. But I must say, I was blown away by the quality of the essays, the consistent, uniform quality of the essays. Your authors are engaging my thought in a very serious way. The effort they have made to understand my ideas and arguments accurately and to engage with what I actually hold is quite extraordinary. I've published a lot, and I've been engaged on hot-button issues with people across the ideological spectrum. So I have a lot of experience of engagement with people from all sorts of different perspectives. I've grown used to some of my ideas being misunderstood or being misrepresented. That doesn't happen in this volume. I'm grateful to you, and I'm grateful to every single one of the authors for the work they put into getting it right. They don't have to agree with what I'm saying, and in some cases, they take issue with what I'm saying. That's fine, and I learn from that. But what is really striking to me is the effort to understand me accurately and to engage with what I actually think and say. Bravo.

WALKER. I'm so glad that you have received this as you have. It's a great personal privilege to have put this together.

GEORGE. I want you to give everyone my warmest and most sincere thanks.

WALKER. The name Robert P. George can conjure up the label of bioethicist, philosopher, general ethicist, and lawyer. You're a public intellectual, if I may employ that broad, encompassing term. If you're asked, "What is the primary intellectual discipline you see yourself operating within?" what do you say?

GEORGE. I see my vocation as that of a teacher; that, I think, is the most important thing I do. It's what I feel called to do. It's at the center of what I do. I've been blessed with such fabulous students. Micah Watson, for example, was my graduate student. A number of the people who get mentioned in the book—Sherif Girgis, Ryan Anderson, Melissa Moschella, on and on—I've been blessed at the undergraduate level and doctoral level with these fabulous students. So teaching is at the center of what I do, and I would regard it as my vocation.

That is related to the other thing I do, which is scholarly research. Here my work has really been at the junction of ethics, law, theology, and politics. Broadly speaking, the term that would encompass the kind of work I do is philosophy. So if you push me against the wall and say, "You have to declare yourself of this or that beyond being a teacher or researcher," I do philosophy. I do moral philosophy. I do political philosophy. I do philosophy of law. I do a bit of work in metaphysics and philosophy of mind and related disciplines. I suppose I have to plead guilty to that term I don't like of "public intellectual."

WALKER. It has become a rather catchall, vacuous phrase, admittedly, but you get called that whenever you appear in print.

GEORGE. I know, and I suppose it's my punishment for failing to keep my mouth shut and stay out of public disputes! I say things that get public attention and get me in trouble. It's one thing to believe things that a Princeton professor, holder of an endowed chair at an Ivy League university, is not supposed to believe. It would be one thing if I were simply to harbor dissenting thoughts in my breast without verbalizing them. Temperamentally, though, I can't stop myself from saying what I think. So when I say what I think, suddenly it's news: "McCormick Professor of Jurisprudence at Princeton says something he's not supposed to think." The next thing you know I'm involved in some sort of controversy, and I'm having to defend my view, which I love doing. You may have noticed that I'm not shy about doing that! I'm the sort of person who is classified by the psychologists as an extreme extrovert. I don't mind at all being out in the public doing intellectual battle. It is a blessing.

I suppose the good part of being a "public intellectual" is that I'm invited to go all over the country and world to talk about the things that are most important to me: the sanctity of human life in all stages and conditions, marriage and the family, the concept of marriage as the conjugal union of husband and wife, religious freedom and the rights of conscience. I suppose it's partly cause and partly effect of the kind of work that I do that I've had the opportunity to give public service, first as a member on the US Commission on Civil Rights—my work on civil rights and civil liberties made that a really valuable thing for me personally when I was able to do it—then as a member on the President's Council on Bioethics and then as chairman of the US Commission on International Religious Freedom. I've enjoyed those dimensions of being a "public intellectual."

WALKER. Let's turn to a little more dour part of the conversation. The consensus among conservative Christians, whether Protestant or Catholic, is that American culture is in a state of disrepair. We are too far gone for us to bring things back, and so there is a temptation to be a pessimist. What is your general attitude toward the culture in which we live?

GEORGE. One of hope. There are, of course, three great theological virtues—faith, hope, and love—and they are integrally connected to each other. You can't fully have one without the other two or two without the other one; you need them all. Saint Paul tells us, and it's revealed to us in Scripture that "the greatest of these is love" (1 Cor. 13:13). But you can't do without hope, and we're required to live in hope. It's not a mere recommendation that God makes. It's an obligation. Hope has got to be distinguished from optimism. Now, I suppose it's true, and again, if the psychologists had me on their couch and analyzed me, they would report that I have an optimistic temperament and personality. But let's never confuse optimism and hope. Optimism is, as Richard Neuhaus used to say, a matter of optics, looking at how things appear. Hope is a virtue. Hope is an active thing. It's hope that inspires us to go out, no matter how bleak things look, even if you're a pessimist temperamentally, and work to set things right, to make things better. It's the virtue that inspires us to go out and make a difference. People of hope never give up, and it would be silly for us as Christians to give up because we've had a peek at the back of the book. We know how the story ends. In fact, we know that the victory has been won already—not by us but by Christ himself with his victory over death, his redeeming act culminating in his resurrection. We Christians sometimes put it in terms of his opening of the gates of heaven, making salvation available to us, his redemptive act. Now at the same time, that doesn't mean that we can then go off and do nothing, that we're not responsible for making a difference in the world. As Mother Teresa says, our job is to be God's instruments in the world, so where there is wrong, it is our job to right it. Where there is injustice, it's our job to bring justice. Where there is suffering and illness, whether it is physical or moral or spiritual, it is our job to bring healing.

To be hopeful doesn't mean we get to stand aside because God's going to do all the work without us. It means to be inspired to act, again, to quote Mother Teresa, to be "God's instruments" in the world—recognizing, of course, our own fallibility and the fact that we'd better proceed with a lot of intellectual humility because we don't want to be too certain we've got God's message right, that we perfectly understand things. We don't. We remain frail and fallen and fallible, but by our best lights—always open to challenge and criticism—we need to speak the truth as we are best able to grasp the truth. We need to be people of conviction who act for the sake of what is right, what is good, what is true, what is beautiful, what is holy, even while recognizing that we're not going to get it perfectly right.

WALKER. To close that question, I have a quote on my desk from your friend Richard John Neuhaus, and it says this, "We have to remember that we are not in charge of making things turn out all right. That's God's job. We are in charge of being faithful. We are just supposed to be faithful. The rest is God's part."[3]

---

3   Kevin Spinale, " 'Sustained by Faith': An Interview with Robert P. George," *America*, November 7, 2011, https://www.americamagazine.org/.

GEORGE. Richard Neuhaus used to quote that to me all the time when I was young and had just started out my scholarly career and became involved with his work at the Institute on Religion and Public Life in New York, which itself had just launched (that's the publisher of *First Things* magazine). Richard would see my enthusiasm, and I tended to be, and still tend to be, a bit on the aggressive side when it comes to acting for causes that I believe are right. He would be all for that. He wouldn't want to tell me not to do that. In fact, I learned a lot from him about how to do that, but he would quote those lines. Throughout our entire relationship, he would always address me by both my names. He would never call me Robby; he would call me Robby George. He would say, "Robby George, your problem is that you think it's up to you to produce the victory. It's not up to you; it's up to God." He said, "It's up to God to produce the victory, and the victory will come on his terms and in his time. Your job is to be faithful, ever faithful. Play your proper role. Don't try to do God's job; do yours."

WALKER. Turning things to the respective corners that we both occupy, there's a growing criticism from what in my world we would call Christian reconstructionism and theonomy and in your world we would call integral-ism. The general criticism is that the rights regime that you and I would promote, the idea that everyone has equal opportunity to make the views they want to voice heard in the public square, that those rights are the cause of our downfall as a culture. What is your response to this criticism that's not just from the left but now from the right? Is that an accurate portrayal of what you think our views are trying to accomplish?

GEORGE. Well, I don't want to stuff people into narrow boxes. There are different people who associate themselves with labels like integralism who believe different things, who make different sorts of arguments, some of whom are critical of the sorts of ideas that I have about political phi-losophy, some of whom don't seem to be all that critical. Their key points and what they say, in which I think they're absolutely right, echo points I myself have made—for example, the idea that our rights are grounded in human goods, that the right is not, as John Rawls and the liberal tradition would say, prior to the good or independent of the good but rather that a sound understanding of the human good is necessary even in shaping our understanding of what rights people have. The civil-libertarian point of view that I represent and that you represent is indeed, in a certain sense, "rights oriented." We do believe in rights and liberties. We believe in the right to freedom of religion. We believe in the right to freedom of speech, the right to freedom of assembly, the right to petition the government for the redress of grievances, the right to due process, the right to equal protection. We believe in those things, but our foundation for those beliefs is not Lockean and not utilitarian.

John Stuart Mill, who I think had some valuable things to say, also made some very grave errors, most importantly his embracing of utilitarianism. He tried to revise and make more sophisticated and plausible the utilitarian philosophy of his own teacher, Jeremy Bentham. But it's not fixable, and he couldn't fix it. My civil libertarianism, like your civil libertarianism, is not what I would think people generally have in mind when you talk about liberalism or liberal civil libertarianism, although the term *liberal* has so many different meanings that it's almost lost its utility. But if we mean by liberal, roughly speaking, Lockean, Rawlsian, Millian, then ours is not a liberal theory of civil liberties but a robust traditionalist theory of civil liberties. As was pointed out in Micah Watson's chapter in the book, the final chapter of my first book, *Making Men Moral: Civil Liberties and Public Morality* (1993), the book that Micah's chapter concentrates on, I tried to adumbrate what I call a perfectionist, nonliberal, and nonutilitarian account of freedoms such as freedom of speech, freedom of religion, freedom of assembly, freedom to protest, to criticize the government.

I build it on the basis of a reflection on the goods that those liberties protect, so our right to freedom of thought and then our right to freedom of speech protect the good of truth and the importance of truth seeking, if we're going to get at the truth, and truth speaking, if we're to speak the truth as best as we understand the truth. The most fundamental reason the government should not restrict our ability to think for ourselves or our right to think for ourselves and to say what we think and to try to persuade others is not that the government's doing that is unfair or that it is contrary to a principle that would be adopted in Rawls's "original position," in which the parties are behind a "veil of ignorance" and don't know anything about what makes them different from anyone else. No, it's because of the goods that are at stake and that need to be protected, above all the good of truth seeking. Truth is not the only one, but when it comes to freedom of speech, that's the good that's most fundamentally protected.

WALKER. Across the board, you've been a stalwart advocate for academic freedom. How do you juggle academic freedom in a confessional context? Obviously, Princeton is different from Southern Seminary, so maybe that difference in itself redefines how you think about it. I would just love for you to explain, What does academic freedom look like in a confessional theological context?

GEORGE. First of all, I want to say that I believe in and support confessional institutions of learning. I am a supporter of Christian classical schools, parochial schools and other Catholic schools, Jewish day schools. I think religiously based education, including at the K–12 level, is a good thing. I also believe in religiously affiliated and grounded and guided colleges and universities—not just seminaries, although those too, of course, but colleges. I support Notre Dame, Wheaton, Brigham Young University, Yeshiva, Zaytuna College. Zaytuna is the Muslim liberal arts college led by my beloved friend Sheikh Hamza Yusuf out in Northern California. I believe in those institutions. Now, I also believe that the specifics, the shape of academic freedom, will differ at a confessional institution from what it is in a nonreligiously affiliated or nonsectarian institution like Princeton or Ohio State or some other universities that might or might not have originally been religiously founded or affiliated but are no longer confessional. I don't mind a confessional university or a university committed to what, using Rawlsian language, one might call a "comprehensive view." If the utilitarians want to set up a utilitarian university, that's fine with me too. I'm not a fan of utilitarianism, but I'd let that flower bloom along with the others. I think if you found a university established on religious beliefs and principles, there is every good reason for that university in its hiring decisions and in its institutional commitments and decisions and in its student life to be guided by those beliefs and principles, and I think that is true whether or not the institution decides to restrict faculty hiring or student admissions to people who share the faith of the college or university.

WALKER. You would say that it's the notion of the particular institution's own concept of its common good that shapes how it's going to conceive of its hiring and membership practices?

GEORGE. That's right. Now I'm going to have a bit more to say about this. So far, so good. I agree with what you just said. I think that if a university says, "Look, we're a Baptist university; to be on this faculty you have to be a Baptist," that's fine with me. It'll be a different kind of university. It'll do a different kind of good, not completely different from other universities but different in some ways. If you want to say we're a Baptist university like Baylor University and we're committed to it, we're serious about our Baptist faith, but we're going to allow non-Baptists, perhaps other Christians, perhaps other people of biblical faiths, perhaps more broadly, to come as students or be faculty members, that's fine too. If they do that, it's also fine to say, "Look, you've got to live, in your personal lives if you want to be a member of the faculty, if you want to be a student, in line with our moral values." That's fine with me too, so long as it's up front, everybody agrees to the terms of the contract, and so forth.

I think those institutions should be guided by their moral beliefs, their religiously inspired moral beliefs. Student life, for example, should be guided by those beliefs, and if you don't like those beliefs and don't want a character or quality of student life that is shaped by those beliefs, then go elsewhere to college. If you're at the Southern Baptist Theological Seminary and you're in a same-sex partnership or in a sexual relationship with a person who's not your spouse, you're in the wrong place because Southern Seminary or Wheaton College or Yeshiva or Zaytuna or Brigham Young or the University of Dallas has a different set of guiding principles. All that's fine, but even where we have religiously affiliated universities that restrict student admission or even faculty membership to people of a particular tradition of faith, my advice, and I've given this advice to religiously affiliated universities of every stripe all over the country, is, do not try to shield your students from ideas that are critical of your faith. That is a mistake. Do not try to brainwash your students. As a matter of fact, take affirmative steps to make sure your students encounter the very best arguments made by people who challenge the fundamental tenets of your faith. If you're Southern Seminary or Baylor or Brigham Young or Yeshiva or Zaytuna or Wheaton or the University of Dallas or Notre Dame, make sure your students know who Nietzsche is, the most powerful atheist thinker of the modern period. Make sure they've read Nietzsche's work, and make sure they've been given a fair account of Nietzsche. Don't distort him. Don't turn him into a straw man. Don't simply present the weakest, most vulnerable version of the Nietzschean argument. Give them the real thing. Same with Hume, same with Voltaire, same with people who challenge their moral views. I wouldn't restrict outside speakers (though the giving of honors, including invitations to give honorific addresses, such as commencement speeches, raises different issues). I don't see any reason why you need to shield students from ideas of any type.

I'm going to say something super controversial that is going to lose a lot of people who've come along with me so far. I don't see any reason why Southern Seminary couldn't invite Richard Dawkins to come and give his criticisms of evangelical Christianity or his criticisms of religious belief. I don't see why the University of Dallas, a great, loyal Catholic university, couldn't invite Peter Singer (I'm going to really upset people), my colleague at Princeton who has defended the morality of infanticide—not just abortion but infanticide—to come and make his argument, and then engage him and treat him respectfully. I don't see why not. I don't think there's any view that we need to shield our young people from at the university level; it's a different thing in K–12. In K–12 you're still equipping young kids with the intellectual tools to be independent thinkers and to be critical thinkers. Once they're in college, they should have those tools, and they should be able to use those tools to engage ideas that are critical of or that challenge the ideas they hold.

I'll say this, and this will be my final comment on the matter. There is not a single view I hold, no matter how deeply I cherish it, no matter how important I think it is or how central it is to my own identity, say, as a Christian, there's not a single view that I hold that I want to immunize against being challenged. None. There's no argument that I don't want to have to face. Whether it's on Twitter or in the classroom or in a faculty seminar or in the public square, I think that truth (and I think we need to dedicate ourselves to the pursuit of truth) is best served by allowing all ideas to be challenged and let people assess them on the merits and decide where they stand based on hearing the best arguments on the competing sides. There. You see, I'm a radical.

WALKER. You've mentioned that your temperament is one of optimism; you're a happy warrior. I think that's one of the reasons I have been attracted to your witness and your work. We need people to look at and say, "Yes, that person is embodying what I think someone ought to be doing around the issues of ideas and activism and institution building. You're happy. But what actually makes you angry? What gets Robert P. George upset to where your cheerful disposition goes away? I recall a YouTube video that went viral. I think you were at Cornell, and a student really went at you for your views on marriage, and you didn't get disrespectful or harsh at all, but I noticed a change in your response. Do you recall what I'm talking about, that scenario?

GEORGE. I might have become a bit . . . intense.

WALKER. Okay, intense perhaps. But what makes you actually come unglued?

GEORGE. Well, praise be to Jesus Christ, that hasn't happened yet, so I'll have to answer that question someday when it happens. Again, I thank God I didn't get the fear gene, and I didn't get the anger gene. It's no virtue on my part, but I'm just not prone to anger. And I'm not afraid; it's not that I have courage. The people who have courage are the people who experience fear and then muster the internal resources, the courage, to do the right thing in the face of fear, but I'm able to speak my mind without having to muster courage because I'm not afraid of these Twitter mobs and cancellation and that kind of stuff. I've never been afraid to speak my mind, and I don't see myself changing. So I tend not to be the kind of person who gets rattled in those ways.

I'll tell you what I don't like. I don't like dishonesty. When I experience someone being dishonest in argument, that makes me a little intense. But I don't assume that because someone deeply disagrees with me, even about an issue that I profoundly care about and think is critically important, life and death, faith, no matter how important the issue is, I don't assume that the person who disagrees with me is being dishonest. I know lots of really honest people who completely disagree with me about the issues I think are most important, and so I want to learn from them. I want to learn from engaging them. If I'm wrong, I want to know why they think I'm wrong. Even if I'm not wrong, if an intelligent, honest person has a different view from mine, I figure I can learn something. I can deepen my understanding of the question even if the belief in question is one on which I'm right and they're wrong. I mean, that's happened in my life countless times. Engaging with Peter Singer, sometimes in person, more often in writing, on life issues has really deepened my understanding of truths that I had believed all along, but I understand them better. I get it more deeply as a result of these engagements. He's forced me to think more deeply. I hope I forced him to think more deeply. He hasn't changed his mind; he still thinks he's right.

I still think I'm right on issues like abortion, euthanasia, infanticide, the equal worth and dignity of the severely disabled. He thinks he's right, I think I'm right, but I think both of us would say—I would certainly say—that our engagement has deepened my understanding of the issue. So I don't like dishonesty, but I don't assume people who disagree with me are dishonest.

I'll tell you what else I don't like, Andrew. I don't like groupthink. I don't like conformism. I'll get a bit intense when I hear a student babbling away in groupthink. If it's clear to me that a student hasn't thought for three seconds, he is just saying what he's picked up from the ether, she is saying what she thinks she is supposed to think because she is of this or that group identity, then I'm probably going to push back with a bit of intellectual force. When you encounter people, whether they are students or not, who seem to have just basically been indoctrinated, to have never considered the arguments on the other side of a question, or are just pontificating (as a Catholic, I hope I can get away with using that word) with no critical thought behind it, well, I get a little intense about that. I don't like conformism, especially intellectual conformism. I'm not saying we should be contrarians. But we shouldn't be intellectual conformists. The motto that I have in the James Madison Program in American Ideals and Institutions, which I had the honor of founding in 2000, is this: "Think deeply, think critically, and think for yourself." That's what I like. Whether people agree with me or not, I want them to think deeply, think critically (and that must include self-critically), and think for themselves.

I also get a little intense when I perceive no intellectual humility and no self-criticism. You know, that means that the person is not really thinking. He's just emoting or spouting opinions. There's no real thinking going on. People who are really thinking are self-critical. They're their own best critics. They've got intellectual humility; they recognize their own fallibility. If people don't recognize their own fallibility, you can't really have much of a discussion with them. They'll just refuse to be challenged. They put up a wall that makes it impossible for them to think and therefore for them to learn from the engagement. I want to learn from my engagement with people I disagree with, but I need people who also want to learn from that engagement. And not just lecture. I'm not interested in just getting a lecture from an interlocutor who's just spouting whatever the dogma is of his or her particular ideological group.

WALKER. It really does seem that intellectual honesty is an issue of personal integrity; it's an issue of resisting conformism or groupthink. It's also how we resist falling into charlatanry (I don't know of a better term) or becoming professional hacks, so to speak. And one of the challenges—and I'd love for you to speak to this—and one of the things that really concerns me about the state of American discourse is that, as far as I perceive it, intellectual honesty is no longer rewarded. Tribalism is rewarded. So this actually gets at one of the questions at the very end I had for you. How essential is the recovery of intellectual virtue, not just for personal virtue but for social and cultural virtue as well?

GEORGE. Critical, it's absolutely critical. And the work that Cornel West and I do together, which is so beautifully outlined in Paul Miller's essay in this volume, is meant to promote the recovery of those intellectual virtues, not only for the good of each of us as individuals but for the overall common good. The common good has been very badly damaged by the loss of serious civility. And by civility, Cornel and I don't mean mere politesse, you know, politely sitting while someone else talks and waiting your turn to talk, not interrupting them or not attacking them physically, and things like that.

By civility, we mean something much deeper: honestly listening with a willingness to learn from the other in a spirit of genuine intellectual humility and curiosity. It's critical not only to the truth-seeking mission of colleges and universities and other institutions but also to the maintenance of our democratic republic. It's critical that we recover these virtues of love of truth, intellectual humility, willingness to learn from people we disagree with, willingness to respect people we disagree with as our fellow citizens and not treating them as mortal enemies. In a republic like ours, the people govern themselves; we govern ourselves. We're not governed by a king or an oligarchy or anything like that. So if we're going to make good decisions, if we're going to govern ourselves wisely and well, we're going to need to be united in some fundamental way. And since we're not a "blood and soil" nation and not a "throne and altar" nation, the source of our unity isn't a common race or even a common history or a common religion; it's got to be a commitment to these principles, principles of civil liberty, principles of the common good and the virtues that Cornel and I are out there trying to promote. I especially encourage anyone reading this interview to have a look at the statement that Cornel West and I put out in 2017 titled "Truth Seeking, Democracy, and Freedom of Thought and Expression." It outlines our reasons for believing that the recovery of the virtues that you and I are talking about here, Andrew, is essential to the flourishing of our country, of our society.

While I'm thinking about it, Andrew, I should also add something to a previous answer. You asked me what makes me angry. And I explained what makes me intense. You might also be interested in what inspires me. What makes me happy? What supports my hope and elevates it, what makes it easier for me to be hopeful? I can tell you exactly what it is. It is getting to work day in and day out, every day, with inspiring young men and women, with young men and women who are brilliant and courageous. I'm speaking, of course, of my students and protégés. Some of them are people I have in classrooms; some I meet going around the country who are interested in my work and what I do or are drawing on it. I include some of the people we mentioned before, such as Sherif Girgis and Ryan Anderson and Melissa Moschella, also Daniel Mark, Micah Watson, and some people who haven't been in my classroom like this fellow Andrew Walker and Matthew Lee Anderson, and so many others who are drawing on my work and who are interested in the same ideas and issues that I'm interested in.

It's not merely that they are brilliant. It would be one thing if they were brilliant. That's great, that's important, that would be inspiring. It's fun to be around brilliant young men and women, and it's encouraging to see it. But they are more than merely brilliant. The even more striking thing about them is that they're brave; they're courageous. They're out there in the public square speaking moral truth to cultural power, advocating un-popular positions, or at least positions that are unpopular with the ruling class, with the power elite, with the intellectual establishment. And they're willing to take the slings and arrows that come with it.

Look at the witness of Ryan Anderson. So extraordinary. You are familiar, I'm sure, with his brilliant books on transgenderism, on religious liberty, on marriage, and on the sanctity of human life. How can one not be inspired to get to work with young people like that? And when I see these brave and brilliant kids, I can't help but think things are going to be okay. It's going be okay. I mean if these kids are out there doing this stuff with this kind of boldness, things are going to be okay. And you know, some of them, Ryan's a good example, are like me in that they're not especially afraid of anything; Ryan, as you know, will speak his mind no matter what. It doesn't bother him to get criticism. But others really do experience the fear, and they are much more to be commended because in the face of the fear—and some are genuinely terrified about the prospect of getting attacked for what they say on social media, for example—they boldly speak the truth as God gives them to grasp the truth. That is inspiring to me.

WALKER. This next question actually builds a little bit on that last question because we're talking about the virtues necessary to continue this project we love called America. I would consider your vision of America and its founding as Aristotelian-Thomistic, as far as the moral contours of the American tradition. America is getting more secular, I would say, broadly speaking, however we wanted to define *secular*. Americans are less religious now than they were previously. Can America continue to be the America that it was in the Aristotelian-Thomistic sense if it secularizes? Can it be America without religion and appreciation for that Aristotelian-Thomistic account undergirding our fabric as a nation?

GEORGE. Well, the answer to the question whether America is in fact becoming more secular—if you mean by *secular* something more than "Do people go to church or affiliate with a particular religion"—is not obvious. If John McWhorter is right, and I think he is, that woke ideology is a religion, it is just a bad religion, a militant-fundamentalist sect, then you know we're not really becoming more secular. There's a different sort of religion that is gaining prominence alongside the traditional faiths that have been part of the American story.

Second, when Thomas Jefferson was asked toward the end of his life where he got the ideas for the Declaration of Independence, that statement of our principles from which our nation begins, he responded, in an 1825 letter to Henry Lee, that he was simply giving voice to "the harmonizing sentiments of the American people."[4] Of course, we know those were sentiments shaped by Christianity, by the Bible—not exclusively but in a very significant part. And then Jefferson went on:

---

4   Thomas Jefferson to Henry Lee [IV], May 8, 1825, in *Thomas Jefferson: Writings*, ed. Merrill D. Peterson (New York: Library of America, 1984), 1500–1501.

The object of the Declaration of Independence . . . was . . . not to find out new principles, or new arguments, never before thought of, not merely to say things which had never been said before; but to place before mankind the common sense of the subject. . . . . Neither aiming at originality of principle or sentiment, nor yet copied from any particular and previous writing, it was intended to be an expression of the American mind. . . . All its authority rests then on the harmonizing sentiments of the day, whether expressed in conversation, in letters, printed essays, or in the elementary books of public right, as Aristotle, Cicero, Locke, Sidney, etc.[5]

Notice the examples: not only Enlightenment figures like John Locke and Algernon Sidney but figures from deeper in our history and tradition, going all the way back to Greek and Roman antiquity. So even Jefferson, who is so often depicted as an Enlightenment secularist, at best a deist, maybe an atheist (although I'm quite sure he wasn't an atheist), even Jefferson who is at one edge among the American founders, the more secular edge, if you will, understands that this American experiment in ordered liberty has its foundations in a complex set of religious and philosophical ideas.

The third thing I'd say is this: ethical monotheism is central to the American idea and our nation's ideals and institutions. The proof of that, again, is in one of Jefferson's own writings, that second sentence of the Declaration of Independence, which is really the foundation of our unity, because we're not a nation in which people are united by a tradition of religion or by blood and soil or by throne and altar. We're united around our shared belief that there are certain God-given, natural human rights: "We hold these truths to be self-evident, that all men are created equal, that they are endowed by their Creator with certain unalienable Rights, and among these are Life, Liberty, and the pursuit of Happiness."[6] It's ethical monotheism that underwrites the idea that there are rights that the government must respect and protect and that the government may not take away because the government didn't give them. In fact, no merely human power gave them. They were conferred not by any merely human power—be it a king, a president, a congress, a parliament—but by the hand of God himself. And

5   Thomas Jefferson to Henry Lee, in *Thomas Jefferson: Writings*, 1500–1501.
6   Declaration of Independence, National Archives, July 4, 1776, https://www.archives.gov/.

because they were not given by any merely human power, they cannot be taken away by any merely human power. It is rather, as the next sentence goes on to say, the obligation of human authority, political authority, to protect those rights—and, I would add, to protect the human goods that those rights protect and the human goods that necessarily shape our understanding of the content of those rights, like the good of truth seeking; the good of friendship, including friendship in political community; the good of seeking and achieving, to the extent that we can, justice and harmony among people; and so forth. You've got a pretty stark binary here. Are our rights the gifts of human powers who may, therefore, take them away? Or are they not? The proposition that they are not is underwritten by the ethical monotheist tradition that we, of course, get from the Bible.

WALKER. We have the Declaration of Independence. We have the Gettysburg Address. I think those might be considered the most quintessentially American documents. I would like to wager that the third quintessential American document to understand America is—

GEORGE. Martin Luther King Jr.'s "Letter from Birmingham Jail."

WALKER. Exactly. So that's my proposition: it's the third most important document to America's identity. I would like you to respond to that proposition.

GEORGE. Yes, I think it is the third most important document (or the fourth if we consider Lincoln's Second Inaugural Address alongside his Gettysburg Address). I think it's a profoundly important document because it is a modern reaffirmation of the principle at the core of the Declaration that human beings, though mere dust of the earth, are made in the very image and likeness of the divine Creator and ruler of all that is. As such, human beings, irrespective of race or sex or ethnicity—and equally irrespective of age or size or stage of development or location or condition of dependency—are bearers of a profound, inherent, and equal dignity.

This is a radical idea, this idea King affirms, this idea at the core of the Declaration of Independence. It's a radical idea because for most of human history and across societies, including our own, people have not been willing genuinely to affirm (or do more than give lip service to) that principle of radical human equality. There's always the temptation to think that there are some people who are in basic dignity better than others and some who are worse, that there are natural inferiors and superiors. We confuse certain, to use the classic philosophical category, accidental qualities (strength, beauty, intelligence, and so forth), things that vary from person to person, in which people are definitely not equal, with what is actually the source of our inherent dignity as human beings. People are not equal in strength, people are not equal in beauty, people are not equal in intelligence, and so forth. To confuse those accidental qualities with basic human dignity, with the quality that actually in the end matters, the thing that ultimately matters, is a deep error that always produces tragic consequences.

To affirm what we are asked by King to affirm, in line with the Declaration of Independence, we have to affirm that, for example, a drug-addicted or demented homeless man or woman living under a bridge, someone who may accost strangers, shout at people, be nasty, someone whom, if he or she disappeared tomorrow, no one would miss, is nevertheless in fundamental worth and dignity the equal of a great athlete like Michael Jordan, a great intellect like Albert Einstein, a great actress like Meryl Streep, or a great singer like Leontyne Price. And we get confused. We have trouble really supposing that that drug-addicted or demented, smelly, nasty homeless person really is the equal in worth and dignity of these magnificent exemplars of the human, these magnificent human beings, because of their strength and beauty, their athletic prowess, intellectual talent, artistic gifts, and so forth. But we must affirm this principle of radical equality. We have to understand that the cognitively disabled child, the child with Down syndrome, the severely physically disabled person who will never walk or run, that these, too, are the equal of every other person in worth and dignity. We have to understand why it would be wrong, why we would be scandalized, as we would be, if someone proposed harvesting the vital organs of, say, a cognitively disabled person to get a heart, two kidneys, and so forth to save the lives of a great physicist and a wonderful singer and a great athlete.

Now, the only explanation for why that would be wrong is that in fundamental worth and dignity the cognitively disabled person is the equal of Albert Einstein or Michael Jordan or Leontyne Price or Meryl Streep or whoever it is. We've got to hold on to that, and not only hold on to it but more fully appreciate its implications. We've gone wrong so often in our country, but it's always when we've strayed from that principle that King reminds us of, that principle in the Declaration. We have nothing to be ashamed of as Americans about when we've been faithful to our principles.

Our problem has never been too much fidelity to the principle of the profound, inherent, and equal dignity of each and every member of the human family. What we have to be embarrassed and ashamed about is that we have often veered from that principle, beginning with slavery. Jefferson himself, of course, owned slaves—the very Jefferson who articulated that principle in the second sentence of the Declaration of Independence. And he knew slavery was wrong. It wasn't that he was in any doubt about it. In another context, speaking of slavery, he famously said, "I tremble for my country when I reflect that God is just: that his justice cannot sleep forever."[7] So even at our nation's founding, when our founders were articulating that great principle of radical equality, we had the inequality of slavery. And then that's followed, when Reconstruction fails after the Civil War, by segregation and Jim Crow. We fought the Civil War to get rid of the worst forms of racial injustice, to get rid of slavery, and we end up with this terrible, vicious regime of Jim Crow falling on our Black fellow citizens. And then we had to work for a century to get rid of legal (*de jure*, as we call it) segregation and Jim Crow laws.

Today, we have the national shame of the denial of the equal worth and dignity of the precious child in the womb. This is a gross violation of the principle that each and every member of the human family is the bearer of profound, inherent, and equal dignity. Just as people are not inferior because of race, people are not inferior because of stage of development. The child in the womb is the equal in worth and dignity of a thirty-year-old person or a sixty-year-old person. So I think King sets the example for us. He's the model of prophetic witness calling us back to our founding principles. And that's why that document, the "Letter from Birmingham Jail," which is a ringing defense of natural law and natural rights invoking the great Christian thinkers in that tradition explicitly (Augustine and Thomas Aquinas), really deserves to be placed in a class with the Gettysburg Address, Lincoln's Second Inaugural Address, which I think is an even more profound statement than Gettysburg, and then, of course, the Declaration.

WALKER. How have you seen Protestantism change over your career?

---

7   Thomas Jefferson, *Notes on the State of Virginia*, in *The Writings of Thomas Jefferson*, ed. Paul Leicester Ford, vol. 3, *1781–1784* (New York: G. P. Putnam's Sons, 1894), 267 (query 18).

GEORGE. Yes, of course. Protestantism must always be understood in relation to Catholicism. After all, the Reformation was about that. So one really important development has been the healing of many of the rifts (especially those rooted in misunderstandings, some of which were to be found on both sides) that came about at the time of the Reformation. We have not united the church; we do not have the unity yet for which Jesus prayed, but the fact that Jesus prayed for that unity means we will get it— the time will come. We just don't know when. Again, we have to remind ourselves, since Richard Neuhaus is no longer here to remind us, that these things come on God's timing and on his terms, but we know that Jesus wants the church to be reunited. And we know that his prayer will not be in vain. I sometimes think we need to just get out of the way of the Holy Spirit of God. The Holy Spirit can do this; we just need to get out of the way. We haven't been reunited yet, but look at the healing that has taken place. Protestants and Catholics no longer think of each other as enemies. I mean, some of them do, but they are fringe figures. There are extremists in both camps, but Protestants and Catholics for the most part—and this wasn't really even true in my boyhood—see each other as fellow disciples of Jesus. This is something that's happened since I was born. They mostly think of themselves as fellow Christians, separated in some important ways, but as fellow Christians.

Here I think the Second Vatican Council of the Catholic Church made important progress. There needed to be some action on the Catholic side, and I think the Second Vatican Council initiated that action. There's been an opening up on the Protestant side to Catholics and Catholicism, people like Chuck Colson reaching across the Catholic-Protestant divide to introduce the work of Catholic thinkers to evangelical scholars and leaders. That's been really valuable—to both sides. I think Catholics and Protestants have figured out that they have a lot to learn from each other.

I'll give you a couple of leading examples on each side. I think Catholics— because of our engagement with Protestants beginning in a certain way in the trenches, the ecumenism of the trenches, in the pro-life struggle, in the struggle to defend marriage and other important moral norms—Catholics have learned from Protestants the importance of the Bible, that the Bible should be part of our personal spiritual lives, that the devotional use of the Bible is important, that reading the Bible for ourselves and not just listening to the proclamations of Scripture Mass on Sunday is necessary. Understanding the Bible is really important.

On the other side, I think Protestants have learned that there is a rich philosophical tradition, a profoundly illuminating and thus valuable tradition of thought about moral questions, political questions, metaphysical issues that has been historically nurtured by Catholicism. They find that it is a tradition that Protestants can benefit from, can draw on, can become part of. Some of the thinkers in this book, in their own work, are drawing really usefully on that tradition. They're appropriating that tradition in a way that I think is illuminating and valuable.

As a contemporary thinker and writer in that tradition, I'm invited to lecture at places like Southern Seminary. Now that wouldn't have happened when I was a boy. Distinguished Protestant thinkers are on the faculty at the University of Notre Dame, holding esteemed chairs, and Catholic kids are learning from them. All this is good. I just think it's great. I'm 100 percent behind it. I couldn't be happier with the direction things are going between evangelical Protestants and Catholics. I feel no distance between myself and my evangelical brothers and sisters. Some on both sides may say that I should, because there are important differences. Those differences do matter. But when I think, "Who are my brothers? Who are the people I confide in? Who am I inspired by? Who are the people I really learn from? With whom do I stand shoulder to shoulder in the most difficult and important struggles? Who are the people I implicitly trust, the people I would trust with my very life?" in so many cases they're evangelical Protestants.

WALKER. Have you noticed an attitude change toward natural law among Protestants in your career?

GEORGE. Oh yes, definitely. Part of that has been scholars like J. Daryl Charles, who contributed to this volume. Part of it has been leaders like Chuck Colson. Chuck, I think, came to believe that the sort of skepticism about natural law found in the work of a great thinker and theologian like Carl F. H. Henry was based on misunderstandings of the tradition of natural law theorizing. When Chuck came to understand that, he became a kind of scout, going out there and looking for ways to introduce Protestant thinkers and Protestants more generally to the treasures of the natural law tradition and to work by contemporary natural law theorists like myself, John Finnis, Joseph Boyle, and many others.

WALKER. One of the projects I'm undertaking is trying to retrieve the Reformed natural law tradition. When we hear Reformers, we tend to think of John Calvin and Martin Luther. But you go and read Peter Martyr Vermigli, Johannes Althusius, and there's a whole other broad strain of Reformed natural law thinking that I'm trying to tell my students: "Go back to our own sources. Yes, read the Catholic tradition on natural law. But we actually have this in our own categories as well." You read someone like Franciscus Junius, and he's using categories strikingly similar to Thomas Aquinas. It's just fascinating how far back even Protestant reflections on natural law actually go.

GEORGE. That's absolutely right.

WALKER. You are simultaneously an intellectual, a writer, a teacher. You're also a coalition builder and an institution builder. Your success is inseparable from those institutions, from those coalitions. The effectiveness of your public life is inseparable from those things. Walk us through how you think about the relationship between ideas, coalitions, and institutions.

GEORGE. You've hit the nail on the head. All three are important, and I've been involved on all three fronts: in doing the intellectual work, the ideas end of things; in building coalitions, including coalitions of people from different religious traditions, denominations, and others; in building institutions, or what I call "infrastructure." It's one thing to have a great idea. It's one thing to understand what's wrong with, say, utilitarianism or Rawlsian liberalism or woke ideology, but you're not going to get anywhere at setting things right, not only in the domain of ideas but also in the culture, unless you can build coalitions of people who are willing to fight for the truth and sacrifice for the truth, who are willing to make the commitments and take the slings and arrows that come.

So it has always seemed to me that building coalitions had to be central to social reform. You saw it, for example, in my work with Chuck Colson and Timothy George on the Manhattan Declaration. There we thought, "We need to bring together the three great traditions within Christianity: the Protestants and the Catholics in the West and the Eastern Orthodox Christians." Whether it should have been even broader is a question that has been debated. But that was a matter of coalition building around a shared set of ideas. And if you look at the Manhattan Declaration, you'll see how deep and rich the sharing is between these Christian traditions on central moral questions that are very urgent today: the sanctity of human life in all stages and conditions, marriage as the conjugal union of husband and wife, religious liberty, and the rights of conscience. These are critical issues on which much has gone wrong. Many unborn babies have been slaughtered. Marriage has been redefined in our country and in many other places. Religious liberty is in jeopardy, not only abroad but at home. And what do we find when these three traditions (Protestantism, Catholicism, and Eastern Orthodoxy) come together? We find that they agree on those issues and are willing to unite to try to set right what has gone wrong.

And then there's the question of institutions (or infrastructure). It's one thing to have a coalition, but it's another thing to have instrumentalities for making coalitions effective. And that's where the institution building comes in. I believe in academic freedom. This is a belief I share not only with fellow Christians but with people of other faiths: Jewish friends, Muslim friends, secular people. It's not a uniquely Christian belief, academic freedom. And so, I have united in creating and building the Academic Freedom Alliance with people representing all faiths and shades of belief, who are on what I regard the right side of the academic freedom issue. That's building infrastructure. It's building institutions, in this case an institution to protect an important value—a value that's not just important as abstract right but important because truth is important, because truth seeking is important. Truth seeking has certain conditions: freedom of thought, inquiry, discussion, speech. You need those freedoms to have truth being sought, pursued, and found, and then appropriated by people. Now the members of our coalition, those in our institution, the Academic Freedom Alliance, don't agree on what the truth is on certain important things. I believe as a Christian that the ultimate and most important truth of all is not a proposition; it's a person. It's the person of Jesus Christ who tells us himself in his self-revelation, "I am the way, and the truth, and the life" (John 14:6). Now my non-Christian colleagues in the Academic Freedom Alliance don't agree with me that the ultimate truth is Jesus Christ, that the truth is a person. But they do agree with me that if we're to get at the truth, we need the conditions of truth seeking, including basic freedoms of thought and inquiry and expression, to be in place.

So I'm willing to unite with them in a coalition and build an institution to protect academic freedom in the cause of truth seeking. And the same is true of other institutions I have built or have been involved in building:

the Witherspoon Institute at Princeton; the Canterbury Institute at Oxford; the Barry Scholarship program, which sends students of all faiths who are independent critical thinkers to Oxford University, very similar to the Rhodes Scholarship program, but we are more truth oriented and more attentive to the independence of thought than the Rhodes program. And there are others I could cite, but that's how I see the relationship between ideas, coalitions, and institutions.

WALKER. What advice would you give to young scholars and public intellectuals right now, in this particular age that we're living in? Courage, I bet, is one of them.

GEORGE. Most fundamentally, I'll sum it up this way: Seek the truth and speak the truth, as God gives you to understand the truth.[8] That's really it. You're not going to get at the truth unless you seek it; you have to ask questions. To do that, you need certain virtues.

First, you need open-mindedness to seek the truth. It doesn't mean you can't have convictions. I have convictions, you have convictions, you can be a truth seeker with convictions, but it means that you're allowing your convictions to be challenged. You yourself have a critical perspective on your convictions. You're asking questions.

Okay, so you need that virtue. You also need the virtue of the love of truth. By that I mean this: Sometimes we fall so deeply in love with our opinions that we prefer them to the truth. We'd rather not know the truth if the truth would disturb our opinions because we have wrapped our emotions so tightly around our opinions that we have become dogmatists. So don't fall so deeply in love with your opinions that you prefer them to truth. You need the virtue of love of truth. The person who has love of truth will want to know the truth, even if it's going to absolutely unsettle everything he believes. Love of truth overcomes the resistance to changing your mind when the weight of argument, evidence, reason shows that you've been mistaken.

Third, you need intellectual humility. As long as you think as a practical matter that you're infallible, you're never going to get at the truth.

8 Here George is alluding to a line from Abraham Lincoln's Second Inaugural Address: "With malice toward none; with charity for all; with firmness in the right, as God gives us to see the right, let us strive on to finish the work we are in." Lincoln, "Second Inaugural Address," March 4, 1865, Teaching American History, accessed May 11, 2022, https://teachingamerican history.org/.

You're never going to be able to seek the truth. All you will seek is to be reinforced in what you already believe. We're not going to get at the truth if we only listen to opinions that reinforce us. So you need, in addition to open-mindedness and love of truth, that intellectual humility that's based on a practical recognition of your own fallibility. I say practical because notionally everyone would admit to fallibility. If I raise the question in one of my classes, "All right, how many of you in this room are fallible?" every hand will go up. But then, if we begin to have a conversation, and I challenge their most cherished, deeply held, identity-forming values, you see as a practical matter that some of them think they are infallible. They couldn't possibly be wrong about the things that they care the most about.

So then the fourth thing that's required is courage. You anticipated this, Andrew. Because most people (there are some outliers here, of course—I've mentioned a couple), most people do feel fear when they suspect that by saying something they are going to be denounced and targeted and called names and made subject to abuse. So most people really need the virtue of courage to overcome that fear, so that they can speak the truth, as God gives them to understand the truth. So courage pertains to truth speaking, but it also pertains to truth seeking in this way: if I'm really seeking the truth, I have to be open to the possibility of learning things that will be upsetting, learning things I might rather not know. It takes courage to be open to that possibility, so we need the courage on the truth-seeking side as well as on the truth-speaking side.

WALKER. You talked about how you think of truth not as a thing but as a person, Jesus. What strikes me about your disposition is that because you believe with intellectual humility that you have arrived at the truth, that doesn't make you fearful or anxious about doing intellectual combat elsewhere. Searching and grasping the truth produces its own form of virtue as a result.

GEORGE. Interesting. I see your point. Yeah, I think there's some truth in that. I will say that what I said about Jesus is that he's the ultimate truth. The ultimate truth is not a proposition but a person. Now there are many propositional truths, including propositional truths about the person of Jesus. So I'm not meaning to downplay propositional truths, but they're not what's ultimate from a Christian point of view. What is ultimate is the truth of the person of Jesus.

WALKER. What do you hope that people make of Robert George's life and work? What do you hope that your lasting impact will be? I know that's a huge question, and I know you're in your sixties, not your nineties. There's still a long time to be configuring your own legacy. But what do you hope people will look back on in your work and see and reflect on?

GEORGE. I hope that they will try to do better than I have done. What I have tried to do is to seek the truth and to speak the truth as God has given me to grasp the truth. I hope they'll correct my errors and practice more fully than I have done in my own life the virtues that are necessary for truth seeking: the intellectual humility, the open-mindedness, the love of truth, the courage. I hope that my ideas and my arguments have advanced the ball when it comes to truth seeking and have shed light on some issues that might have been a little more obscure. I'm sure there are some errors mixed in with whatever truth I've been able to get at, and I do want people who look at my work in the future to correct those errors. But if I've gotten some truths, and I think I have, I hope they'll use them and build on them.

I see the work being done by my own former students and my protégés, and I'm enormously heartened by it. They are better than I am. They are moving the ball forward. Sometimes, where I've only been able to outline something, almost like a sketch, they've been building, supplying the rich detail, so that now it's not a sketch anymore, but it's more like a full-blown painting with all the textures and colors and the complexities. I know that even if I'm given thirty more years—and I'd love to keep at this work—some of what I will contribute will be just thoughts, just suggestions. And it will be up to someone else to take them and see if there's any merit to them and then build on them. One thing is that I work in too many areas. So I haven't concentrated so much in any one area to develop my thought in that area as fully as I might have done had I been more narrowly focused. But the advantage of working in all these areas is that I can get some ideas out in all these areas, and then my students and others can see what's of any value there and build on it.

Robert P. George Selected Bibliography

Books

Barber, Sotirios A., and Robert P. George, eds. *Constitutional Politics: Essays on Constitution Making, Maintenance, and Change*. Princeton, NJ: Princeton University Press, 2001.

George, Robert P., ed. *The Autonomy of Law: Essays on Legal Positivism*. Oxford: Oxford University Press, 1996.

George, Robert P. *The Clash of Orthodoxies: Law, Religion, and Morality In Crisis*. Wilmington, DE: ISI Books, 2001.

George, Robert P. *Conscience and Its Enemies: Confronting the Dogmas of Liberal Secularism*. Wilmington, DE: ISI Books, 2013.

George, Robert P., ed. *Great Cases in Constitutional Law*. Princeton, NJ: Princeton University Press, 2000.

George, Robert P. *In Defense of Natural Law*. Oxford: Oxford University Press, 1999.

George, Robert P. *Making Men Moral: Civil Liberties and Public Morality*. Oxford: Oxford University Press, 1993.

George, Robert P., ed. *Natural Law, Liberalism, and Morality*. Oxford: Oxford University Press, 1996.

George, Robert P., ed. *Natural Law and Moral Inquiry: Ethics, Metaphysics, and Politics in the Work of Germain Grisez*. Washington, DC: Georgetown University Press, 1998.

George, Robert P., ed. *Natural Law Theory: Contemporary Essays*. Oxford: Oxford University Press, 1992.

George, Robert P., and Jean Bethke Elshtain, eds. *The Meaning of Marriage: Family, State, Market, and Morals*. Dallas: Spence, 2006.

George, Robert P., and Christopher Tollefsen. *Embryo: A Defense of Human Life*. 2nd ed. Princeton, NJ: Witherspoon Institute, 2011.

George, Robert P., and Christopher Wolfe, eds. *Natural Law and Public Reason*. Washington, DC: Georgetown University Press, 2000.

Girgis, Sherif, Ryan T. Anderson, and Robert P. George. *What Is Marriage? Man and Woman: A Defense*. New York: Encounter Books, 2012.

Keown, John, and Robert P. George, eds. *Reason, Morality, and Law: The Philosophy of John Finnis*. Oxford: Oxford University Press, 2013.

Lee, Patrick, and Robert P. George. *Body-Self Dualism in Contemporary Ethics and Politics*. Cambridge: Cambridge University Press, 2008.

Lee, Patrick, and Robert P. George. *Conjugal Union: What Marriage Is and Why It Matters*. Cambridge: Cambridge University Press, 2014.

Snell, R. J., and Robert P. George, eds. *Mind, Heart, and Soul: Intellectuals and the Path to Rome*. Charlotte, NC: TAN Books, 2018.

Journal Publications

Anderson, Ryan T., and Robert P. George. "The Baby and the Bathwater." *National Affairs* 41 (Fall 2019): 172–84. https://nationalaffairs.com/.

George, Robert P. "The Concept of Public Morality." *American Journal of Jurisprudence* 45, no. 1 (January 2000): 17–31.

George, Robert P. "Liberty and Conscience." *National Affairs* 17 (Fall 2013): 128–39. https://nationalaffairs.com/.

George, Robert P. "Natural Law." *Harvard Journal of Law and Public Policy* 31, no. 1 (Winter 2008): 171–96.

George, Robert P. "Natural Law, God, and Human Dignity." *Chautauqua Journal* 1, art. 8 (2016). https://encompass.eku.edu/tcj/.

George, Robert P. "Natural Law, the Constitution, and the Theory and Practice of Judicial Review." *Fordham Law Review* 69, no. 6 (2001): 2269–84.

George, Robert P. "The 1993 St. Ives Lecture—Natural Law and Civil Rights: From Jefferson's 'Letter to Henry Lee' to Martin Luther King's 'Letter from Birmingham Jail.'" *Catholic University Law Review* 43, no. 1 (1993): 143–57.

George, Robert P. "Public Reason and Political Conflict: Abortion and Homosexuality." *Yale Law Journal* 106, no. 8 (June 1997): 2475–2504. https://doi.org/10.2307/797225.

George, Robert P. "Religious Liberty and the Human Good." *International Journal for Religious Freedom* 5, no. 1 (2012): 35–44.

George, Robert P. "What's Sex Got to Do With It? Marriage, Morality, and Rationality." *American Journal of Jurisprudence* 49, no. 1 (2004): 63–86.

Lee, Patrick, and Robert P. George. "The Nature and Basis of Human Dignity." *Ratio Juris* 21, no. 2 (June 2008): 173–93.

Essays, Commentaries, and Editorials

Anderson, Ryan T., and Robert P. George. "Liberty and SOGI Laws: An Impossible and Unsustainable 'Compromise.'" *Public Discourse*. January 11, 2016. https://www.thepublicdiscourse.com/.

George, Robert P. "Could America Survive without Religion?" *Public Discourse*, November 19, 2015. https://www.thepublicdiscourse.com/.

George, Robert P. "Counterfeit Textualism." *National Review*, November 19, 2019. https://www.nationalreview.com/.

George, Robert P. "Gnostic Liberalism." *First Things*, December 2016, 33–38.

George, Robert P. "Immigration and American Exceptionalism." *Mirror of Justice* (blog). Program on Church, State, and Society at Notre Dame Law School, July 21, 2019. https://mirrorofjustice.blogs.com/.

George, Robert P. "Public Morality, Public Reason." *First Things*, November 2006, 21–26.

George, Robert P. "Religious Freedom and Why It Matters." *Touchstone*, May/June 2014, 22–29.

George, Robert P. "'A Republic . . . If You Can Keep It': Why Lincoln Defied *Dred Scott* and We Must Defy *Roe*." *First Things*, January 22, 2016. https://www.firstthings.com/.

George, Robert P. "*Roe* Will Go." *First Things*, October 2021. https://www.firstthings.com/.

George, Robert P. "What Is Law? A Century of Arguments." *First Things*, April 2001, 23–29.

George, Robert P. "What Is Religious Freedom?" *Public Discourse*, July 24, 2013. http://www.thepublicdiscourse.com/.

George, Robert P., and Ramesh Ponnuru. "Why We Shouldn't Punish Mothers for Abortion." *National Review*, May 12, 2016. https://www.nationalreview.com/.

Girgis, Sherif, Ryan T. Anderson, and Robert P. George. "The Wisdom of Upholding Tradition." *Wall Street Journal*, November 20, 2012. https://www.wsj.com/.

Contributors

Adeline A. Allen, JD, is an associate professor of law at Trinity Law School. She was a 2017–2018 visiting fellow at the James Madison Program in American Ideals and Institutions at Princeton University. She and her family live in Southern California.

Matthew Lee Anderson, DPhil, is an assistant research professor of ethics and theology at Baylor University's Institute for Studies of Religion, the associate director of Baylor in Washington, and an associate fellow at the McDonald Centre for Theology, Ethics, and Public Life. He holds a DPhil from Oxford University and is a perpetual member of Biola University's Torrey Honors College. He is the founder of Mere Orthodoxy and has authored two books.

Hunter Baker, JD, PhD, is the dean of arts and sciences and a professor of political science at Union University. He is a fellow at the Ethics and Religious Liberty Commission and at the Center for Religion, Culture, and Democracy. Baker is also a contributing editor of *Touchstone: A Journal of Mere Christianity*.

J. Daryl Charles, PhD, is the Acton Institute affiliate scholar in theology and ethics, a contributing editor of *Providence: A Journal of Christianity and American Foreign Policy* and the journal *Touchstone*, and the author or editor of twenty books. The focus of Charles's research and writing is religion and society, Christian social ethics, the just-war tradition, and natural law. Prior to entering the university classroom, Charles did public policy work in criminal justice in Washington, DC.

David S. Dockery, PhD (University of Texas System), serves as president of the International Alliance for Christian Education and as Distinguished Professor of Theology at Southwestern Baptist Theological Seminary. The author or editor of more than thirty books, Dockery previously served as president of Union University and of Trinity Evangelical Divinity School.

Scott Klusendorf is president of Life Training Institute and the author of *The Case for Life: Equipping Christians to Engage the Culture*. Scott is a graduate of UCLA and holds a master's degree in Christian apologetics from Biola University. He and his wife, Stephanie, have been married since 1985, and they have four children.

Adam J. MacLeod, JD, is professor of law at Faulkner University and research fellow of the Center for Religion, Culture, and Democracy. He has been a visiting fellow at Princeton University and a research fellow at George Mason University, a special deputy attorney general of Alabama, and law clerk to state and federal judges. He coedited the fourth edition of Christie and Martin's *Jurisprudence* (West Academic, 2020) and has authored *Property and Practical Reason* (Cambridge University Press, 2015), *The Age of Selfies* (Rowman & Littlefield, 2020), and more than a hundred articles, essays, and book reviews.

Paul D. Miller, PhD, is a professor of the practice of international affairs at Georgetown University. He is a senior nonresident fellow at the Atlantic Council and a research fellow at the Ethics and Religious Liberty Commission. His most recent books are *Just War and Ordered Liberty* (Cambridge University Press, 2021) and *The Religion of American Greatness* (IVP Academic, 2022).

Jennifer Marshall Patterson is a visiting lecturer and the director of the Institute of Theology and Public Life at Reformed Theological Seminary, Washington, DC. She has worked in public policy for more than twenty-five years. She is currently a PhD candidate in moral theology and ethics at the Catholic University of America.

Mark Tooley is president of the Institute on Religion and Democracy in Washington, DC, and editor of *Providence: A Journal of Christianity and American*

Foreign Policy. He's the author of three books: *Taking Back the United Methodist Church* (Bristol, 2008), *Methodism and Politics in the Twentieth Century: From William McKinley to 9/11* (Bristol, 2012), and *The Peace That Almost Was: The Forgotten Story of the 1861 Washington Peace Conference and the Final Attempt to Avert the Civil War* (Nelson Books, 2015).

Carl R. Trueman, PhD, teaches at Grove City College in Pennsylvania. He is a graduate of the University of Cambridge (MA) and the University of Aberdeen (PhD). He is a fellow at the Ethics and Public Policy Center in Washington, DC, and a contributing editor at *First Things.*

Andrew T. Walker, PhD, is associate professor of Christian ethics at the Southern Baptist Theological Seminary. He serves as an associate dean in the school of theology and as the director of the Carl F. H. Henry Institute for Evangelical Engagement. He is also the managing editor of the Opinions section of *WORLD* magazine and a fellow at the Ethics and Public Policy Center in Washington, DC. He is the author or editor of several volumes on Christian ethics and public theology. Prior to entering academia, he worked for a number of public policy organizations. He resides in Louisville, Kentucky.

Micah J. Watson, PhD, is Paul Henry Professor of Christianity and Politics at Calvin University, where he also directs the politics, philosophy, and economics program. He has written several chapters for edited volumes and is the coauthor of *C. S. Lewis on Politics and the Natural Law* (Cambridge University Press, 2017). He received an MA and PhD in politics from Princeton University and an MA in church-state studies from Baylor University. He and his wife, Julie, are natives of California but make their home in Grand Rapids, Michigan, with their five children.

John D. Wilsey, PhD, is associate professor of church history and philosophy at the Southern Baptist Theological Seminary and research fellow at the Center for Religion, Culture, and Democracy. He was the 2017–2018 William E. Simon Visiting Fellow in Religion and Public Life at the James Madison Program in American Ideals and Institutions at Princeton University. He is the author of *God's Cold Warrior: The Life and Faith of John Foster Dulles* (Eerdmans, 2021).

General Index

abolition of slavery, 229, 244, 258
abortion, 21–22, 57, 60–65, 124–25, 139, 209
  cobelligerency against, 49
  as health care, 22
  and modern gnosticism, 22
  Rawls on, 126–27
  and worldview, 181–82
academic freedom, 27–28, 268, 292, 307
Academic Freedom Alliance, 307
accidental property, 137
accommodation, of religion, 216–17
acorn–oak tree analogy, 137–38
Adams, John, 255, 257
Adams, Robert, 164
adoption, 257
aesthetic appreciation, 79
Aid to the Church in Need International, 221
Alcorn, Randy, 51
Algernon Society, 300
Alito, Samuel, 189
Allen, Adeline, 19
Alliance Defending Freedom, 183
Althusius, Johannes, 306
Alzheimer's disease, 137, 141
America
  as experiment, xii
  secularization of, 299
American College of Obstetrics and Gynecology (ACOG), 21–22
American Council of Churches, 41

American democracy, 226
  future of, 229–33
  and justice, 223
Anderson, Matthew Lee, 298
Anderson, Ryan T., 3, 51, 65, 189, 191, 233–39, 284, 287, 298–99
anger, 295, 298
Anglicans, 39
Anglo-liberalism, 236
Anscombe Society, 190
Anselm, 57, 59
antiaging therapies, 158
Antiochene Orthodox tradition, 15
antiperfectionism, 99, 102, 108–9
  neutrality of, 113–14
antitribalism, 278–80
apostasy, 40
Apostle, The (film), 266
Aristotle, 18, 28, 100–101, 102, 104, 106, 230, 245
  focal-meaning analysis, 249
  on friendship, 270–71, 273, 280
  hylomorphism of, 159–60
  on order of making, 252
  as truth seeker, 285–86
Arkes, Hadley, 123, 183
Ashford, Bruce, 51
atheism, 86
Athletes in Action, 20
Augustine, 236, 252, 264, 303
"autonomist" liberalism, 107
autonomous reason, 24

Scripture Index